PENGUIN REFERENCE

The Penguin Book of Baby Names

David Pickering is an experienced writer, editor and illustrator. He has broadcast many times on radio and television and lives in Buckingham with his wife and two sons. He has compiled or contributed to well over 200 reference books, mostly in the area of the arts, English language, history, folklore, entertainment and popular interest. As author, these include a *Dictionary of First Names* (Penguin, 1999, 2004), *Sports Quotations* (2000), a *Dictionary of Proverbs* (2001), the *Pears Factfinder* (Penguin, 2002), a *Dictionary of Saints* (2004), *Pirates* (2006), *Jokes* (Penguin, 2006), *Perfect Pub Quiz* (2007) and *Buttering Parsnips, Twocking Chavs* (2007).

# The Penguin Book of
# BABY NAMES

David Pickering

PENGUIN BOOKS

PENGUIN BOOKS

Published by the Penguin Group
Penguin Books Ltd, 80 Strand, London WC2R 0RL, England
Penguin Group (USA) Inc., 375 Hudson Street, New York, New York 10014, USA
Penguin Group (Canada), 90 Eglinton Avenue East, Suite 700, Toronto, Ontario, Canada M4P 2Y3
(a division of Pearson Penguin Canada Inc.)
Penguin Ireland, 25 St Stephen's Green, Dublin 2, Ireland (a division of Penguin Books Ltd)
Penguin Group (Australia), 250 Camberwell Road, Camberwell, Victoria 3124, Australia
(a division of Pearson Australia Group Pty Ltd)
Penguin Books India Pvt Ltd, 11 Community Centre, Panchsheel Park, New Delhi – 110 017, India
Penguin Group (NZ), 67 Apollo Drive, Rosedale, North Shore 0632, New Zealand
(a division of Pearson New Zealand Ltd)
Penguin Books (South Africa) (Pty) Ltd, 24 Sturdee Avenue, Rosebank, Johannesburg 2196, South Africa

Penguin Books Ltd, Registered Offices: 80 Strand, London WC2R 0RL, England

www.penguin.com

First published 2009
7

Set in ITC Stone Sans and ITC Stone Serif
Typeset by Data Standards Ltd, Frome, Somerset
Printed in England by Clays Ltd, St Ives plc

ISBN: 978-0-141-04085-1

www.greenpenguin.co.uk

# CONTENTS

# INTRODUCTION

Choosing a name for a baby is a matter most new parents naturally take very seriously. After all, a person's name can affect their whole life and career, and an inappropriate choice may cause lasting embarrassment or difficulty whatever that person's age or other qualities. A fanciful or frivolous name, for example, may suggest a likeable, cheerful nature but is not likely to promote a person's chances of being taken seriously, while a plainer, monosyllabic name might.

A person's name is a stamp of their individuality, though in reality it may well say more about the parents' prejudices, class background or social pretensions than it does about the bearer. People tend to make instant judgements about strangers based on names, although these judgements may be modified later. Children in particular may focus on unusual names in order to emphasize their own unique personality or make fun of others. Some names 'fit in' in certain regions or communities, but would look out of place elsewhere. Others change with fashion, being in vogue with one generation, but old-fashioned to the next (although they may well come back into fashion years later).

Examination of the latest lists of newly registered first names published by various government agencies around the English-speaking world each year (and contained in an appendix at the end of this book) reveals much about current trends and changing tastes in the naming of children. Parents continue to be attracted both to traditional choices that have been popular for generations and to revivals of neglected favourites as well as to newer coinages, typically ones that have been promoted in various branches of the media. Thus, lists of the most popular names over the past few years have featured such well-established choices as Jack, Thomas, Olivia and Emily alongside such new or rediscovered names as Ethan, Callum, Ruby and Mia.

Modern parents tend to be more conservative in naming their sons than they are in naming their daughters and there is consequently a somewhat wider choice of names available for girl babies. They are, however, more than happy to consider unusual alternatives for either sex alongside more conservative traditional choices or to take up a diminutive form of an old name rather than the root name itself (for instance, Jake rather than Jacob or Evie rather than Eve). Several long-standing favourites for both sexes, which might have been expected to remain top choices for years to come, have gone into decline as a result, notable amongst them such examples as David (ending some fifty years as one of the top-ten favourite choices) and Sarah. Also languishing in the lower reaches of the tables are such former staples as Robert, Andrew, John, Susan and Alexandra. Other names that were briefly at a peak a decade ago (among them Jason, Kylie and Chelsea) have returned to relative obscurity. Only time will tell if a similar fate awaits Madison, Jayden, Tyler, Keira, Ava and other recently emerged choices that have taken their place.

Parents continue to range widely for inspiration. For some the easiest route, in time-honoured fashion, is to look at a list of saints' days (as given in the appendices of this book) and select a name appropriate to the baby's birthday or else to pick a name with family or religious significance. While names from the Bible (Joshua, Matthew, Rebecca and so on) continue to play an important role, many of the other names in the lists of the most popular baby names reflect the influence of contemporary society, with bursts of interest in names borne by top sports players, film stars, fictional characters and so forth. In the last few years television has provided several candidates, including the girls' name Chardonnay, as featured in the drama series *Footballers' Wives*, and Leona, familiar through Leona Lewis, winner of *The X Factor* talent show. The cinema, meanwhile, has suggested, among others, Angelina (after actress Angelina Jolie), Erin (from the film *Erin Brockovich*) and Maximus (after the name of the hero in *Gladiator*). Children's literature has inspired a renewal of interest in the old favourite Harry (as a result of the success of the *Harry Potter* stories) and in politics the election of Barack Obama as US president may well boost the status of Barack as a popular choice.

Many people have followed the lead of various celebrities in taking up, with varying degrees of enthusiasm, the often adventurous names that the famous select for their own children. Highlights in this category have included such names as Brooklyn, Romeo and Cruz (as bestowed upon David and Victoria Beckham's offspring), Mia (the name of Kate Winslet's daughter) and Daisy (Jamie Oliver's choice for his daughter).

A natural conservatism has continued to exert itself with regard to more outlandish choices and parents seem to have been on the whole reluctant to accept the baton proffered by the late Paula Yates, who named her four daughters Fifi Trixibelle, Peaches, Little Pixie and Heavenly Hiraani Tiger Lily (see the appendices for a list of celebrity baby names for further inspiration). Other recently recorded names that seem destined to remain unique include those of three Brazilian sisters who were called Xerox, Photocopier and Authenticated (reportedly because their birth resulted from a romp on a photocopying machine) and the British baby girl born in the 1990s with the name Room 21A (named apparently for similar reasons).

Lists of the most popular first names from different parts of the English-speaking world reveal the extent to which first names appear to be becoming increasingly universal, perhaps through the influence of the international media. There remain, however, some regional preferences, examples including Logan, Ryan and Caitlin in Scotland, Brandon and Taylor in the USA, and Lachlan and Mackenzie in Australia. If richness of choice is to be preserved in the future such divergences are only to be welcomed.

Unlike some other countries, the UK does not have a formal list of names from which new parents must choose. It should be noted, however, that the authorities may suggest parents reconsider if they find the proposed names particularly provocative or offensive. Births must be registered with the local register office within forty-two days (twenty-one in Scotland), although it is possible to delay for a whole year before notifying the authorities of the child's actual name.

The aim of this book is to expand the number of possibilities available to parents seeking names for their children without swamping them with ridiculous names that virtually no one would ever consider. To inform their choices, entries include brief information about the meaning of each name and its origins as well as cross-references to variant forms and (where appropriate) a guide to pronunciation.

Finally, it may be reassuring to know that if a baby grows up to hate his or her name there remains the option of changing it, for a small fee (currently £34), by deed poll at a Registrar's Office.

# GIRLS

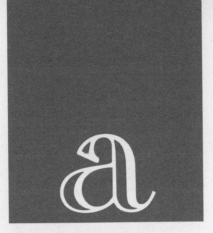

# GIRLS' NAMES

**Aaliyah** *See* ALIYAH.

**Abbey** English name that was taken up as an informal version of ABIGAIL and in time came to be considered a name in its own right. Also found as **Abbie** or **Abby**.

**Abbie/Abby** *See* ABBEY.

**Abigail** Biblical name based on the Hebrew Abigayil, meaning 'my father rejoices' or 'father's joy'. It appears in the Bible as the name of both King David's sister and his wife and was consequently taken up by English Puritans in the seventeenth century. Familiar forms include **Abbie**, **Abby**, **Gale** and **Gayle**. *See also* ABBEY; GAIL.

**Abilene** English name based ultimately on a Hebrew place name thought originally to have meant 'grass'. It appears in the Bible and was consequently adopted as a name for various settlements in the USA, including a city in Kansas.

**Acacia** English name based on the Greek for 'immortality' or 'resurrection', best known as the name of a flowering shrub.

**Ad** *See* ADA.

**Ada** English name possibly based on the Old German *adal* ('noble') under the influence of the biblical ADAH. **Ad**, **Addi**, **Addie** and **Adie** are shortened forms. *See also* ADELAIDE.

**Adah** Hebrew name meaning 'decorated' or 'ornamented'. It appears in the Bible as the name of the wives of Lamech and Esau.

**Addi/Addie/Addy** *See* ADA; ADELAIDE; ADELINE.

**Adela** English and German name based on the Old German *adal* ('noble'). It came to England with the Normans in the eleventh century, being borne by William the Conqueror's daughter Adela (1062–1137) among others. Also encountered as **Adella**, **Adele**, **Adelle** or the French **Adèle**. *See also* DELLA.

**Adelaide** English name based on the Old German *adal* ('noble') and *heit* ('kind', 'state' or 'condition') and thus meaning 'woman of noble estate'. It became well known through William IV's German-born wife Queen Adelaide (1792–1849). Also found as **Adelia**. Shortened to **Addi**, **Addie** or **Addy**. *See also* HEIDI.

**Adele/Adèle/Adelia** *See* ADELA.

**Adeline** French name that developed as a variant of ADELA and has been in occasional use among English speakers since the eleventh century. Shortened to **Addi**, **Addie**, **Addy** or **Aline**.

**Adella/Adelle** *See* ADELA.

**Adie** *See* ADA.

**Adriana/Adriane/ Adrianna/Adrianne** *See* ADRIENNE.

**Adrienne** French name taken up by English speakers as a feminine version of ADRIAN, itself from the Latin for 'man of Adria' (a reference to a town in northern Italy). Variants include **Adriane**, **Adrianne**, **Adrianna** and **Adriana**. Shortened to **Drena** or **Drina**.

**Aeronwen** *See* AERONWY.

**Aeronwy** Welsh name meaning 'berry stream'. The name refers to the River Aeron in Ceredigion. Also encountered as **Aeronwen**.

**Afra** *See* APHRA.

**Africa** English name based on that of the continent. **Afrika** is a variant.

**Afrika** *See* AFRICA.

**Agatha** English name descended from the Greek Agathe, itself based on the Greek *agathos* ('good'). It was introduced to England by the Normans and was in widespread use throughout medieval times. Shortened to Aggie.

**Aggie** *See* AGATHA; AGNES.

**Agnes** English, German, Dutch and Scandinavian name descended from the Greek Hagne, itself based on *hagnos* ('chaste' or 'pure'). Its popularity may owe something to the influence of the Latin *agnus* ('lamb'), with its Christian associations. Familiar forms include **Aggie**, **Nessa**, **Nessie** and **Nesta** (or **Nest**). *See also* ANNIS; INEZ.

**Aileen** *See* EILEEN.

**Ailie** *See* AILSA.

**Ailis/Ailish** *See* ALICE.

**Ailsa** ('ailsa'/'ighla') Scottish name that originated as a place name (from the isle of Ailsa Craig in the Firth of Clyde), presumably under the influence of ELSA and similar names. The original place name came from the Old Norse Alfsigesey (meaning 'island of Alfsigr'). **Ailie** is a variant form.

**Aimée/Aimi** *See* AMY.

**Aine** ('anyeh') Irish name based on the Gaelic for 'brightness'. It appears in Irish folklore as the name of a fairy queen.

**Aisha** ('eye-eesha') Arabic name meaning 'alive'. It was borne by Muhammad's third and favourite wife and consequently became a favourite choice of name in the Arabic world. Also encountered as **Ayesha** – as in the H. Rider Haggard novel *Ayesha* (1905) – and as **Asia**.

**Aisling** ('ashling') Irish first name based on the Gaelic for 'dream' or 'vision'. It became popular in Ireland in the 1960s. Also found as **Aislinn**, **Ashling** or **Isleen**.

**Aislinn** *See* AISLING.

**Aithne** *See* EITHNE.

**Al** Shortened form of such names as ALANA, ALICE and ALISON. It entered general usage in the USA in the nineteenth century. **Allie** and **Ally** are variants.

**Alana** Feminine version of ALAN, itself supposedly from the Celtic *alun* ('concord' or 'harmony') or otherwise interpreted as meaning 'rock'. Also found as **Alannah**. Shortened to AL.

**Alanis** English name based on the German ALANA, meaning 'precious' or 'awakening'. Notable bearers of the name include Canadian pop singer Alanis Morrisette (b. 1974).

**Alannah** *See* ALANA.

**Alberta** English name that developed as a feminine equivalent of ALBERT, itself from the Old German *adal* ('noble') and *beraht* ('bright' or 'famous') and thus meaning 'nobly famous'. Variants include **Albertina** and **Albertine**.

**Albertina/Albertine** *See* ALBERTA.

**Aleta/Aletha** *See* ALETHEA.

**Alethea** English name based on the Greek *aletheia* ('truth'). It seems to have made its first appearances among English speakers in the seventeenth century. Also rendered as ALTHEA, although the two names are otherwise unconnected, and as **Aleta** (or **Aletha**) or **Oleta** (or **Olethea**). **Letty** is an informal version.

**Alex** Shortened form of ALEXANDRA or ALEXIS. It appears to have been an early twentieth-century introduction. Also encountered as **Alix**. **Lex** and LEXIE are informal versions of the name.

**Alexa** *See* ALEXANDRA; ALEXIS.

**Alexandra** Feminine version of ALEXANDER, itself from the Greek *alexein* ('to defend') and *anēr* ('man') and thus meaning 'defender of men'. Variants include **Alexandria** and **Alexandrina**. Shortened to ALEX, **Alexa**, **Alexia**, SANDRA, SASHA or **Zandra**. *See also* ALEXIS.

**Alexandria/ Alexandrina** *See* ALEXANDRA.

**Alexia/Alexie/Alexina** *See* ALEXIS.

**Alexis** English and Russian name descended from the Greek Alexios, itself like ALEXANDRA based on the Greek *alexein* ('to defend'). **Alexa**, **Alexia** and **Alexie** are relatively rare variants. LEXIE and **Lexy** are familiar forms.

Variants include the Scottish **Alexina**.

**Alfa** *See* ALPHA.

**Alfonsine** *See* ALPHONSINE.

**Alfreda** English name descended from the Old English ELFREDA, meaning 'elf strength', but now generally regarded as a feminine equivalent of ALFRED, itself from the Old English *aelf* ('elf') and *raed* ('counsel'). FREDA is a shortened form of the name.

**Ali** *See* ALICE; ALISON.

**Alice** English and French name descended from the Old German Adalheit, meaning 'noble woman'. It enjoyed renewed popularity after the publication of Lewis Carroll's stories *Alice's Adventures in Wonderland* (1865). Variants include the Welsh **Alys** and the Irish **Alis**, **Ailis** or **Ailish**. Shortened to AL or **Ali**. *See also* ALICIA; ALISON.

**Alicia** English name that was taken up as a Latinized variant of ALICE in the nineteenth century. It has continued to appear alongside other forms of the name up to the present. Variant forms include **Alisa**, **Alissa**, **Alisha**, **Alyssa** and **Lyssa**.

**Alida** English name based on the Latin for 'little bird'. **Alita** is a variant.

**Aline** *See* ADELINE.

**Alis** *See* ALICE.

**Alisa** *See* ALICIA.

**Alisha** *See* ALICIA.

**Alison** English and French name that developed as a Norman French variant of ALICE. It was taken up during the medieval period and enjoyed a substantial revival throughout the English-speaking world from the 1920s. Also spelled **Allison** or **Alyson**. Shortened to AL, **Ali**, **Allie** or **Ally**.

**Alissa** *See* ALICIA.

**Alita** *See* ALIDA.

**Alix** *See* ALEX.

**Aliyah** Hebrew name

meaning 'rising' or 'ascending'. Also found as **Aaliyah**.

**Allegra** English and Italian name based on the Italian *allegro* ('happy', 'lively' or 'merry'). It is possible that the name was actually invented by the British poet Lord Byron, who bestowed it upon his daughter Allegra Byron (1817–22).

**Allie** *See* AL; ALISON.

**Allison** *See* ALISON.

**Allula** *See* ALULA.

**Ally** *See* AL; ALISON.

**Alma** English name of obscure origin, possibly based on the Latin *alma* ('kind') but often associated with the Italian *alma* ('soul'). It became popular among English speakers in tribute to the British Army's victory at the Battle of Alma (1854) during the Crimean War.

**Almira** English name probably based on the Arabic *amiri* ('princess').

**Alpha** English name based on the first letter of the Greek alphabet and thus suggesting excellence or prime importance. Its use as a first name in the English-speaking world goes back to the nineteenth century. Also spelled **Alfa**. *See also* OMEGA.

**Alphonsine** Feminine version of ALPHONSE, itself based on the Old German *adal* ('noble') and *funs* ('ready' or 'prompt'), or else *ala* ('all') and *hadu* ('struggle') or *hild* ('battle'). Variants include **Alfonsine**.

**Althea** English name descended from the Greek Althaia, itself based on the Greek *althein* ('to heal') and thus meaning 'wholesome'. It appeared in Greek mythology and was taken up as a poetic name by English speakers in the seventeenth century. *See also* ALETHEA.

**Alula** English name based on the Latin meaning 'winged one' or the Arabic for 'first'. Variants include **Allula**.

**Alva** English name descended from the Hebrew Alvah, meaning 'height' or 'exalted', but also in use as a feminine equivalent of ALVIN.

**Aly** *See* ALISON.

**Alys** *See* ALICE.

**Alyson** *See* ALISON.

**Alyssa** *See* ALICIA.

**Amabel** English name based on the Latin *amabilis* ('lovable'). It made early appearances among English speakers during the medieval period. *See also* ANNABEL; MABEL.

**Amalia** *See* AMELIA.

**Amalinda** *See* AMELINDA.

**Amanda** English name based ultimately on the Latin *amanda* ('lovable'), apparently under the influence of MIRANDA. Its first appearance seems to have been as the name of a character in the Colley Cibber play *Love's Last Shift* (1696). Commonly abbreviated to **Manda** or **Mandy** (or **Mandi**).

**Amaryllis** Greek name possibly based on the Greek *amaryssein* ('to sparkle') and thus a reference to sparkling

eyes. The name appeared in both Virgil and Ovid. Its revival in the nineteenth century probably owed much to its use as a flower name.

**Amata** Italian name based on the Latin for 'beloved'.

**Amber** English name based on that of the yellow translucent fossil resin. It was taken up along with other jewel names towards the end of the nineteenth century. **Ambretta** is a rare variant.

**Ambretta** *See* AMBER.

**Amelia** English name descended from the Roman Aemilius under the influence of the Old German *amal* ('labour'). It became familiar to English speakers in the nineteenth century through William IV's wife Queen Adelaide (1792–1849), whose full name was Adelaide Louise Theresa Caroline Amelia. Also found as **Amalia** or in the French form **Amelie** (or **Amélie**). **Millie** and **Milly** are familiar forms. *See also* EMILIA.

**Amelie/Amélie** *See* AMELIA.

**Amelinda** Spanish name meaning 'beloved and pretty'. Also found as **Amalinda**.

**Amethyst** English name based on that of the semi-precious stone.

**Amey/Amie** *See* AMY.

**Aminta** *See* ARAMINTA.

**Amita** *See* AMITY.

**Amity** English name based on the Latin *amitia* ('friendship'). Variants include **Amita**, a relatively modern version of the name.

**Amy** English name based on the Old French *amee* ('beloved'), itself descended from the Latin *amare* ('to love'). Variants of the name include **Aimi**, **Amey**, **Amie** and the French **Aimée**.

**Anaïs** French name based on the Greek for 'fruitful'. Famous bearers of the name in the English-speaking world have included US writer Anaïs Nin (1903–77).

**Anarawd** ('anarod') Welsh name meaning 'most eloquent'.

**Anastacia** *See* ANASTASIA.

**Anastasia** English and Russian name descended from the Greek Anastasios, itself based on the Greek *anastasis* ('resurrection'). Because of its meaning the name was popular among early Christians. Also found as **Anastacia**. Shortened to STACEY. *See also* TANSY.

**Andi/Andie** *See* ANDREA.

**Andrea** Feminine equivalent of ANDREW, possibly influenced by the Greek Andreas. It was not until after the Second World War that the name began to appear with any regularity. Variants include **Andreana**, **Andrena**, **Andrine** and **Andrene**. Shortened to **Andi** or **Andie**.

**Andreana/Andrena/ Andrene/Andrine** *See* ANDREA.

**Aneka** *See* ANNEKA.

**Ange** *See* ANGEL; ANGELA; ANGELICA.

**Angel** English name descended via Latin from the Greek *angelos* ('messenger') and meaning 'messenger of God' or simply 'angel'. **Ange** and **Angie** are familiar forms of the name. *See also* ANGELA.

**Angela** English and Italian name that developed as a variant of ANGEL. In its early history it was often reserved for children born on 29 September, the feast of St Michael and All Angels. Shortened to **Ange**, **Angie** or **Angy**. *See also* ANGELICA.

**Angelica** English and Italian name based on the Latin *angelicus* ('angelic') but often regarded as a variant of ANGELA. It was imported to England from Italy in the seventeenth century. Variants of the name include **Anjelica**, **Angelina**, **Angeline** and **Angelita**. Shortened to **Ange** or **Angie**.

**Angelina/Angeline/ Angelita** *See* ANGELICA.

**Angharad** ('anharad') Welsh name based on the Welsh *an* ('more') and *car* ('love') and meaning 'much loved'. Its history among Welsh speakers goes back at least to the twelfth century.

**Angie/Angy** *See* ANGEL; ANGELA; ANGELICA.

**Anika** *See* ANNEKA.

**Anila** Indian name based on the Sanskrit for 'wind'.

**Anis** *See* ANNIS.

**Anita** Spanish name that evolved as a variant of ANNE. It was taken up by English speakers in the nineteenth century, initially in the USA. **Nita** is a familiar form.

**Anjelica** *See* ANGELICA.

**Ann** English name that developed as a variant of the Hebrew HANNAH and thus means 'grace' or 'favour'. It has been eclipsed in recent decades by the French form of the name, ANNE. Familiar forms of the name include **Annie**, **Nan**, **Nana**, NANCY and NINA.

**Anna** English, French, Dutch, German, Italian, Scandinavian and Russian name that began life as the Greek or Latin form of HANNAH and thus interpreted as meaning 'grace' or 'favour'. It was taken up by English speakers in the nineteenth century, alongside ANN and other variants, such as **Anya**.

**Annabel** English name that came about through the combination of ANN or ANNA with the French *belle* ('beautiful'), possibly under the influence of AMABEL. It made its first appearances in Scotland as early as the twelfth century. Also encountered as **Annabella** or **Annabelle**. Shortened to **Bel** or **Belle**.

**Annabella/Annabelle** *See* ANNABEL.

**Annalisa** English version of the German and Scandinavian Anneliese, which resulted from the combination of ANNE and Liese (a variant of ELIZABETH). **Annalise** is a variant.

**Annalise** *See* ANNALISA.

**Anne** French name that was taken up by English speakers as a variant of ANN during the medieval period. Variants include ANNETTE, ANITA and ANNEKA. It is also found in combination with various other names, as in **Mary Anne** or **Anne-Marie**. Familiar forms of

the name include ANNIE, **Nan**, **Nana** and NANCY.

**Anneka** Swedish variant of ANNE that was adopted by English speakers in the 1950s. Other forms of the name include **Aneka**, **Anika** and **Annika**. Commonly abbreviated to **Annie**.

**Anne-Marie** *See* ANNE.

**Annett/Annetta** *See* ANNETTE.

**Annette** French variant of ANNE that has been in use as a first name among English speakers since the nineteenth century. Also encountered as **Annetta** or **Annett**. Familiar forms include **Netta** and **Nettie**.

**Annice** *See* ANNIS.

**Annie** Informal version of ANN, ANNE and their many variants that is sometimes treated as a name in its own right. It was taken up by English speakers around the middle of the nineteenth century, popularized by the Scottish song 'Annie Laurie'

(1838). **Anny** is a rare variant, confined largely to Ireland.

**Annika** *See* ANNEKA.

**Annis** English name that was taken up during the medieval period as a variant of AGNES. Also encountered as **Anis**, **Annys** or **Annice**.

**Annunciata** Italian name based on *nuntius* ('bringer of news'). It is traditionally given to children born on Lady Day (25 March).

**Anny** *See* ANNIE.

**Annys** *See* ANNIS.

**Anona** English name of uncertain origin, based either on the Latin for 'harvest' or else the result of the combination of ANN and FIONA or similar names.

**Anouk** French variant of ANN, interpreted to mean 'favoured grace'.

**Anoushka** *See* ANOUSKA.

**Anouska** Russian variant of ANN. Also encountered as **Anoushka** or **Anushka**.

**Anthea** English name descended from the Greek Antheia, itself based on the Greek *antheios* ('flowery') and borne in Greek mythology as a title of the goddess Hera. It made early appearances in seventeenth-century English literature.

**Antoinette** Feminine equivalent of Antoine, the French equivalent of ANTHONY, which is itself popularly (although mistakenly) linked to the Greek *anthos* ('flower') but is otherwise of obscure (possibly Etruscan) origin. It is usually associated with the French queen Marie-Antoinette (1755–93). Shortened to **Toni** or **Toinette**.

**Antonella** *See* ANTONIA.

**Antonia** Feminine form of ANTHONY, which is itself popularly (although mistakenly) linked to the Greek *anthos* ('flower') but is otherwise of obscure (possibly Etruscan) origin. Variants include **Antonina** and **Antonella**. Shortened to **Toni** and less commonly to **Tonia** or **Tonya**.

**Antonina** *See* ANTONIA.

**Anusha** Indian name based on the Hindi for 'star'.

**Anushka** *See* ANOUSKA.

**Anwen** Welsh first name meaning 'very beautiful'.

**Anya** *See* ANNA.

**Aphra** English name that may have evolved from an ancient Irish name or else from the Roman **Afra** (denoting a woman from Africa), a name that was applied to people with dark hair or swarthy colouring. It appears in the Bible as a place name derived from the Hebrew for 'dust'.

**Apolline** *See* APOLLONIA.

**Apollonia** Feminine equivalent of the Greek Apollonius, itself a variant of Apollo, the name of the Greek god of the sun. The name was borne by a third-century Christian martyr. **Apolline** is a variant.

**April** English name based on the name of the month, presumably inspired by its associations with the spring and new growth. Variants include the French AVRIL.

**Arabel** *See* ARABELLA.

**Arabella** English name that is thought to have evolved from Annabella (*see* ANNABEL) or else from the Latin *orabilis* ('entreatable', 'obliging' or 'yielding to prayer'). Variants include **Arabel** and **Arabelle**. Commonly abbreviated to BELLA or **Belle**.

**Arabelle** *See* ARABELLA.

**Araminta** English name of obscure origin, possibly the result of the combination of ARABELLA and the older Aminta or Amynta, itself from the Greek for 'protector'. **Aminta** is a variant. Familiar forms of the name are **Minta** and **Minty**.

**Aretha** English name descended from the Greek Arete, itself based on the Greek *aretē* ('excellence'). It became widely known through US soul singer Aretha Franklin (b. 1942).

**Aria** Italian name meaning 'beautiful song'.

**Ariadne** Greek name possibly based on the Greek *ari* ('more') and *agnos* ('chaste' or 'pure') and thus meaning 'very holy'. It appears in Greek mythology as the name of the daughter of King Minos who shows Theseus how to escape the labyrinth. Variants include the French **Arianne** and the Italian **Arianna**.

**Ariane** *See* ORIANA.

**Arianna/Arianne** *See* ARIADNE.

**Arianrhod** Welsh name meaning 'silver disc'. The allusion is to the moon and the name appears in the *Mabinogion* as that of the moon goddess.

**Ariella** *See* ARIELLE.

**Arielle** Feminine version of ARIEL, itself a Jewish name based on the Hebrew for 'lion of God'. **Ariella** is a variant form.

**Arleen/Arlena** *See* ARLENE.

**Arlene** English name that appears to have evolved as a shortened form of such names as CHARLENE and MARLENE. It has also made appearances in such variant forms as **Arline**, **Arleen** and **Arlena**.

**Arlette** French name that may have evolved as a variant of CHARLOTTE or CHARLES. It was the name of William the Conqueror's mother.

**Arline** *See* ARLENE.

**Armani** English name that probably developed out of the German Herman. It is popularly associated with Italian fashion designer Giorgio Armani (b. 1934).

**Artemis** Greek name borne by the Greek goddess of the moon and of the hunt.

**Ash** *See* ASHLEY.

**Ashantay/Ashantee** *See* ASHANTI.

**Ashanti** Ghanaian name that originated as a surname taken from that of a historical African empire. Variants include **Ashantay** and **Ashantee**.

**Ashia** English name that may have evolved either from AISHA or ASHLEY.

**Ashlea/Ashlee/ Ashleigh** *See* ASHLEY.

**Ashley** English name that originated as a place name based on the Old English *aesc* ('ash') and *leah* ('clearing' or 'wood'). It enjoyed a considerable boost through the 1939 film *Gone with the Wind*, in which the name appears. Its use as a feminine name appears to date from the 1940s. Also found as **Ashleigh**, **Ashlee** or **Ashlea**. Shortened to **Ash**.

**Ashling** *See* AISLING.

**Ashton** English name that originated as a place name meaning 'ash tree town'. Shortened to **Ash**.

**Asia** *See* AISHA.

**Aspasia** Greek name meaning 'welcome one'. It appears in classical history as the name of the lover of the fifth-century Athenian statesman Pericles.

**Asta** *See* ASTRID.

**Astra** English name based ultimately on the Greek *aster* ('star') but often considered to be a variant of ESTHER, STELLA or other names sharing the same source.

**Astrid** English and Scandinavian name descended from the Old Norse Astrithr, itself from the Norse *ans* ('god') and *frithr* ('fair') and thus meaning 'divinely beautiful'. **Asta** and **Sassa** are shortened forms.

**Atalanta** *See* ATLANTA.

**Atlanta** English name based on the Greek **Atalanta**, meaning 'secure'.

**Aub** *See* AUBREY.

**Aubrey** English and French name descended from the Old German Alberic, itself from the Old German *alb* ('elf') and *richi* ('riches' or 'power') and thus meaning 'elf ruler' or 'supernaturally powerful'. It has been used as a girls' name since

the late nineteenth century.
Shortened to **Aub**.

## Aud/Audi/Audie/
**Audra** *See* AUDREY.

**Audrey** English name
descended from the Old
English Aethelthryth, itself
based on the Old English *aethel*
('noble') and *thryth* ('strength')
and thus meaning 'noble
strength'. Also found as **Audrie**
or **Audry**. **Audra** and **Audrina**
are rarer variants. Shortened to
**Aud**, **Audi** or **Audie**.

## Audrie/Audrina/Audry
*See* AUDREY.

**Augusta** Feminine
equivalent of the Roman
AUGUSTUS. Roman emperors
traditionally styled themselves
*Augustus* and the feminine form
of the title was bestowed upon
female members of their
families. **Augustina** and
**Augustine** are variants.
Familiar forms include **Gus**,
**Gussie** and **Gusta**.

## Augustina/Augustine
*See* AUGUSTA.

**Aurelia** Feminine equivalent
of the Roman Aurelius, itself
based on the Latin *aurum*
('gold') and thus meaning
'golden-haired'. It was taken
up by English speakers in the
seventeenth century.

**Aurie** *See* AURIOL.

**Auriel** *See* AURIOL; ORIEL.

**Auriol** English name based
on the Latin *aureus* ('golden'),
although also associated with
the Roman clan name
Aurelius. Also spelled **Auriel** or
**Auriole**. **Aurie** and **Aury** are
familiar forms. *See also* ORIEL.

**Auriole** *See* AURIOL.

**Aurora** English, German and
French name based on the
Latin *aurora* ('dawn'). It appears
in Roman mythology as the
name of the goddess of the
dawn and was revived
throughout Europe during the
Renaissance.

**Aury** *See* AURIOL.

**Autumn** English name based
on that of the season.

**Ava** English name that is
thought to have evolved as a
variant of EVE, although it is

often assumed to have links with the Latin *avis* ('bird'). It was revived among English speakers in the mid-twentieth century, promoted by the fame of US film actress Ava Gardner (Lucy Johnson; 1922–90).

**Avaril** *See* AVERIL.

**Aveline** French name descended from the Old German Avila, itself a variant of AVIS. It was among the many historical names revived in the nineteenth century.

**Averell** *See* AVERIL.

**Averil** English name that evolved either as a variant of AVRIL or else from the Old English Eoforhild (or Everild), itself based on the Old English *eofor* ('boar') and *hild* ('battle') and thus meaning 'boarlike in battle'. Variants include **Avaril**, **Averill** and **Averell**.

**Averill** *See* AVERIL.

**Avice** *See* AVIS.

**Avis** English name of obscure origin, possibly related to the German Hedwig (meaning 'struggle') or else based on the Latin *avis* ('bird'). **Avice** is a variant.

**Avril** English name based on the French *avril* ('April'), or otherwise descended from the Old English Eoforhild, itself based on the Old English *eofor* ('boar') and *hild* ('battle') and meaning 'boarlike in battle'. It is often reserved for girls born in April. *See also* APRIL; AVERIL.

**Ayesha** *See* AISHA.

**Azalea** English flower name that was taken up as a first name among English speakers towards the end of the nineteenth century.

**Azura** *See* AZURE.

**Azure** French name meaning 'sky-blue'. **Azura** is a variant form.

# GIRLS' NAMES

**Bab** *See* BARBARA.

**Babette** French variant of ELIZABETH or BARBARA.

**Babs** *See* BARBARA.

**Bailey** English name variously meaning 'berry clearing', 'bailiff' or 'town fortification'. Also found as **Baillie** or **Bayley**.

**Baillie** *See* BAILEY.

**Bambi** Italian name based on *bambino* ('child'). It became familiar from the animated Disney film *Bambi* (1942).

**Bar/Barb** *See* BARBARA.

**Barbara** English, German and Polish name based ultimately on the Greek *barbaroi* ('strange' or 'foreign') and thus meaning 'foreign woman'. It is thought that the Greek word *barbaroi* imitated the stammering of foreigners unable to speak Greek. Also rendered as **Barbra**. Shortened to **Bab**, **Babs**, **Bar**, **Barb**, **Barbie** or BOBBIE.

**Barbie/Barbra** *See* BARBARA.

**Bathsheba** Hebrew name variously interpreted as meaning 'seventh daughter' or 'daughter of the oath'. It appears in the Bible as the name of the wife of King David and was taken up by English Puritans in the seventeenth century. Shortened to **Sheba**.

**Bayley** *See* BAILEY.

**Bea** *See* BEATA; BEATRICE.

**Beata** Italian name based on the Latin for 'blessed one'. Shortened to **Bea**.

**Beatrice** Italian, French and English name based on the Latin *beatus* ('blessed' or 'lucky'). It became lastingly famous through Beatrice Portinari (1266–90), the model for Beatrice in Dante's *Divine Comedy*. Variants include the Welsh **Betrys** or **Bettrys**. Among familiar forms are **Bee**, **Bea**, **Beattie** (or **Beatty**), **Tris** and **Trissie**. *See also* BEATRIX.

**Beatrix** English, German and Dutch name descended like BEATRICE from the Latin *beatus* ('happy' or 'blessed'). Records of the name's use among English speakers go back to the Norman Conquest. Informal versions of the name include **Trix** and **Trixie**.

**Beattie/Beatty** *See* BEATRICE.

**Becca/Becky** *See* REBECCA.

**Bee** *See* BEATRICE.

**Bel** *See* ANNABEL; BELINDA; ISABEL.

**Belinda** English name based either on the Italian *bella* ('beautiful') or possibly on the Old German *lint* ('snake') and thus suggestive of a cunning nature. Today it is often assumed to have resulted from the combination of BELLA and LINDA. Shortened to **Bel**, **Bindy**, LINDA or **Lindy**.

**Bella** English and Italian name that developed as a shortened form of such names as ARABELLA and ISABELLA, apparently promoted through association with the French and Italian *bella* ('beautiful'). Variants in other languages include the French **Belle**.

**Belle** *See* ARABELLA; BELLA.

**Benita** Feminine version of the Italian and Spanish **Benito**, equivalent to BENEDICT.

**Berenice** *See* BERNICE.

**Bernadetta** *See* BERNADETTE.

**Bernadette** Feminine equivalent, of French origin, of BERNARD. Borne by St Bernadette of Lourdes (Marie-Bernarde Soubirous; 1844–79), whose visions made Lourdes a place of pilgrimage, it became popular among Roman Catholics, especially in Ireland. Variants include **Bernardette**, **Bernardine** and the Italian

**Bernadetta.** Shortened to **Bernie** or **Detta.**

**Bernardine** *See* BERNADETTE.

**Bernice** English and Italian name descended ultimately from the Greek Pherenike, meaning 'victory bringer'. It appears in the Bible and was taken up by English speakers after the Reformation. Also found as **Berenice.** Informal versions include **Bernie,** BERRY, **Binnie** and **Bunny.**

**Bernie** *See* BERNADETTE; BERNICE.

**Berry** English name based on the ordinary vocabulary word 'berry' that enjoyed modest popularity among English speakers towards the end of the nineteenth century. *See also* BERNICE; BERYL.

**Bert** *See* BERTHA.

**Bertha** English and German name based on the Old German *beraht* ('bright' or 'famous'). Early records of the name's use among English speakers go back to the eleventh century. Familiar forms of the name include **Bert** and **Bertie.** *See also* BIRDIE.

**Bertie** *See* BERTHA.

**Beryl** English name based on that of the precious gem. It was among the many jewel names that were adopted by English speakers towards the end of the nineteenth century. **Berry** is a diminutive form.

**Bess** English name that developed as a shortened form of ELIZABETH. Queen Elizabeth I was nicknamed 'Good Queen Bess' but the name did not establish itself as a particular favourite until the seventeenth century. Also encountered as **Bessie** (or **Bessy**).

**Bessie/Bessy** *See* BESS.

**Bet** *See* BETH; BETSY; ELIZABETH.

**Beth** English name that developed as a shortened form of ELIZABETH or BETHANY. Sometimes abbreviated to **Bet.** Also found in combination with various other names, as in **JoBeth** and **Mary Beth.**

Variants include the Welsh **Bethan**. *See also* BETHIA.

**Bethan** *See* BETH.

**Bethany** English name based on a Hebrew place name meaning 'house of figs'. It appears in the New Testament as the name of a village near Jerusalem that Christ passed through shortly before his crucifixion. Sometimes abbreviated to BETH.

**Bethia** English name based on the Hebrew *bith-yah* ('daughter of God'), or alternatively on the Gaelic *beath* ('life'). Sometimes abbreviated to BETH.

**Betrys** *See* BEATRICE.

**Betsey** *See* BETSY.

**Betsy** English name that developed as an informal version of ELIZABETH, apparently through the combination of **Bet** and **Bessie**. Also encountered as **Betsey**.

**Bette** ('bet' or 'bettee') English name that developed as a shortened form of ELIZABETH (*see also* BETTY). Originally French, it is today often associated with the US film actress Bette Davis (Ruth Elizabeth Davis; 1908–89).

**Bettina** *See* BETTY.

**Bettrys** *See* BEATRICE.

**Betty** English name that developed as a shortened form of ELIZABETH. Variants include the Italian and Spanish **Bettina**, which enjoyed some popularity in the English-speaking world in the 1960s. *See also* BETTE.

**Beulah** Hebrew name for Israel, meaning 'she who is married', that was taken up as a first name among English speakers in the seventeenth century, becoming particularly popular within the black community in the USA. The original Hebrew 'land of Beulah' is also sometimes interpreted to be a reference to heaven.

**Bev** *See* BEVERLY.

**Beverley** *See* BEVERLY.

**Beverly** English name that developed as a feminine equivalent of BEVERLEY and is now more widespread than the original from which it evolved. Occasionally also encountered as **Beverley**. Often abbreviated to **Bev**.

**Beyoncé** English name apparently coined for US singer Beyoncé Knowles (b. 1981). The name is based on her mother's maiden name, Tina Beyincé.

**Bianca** Italian name based on the Italian *bianca* ('white' or 'pure'). English speakers adopted the name in the sixteenth century, when it also appeared in the plays of William Shakespeare. *See also* BLANCHE; CANDIDA.

**Biddie/Biddy/Bidelia** *See* BRIDGET.

**Billie** English name taken up as a feminine version of the masculine Billy (*see* WILLIAM). Notable bearers of the name include British television actress Billie Piper (b. 1982).

**Bina** *See* SADHBH.

**Bindy** *See* BELINDA.

**Binnie** English name that developed as an informal version of BERNICE or any longer name ending '-bina' but may also be encountered as a familiar form of several other names with no apparent connection.

**Birdie** English name based on the ordinary vocabulary word 'bird' and also encountered as a variant of BERTHA and other names.

**Birgit** *See* BRIDGET.

**Blair** Scottish name that originated as a place name based on the Gaelic *blar* ('field' or 'plain'). It has enjoyed a modest revival since the middle of the twentieth century, chiefly in Canada and the USA.

**Blanche** English and French name based on the French *blanc* ('white' or 'pure') and originally normally bestowed upon blondes. *See also* BIANCA.

**Blase/Blaze** *See* BLAISE.

**Bliss** English name based on the ordinary vocabulary word 'bliss'. Recorded in use since medieval times.

**Blod** *See* BLODWEN.

**Blodwen** Welsh name based on the Welsh *blodau* ('flowers') and *gwyn* ('white') and possibly first taken up under the influence of the French Blanchefleur. It was fairly common in medieval times but remains confined chiefly to Wales. Also encountered as **Blodwyn**. Shortened to **Blod**.

**Blodwyn** *See* BLODWEN.

**Blondie** English name that evolved as a nickname for anyone with blonde hair. It appears to have made its first appearances in the 1920s.

**Blossom** English name based on the ordinary vocabulary word 'blossom'. It was among the various flower names and related terms that were adopted as first names towards the end of the nineteenth century. *See also* FLEUR; FLORA; FLOWER.

**Bluebell** English name based on that of the bluebell flower. It has made rare appearances among English speakers since the late nineteenth century.

**Blythe** English name probably derived from the ordinary vocabulary word 'blithe'. It has made occasional appearances since the 1940s.

**Bo** Scandinavian name that is often treated as a shortened form of BONITA and other names. Notable bearers of the name include US film actress Bo Derek (Mary Cathleen Collins; b. 1956).

**Bobbie** English name that was taken up as a shortened form of ROBERTA. It is sometimes also encountered as an informal version of BARBARA or as a feminine form of BOBBY.

**Bonita** English name based on the Spanish *bonito* ('pretty'). The name does not appear to have originated in Spain itself, having made its first appearances among English speakers in the USA in the 1920s. *See also* BONNIE.

**Bonnie** English name based on the Scottish 'bonny' (meaning 'pretty' or 'fine'), itself ultimately from the Latin *bonus* ('good'). It is also in use as a shortened form of BONITA. Also encountered as **Bonny**.

**Bonny** *See* BONNIE.

**Brandi** *See* BRANDY.

**Brandy** English name variously considered an informal feminine equivalent of BRANDON or simply based upon the ordinary vocabulary word for distilled wine. Also found as **Brandi**.

**Branwen** Welsh name based on the Welsh *bran* ('raven') and *gwyn* ('white' or 'blessed'), but also in existence as a variant of BRONWEN. It appears in the *Mabinogion* as the name of the beautiful sister of King Bran and is still in occasional use in Wales.

**Breanna** *See* BRIANNA.

**Bree** Irish name that evolved as a variant of BRIDGET, but also in use as a shortened form of various other names. It has had increased exposure in recent years as the name of a character in the US television series *Desperate Housewives*.

**Bren** *See* BRENDA.

**Brenda** English name based on the Old Norse *brandr* ('sword' or 'torch'), but also sometimes regarded as a feminine equivalent of the Irish BRENDAN. It was taken up initially as a first name in the Shetland Isles. Commonly shortened to **Bren**.

**Brenna** Irish name based on the Irish Gaelic for 'raven-haired beauty'.

**Brianna** Irish name meaning 'high', 'noble' or 'strong'. Also treated as a feminine version of BRIAN. Variant forms include **Breanna**, **Briannah** and **Bryanna**.

**Briannah** *See* BRIANNA.

**Bride** *See* BRIDGET.

**Bridget** English name based on the Gaelic Brighid, itself from the Celtic *brigh* ('strength' or 'power'). In its Gaelic form it was the name of a Celtic fire goddess and consequently became popular in Ireland and Scotland. Also encountered as **Birgit**, **Brigit**, **Brigid** or **Brigitte**. **Bidelia** is a fanciful elaboration of the name. Informal versions include **Gita**, **Bride**, **Bridie** and **Biddie** or **Biddy**. *See also* BREE; BRITT.

## Bridie/Brigid/Brigit/Brigitte *See* BRIDGET.

## Briony *See* BRYONY.

## Britney

English name that may have evolved from BRITTANY. Its popularity has been promoted in recent years through US pop singer Britney Spears (b. 1981).

## Britt

Swedish equivalent of BRIDGET. Notable bearers of the name have included Swedish film actress Britt Ekland (b. 1942).

## Brittany

English name based on the name of the province of Bretagne (anglicized as Brittany). It has enjoyed modest popularity among English speakers since the middle of the twentieth century.

## Bron *See* BRONWEN.

## Bronwen

Welsh name based on the Welsh *bron* ('breast') and *gwen* ('white') and thus meaning 'fair-bosomed'. Also encountered as **Bronwyn** and sometimes confused with the otherwise unrelated BRANWEN. Shortened to **Bron**.

## Bronwyn *See* BRONWEN.

## Brooke

English name based on the ordinary vocabulary word 'brook'. Notable bearers of the name include US film actress Brooke Shields (b. 1965).

## Brooklyn

English name based on that of the Brooklyn district of New York City. Also found as **Brooklynn** or **Brooklynne** when applied to girls.

## Brooklynn/Brooklynne *See* BROOKLYN.

## Bryanna *See* BRIANNA.

## Bryony

English name based on that of the wild hedgerow plant, although also in occasional use as a feminine equivalent of BRIAN. Also found as **Briony**.

## Bunny *See* BERNICE.

**Buntie** *See* BUNTY.

**Bunty** English name of uncertain origin, possibly with its roots in a nickname based on a dialect term for a lamb. It became fairly common in the UK in the wake of the popular play *Bunty Pulls the Strings* (1911). Also encountered as **Buntie**.

# GIRLS' NAMES

**Caddy** *See* CANDICE; CAROLINE.

**Cadena/Cadence** *See* CADENZA.

**Cadenza** English name based on the Latin for 'with rhythm'. It developed as a variant of **Cadence**. Also found as **Cadena**.

**Caitlin** *See* CATHERINE; KATHLEEN.

**Cal** *See* CALANDRA; CALANTHA.

**Calandra** English name of Greek origin, meaning 'lark'. Variants include **Calandria**, **Calinda** and the French Calandre. Shortened to **Cal**, **Callie** or **Cally**.

**Calandre/Calandria** *See* CALANDRA.

**Calantha** Greek name meaning 'beautiful blossom'. Shortened to **Cal**, **Callie** or **Cally**.

**Caledonia** English name based on the Roman name for Scotland.

**Calico** English name that originated as an Indian place name (the port of Calicut in Kerala from which calico fabric was imported).

**Calinda** *See* CALANDRA.

**Calista** *See* CALLISTA.

**Callie** *See* CALANDRA; CALANTHA; CALLIOPE.

**Calliope** ('kaleeohpee') Greek name meaning 'beautiful face'. Borne by the ancient Greek muse of epic poetry, it has made occasional reappearances among English speakers over the centuries. Shortened to **Cally**.

**Callista** Feminine equivalent of the Italian Callisto, itself descended from the Roman Callistus, which came from the Greek *kalos* ('fair' or 'good'). In the altered form **Calista** it became widely known in the late 1990s through the US actress Calista Flockhart (b. 1964).

**Cally** *See* CALANDRA; CALANTHA; CALLIOPE.

**Calypso** Greek name meaning 'concealer'. In Greek myth, Calypso was a sea nymph who kept Odysseus prisoner for seven years. Also found as **Kalypso**.

**Cam/Camellia** *See* CAMILLA.

**Cameron** Scottish name based on the Gaelic *cam shron* ('crooked nose'). It has retained its strong Scottish connections, being well known as a clan name. Its use as a feminine name, as borne by US film actress Cameron Diaz (b. 1972), is a relatively recent phenomenon.

**Camilla** Feminine version of the Roman Camillus, thought

to mean 'attendant at a sacrifice'. Also spelled **Camellia**, it was regarded initially as a literary name. **Camille** is a French variant. Shortened to **Cam**, **Cammie**, **Millie** or **Milly**.

**Camille/Cammie** *See* CAMILLA.

**Candace** *See* CANDICE.

**Candi** *See* CANDIDA; CANDY.

**Candia** *See* CANDIDA.

**Candice** English name of uncertain origin. It represents a modern variant of **Candace**, in which form the name appears in the Bible as that of a queen of Ethiopia. As Candice it was adopted early in the twentieth century, becoming particularly popular in the USA. Shortened to **Caddy** or CANDY. Variants include **Candis**.

**Candida** Roman name based on the Latin *candidus* ('white'). It enjoyed a peak in popularity in the early twentieth century, promoted by the George Bernard Shaw play *Candida* (1894). Familiar forms include **Candi**, **Candia**, **Candie** and CANDY.

**Candie** *See* CANDIDA.

**Candis** *See* CANDICE.

**Candy** Familiar form of CANDICE and CANDIDA, possibly influenced by the ordinary vocabulary word 'candy' (a word of Indian origin). Also spelled **Candi**.

**Caprice** English name apparently based on the ordinary vocabulary word meaning 'whim'. It has become widely familiar through US glamour model Caprice Bourret (b. 1971).

**Cara** English name based on the Latin or Italian *cara* ('dear'). It is also possible to trace the name back to the Irish *cara* ('friend' or 'dear one'). Variants include **Kara** and **Carita**. *See also* CARINA.

**Careen** English name of uncertain origin. It appears to have been created by the US novelist Margaret Mitchell in her novel *Gone with the Wind* (1936), perhaps under the influence of CARA or CARINA.

**Carey** English name that developed as a variant of CARY in the nineteenth century. In Irish use it may have evolved from the Gaelic O Ciardha ('descendant of the dark one'). The Welsh may trace it back to the place name Carew. Since the 1950s has been reserved almost exclusively for girls.

**Cari** *See* CERI.

**Carina** Scandinavian, German and English name that developed out of CARA. Variants include **Karina** and **Karine**.

**Carissa** English name based on the Latin for 'dear one'.

**Carita** *See* CARA.

**Carla** English, German and Italian name that evolved as a feminine form of CARL, itself based on the Old English *ceorl* ('man'), or otherwise encountered as a shortened form of CARLTON. Familiar forms of the name include **Carlie**, **Carley**, **Carly** – as borne by US pop singer Carly Simon (b. 1945) – and **Karly**.

**Carleen** *See* CARLENE.

**Carlene** English name that developed as a variant form of CARL under the influence of such names as CHARLENE and DARLENE. Famous bearers of the name have included the US singer-songwriter Carlene Carter (b. 1955). Also spelled **Carleen**.

**Carley/Carlie** *See* CARLA.

**Carlotta** *See* CHARLOTTE.

**Carly** *See* CARLA.

**Carlyn** *See* CAROLINE.

**Carmel** Hebrew name that originated as a place name meaning 'vineyard' or 'garden'. It appears in the Bible as the name of the sacred Mount Carmel in Israel. Variants of the name include **Carmela**, **Carmelina** and **Carmelita**. *See also* CARMEN.

**Carmela/Carmelina/ Carmelita** *See* CARMEL.

**Carmen** Spanish equivalent of CARMEL that is often associated with the Latin *carmen* ('song'). The huge success of Bizet's opera *Carmen* (1873–4) made the name popular among English speakers in the nineteenth century.

**Caro** *See* CAROLINE.

**Carol** English name that developed as a shortened form of CAROLINE, although it is also associated with the ordinary vocabulary word 'carol' and has thus often been reserved for children born at Christmas. Variants of the feminine version include CAROLE, CARROLL and CARYL.

**Carole** English and French name that evolved as a variant of CAROL. English speakers adopted the name from the French around the middle of the twentieth century.

**Carolina** *See* CAROLINE.

**Caroline** English name based on the Italian **Carolina**, itself a feminine equivalent of Carlo (*see* CHARLES). It came to England with George II's wife, Queen Caroline of Ansbach (1683–1737). Among the name's familiar forms are **Caddy**, **Carlyn**, **Caro** and LINA. Also encountered as

**Carolyn** or, more rarely, **Carolyne**. *See also* CARRIE.

**Carolyn/Carolyne** *See* CAROLINE.

**Caron** Welsh name based on the Welsh *caru* ('to love') but also in use as a variant of KAREN, perhaps under the influence of CAROL.

**Carri** *See* CARRIE.

**Carrie** English name that emerged as a shortened form of CAROLINE in the nineteenth century. Interest in the name reached a peak in the USA during the 1970s, possibly under the influence of the Stephen King horror novel *Carrie* (1974). Also found as **Carri** or **Carry**. Sometimes combined with other names, as in **Carrie-Ann**.

**Carrie-Ann** *See* CARRIE.

**Carroll** *See* CAROL.

**Carry** *See* CARRIE.

**Carson** English name that may have been based on an unidentified place name. As a first name, it is associated primarily with people with Irish or Scottish connections. Famous bearers of the name have included US novelist Carson McCullers (Lula Carson McCullers; 1917–67).

**Cary** English name that originated as a place name (the River Cary in the counties of Devon and Somerset). *See also* CAREY.

**Caryl** Variant of CAROL, possibly influenced by BERYL and other similar names. It was taken up by English speakers in the nineteenth century.

**Caryn** *See* KAREN.

**Carys** Welsh name based on the Welsh *car* ('love') that developed under the influence of such names as GLADYS. **Cerys** is a variant form.

**Casey** English name that can be traced back to an Irish surname meaning 'vigilant in war'. Also spelled **Kasey**.

**Cass** *See* CASSANDRA.

**Cassandra** Greek name meaning 'ensnaring men'. It appears in Greek mythology as the name of a celebrated prophetess, whose prophecies were fated never to be believed. Shortened to **Cass** or **Cassie**. *See also* SANDRA.

**Cassia** *See* KEZIA.

**Cassidy** English name based on the Irish O Caiside. A relatively recent introduction, it has been applied to both sexes but remains confined largely to the USA.

**Cassie** *See* CASSANDRA.

**Cat** English name that evolved initially as a nickname for anyone with a tempestuous character or as an abbreviation of CATHERINE. It has appeared in generally informal use among English speakers since the early twentieth century.

**Catalina/Cate/Cath/ Catha** *See* CATHERINE.

**Catharine** *See* CATHERINE.

**Catherine** English name descended from the Greek Aikaterina, which is itself of unknown meaning. The link with St Catherine of Alexandria, who was tortured

on a spiked wheel before being beheaded, has led to the name being linked with the Greek *aikia* ('torture'), although it has also been related to the Greek *katharos* ('pure'), hence the alternate spellings **Katherine**, **Katharine** and **Catharine**. Other variants include **Kathryn** (or **Cathryn**), **Catrine**, KATRINA (or **Catrina**), **Catalina**, the Welsh **Catrin** and the Irish **Caitlin** (from which KATHLEEN and **Cathleen** evolved). Shortened to CAT, **Cath** (or **Kath**), **Catha**, **Cate**, KATE, **Katie** (or **Katy**), **Cathi**, **Cathy** (or **Kathy**), KAY, **Kit** and KITTY. *See also* CATRIONA; KAREN.

**Cathi** *See* CATHERINE.

**Cathleen** *See* CATHERINE; KATHLEEN.

**Cathryn/Cathy/Catrin** *See* CATHERINE.

**Catrina/Catrine** *See* CATHERINE; CATRIONA.

**Catriona** ('catreena') Scottish and Irish name that developed as a variant of CATHERINE. It was adopted more widely throughout the

English-speaking world in the nineteenth century. Also found as **Catrina**, **Catrine** or KATRINA. Shortened to **Trina** or, chiefly among the Irish, to **Riona**.

**Cayla** *See* KAYLEIGH.

**Ceallagh** *See* KELLY.

**Ceara** *See* CERA.

**Cecil/Cécile** *See* CECILIA.

**Cecilia** English name descended from the Roman Caecilia, itself from the Latin *caecus* ('blind'). Variants include **Cicely** and **Cecily** (or **Cecilie**) as well as the French **Cécile**. A less well-known variant is **Sisley**. **Cecil**, **Ciss** (or **Sis**), CISSIE (or **Cissy**) and **Sissie** (or **Sissy**) are familiar forms. *See also* CELIA.

**Cecilie/Cecily** *See* CECILIA.

**Ceinwen** ('kainwen') Welsh name based on *cain* ('fair') and *gwen* ('white' or 'blessed') and sometimes interpreted as meaning 'beautiful gems'.

**Celandine** English name based on the name of the plant, itself from the Greek for 'swallow'.

**Celeste** English name descended via the masculine French name Céleste from the Roman Caelestis, itself from the Latin *caelestis* ('heavenly'). It was taken up by English speakers in the twentieth century, though only as a name for girls. Variants include **Celestina** and **Celestine**.

**Celestina/Celestine** *See* CELESTE.

**Celia** English and Italian name descended from the Roman Caelia, itself probably from the Latin *caelum* ('heaven'), but often also treated as a shortened form of CECILIA. *See also* CÉLINE; SHEILA.

**Celina** *See* CÉLINE; SELINA.

**Céline** French name descended from the Roman Caelina, itself probably from the Latin *caelum* ('heaven'). Often treated as an elaboration of CELIA. Variants include **Celina**. *See also* SELINA.

**Cera** ('keera') Irish name of obscure meaning. It was borne by a queen of ancient Irish legend and by three Irish saints. Also spelled **Ceara**.

**Ceri** Welsh name based on the Welsh *caru* ('to love') and meaning 'loved one', also encountered as a shortened form of CERIDWEN or as a variant of KERRY. It does not appear to have been in use before the 1940s.

**Ceridwen** Welsh name based on the Welsh *cerdd* ('poetry') and *gwen* ('white' or 'blessed') and thus meaning 'poetically fair'. It was borne by the Celtic goddess of poetical inspiration. Sometimes abbreviated to CERI.

**Cerise** English name of French origin, based on the cherry-red colour of the same name.

**Cerys** *See* CARYS.

**Chandra** Indian name based on the Sanskrit for 'moon'.

**Chantal** French name based on the Old Provençal *cantal* ('stone' or 'boulder') but popularly associated with the French *chant* ('song'). English speakers took up the name in the twentieth century. Variants include **Chantale**, **Chantalle**, **Chantelle**, **Shantel** and **Shantelle**.

**Chantale / Chantalle / Chantelle** *See* CHANTAL.

**Chardonay** *See* CHARDONNAY.

**Chardonnay** English name alluding to Chardonnay wine. It became widely known in 2001 through the popular television series *Footballers' Wives*, which featured a character of that name. Also found as **Chardonay**.

**Charis** ('kariss') English name based on the Greek *kharis* ('grace'). It was borne in classical mythology by one of the three Graces. In the variant form **Charissa** (possibly influenced by CLARISSA) it made an early appearance in Edmund Spenser's *The Faerie Queen* (1590).

**Charissa** *See* CHARIS.

**Charity** English name based

on the ordinary vocabulary word 'charity'. It was among the many 'virtue' names taken up by English Puritans after the Reformation. CHERRY and **Chattie** are informal versions of the name.

**Charleen** *See* CHARLENE.

**Charlene** ('sharleen') English name that developed as a feminine variant of CHARLES, itself ultimately from the Old German *karl* ('free man'). It is a relatively recent coinage, dating only to the middle of the twentieth century. Variants include **Charleen, Charline** and **Sharlene**. Shortened to **Charlie, Charley** or **Charly**.

**Charley** *See* CHARLENE; CHARLOTTE.

**Charlice** *See* CHARLIZE.

**Charlie/Charline** *See* CHARLENE.

**Charlisa** *See* CHARLIZE.

**Charlize** ('sharleece') English variant of CHARLES. Charlize Theron (b. 1975) is a well-known South African-born US

film actress. Variants include **Charlice** and **Charlisa**.

**Charlotta** *See* CHARLOTTE.

**Charlotte** ('sharlot') English and French version of the Italian Carlotta, itself a feminine variant of Carlo (the Italian equivalent of CHARLES). Among variants are **Charlotta, Carlotta** and the rare **Sharlott**. Informal versions include **Charley, Charlie, Charly, Chattie, Lotta, Lottie, Lotty, Tottie** and **Totty**.

**Charly** *See* CHARLENE; CHARLOTTE.

**Charmain** *See* CHARMAINE.

**Charmaine** ('sharmain') English name that is thought to have evolved either as a variant of CHARMIAN or else from the ordinary vocabulary word 'charm'. Its popularity was promoted by the song 'Charmaine' (1926). Variants include **Charmain, Sharmain, Sharmaine** and **Sharmane**.

**Charmian** English name descended from the Greek Kharmion, itself from the Greek *kharma* ('joy' or 'delight'). It became widely known as the name of Cleopatra's lady-in-waiting in William Shakespeare's *Antony and Cleopatra* (1606–7). *See also* CHARMAINE.

**Chastity** English name based on the ordinary vocabulary word 'chastity'. It was among the 'virtue' names adoped in the seventeenth century.

**Chattie** *See* CHARITY; CHARLOTTE.

**Chayanne** *See* CHEYENNE.

**Chelle** *See* MICHELLE.

**Chelsea** English name that originated as a place name (Chelsea in central London) meaning 'landing-place for limestone'. It emerged as a first name in the 1950s, initially in Australia and the USA. Also encountered as **Chelsie**.

**Chelsie** *See* CHELSEA.

**Cher** French name based on the French *chère* ('dear'), but sometimes also employed as a shortened form of such names as CHERRY and CHERYL. It enjoyed a boost in the 1960s through US pop singer and film actress Cher (Cherilyn Sarkasian LaPierre; b. 1946).

**Cheralyn** *See* CHERYL.

**Cherelle** *See* CHERRY.

**Cherida** English name that appears to have resulted from the combination of CHERYL and PHYLLIDA. It is a relatively recent coinage, possibly influenced by the Spanish *querida* ('dear').

**Cherie** ('sheree') French name based on the French *chérie* ('dear one' or 'darling'). Also spelled **Sheree, Sheri, Sherie** or **Sherry**. *See also* CHER; CHERRY; CHERYL.

**Cherill/Cherilyn** *See* CHERYL.

**Cherish** English name based on the ordinary vocabulary word 'cherish'. As a first name it is a relatively recent introduction.

**Cherrie** *See* CHERRY.

**Cherry** English name that developed as an informal version of such names as

CHARITY, CHERIE and CHERYL but is also associated with the fruit of the same name. Variants include **Cherrie** and **Cherelle**.

**Cheryl** ('sherril') English name that is thought to have resulted from the combination of CHERRY and BERYL (or other similar names) perhaps under the influence of CHERIE. Variants include **Cheryll**, **Cherill**, **Sherill**, **Sheryl** and various combinations with LYNN, including **Cheralyn**, **Cherilyn** and **Sherilyn**.

**Cheryll** *See* CHERYL.

**Chevonne** *See* SIOBHAN.

**Cheyenne** Native American name based on that of the Cheyenne Native American tribe. Also found as **Chayanne**, **Chyanne** and **Shyanne**.

**Chiquita** ('chickeeta') Spanish name meaning 'little one'.

**Chloe** English name descended from the Greek Khloe, meaning 'young green shoot'. It appeared in Greek mythology as an alternative name for the goddess of agriculture Demeter and in the legend of Daphnis and Chloë. Also spelled **Chloë**. Sometimes abbreviated to **Clo**.

**Chloris** Greek name based on *khloros* ('green' or 'fresh'). Representing fertility, it appears in the poetry of the Roman poet Horace and was consequently taken up by English poets in the seventeenth and eighteenth centuries. Also spelled **Cloris**.

**Chris** Shortened form of various longer names, including CHRISTINE, CHRISTABEL and CRYSTAL. Variants include **Chrissie** and **Chrissy**.

**Chrissie/Chrissy** *See* CHRIS; CHRISTABEL; CRYSTAL.

**Christa** *See* CHRISTINA; CHRISTINE.

**Christabel** English name based on the Roman Christus ('Christ') and the Latin *bella* ('beautiful') and thus meaning 'beautiful Christian'. It became popular on the publication of Samuel Taylor Coleridge's poem *Christabel* (1797).

Variants include **Christobel**, **Christabelle** and **Christabella**. Shortened to CHRIS, **Chrissie**, **Chrissy**, **Christie**, **Christy**, BELLA or **Belle**.

**Christabella/ Christabelle** *See* CHRISTABEL.

**Christelle** *See* CRYSTAL.

**Christiana** Feminine equivalent of CHRISTIAN, itself from the Latin for 'Christian'. It seems to have made its first appearances among English speakers in the seventeenth century. Variants include **Christiania** and **Christianna**. Shortened to CHRIS or **Christie** (or **Christy**). *See also* CHRISTINA.

**Christiania/Christianna** *See* CHRISTIANA.

**Christie** *See* CHRISTABEL; CHRISTIANA; CHRISTINE.

**Christina** English name that developed as a variant of CHRISTIANA. It was taken up alongside the older form of the name as early as the eighteenth century. Shortened forms of the name include CHRIS, **Christa**, KIRSTY and TINA.

**Christine** English and French variant of CHRISTINA and CHRISTIANA. This modern variant established itself towards the end of the nineteenth century. Variants include the Welsh **Crystin**. Shortened to CHRIS, **Chrissie**, **Chrissy**, **Christa**, **Christie**, **Christy** or KIRSTY.

**Christobel** *See* CHRISTABEL.

**Christy** *See* CHRISTINE.

**Chrystal/Chrystalla** *See* CRYSTAL.

**Chyanne** *See* CHEYENNE.

**Ciara** ('keera') Irish name based on the Irish Gaelic *ciar* ('dark').

**Cicely** *See* CECILIA.

**Cilla** Shortened form of PRISCILLA and of the less frequent DRUSILLA. It has become well known in the UK through British pop singer and television presenter Cilla Black (Priscilla White; b. 1943).

**Cimmie** *See* CYNTHIA.

**Cinderella** English version of the French Cendrillon, meaning 'little cinders'. Best known from the classic fairytale *Cinderella*, it has made occasional appearances as a first name. CINDY is a shortened form.

**Cindi/Cindie** *See* CINDY.

**Cindy** Shortened form of such names as CYNTHIA, LUCINDA and even CINDERELLA, which is now often encountered as a name in its own right. It began to appear with increasing frequency among English speakers in the 1950s. Variants include **Cindie**, **Cindi**, **Cyndi** and **Sindy**.

**Cis/Ciss** *See* CECILIA; CISSIE.

**Cissie** English name that developed as a shortened form of CECILIA and its variants. Also found as **Cissy**, **Sissie** or **Sissy**. Commonly abbreviated to **Cis** or **Ciss**.

**Cissy** *See* CECILIA; CISSIE.

**Clair** *See* CLAIRE.

**Claire** English and French name descended from the Roman Clara, itself based on the Latin *clarus* ('clear' or 'pure'). It came to England with the Normans, often appearing as **Clare** as well as in the French form Claire. Also found as **Clair** or, more rarely, **Clarette** or **Claretta**. *See also* CLARA.

**Clara** English, German and Italian name based on the Latin *clarus* ('clear' or 'pure') that was taken up in the English-speaking world as a Latinized version of **Clare** (*see* CLAIRE). In Scotland it is sometimes considered to be an anglicized form of SORCHA. **Clarrie** is a shortened form. *See also* CLARIBEL; CLARICE; CLARINDA.

**Clarabel** *See* CLARIBEL.

**Clare** *See* CLAIRE; CLARA.

**Claretta/Clarette** *See* CLAIRE.

**Claribel** English name that resulted from the combination of CLARA and such names as

ANNABEL and ISABEL. It was adopted as a literary name in the sixteenth century. Also found as **Clarabel**.

**Clarice** English and French name descended from the Roman Claritia, itself from the Latin *clara* ('clear' or 'pure') or else from *clarus* ('famous' or 'renowned'). It was taken up by English speakers in medieval times. *See also* CLARISSA.

**Clarinda** English name that appears to have resulted from the combination of CLARA and BELINDA, LUCINDA or other similar names. It emerged in the late sixteenth century, appearing possibly for the first time in Edmund Spenser's epic poem *The Faerie Queene* (1590, 1596), perhaps on the model of **Clorinda**.

**Claris** *See* CLARISSA.

**Clarissa** English name that developed from CLARICE. The name became well known through the Samuel Richardson novel *Clarissa* (1748). Sometimes abbreviated to **Clarrie**, **Clarry** or **Claris**.

**Clarrie** *See* CLARA; CLARISSA.

**Clarry** *See* CLARISSA.

**Claudette** *See* CLAUDIA.

**Claudia** English, French and German name descended from the Roman Claudius, itself based on the Latin *claudus* ('lame'). In Wales it is sometimes treated as an equivalent of GLADYS. Variants include the French **Claudette** and **Claudine**. *See also* CLODAGH.

**Claudine** *See* CLAUDIA.

**Clelia** English and Italian name descended from the Roman Cloelia. It appears in Roman mythology as the name of a legendary heroine who escaped capture by the Etruscans.

**Clem** *See* CLEMENTINA.

**Clementina** Feminine version of CLEMENT, itself based on the Latin *clemens* ('merciful'). The French variant **Clementine** is best known through Lady (Clementine) Spencer-Churchill

(1885–1977), wife of British Prime Minister Winston Churchill. Shortened to **Clem**, **Clemmie**, **Clemmy** and **Cleo**.

## Clementine/Clemmie/Clemmy *See* CLEMENTINA.

**Cleo** *See* CLEMENTINA; CLEOPATRA.

**Cleopatra** English version of the Greek Kleopatra, based on the Greek *kleos* ('glory') and *pater* ('father') and thus meaning 'father's glory'. Universally associated with the historical queen of Egypt famed for her love affairs with Julius Caesar and Mark Antony. Shortened to **Cleo** or CLIO.

**Clio** English first name descended from the Greek Kleio, itself based on the Greek *kleos* ('glory' or 'praise'). Borne in classical mythology by one of the Muses, it is sometimes encountered today as a shortened form of CLEOPATRA.

**Cliona** Irish name descended from the Gaelic Cliodhna (or Clidna). Borne in Irish legend by a beautiful fairy princess, it was taken up with some enthusiasm as a first name in

the twentieth century, although chiefly confined to the Irish community.

**Clo** *See* CHLOE; CLODAGH.

**Clodagh** ('cloda') Irish name that originated as the name of a river in County Tipperary, Ireland. Sometimes treated as an Irish equivalent of CLAUDIA, its introduction as a first name appears to date from the early twentieth century. Sometimes abbreviated to **Clo**.

**Clorinda** *See* CLARINDA.

**Cloris** *See* CHLORIS.

**Clotilda** English version of the French Clothilde, which was itself based on the Old German *hlod* ('famous' or 'loud') and *hild* ('battle'). Variants include **Clotilde**.

**Clotilde** *See* CLOTILDA.

**Clova** *See* CLOVER.

**Clover** English name based on that of the wild flower. It enjoyed some exposure in the nineteenth century as the name of a character in the *Katy* books of US children's writer

Susan Coolidge (Sarah Chauncy Woolsey; 1835–1905). Also spelled **Clova**.

**Coco** Spanish name that developed as a shortened version of Soccoro. Notable bearers of the name have included the French fashion designer Coco Chanel (1883–1971).

**Codey** *See* CODY.

**Cody** English name that is thought to have evolved from an Irish surname meaning 'descendant of a helpful person'. Also spelled **Codey** or **Kody**.

**Coleen/Colene** *See* COLLEEN.

**Colette** French name that developed out of Nicolette (a French equivalent of NICOLA). Borne by a fifteenth-century French saint, it became well known through French novelist Colette (Sidonie Gabrielle Colette; 1873–1954). Also spelled **Collette**.

**Colleen** Irish name based on the Gaelic *cailin* ('girl').

Sometimes considered to be a feminine form of COLIN, it was adopted by English speakers in the nineteenth century. Despite its strong Irish connections it is not very common in Ireland itself. Variants include **Coleen** and **Colene**.

**Collette** *See* COLETTE.

**Columbine** English and French version of the Italian Columbina, itself descended from the Roman Columba, from the Latin for 'dove'. It became well known as the name of Harlequin's lover in traditional harlequinade entertainments. The name was also promoted through its association with the flower columbine.

**Comfort** English name that enjoyed some popularity among English speakers after the Reformation. It continued to make rare appearances among both sexes into the nineteenth century.

**Con** *See* CONNIE; CONSTANCE.

**Concetta** Italian name descended from the Roman

Conceptua, itself based on the Latin *concepta* ('conceived'). A reference to the Immaculate Conception, it may also be encountered in the Spanish form **Conchita**.

**Conchita** *See* CONCETTA.

**Connee** *See* CONNIE.

**Connie** English name that evolved as a shortened form of CONSTANCE and is now sometimes considered a name in its own right. Commonly abbreviated to **Con**. Also spelled **Connee**.

**Constance** English and French name descended from the Roman Constantia, meaning 'constancy' or 'perseverance'. Borne by a daughter of William the Conqueror, it was among the 'virtue' names favoured by the Puritans. Variants include **Constancy**, **Constantina** and **Constanza**. Shortened to **Con** or CONNIE.

**Constancy/ Constantina/Constanza** *See* CONSTANCE.

**Cora** English name based on the Greek *korē* ('girl'). In the Greek form Kore, it appeared in classical mythology as an alternative name for Persephone, goddess of the underworld. Variants include **Coretta** and **Kora**. *See also* CORAL; CORALIE; CORINNE.

**Coral** English name that appears to have been adopted as a result of the fashion for coral jewellery in the late nineteenth century. It is sometimes suggested, however, that the name can be considered a variant of CORA. **Cory** is an informal version. *See also* CORALIE.

**Coralie** French name of uncertain meaning that has also made occasional appearances among English speakers. It is sometimes regarded as a variant of CORA or CORAL (both of which it apparently predates).

**Cordelia** English name of obscure origin, possibly a variant of the Celtic Cordula, itself based on the Latin *cor* ('heart'). Best known from Cordelia in William Shakespeare's tragedy *King Lear* (1604–5). Informal versions include **Cordy** and DELIA.

**Cordy** *See* CORDELIA.

**Coretta** *See* CORA.

**Corinna** *See* CORINNE.

**Corinne** English and French name descended ultimately from the Greek Korinna, itself probably from the Greek *korē* ('girl'). It is often considered a variant of CORA. The variant **Corinna** became well known from Robert Herrick's poem 'Corinna's going a–Maying' (1648).

**Cornelia** Feminine equivalent of the Roman CORNELIUS, itself possibly based on the Latin *cornu* ('horn'). Shortened forms of the name include **Cornie**, **Corrie** and **Nellie**.

**Cornie/Corrie** *See* CORNELIA.

**Cory** *See* CORAL.

**Cosima** Feminine version of COSMO, itself descended from the Greek Kosmas, based on the Greek *kosmos* ('order', 'harmony' or 'beauty').

**Courtenay/Courteney** *See* COURTNEY.

**Courtney** English name that originated as the Norman French place name Courtenay (meaning 'domain of Curtius'), although it was also a nickname based on the French *court nez* ('short nose'). As a name for girls it appears to have been adopted around the middle of the twentieth century. Variants include **Courtenay** and **Courteney**.

**Cressida** English version of the Greek Khryseis, itself based on the Greek *khrysos* ('gold'). It became well known through the legend of Troilus and Cressida, as related by Chaucer and Shakespeare. Shortened to **Cressy**.

**Cressy** *See* CRESSIDA.

**Cristal** *See* CRYSTAL.

**Cruz** ('crooth') Spanish and Portuguese name meaning 'cross'. **Cruzito** is a variant.

**Cruzito** *See* CRUZ.

**Crystal** English name based on the ordinary vocabulary

word 'crystal'. Also
encountered as **Chrystal,
Christel, Cristal, Crystle,
Krystle** or **Krystal** and, more
rarely, as **Christelle** or
**Chrystalla**. Commonly
abbreviated to CHRIS or
**Chrissie**.

**Crystin** *See* CHRISTINE.

**Crystle** *See* CRYSTAL.

**Cybill** *See* SYBIL.

**Cyndi** *See* CINDY.

**Cynthia** English version of
the Greek Kynthia, a name
borne in mythology by the
goddess Artemis whose
birthplace was supposed to
have been Mount Kynthos (a
name of obscure origin) on the
island of Delos. Shortened to
**Cimmie** or CINDY.

**Cyra** Feminine version of
CYRUS, itself based on the
Greek Kyros, which may have
evolved from the Greek *kurios*
('lord') or come from Persian
words meaning 'sun' or
'throne'. **Cyrilla** is a variant
form.

**Cyrena** Greek name that was
borne in classical Greek
mythology by a water nymph
of Cyrene with whom Apollo
fell in love.

**Cyrilla** *See* CYRA.

# GIRLS' NAMES

**Daff** *See* DAFFODIL; DAPHNE.

**Daffodil** English name based on that of the flower. Like other flower names it made its first appearances towards the end of the nineteenth century. **Daff** and **Dilly** are informal versions.

**Daffy** *See* DAPHNE.

**Dagmar** Scandinavian name based either on *dag* ('day') and *mar* ('maid') or on the Slavonic *dorog* ('dear') and *meri* ('great' or 'famous').

**Dahlia** ('dayleea') English name based on that of the flower. The flower itself was named in honour of the celebrated Swedish botanist

Anders Dahl (1751–89). Also spelled **Dalia** or **Dalya**.

**Daireann** *See* DARINA.

**Daisy** English name based on that of the flower, itself from the Old English *daegeseage* ('day's eye') – so called because it opens its petals at daybreak. Through association with the French *marguerite*, the French name for the daisy, it came to be regarded as a familiar form of MARGARET.

**Dakoda** *See* DAKOTA.

**Dakota** Native American name that originated as a tribal name meaning 'friend' or 'ally'. Also found as **Dakotah** or **Dakoda**.

**Dakotah** *See* DAKOTA.

**Dale** English name that originated as a surname originally borne by people living in a dale or valley. As a name for girls it appears to have made early appearances in the first decade of the twentieth century. It is confined chiefly to the USA.

**Dalia/Dalya** *See* DAHLIA.

**Damaris** Greek name based on the Greek *damar* ('wife') or *damalis* ('calf' or 'heifer') and thus signifying gentleness. It appears in the Bible as the name of an Athenian convert of St Paul.

**Dan** *See* DANIELLE.

**Dana** English name that evolved out of DANIEL in the nineteenth century. Today it is more often bestowed upon girls than boys and treated as a variant of DANIELLE.

**Dandie** *See* DANDY.

**Dandy** English name based on the ordinary vocabulary word 'dandy', but also in use as a familiar form of such names as DANIELLE. It has made occasional appearances among both sexes since the early twentieth century. Also found as **Dandie**.

**Danette/Dani** *See* DANIELLE.

**Danica** *See* DANIKA.

**Daniela/Daniella** *See* DANIELLE.

**Danielle** Feminine equivalent, of French origin, of DANIEL, itself based on the Hebrew for 'God is my judge' or 'God has judged'. It has been popular among English speakers since the 1940s. Variants include **Danette**, **Daniela**, **Daniella** and **Danita**. Among shortened forms are **Dan**, **Danny**, **Dannie** and **Dani**. *See also* DANA.

**Danika** Slavonic name based on that of the morning star. Also found as **Danica**.

**Danita/Dannie/Danny** *See* DANIELLE.

**Daph** *See* DAPHNE.

**Daphne** Greek name meaning 'laurel tree'. Borne in Greek mythology by a nymph who was transformed by her father into a laurel tree when pursued by Apollo, it was taken up among English speakers in the eighteenth century. Shortened to **Daff**, **Daffy** or **Daph**.

**Dara** Jewish name for girls based on the Hebrew for 'pearl of wisdom' (although when it appears in the Old Testament it is given as a boys' name).

**Darcey** Feminine equivalent of the masculine DARCY. It has made irregular appearances among English speakers since the early twentieth century, primarily in the USA. Famous bearers of the name have included the British ballerina Darcey Bussell (b. 1969).

**Darline** *See* DARLENE.

**Daria** English, Italian and Polish name that evolved originally as a feminine equivalent of the Roman DARIUS, meaning 'protector' or 'wealthy'. It has made irregular appearances among English speakers into modern times.

**Darina** Irish name based on the Irish Gaelic *daireann* ('fruitful'). Also found as **Daireann, Doirend** or **Doirenn**.

**Darleen** *See* DARLENE.

**Darlene** English name that is thought to have evolved from the ordinary vocabulary word 'darling' under the influence of such similar coinages as CHARLENE. It became fairly popular in the USA in the 1950s. Also found as **Darleen** or **Darline**.

**Darelle** *See* DARYL.

**Daryl** Feminine version of DARRYL, an English name based on the Norman baronial surname d'Airelle (referring to Airelle in Calvados). An alternative derivation traces the name back to the Old English *deorling* ('darling'). Also found as **Darrelle**.

**Davena/Davida** *See* DAVINA.

**Davina** Scottish feminine variant of DAVID, itself based on the Hebrew for 'favourite', 'beloved' or 'darling'. It appears to be a fairly recent introduction of early twentieth-century coinage. Variants include **Davida, Davena** and **Davinia**. Sometimes shortened to **Vina**. *See also* DIVINA.

**Davinia** *See* DAVINA; DIVINA.

**Dawn** English name based on

the ordinary vocabulary word 'dawn'. It seems to have made its first appearances among English speakers in the 1920s. *See also* AURORA.

**Deanna** English name that evolved as a variant of DIANA in the early twentieth century but is also occasionally encountered as a feminine equivalent of DEAN. Famous bearers of the name have included Canadian-born US film actress and singer Deanna Durbin (Edna Mae Durbin; b. 1921).

**Deanne** *See* DIANE.

**Dearbhail** *See* DERVLA.

**Deb** *See* DEBORAH.

**Debbie** Shortened form of DEBORAH that is sometimes treated as a name in its own right. It enjoyed a peak in popularity in the 1960s and 1970s. Also found as **Debby**.

**Debby** *See* DEBBIE; DEBORAH.

**Debo** *See* DEBORAH.

**Deborah** English name

based on the Hebrew for 'bee' and thus suggestive of a diligent, industrious nature. It appears in the Bible and was consequently taken up with some enthusiasm by Puritans in the seventeenth century. **Debra** is a variant form of the name. Shortened to **Deb**, **Debs**, **Debo** or DEBBIE (or **Debby**).

**Debra/Debs** *See* DEBORAH.

**Dee** English name that evolved as a shortened form of various names beginning with the letter 'D', including DEIRDRE and DOROTHY. Variants include **DeeDee** (or **Didi**).

**DeeDee** *See* DEE.

**Deidra/Deidre** *See* DEIRDRE.

**Deirbhile** *See* DERVLA.

**Deirdre** Irish name based on the Irish *deardan* ('storm') and thus meaning 'raging' or 'tempestuous'. The name has featured prominently in Irish literature through retellings of the tragic legend of the

beautiful Deirdre of the
Sorrows. Also found as **Deidre**,
**Diedre** or **Deidra**.

**Delainey/Delainie** *See*
DELANEY.

**Delaney** English name
drawing on Irish Gaelic and
Old French origins and
variously meaning 'dark
challenger' or 'from the elder
grove' or else based on a
reference to the Slaney river.
Variants include **Delainey**,
**Delainie** and **Delany**.

**Delany** *See* DELANEY.

**Delfina** *See* DELPHINE.

**Delia** English name based
ultimately on that of the Greek
island of Delos, which in
Greek mythology was the
home of Artemis and Apollo. It
is occasionally encountered as a
shortened form of such names
as CORDELIA. DELLA is a
variant form. Sometimes
abbreviated to DEE.

**Délice** *See* DELICIA.

**Delicia** English name
descended from the Roman
Delicius, itself from the Latin

*deliciae* ('delight'). Variants
include **Délice** and **Delys**.

**Delight** English name based
on the ordinary vocabulary
word denoting 'joy' or
'pleasure'.

**Delila** *See* DELILAH.

**Delilah** Hebrew name
meaning 'delight', possibly
from the Arabic *dalla* ('to flirt'
or 'to tease'). It appears in the
Bible as the name of Samson's
deceitful lover and the cause of
his downfall. **Delila** is a variant
form.

**Dell** *See* DELLA.

**Della** Variant form of ADELA
and DELIA among other names.
It made its first appearances
towards the end of the
nineteenth century.
Commonly shortened to **Dell**.

**Delma** *See* FIDELMA.

**Delora/Delores** *See*
DOLORES.

**Delphina** *See* DELPHINE.

**Delphine** French name
descended from the Roman

Delphina, meaning 'woman of Delphi'. Madame de Staël's use of the name in her novel *Delphine* (1802) undoubtedly promoted awareness of it. Variants include **Delfina**, **Delphina** and **Delvene**.

**Delvene** *See* DELPHINE.

**Delwen** *See* DELWYN.

**Delwyn** Welsh name based on the Welsh *del* ('pretty' or 'neat') and *wyn* ('white' or 'blessed'). Also encountered as **Delwen**.

**Delys** *See* DELICIA.

**Delyth** ('dellith') Welsh name based on the Welsh *del* ('pretty' or 'neat'). It remains confined largely to Wales itself.

**Demelza** English name that originated as a Cornish place name meaning 'hill-fort of Maeldaf'. It became popular after being selected by British novelist Winston Graham for the name of a character in his *Poldark* series of novels set in historical Cornwall, beginning with *Demelza* (1946).

**Demi** English name that

evolved as a shortened form of the Roman Demetra, itself descended from Demeter, the name of the goddess of the harvest in Greek mythology. It has become well known in recent years through US film actress Demi Moore (b. 1962).

**Dena** English name meaning 'valley'. Variant forms include **Dina**.

**Deneice/Denice/
Deniece** *See* DENISE.

**Denise** French name that developed as a feminine version of Denis (*see* DENNIS). It enjoyed a peak in popularity in the 1950s and 1960s. **Dennie** is a familiar form of the name. Variants include **Deneice**, **Denice** and **Deniece**.

**Dennie** *See* DENISE.

**Dervila** *See* DERVLA.

**Dervla** Irish name possibly based on the Irish *dear* ('daughter') and *file* ('poet') or *Fal* ('Ireland') and thus meaning 'daughter of Ireland'. Variants include **Dearbhail**, **Deirbhile** and **Dervila**.

**Deryn** Welsh name possibly based on *aderyn* ('bird'). It seems to have made its first appearance in Wales around the middle of the twentieth century.

**Desdemona** English name apparently based on the Greek *dusaimon* ('ill-fated'). It is famous as the name of the doomed wife of the central character in William Shakespeare's tragedy *Othello* (1602–4).

**Désirée** French name meaning 'desired'. It can be traced back ultimately to the Roman Desiderata, meaning 'desired' in Latin. Often rendered without the accents.

**Destinee/Destinie** *See* DESTINY.

**Destiny** English name based on the ordinary vocabulary word 'destiny'. It appears to be a relatively recent introduction. Variants include **Destinee** and **Destinie**.

**Detta** *See* BERNADETTE.

**Deva** English, Welsh, Scottish and Irish name based on the Latin name for the River Dee.

**Devon** English name based on that of the county of Devon.

**Di** *See* DIANA; DIANE; DINAH.

**Diahann** *See* DIANE.

**Diamond** English name based on that of the gemstone. It was among the various jewel names that enjoyed some popularity in the nineteenth century.

**Dian** *See* DIANE.

**Diana** English name that refers to the name of the Roman goddess of the moon and the hunt. Despite its pagan associations, it was taken up by English speakers after the Reformation. Notable bearers of the name have included Diana, Princess of Wales (1961–97). Shortened to **Di**. *See also* DEANNA; DIANE; DINAH.

**Diane** French version of the English DIANA that was taken up alongside the existing form of the name by English speakers in the 1930s. Variants include **Dian**, **Dianne**, **Deanne**, **Diahann** and **Dyan** (or **Dyanne**). Shortened to **Di**. *See also* DIONNE.

**Dianne** *See* DIANE.

**Didi** *See* DEE.

**Dido** Greek name meaning 'teacher'. It is famous in Greek mythology as the name of a queen of Carthage who killed herself after she was deserted by the hero Aeneas.

**Diedre** *See* DEIRDRE.

**Dil/Dill** *See* DILYS.

**Dilly** *See* DAFFODIL; DILWEN; DILYS.

**Dilwen** Welsh name that is thought to have resulted from the combination of DILYS and *gwyn* ('white') and meaning 'fair' or 'holy'. It appears to be an introduction of twentieth-century origin. Also found as **Dilwyn**. **Dilly** is an informal version.

**Dilwyn** *See* DILWEN.

**Dilys** Welsh name based on *dilys* ('genuine', 'steadfast' or 'sincere'). It appears to have been a nineteenth-century introduction that soon found favour beyond Welsh borders. **Dylis** and **Dyllis** are variant forms of the name. Shortened to **Dil**, **Dill** or **Dilly**.

**Dina** *See* DENA; DINAH.

**Dinah** Hebrew name based on *din* ('judgement' or 'lawsuit') and interpreted as meaning 'vindicated'. It often appears as a variant of DIANA, despite the fact that the two names have distinct origins. **Dina** is a variant form. Shortened to **Di**.

**Dione/Dionna** *See* DIONNE.

**Dionne** Feminine version of DION, itself descended via the Roman Dionysius from the Greek Dionysios or some other similar Greek source. Variants include **Dione** and **Dionna**.

**Divina** English name that developed as a variant of DAVINA, possibly under the influence of the ordinary vocabulary word 'divine'.

Variants include **Davinia**, which may reflect the influence of LAVINIA.

**Dixee** *See* DIXIE.

**Dixie** English name based on the French *dix* ('ten'). It is popular chiefly in the USA, where it is best known as the nickname of the southern states. Also found as **Dixee**.

**Dod/Dodie/Dodo** *See* DOROTHY.

**Doireann** *See* DOREAN.

**Doirend/Doirenn** *See* DARINA.

**Doll/Dolley** *See* DOLLY.

**Dolly** English name that evolved as an informal version of DOROTHY or DOLORES and is sometimes presumed (inaccurately) to have been inspired by the ordinary vocabulary word 'doll'. Shortened to **Doll**. Also spelled **Dolley**, chiefly in the USA.

**Dolores** Spanish name meaning 'sorrows' and thus referring to the title *Maria de los Dolores* ('Mary of the Sorrows') borne by the Virgin Mary. It became popular in the twentieth century, when it spread with Spanish emigrants to many parts of the English-speaking world. Also found as **Delores** or **Delora**. *See also* DOLLY; LOLA; LOLITA.

**Dominica** *See* DOMINIQUE.

**Dominique** Feminine equivalent, of French origin, of the male DOMINIC, itself based on the Latin *dominus* ('lord'). English speakers first took up the name in this French incarnation in the 1960s. The related **Dominica** is somewhat older.

**Donna** English name based on the Italian *donna* ('lady'). It was taken up by English speakers in the 1920s, initially in the USA. *See also* MADONNA.

**Dora** English name that developed as a shortened form of such names as **Dorothea**, ISADORA and THEODORA, which all share common origins in the Greek word *dōron* ('gift'). **Doria**, **Doretta**, **Dorette** and **Dorita** are rare variants. Familiar forms of the name include **Dorry** and **Dory**.

**Dorcas** English name based on the Greek *dorkas* ('doe' or 'gazelle'). It appears in the Bible as an interpretation of the Aramaic TABITHA. English Puritans adopted it as a first name after the Reformation. In Scotland it is sometimes employed as an anglicization of Deoiridh.

**Dorean** Irish name that developed as an anglicization of the Gaelic **Doireann**, itself resulting from the combination of the Gaelic *der* ('daughter') and the name of the legendary Irish hero Finn. It emerged as a popular choice among Irish speakers in the twentieth century, perhaps influenced by the English DOREEN.

**Doreen** English name that resulted from the combination of such names as DORA, KATHLEEN and MAUREEN. English speakers took up the name towards the end of the nineteenth century. Variants include **Dorene** and **Dorine**. *See also* DOREAN.

**Dorene** *See* DOREEN.

**Doretta/Dorette/Doria** *See* DORA.

**Dorice** *See* DORIS.

**Dorinda** English name that resulted from the combination of DORA and the suffix '-inda', as found in such names as BELINDA and CLARINDA. It was introduced as the name of a character in George Farquhar's play *The Beaux Stratagem* (1707).

**Dorine** *See* DOREEN.

**Doris** English name based on the Greek for 'bountiful' or else meaning 'person from Doris' (Doris being a region in ancient Greece), but also treated as a combination of DOROTHY and PHYLLIS. It appears in mythology as the name of a minor goddess. Also found as **Dorice**. **Dorrie** is a familiar version.

**Dorita** *See* DORA.

**Dorothea** *See* DOROTHY.

**Dorothy** English name descended via **Dorothea** from

the Greek *dōron* ('gift') and *theos* ('god') and thus meaning 'gift of God'. As Dorothea, it was taken up by English speakers in the sixteenth century. Dorothy eclipsed Dorothea from the late nineteenth century. Shortened to **Thea, Dee, Dot, Dottie** (or **Dotty**), **Dod, Dodo** or **Dodie**. *See also* DOLLY; DORA.

**Dorrie** *See* DORA; DORIS.

**Dorry/Dory** *See* DORA.

**Dot/Dottie/Dotty** *See* DOROTHY.

**Dreda** *See* ETHELDREDA.

**Drena** *See* ADRIENNE.

**Drew** English name that evolved as a shortened form of ANDREW or otherwise out of DROGO. Initially a name for boys, it has been bestowed upon girls in relatively recent times. Famous bearers of the name include US film actress Drew Barrymore (b. 1975).

**Drina** *See* ADRIENNE.

**Drucilla/Druscilla** *See* DRUSILLA.

**Drusilla** English name descended from the Roman Drusus, itself supposedly from the Greek *drosos* ('dew') and meaning 'fruitful' or 'dewy-eyed'. It appears in the Bible and was taken up by English speakers in the seventeenth century. Also found as **Drucilla** or **Druscilla**. *See also* CILLA.

**Dulce** *See* DULCIE.

**Dulcie** English name based on the Latin *dulcis* ('sweet'). Recorded in use among English speakers in medieval times in such forms as Duce or Dowse, it was revived in its modern form towards the end of the nineteenth century. **Dulce** is a shortened form.

**Dusty** English name that emerged either as a feminine equivalent of the masculine DUSTIN or else as a borrowing of the ordinary vocabulary word 'dusty' (referring to the colour of a person's hair or complexion). It has made occasional appearances as a first name since the 1950s.

**Dyan/Dyanne** *See* DIANE.

**Dylis/Dyllis** *See* DILYS.

**Dymphna** Irish name that is thought to have evolved from the Gaelic Damhnait, itself from *damh* ('fawn' or 'stag') and *damh* ('poet'). It is little known outside Ireland itself. **Dympna** is a variant form.

**Dympna** *See* DYMPHNA.

# GIRLS' NAMES

**Eadan** ('aidan' or 'adan') Irish name based on the Old Irish Etain, possibly based on the Old Irish *et* ('jealousy'). It features in Irish legend as the name of a sun goddess. Also encountered as **Etan**.

**Earlean/Earlena** *See* EARLENE.

**Earlene** Feminine equivalent of EARL. Variants include **Earlena**, **Erlean**, **Erleen** and **Erlinda**.

**Eartha** English name based on the ordinary vocabulary word 'earth'. Famous bearers of the name have included US jazz singer and actress Eartha Kitt (b. 1928). Variants include **Ertha** and **Erthel**.

**Easter** English name based on the name of the Christian festival of Easter, itself a reference to the Germanic spring goddess Eostre. Sometimes treated as a variant of ESTHER.

**Ebo** *See* EBONY.

**Ebony** English name based on the name of the black wood ebony. It was taken up chiefly among black Americans in the 1970s and by the 1980s ranked among the top three most popular names among female members of the black community in the USA. Shortened to **Ebo**.

**Echo** English name based on the ordinary vocabulary word 'echo'. In Greek legend, Echo was a nymph whose unceasing chatter irritated the goddess Hera, who robbed her of the power of independent speech and allowed her only to repeat the last fragment of what others said.

**Eda** *See* ADA; EDITH.

**Edana** Feminine equivalent of the Irish AIDAN, meaning 'fire'.

**Ede** *See* EDITH.

**Eden** English name that is descended either from the Old English **Edun** or **Edon**, which came in turn from the Old English *ead* ('riches') and *hun* ('bearcub'), or from the name of the biblical paradise.

**Edie** *See* EDITH.

**Edina** *See* EDNA; EDWINA.

**Edith** English, French, German and Scandinavian descended from the Old English Eadgyth, itself based on the Old English *ead* ('riches') and *gyth* ('strife') and thus meaning 'rich in war'. Shortened to **Edy**, **Edie** or **Eda**.

**Edlyn** English name based on the Old English for 'noble maid'.

**Edmé** *See* ESMÉ.

**Edna** English name possibly based on the Hebrew *ednah* ('rejuvenation' or 'pleasure') or else on the Irish EITHNE, itself from the Irish Gaelic for 'kernel'. It appears in the Apocrypha as the name of

Sarah's mother and is sometimes considered a feminine equivalent of EDEN. Variants include **Edina**.

**Edweena/Edwena** *See* EDWINA.

**Edwina** Feminine form of EDWIN. It does not seem to have been in use in medieval times and probably made its first appearances in the nineteenth century when Edwin was revived. Variants include **Edweena** and **Edwena**.

**Edy** *See* EDITH.

**Effie** *See also* EPHRAIM; EUPHEMIA.

**Eglantina** *See* EGLANTINE.

**Eglantine** English flower name based on that of the plant usually identified as sweetbrier (which has the French name *aiglent*) but often confused with honeysuckle. Variants include **Eglantina**, **Eglantyne** and **Eglentyne**.

**Eglantyne/Eglentyne** *See* EGLANTINE.

**Eibhlin** *See* EILEEN.

**Eilean** *See* EILEEN.

**Eileen** English name based
on the Irish **Eibhlin**, an Irish
equivalent of AVELINE or
EVELYN, but also treated as an
Irish form of HELEN. It was
widely exported by Irish
emigrants towards the end of
the nineteenth century.
Variants include **Aileen** (a
Scottish variant), **Eilean**,
**Eilene**, **Ilean**, **Ileen**, **Ileene**
and **Ilene**. **Eily** is a familiar
form.

**Eilene** *See* EILEEN.

**Eiluned** *See* ELUNED.

**Eilwen** Welsh name meaning
'fair brow'.

**Eily** *See* EILEEN.

**Eira** ('eera' or 'ighra') Welsh
name meaning 'snow'. It is a
relatively recent introduction
that has yet to win acceptance
outside Wales.

**Eireen** *See* EIRIAN.

**Eirian** ('ighreean') Welsh
name meaning 'bright',
'beautiful' or 'silver'. Variants
include **Eireen**, **Arian** and
**Ariane**.

**Eirlys** ('airlees' or 'igherliss')
Welsh name meaning
'snowdrop'.

**Eirwen** Welsh name
meaning 'snow white'.

**Eithne** ('ethnee' or 'eenya')
Irish name probably based on
the Gaelic *eithne* ('kernel'),
although often treated as a
feminine version of AIDAN.
Borne by an Irish goddess,
several Irish queens and nine
saints, the name remains rare
outside Ireland. Variants
include **Enya**, **Ethna**, **Ethne**,
**Etna** and **Aithne**. *See also* ENA.

**Elain** Welsh name meaning
'fawn' or 'hind'. Sometimes
confused with the otherwise
unrelated ELAINE.

**Elaine** English name
descended via Old French from
HELEN. It appeared with
increasing frequency among
English speakers from the late
nineteenth century following
its appearance in Alfred, Lord
Tennyson's *Idylls of the King*
(1859). Variants include
**Elayne**.

**Elayne** *See* ELAINE.

**Eleanor** English name of disputed origin. It probably evolved as a French version of HELEN, itself based on the Old German *al* ('all'). The name came to England with Henry II's wife, Eleanor of Aquitaine (1122–1204). Variants include **Eleanora, Elenora, Eleonora, Eleonore, Lenore** and **Elinor**. **Ellie,** NELL, **Nellie, Nelly,** NORA and **Norah** are familiar forms.

**Eleanora** *See* ELEANOR.

**Electra** English version of the Italian Elettra, itself based on the Greek *elektor* ('brilliant'). It is usually associated with the legend of Orestes and Electra, the children of Agamemnon who avenged their father's murder.

**Elen** Welsh equivalent of HELEN. The name may have developed not directly from Helen but perhaps from the Welsh *elen* ('nymph'). Variants include **Elin**.

**Elena** *See* HELEN.

**Elenora/Eleonora/ Eleonore** *See* ELEANOR.

**Eleri** Welsh name of uncertain meaning. It appears in Welsh mythology as the name of the daughter of Brychan.

**Elfleda** English name descended from the Old English Aethelflaed, itself based on the Old English *aethel* ('noble') and *flaed* ('beauty').

**Elfreda** English name descended from the Old English Aelfthryth, itself based on the Old English *aelf* ('elf') and *thryth* ('strength'). Also found as **Elfrida** or ALFREDA. Shortened to FREDA or **Friede**.

**Elfrida** *See* ELFREDA.

**Elin** *See* ELEN.

**Elined** *See* ELUNED.

**Elinor** *See* ELEANOR.

**Elisabeth** *See* ELIZABETH.

**Elise/Elissa** *See* ELIZA.

**Elita** English name based on the French *élite* ('chosen').

**Eliza** English name that evolved as a shortened form of ELIZABETH. **Elise** and **Elissa** are popular variants. *See also* LISA.

**Elizabeth** English name based on the Hebrew Elisheba, meaning 'oath of God' or 'God has sworn'. It was the name of John the Baptist's mother and in 1600 one in five females born in England was given the name. Also found as **Elisabeth**. Variants in other languages include the Welsh **Bethan**. Shortened to **Lib**, **Libby**, LISA, **Lisbeth**, **Liz**, **Liza**, **Lizzie**, **Lizzy** and **Tetty**. *See also* BESS; BETH; BETSY; BETTY; ELIZA; ELSA; ELSIE; ELSPETH; ISABEL.

**Elke** Jewish name based on the Hebrew *elkahan* ('possessed by God'), although it is also regarded as a Yiddish version of ELAINE or as a German equivalent of ALICE. Also found as **Elkie**.

**Elkie** *See* ELKE.

**Ella** English name descended via French from the Old German Alia, itself from the German *al* ('all'). It is also used as a shortened form of such

names as ELEANOR and ELLEN. It came to England with the Normans. **Ellie** is a familiar form of the name.

**Ellar** Scottish name that developed as an anglicization of the Gaelic Eallair, itself from the Latin *cella* ('cellar'). The name was originally borne by butlers or stewards in monasteries.

**Ellen** English name that was taken up as a variant of HELEN in the sixteenth century. Variants include **Ellie**, NELL, **Nellie** and **Nelly**.

**Ellerie** Feminine equivalent of ELLERY.

**Ellie** *See* ELEANOR; ELLA; ELLEN; ELSA; HELEN.

**Ellis** English name that evolved either from the identical surname, based on ELIAS, or else as a variant of ISABEL or ALICE or as an anglicization of the Irish Eilis or the Welsh Elisud, itself from *elus* ('kind').

**Elly** *See* ELEANOR; ELLA; ELLEN; HELEN.

**Elma** English name that is thought to have evolved through the combination of ELIZABETH and MARY. Largely confined to the USA, it is also found as a shortened form of WILHELMINA and other names ending '-elma' and occasionally as a feminine equivalent of ELMER.

**Elodia** *See* ÉLODIE.

**Élodie** French name based on the Germanic *ali* ('other' or 'foreign') and *od* ('riches'). Elodia is a variant.

**Eloisa** *See* ÉLOISE.

**Éloise** French name of uncertain Germanic origin has made irregular appearances (usually without the accent) among English speakers over the centuries. It may come from the Old German for 'hale' or 'wide' and is sometimes treated as a feminine equivalent of LOUIS. Also found as **Eloisa**.

**Elsa** English, German and Swedish name based on ELIZABETH. Variants include **Ilsa** and **Ilse**. **Ellie** is a familiar form of the name. *See also* AILSA.

**Else** *See* ELSIE.

**Elsie** English name that developed via **Elspie** as a familiar form of ELSPETH, although it is also sometimes encountered as a shortened form of ELIZABETH. Sometimes abbreviated to **Else**.

**Elspeth** English and Scottish name that developed as a variant of ELIZABETH in the nineteenth century. **Elspie** is a familiar form of the name. *See also* ELSIE.

**Elspie** *See* ELSPETH.

**Eluned** Welsh name that is thought to have evolved out of the earlier **Luned** or **Lunet**, names which may have evolved out of the Welsh *eilun* ('idol'). Also encountered as **Eiluned** or **Elined**.

**Elvira** Spanish name of uncertain origin, possibly descended from the Old German Alwara, itself from the Old German *al* ('all') and *wer* ('true') and thus meaning 'true to all'.

**Elysia** English name based on the Greek for 'blissful'. It evolved as a feminine version of Elysium, the name of heaven in Greek mythology.

**Em** *See* EMILY; EMMA; EMMELINE.

**Emanuela** *See* EMANUELLE.

**Emanuelle** Feminine version of EMANUEL, itself based on the Hebrew Immanuel, meaning 'God with us'. Variants include **Emanuela** and **Emmanuela**.

**Emblem/Emblin/ Emblyn/Emeline/ Emelyn** *See* EMMELINE.

**Emer** Irish name of uncertain origin. It is famous in Irish mythology as the name of the hero Cuchulain's beloved, who was depicted as the personification of all female qualities. **Emir** is a rare variant form.

**Emerald** English name based on that of the gem. Like other jewel names, it enjoyed some popularity among English speakers towards the end of the nineteenth century. Occasionally encountered as a familiar form of ESMERALDA.

**Emilia** English name that developed as a variant of AMELIA. It emerged during medieval times and is still in use today. Well-known bearers of the name include three characters in the plays of William Shakespeare.

**Emily** English first name descended from the Roman Aemilia, itself from the Latin for 'striving' or 'eager'. **Em, Emmie, Emmy** and **Milly** (or **Millie**) are shortened forms of the name. *See also* AMELIA.

**Emir** *See* EMER.

**Emlyn** Welsh name that is sometimes traced back to the Roman Aemilius, itself from the Latin for 'striving' or 'eager', or else from unknown Celtic roots. It is usually considered a boys' name but is occasionally given to girls.

**Emma** English name based on Old German *ermen* ('entire' or 'universal'). It has been in regular use among English speakers since medieval times. **Em, Emmie** and **Emmy** are familiar forms of the name.

**Emmanuela** *See*
EMANUELLE.

**Emmeline** English name
that developed as a variant of
EMMA but can also be traced
back via the Old French
Ameline to the Old German
*amal* ('labour'). Also
encountered as a rare variant of
EMILIA or EMILY, it may also
be found as **Emeline** or
**Emelyn** as well as the rarer
**Emblem, Emblin** or **Emblyn**.

**Emmie/Emmy** *See*
EMILY; EMMA; EMMELINE.

**Ena** English version of the
Irish EITHNE that is also in use
as a shortened form of
EUGENIA, HELENA and other
names with similar endings. It
became popular at the end of
the nineteenth century after it
was bestowed upon Queen
Victoria's granddaughter,
Princess Ena (Victoria Eugénie
Julia Ena; 1887–1969). Also
found as INA.

**Enid** English name that may
have developed from the
Welsh *enaid* ('soul' or 'life') or
possibly from *enit* ('woodlark').
It became popular among
English speakers towards the
end of the nineteenth century
in reference to the Arthurian
legend of Enid and Geraint.

**Enola** English name of
uncertain meaning. A late
nineteenth-century
introduction, it acquired some
notoriety through the 'Enola
Gay', the nickname of the US
Superfortress bomber that
dropped an atomic bomb on
Hiroshima on 6 August 1945.

**Enya** *See* EITHNE.

**Eppie** *See* EUPHEMIA;
HEPHZIBAH.

**Erica** Feminine equivalent of
ERIC, itself from *ei* ('ever' or
'always') or *einn* ('one') and *rikr*
('ruler') and thus meaning
'ever-ruling'. It may have been
influenced by *erica*, the Latin
name for the plant heather. In
Scotland it may be treated as an
anglicization of the Gaelic
**Oighrig**. Also found as **Erika.
Rica, Ricki, Rika** and **Rikki**
are shortened forms.

**Erika** *See* ERICA.

**Erin** Irish name based on
Eire, the traditional Gaelic
name for Ireland itself. It has

made occasional appearances as a first name since the late nineteenth century, not only in Ireland but also in Australia, the USA and elsewhere. **Errin** and **Eryn** are variant forms.

**Erlean/Erleen/Erlinda** *See* EARLENE.

**Erma** *See* IRMA.

**Ermintrude** English, French and German name based on the Old German *ermen* ('entire' or 'universal') and *traut* ('beloved') and thus meaning 'wholly beloved'. Shortened to **Trudie**, **Trudi** or TRUDY.

**Erna** English name that developed as a shortened form of ERNESTA and **Ernestine**. It was taken up by English speakers in the nineteenth century.

**Ernesta** Feminine equivalent of ERNEST, itself based on the Old German *eornost* ('earnestness' or 'seriousness'). It made its first appearances among English speakers at the time of accession of the Hanoverian George I.

**Ernestina** and **Ernestine** are variant forms. *See also* ERNA.

**Ernestina/Ernestine** *See* ERNESTA.

**Errin** *See* ERIN.

**Ertha/Erthel** *See* EARTHA.

**Eryn** *See* ERIN.

**Esmaralda** *See* ESMERALDA.

**Esmé** French name based on the Old French *esme* ('loved' or 'esteemed'). As a name for girls, also spelled **Esmée**, it was taken up by English speakers in the eighteenth century. Sometimes treated as an abbreviated form of ESMERALDA. *See also* AIMÉE.

**Esmée** *See* ESMÉ.

**Esmeralda** English name based on the Spanish *esmeralda* ('emerald'). Borne by the gypsy girl in Victor Hugo's *The Hunchback of Notre Dame* (1831), it is sometimes shortened to ESMÉ. Also rendered as **Esmerelda** or **Esmaralda**. *See also* EMERALD.

**Esmerelda** *See* ESMERALDA.

**Esperanza** Spanish name descended from the Roman Sperantia, itself based on the Latin *sperans* ('hope').

**Ess/Essa** *See* ESTHER.

**Essie** *See* ESTELLE; ESTHER.

**Essylt** *See* ISOLDE.

**Esta** *See* ESTHER; HESTER.

**Estella** *See* ESTELLE.

**Estelle** French name based on STELLA and thus meaning 'star'. Before Estelle became the dominant form in the twentieth century it was usually encountered as **Estella**. **Essie** is a familiar form of the name.

**Esther** Biblical name that may have had its roots in the Persian *stara* ('star') but is otherwise associated with the Hebrew Hadassah, meaning 'myrtle' or 'bride'. Another theory suggests it is a Hebrew version of Ishtar, the name of the Persian goddess of love. **Ess**, **Essa**, **Essie**, **Esta**, **Ettie**, **Etty**, **Hester** and **Hetty** are familiar forms of the name.

**Esyllt** *See* ISOLDE.

**Etan** *See* EADAN.

**Eth** *See* ETHEL.

**Ethel** English name based ultimately on the Old German *ethel* ('noble'). It is thought to represent a shortened version of Anglo-Saxon names like Ethelburga and Ethelthryth. Shortened to **Eth** and, more rarely, to **Thel**.

**Etheldreda** English name based on the Old English *aethel* ('noble') and *thryth* ('strength'). It was borne by a seventh-century English saint and remained in occasional use before giving way to the related AUDREY around the sixteenth century. **Dreda** is a shortened version.

**Ethna/Ethne/Etna** *See* EITHNE.

**Etta** *See* HENRIETTA.

**Ettie/Etty** *See* ESTHER; HENRIETTA.

**Eudora** Greek name based on *eu* ('good') and *dōron* ('gift') and thus meaning 'good gift'. Commonly shortened to DORA.

**Eugenia** *See* EUGENIE.

**Eugenie** French name (Eugénie) adopted as a feminine equivalent of EUGENE. Famous from Napoleon III's wife, the Empress Eugénie (1826–1920), who spent much of her life in England, it was taken up by English speakers in the nineteenth century. **Eugenia** is a rare variant. Shortened to **Gene** or **Genie**. *See also* ENA.

**Eulalia** English, Italian and Spanish name based on the Greek *eu* ('good') and *lalein* ('chatter' or 'talk') and thus meaning 'sweetly speaking'. **Lallie** and **Lally** are familiar forms.

**Eunice** ('yoonis') Biblical name based on the Greek *eu* ('good') and *nike* ('victory') and thus meaning 'good victory'. Also found as **Unice**.

**Euphemia** Greek name based on *eu* ('well') and *phenai* ('to speak') and thus meaning 'well spoken of', 'well regarded' or 'of good repute'. **Effie**, **Eppie**, **Phamie**, **Phemie** and FANNY are familiar forms of the name.

**Eustacia** Feminine equivalent of EUSTACE, itself descended via French from the Greek Eustakhios, from the Greek *eu* ('good') and *stakhus* ('ear of corn' or 'grapes') and thus interpreted as meaning 'fruitful'. **Stacy** is a familiar form of the name.

**Eva** Roman name based on the Hebrew Havvah, meaning 'living'. The usual form of the English EVE in many non-English-speaking cultures, it was taken up by English speakers as an alternative form of the name around the middle of the nineteenth century. A variant is **Evita**, made famous as the nickname of Eva Perón, wife of the Argentine President Juan Perón. *See also* AVA; EVANGELINE.

**Evadne** Greek name based on *eu* ('well') in combination with another unknown root. It appears in Greek mythology and has made occasional appearances among English speakers since the seventeenth century.

**Evalina/Evaline/Evalyn** *See* EVELYN.

**Evangelina** *See*
EVANGELINE.

**Evangeline** English name based on the Latin *evangelium* ('gospel'). It appears to have been popularized through Henry Wadsworth Longfellow's narrative poem *Evangeline* (1847). Also found as **Evangelina**. Shortened to EVA or **Evie**.

**Eve** English and French name based on the Hebrew Havvah, itself from the Hebrew *hayya* ('living'). As the name of the female companion of the biblical Adam, the name has always had special religious significance among Christians. **Evie** is a familiar form of the name. *See also* EVA; EVELYN.

**Eveleen/Evelina/ Eveline** *See* EVELYN.

**Evelyn** English name that is bestowed upon both sexes. As a name for girls, possibly a combination of EVE and LYNN or influenced by the French AVELINE, it was in use among English speakers by the late nineteenth century. Variants include **Evalina**, **Evaline**, **Evalyn**, **Evelyne**, **Eveline**, **Eveleen** and **Eibhlin**. Shortened to **Evie** or EVE.

**Evelyne** *See* EVELYN.

**Evie** *See* EVA; EVANGELINE; EVE; EVELYN.

**Evita** *See* EVA.

**Evonne** *See* YVONNE.

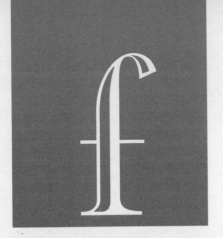

# GIRLS' NAMES

**Fabia** Feminine version of the Roman Fabianus (*see* FABIAN), which was itself based on the Latin *faba* ('bean'). **Fabienne** is a French equivalent.

**Fabienne** *See* FABIA.

**Fae** *See* FAY.

**Faith** English virtue name that was taken up by the Puritans in the seventeenth century, initially as a name for either sex. Unlike some of the other virtue names, Faith has remained in use, although it is now reserved for females. Familiar forms include FAY and **Faithie**.

**Faithie** *See* FAITH.

**Fallon** English name that originated as the Irish surname O Fallamhain, which means 'leader'.

**Fan** *See* FANNY.

**Fancy** English name that may have arisen as a variant of FANNY, or possibly under the influence of the ordinary vocabulary word 'fiancée'.

**Fannie** *See* FANNY.

**Fanny** English name that developed as a shortened form of such names as EUPHEMIA, FRANCES and MYFANWY. Also found as **Fannie**, it appeared with considerable frequency among English speakers from the late seventeenth century. Shortened to **Fan**. *See also* FANCY.

**Farah** Arabic name meaning 'joy' or 'cheerfulness'.

**Farrah** English name ultimately based on the Latin for 'iron'. The name became widely known in the 1970s through US actress Farrah Fawcett-Majors (b. 1947).

**Fatima** Arabic name meaning 'weaning' or 'abstaining', often interpreted as meaning 'chaste' or 'motherly'. Borne by the favourite daughter of Muhammad, it has long been a popular choice among Muslims.

**Faustina** *See* FAUSTINE.

**Faustine** French name based on the Latin *faustus* ('fortunate'). **Faustina** is a rare English variant. Both versions of the name are closely associated with the Faust legend as recounted in Christopher Marlowe's play *Doctor Faustus* (c. 1592).

**Fawn** English name that evolved either from the ordinary vocabulary word for a young deer or else through the combination of FAY and DAWN or similar names.

**Fay** English name based on the traditional name for a fairy. It may also be encountered as a shortened form of FAITH. **Faye** and **Fae** are variant forms.

**Faye** *See* FAY.

**Fearne** *See* FERN.

**Fedelma** *See* FIDELMA.

**Fedora** *See* THEODORA.

**Felicia** *See* FELICITY.

**Felicity** English name based on the ordinary vocabulary word meaning 'good luck' or 'good fortune'. Often treated as a feminine equivalent of FELIX, it was among the virtue names adopted by Puritans in the seventeenth century. Familiar forms include **Flick, Liss, Lissa, Lissie, Phil** and LUCKY. **Felicia** is a rare variant of eighteenth-century origin.

**Femie** *See* EUPHEMIA.

**Fenella** Irish name that developed out of **Fionnuala**, itself based on the Gaelic *fionn* ('fair' or 'white') and *guala* ('shoulder') and thus meaning 'fair-shouldered'. In Irish legend Fionnuala is turned into a swan by her wicked stepmother and is only released from the spell when Ireland adopts Christianity. Variants include **Finella, Finola** and

**Fionola**. Shortened to **Nella**, **Nola** or **Nuala**. *See also* PENELOPE.

**Feodora** *See* THEODORA.

**Fern** English name based on that of the plant. It is thought to have made its first appearance among English speakers along with other flower and plant names in the nineteenth century. Also found as **Fearne**.

**Fernanda** Feminine version of the Spanish Fernando (*see* FERDINAND).

**Ffion** ('feeon') Welsh name meaning 'rose' or 'foxglove finger'.

**Fi** *See* FIONA.

**Fidelia** English name based on the Latin *fidelis* ('faithful'). It was included among the virtue names taken up by English Puritans in the seventeenth century.

**Fidelma** Irish name based on the Gaelic Feidhelm (or Fedelm), which may have originally meant 'beauty'. It was borne by an early Irish saint who was converted to Christianity by St Patrick. **Fedelma** is a variant. Shortened to **Delma**.

**Fifi** French name that developed as a shortened form of JOSEPHINE and various other names incorporating 'fi', such as FIONA and YVONNE.

**Fina** *See* FIONA; SERAPHINA.

**Finella/Finola** *See* FENELLA.

**Fiona** English name based on the Scottish Gaelic *fionn* ('fair' or 'white'). It became well known through its appearance in the Ossianic poems of James Macpherson (1736–96), who seems to have been the first person to use the name. Variants include **Fina** and the rare **Tiona**. Shortened to **Fi**.

**Fionnuala/Fionola** *See* FENELLA.

**Flame** English name based on the ordinary vocabulary word 'flame'. A relatively recent introduction.

**Flave** *See* FLAVIA.

**Flavia** Roman name based
on the Latin *flavus* ('yellow' or
'golden'), probably a reference
to blonde hair. Records of its
use among English speakers go
back to the sixteenth century.
Shortened to **Flave** or **Flavie**
(also a French variant of the
name). *See also* FULVIA.

**Flavie** *See* FLAVIA.

**Fleur** French name meaning
'flower'. Its adoption by
English speakers owed much to
the popularity of a character
bearing the name in John
Galsworthy's *Forsyte Saga*
novels (1906–22). A variant
form is **Fleurette**. *See also*
BLOSSOM; FLORA; FLOWER.

**Fleurette** *See* FLEUR.

**Flick** *See* FELICITY.

**Flo** *See* FLOELLA; FLORA;
FLORENCE.

**Floella** English name that is
thought to have resulted from
the combination of FLORA and
FLORENCE with ELLA or
similar names. Commonly
shortened to **Flo**.

**Flora** Roman name based on

the Latin *flos* ('flower'). The
name of the Roman goddess of
the spring, it became popular
in Scotland in tribute to Flora
MacDonald (Fionnaghal
MacDonald; 1722–90), who in
1746 helped Bonnie Prince
Charlie escape from Scotland.
Variants include **Floretta**,
**Florette** and **Florinda**. **Flo**,
**Florrie**, **Floss** and **Flossie** are
informal versions.

**Florence** English name
descended from the Roman
Florentia, itself based on the
Latin *florens* ('blossoming' or
'flourishing'). It was first taken
up by English speakers in the
medieval period (when it was
also used as a name for boys).
**Florentina** is a rare variant.
Shortened to **Flo**, **Florrie**,
**Floss**, **Flossie** and **Floy**.

**Florentina** *See* FLORENCE.

**Floretta/Florette/**
**Florinda** *See* FLORA.

**Florrie/Floss/Flossie** *See*
FLORA; FLORENCE.

**Flower** English name based
on the ordinary vocabulary
word 'flower'. *See also*
BLOSSOM; FLEUR; FLORA.

**Floy** *See* FLORENCE.

**Fortune** English name based on the Latin *fortuna* ('fortune' or 'fate'). It was taken up by English Puritans in the seventeenth century but is rare today.

**Fran** *See* FRANCES; FRANCESCA.

**Francene** *See* FRANCES.

**Frances** Feminine version of FRANCIS, initially in use for boys as well as girls. Variants of the name include **Francine** (or **Francene**). Shortened to **Fran**, **Frannie** (or **Franny**), **Francie**, **Frankie** or FANNY. *See also* FRANCESCA.

**Francesca** Italian name that developed as a feminine form of the Italian FRANCESCO, which was itself descended from the Roman Franciscus, meaning 'Frenchman'. Shortened to **Fran** or **Franny**.

**Francie/Francine** *See* FRANCES.

**Françoise** ('fronswahz') Feminine version of the French FRANÇOIS, descended ultimately from the Roman Franciscus.

**Frankie/Frannie/ Franny** *See* FRANCES; FRANCESCA.

**Frea** *See* FREYA.

**Fred** *See* FREDA; FREDERICA.

**Freda** English name that developed as a shortened form of such names as ALFREDA, FREDERICA and WINIFRED, although it is often treated as a feminine equivalent of FRED or FREDERICK. Sometimes encountered as **Frida** and/or **Frieda**. Informal versions include **Fred** and **Freddie**.

**Freddie** *See* FREDA; FREDERICA.

**Frederica** English name that evolved as a feminine form of FREDERICK. Variant forms include **Fritzi**. Shortened to **Fred**, FREDA, **Freddie**, **Rickie**, **Ricky** or **Rica**.

**Freya** Scandinavian name based on that of the Norse goddess of love (after whom Friday was named). It is thought to have come originally from the German *frau* ('woman'). It is particularly popular in Scotland and the Shetland Islands. Variants include **Frea**.

**Frida** *See* ELFREDA; FREDA.

**Frieda** *See* FREDA.

**Fritzi** *See* FREDERICA.

**Fulvia** Italian and English name that developed originally as the feminine form of the Roman Fulvius, itself based on the Latin *fulvus* ('dusky' or 'tawny').

## GIRLS' NAMES

**Gab/Gabby/Gabi/ Gabriella** *See* GABRIELLE.

**Gabrielle** French name that developed as a feminine equivalent of GABRIEL, meaning 'my strength is God' or 'man of God'. English speakers adopted the name towards the end of the nineteenth century. Variants include **Gabriella**. Shortened to **Gab**, **Gabby**, **Gabi** or **Gaby**. *See also* GAY.

**Gaby** *See* GABRIELLE.

**Gae** *See* GAY.

**Gaea** *See* GAIA.

**Gaenor** *See* GAYNOR.

**Gaerwen** Welsh name meaning 'white castle'.

**Gaia** Greek name based on the Greek *gē* ('earth'). In classical mythology it was borne by the goddess of the earth who gave birth to the Titans. Also found as **Gaea**.

**Gail** English name that evolved as a shortened form of ABIGAIL. It began to appear among English speakers during the 1930s. Also found as **Gale** or **Gayle**.

**Gala** *See* GALINA.

**Galatea** Greek name meaning 'milky white'. The name was borne in Roman mythology by a statue that was brought to life by the goddess Venus.

**Gale** *See* GAIL.

**Galina** Russian name of uncertain origins, though possibly based on the Greek *galēnē* ('calm'). Variants include **Gala**, as borne by Spanish artist Salvador Dalí's wife Gala (Yelena Diakonov; 1904–84).

**Gardenia** English flower name that has made irregular appearances as a first name since the nineteenth century. The flower itself was named after an eighteenth-century naturalist called Dr Alexander Garden.

**Garnet** English name that was taken up as a first name in the nineteenth century at a time when many other jewel names came into fashion.

**Gay** English name based on the French *gai* ('joyful' or 'cheerful'). It became popular among English speakers in the 1930s and in its early history was occasionally borne by men as well as women. Variants include **Gaye** and the rarer **Gae**.

**Gaye** *See* GAY.

**Gayle** *See* GAIL.

**Gaynor** English name that evolved in medieval times as a variant of GUINEVERE. **Gaenor** is a Welsh variant.

**Geena** *See* GINA.

**Geeta** *See* GITA.

**Gem** *See* GEMMA.

**Gemma** English, Irish and Italian name based on the Italian for 'gem' or 'jewel'. A long-established favourite in Italy, it has become relatively common in the English-speaking world, perhaps under the influence of EMMA. Also found as **Jemma**. Shortened to **Gem**.

**Gena** *See* GINA.

**Gene** English name that developed as a shortened form of EUGENIE or a variant of JEAN.

**Genette** *See* JEANETTE.

**Geneva** English name that may have been inspired by the name of the city in Switzerland, although it has also been suggested that it developed as a variant of GENEVIEVE or JENNIFER.

**Genevieve** French name possibly based on the Old German *geno* ('people' or 'race') and *wefa* ('woman') and thus meaning 'lady of the people'. It was adopted by English speakers (usually without the accent of the French **Geneviève**) in the nineteenth century. Shortened to **Ginny**, GINA, **Ginette** or **Veva**.

**Genie** *See* EUGENIE.

**Gentian** English name based on that of the flower, which itself may have been named after Gentius, a king of classical Illyria who studied the plant's medicinal uses.

**George** *See* GEORGETTE; GEORGIA; GEORGINA.

**Georgene** *See* GEORGINA.

**Georgette** French variant of the masculine GEORGE, itself based ultimately on the Greek *geōrgos* ('farmer'). It was taken up by English speakers in the early twentieth century. Shortened to **Georgie** or **George**.

**Georgia** Feminine equivalent of GEORGE, itself based ultimately on the Greek *geōrgos* ('farmer'). It was promoted in the USA through association with the state of Georgia but is popular elsewhere, often linked with such similar names as GEORGINA. Also found as **Giorgia**. Informal versions include **Georgie** and **George**.

**Georgiana** English name that developed from GEORGIA or GEORGINA as a feminine version of GEORGE, perhaps under the influence of JULIANA. This Latinate form of the name enjoyed considerable popularity in the eighteenth century. Shortened to **Georgie** or **Georgy**.

**Georgie** *See* GEORGETTE; GEORGIA; GEORGIANA; GEORGINA.

**Georgina** Feminine version of GEORGE itself based ultimately on the Greek *geōrgos* ('farmer'). It was taken up by English speakers in the eighteenth century, becoming especially popular in Scotland. It largely replaced GEORGIANA in the nineteenth century. **Georgene** and **Georgine** are variant forms. Shortened to **Georgie**, **George** or GINA.

**Georgine** *See* GEORGINA.

**Georgy** *See* GEORGIANA.

**Geraldine** Feminine version of GERALD, itself based on the Old German *ger* ('spear') and *wald* ('rule') and thus meaning 'spear rule'. It entered general usage in the English-speaking world in the nineteenth century, partly due to its appearance in Samuel Taylor Coleridge's poem *Christabel* (1816). Shortened forms include **Gerrie**, GERRY, **Jerrie** and **Jerry**.

**Geranium** English name based on that of the popular garden flower.

**Gerda** Scandinavian name that was probably based on the Old Norse *garthr* ('enclosure' or 'guardian'). Borne by a beautiful Norse goddess of peace and fertility, it is also employed as a variant of GERTRUDE.

**Geri** *See* GERRY.

**Gerrie** *See* GERALDINE; GERRY.

**Gerry** English name that evolved as a shortened form of GERALDINE and now often considered a name in its own right. Also found as **Gerrie**, **Geri** or **Jerry**.

**Gert/Gertie** *See* GERTRUDE.

**Gertrude** English, French, German and Dutch name based on the Old German *ger* ('spear') and *traut* ('strength') and thus meaning 'strong with the spear' or 'ruler of the spear'. It was taken up by English speakers towards the end of the medieval period. Shortened to **Gert**, **Gertie**, TRUDY, **Trudi** or **Trudie**.

**Ghislain** *See* GHISLAINE.

**Ghislaine** ('gilane' or 'gilan') French name that developed as a variant of GISELLE. It has made occasional appearances among English speakers since the 1920s. Sometimes shortened to GIGI. Variants include **Ghislane** and **Ghislain**.

**Ghislane** *See* GHISLAINE.

**Gigi** ('jeejee') French name that developed as a shortened form of GHISLAINE and other names. In Colette's novel *Gigi* (1958) it is treated as a familiar form of the French **Gilberte**,

the feminine version of
GILBERT.

**Gilberte** *See* GIGI.

**Gilda** Italian name that may
have developed from an Old
German name based on *hild* or
*gild* ('sacrifice'), from the Gaelic
for 'servant of God' or from
the Old English for 'golden'.
The name was known in
Anglo-Saxon England.

**Gill** *See* GILLIAN.

**Gillian** English name that
developed either as an
elaboration of JILL or as a
feminine version of JULIAN.
Another theory suggests it
evolved from the Scottish
Gaelic for 'servant of St John'.
Also found as **Jillian,** a
relatively modern form of the
name. Commonly shortened to
**Gill, Gillie** or **Gilly.**

**Gillie/Gilly** *See* GILLIAN.

**Gina** Italian and English
name that developed as a
shortened form of GEORGINA
and REGINA. It was taken up
by English speakers in the
1920s. Also found as **Gena** or
**Geena** – as borne by US actress

Geena Davis (b. 1957). *See also*
GENEVIEVE.

**Ginette** *See* GENEVIEVE.

**Ginger** English name that
developed as a nickname for
anyone with red hair or a
tempestuous character. As a
girls' name it is sometimes used
as a familiar form of VIRGINIA.

**Gini/Ginnie/Ginny** *See*
GENEVIEVE; VIRGINIA.

**Giorgia** *See* GEORGIA.

**Gipsy** *See* GYPSY.

**Giselle** French and English
name based on the Old
German *gisil* ('pledge'). Like
other names derived from the
same source it may have come
about through the medieval
practice of handing over
children to foreign courts as
pledges or guarantees of
alliances.

**Gita** Indian name based on
the Sanskrit *gita* ('song'). Also
found as **Geeta.**

**Glad** *See* GLADYS.

**Gladys** English name based

on the Welsh Gwladys, itself possibly from the Welsh *gwledig* ('princess'). It is also encountered as a variant of CLAUDIA. Known in Wales in various forms since before the Norman Conquest, it was taken up by English speakers elsewhere towards the end of the nineteenth century. Shortened to **Glad**.

**Glen** *See* GLENDA; GLENYS.

**Glenda** Welsh name based on the Welsh *glan* ('clean' or 'holy') and *da* ('good'). The most famous bearer of the name to date has been the British actress and politician Glenda Jackson (b. 1936). Shortened to **Glen**.

**Glenice/Glenis** *See* GLENYS.

**Glenn** Scottish and English name based on the Gaelic *gleann* ('valley') that was taken up as a first name for girls from the 1940s. Famous bearers of the name have included US film actress Glenn Close (b. 1945). **Glenna** is a rare variant. *See also* GLYNIS.

**Glenna** *See* GLENN.

**Glenys** Welsh name that is thought to have evolved relatively recently as a variant of GLYNIS. Other theories suggest that it may have come about through the combination of GLADYS and GLENDA. Also found as **Glenice** or **Glenis**. Shortened to **Glen**.

**Glinys** *See* GLYNIS.

**Gloria** English name based on the Latin *gloria* ('glory'). It seems to have made its first appearance as the name of a character in the George Bernard Shaw play *You Never Can Tell* (1889). Sometimes rendered as **Glory**.

**Glory** *See* GLORIA.

**Glyn** *See* GLYNIS.

**Glynis** Welsh name that is thought to have developed from the Welsh *glyn* ('valley') under the influence of GLADYS. Sometimes rendered as **Glinys**, **Glynnis** or **Glynys**. Commonly shortened to **Glyn** or **Glynn**.

**Glynn** *See* GLYNIS.

**Glynnis/Glynys** *See*
GLYNIS.

**Godiva** English name
meaning 'gift of God'. It is
most familiar from the ancient
story of Godiva, a queen who
rode naked through the streets
of Coventry to dissuade her
husband from imposing a new
tax.

**Golda** Jewish name based on
a Yiddish nickname meaning
'gold'. Also found as GOLDIE.

**Goldie** English name of
uncertain origin, though
usually assumed to be from the
ordinary vocabulary word
'gold'. It may have been
derived from an identical
surname or else have been
taken up as a name for anyone
with blonde hair. Famous
bearers of the name have
included US film actress Goldie
Hawn (b. 1945). *See also*
GOLDA.

**Grace** English name based on
the ordinary vocabulary word
'grace'. It was among the many
virtue names adopted by
Puritans in the seventeenth
century. In Ireland the name
sometimes appears as an
anglicization of the Gaelic
GRAINNE. The name has
ranked high among the most
popular girls' names since the
year 2000. **Gracie** is an
informal version of the name.

**Gracie** *See* GRACE.

**Grainne** ('grawnya') Irish
name probably based on the
Gaelic *graidhne* ('love'). The
name appears in Irish legend as
that of the daughter of King
Cormac, who killed herself
after her lover Dermot died
following a long pursuit by the
jealous Finn MacCool. It is
sometimes anglicized as
GRACE. Variants include
**Grania** and **Granya**.

**Grania/Granya** *See*
GRAINNE.

**Greer** Scottish name based
on the masculine Gregor (*see*
GREGORY). The most famous
bearer of the name to date has
been the Anglo-Irish actress
Greer Garson (1908–96),
whose mother bore it as her
maiden name. Occasionally
found as **Grier**.

**Greta** Scandinavian and
German name that developed

as a shortened form of Margareta (*see* MARGARET). The name was made internationally famous through the Swedish film actress Greta Garbo (Greta Lovisa Gustafsson; 1905–90). Also found as **Gretta**.

**Gretchen** German name that developed as a variant of Margarete (*see* MARGARET). It has made occasional appearances among English speakers since the nineteenth century, when it was boosted through a character of the name in Goethe's *Faust* (1808).

**Grete** *See* GRETEL.

**Gretel** German name that developed as a variant of Margarete (*see* MARGARET). It is best known through the fairytale of Hansel and Gretel. Sometimes found as **Grete**.

**Gretta** *See* GRETA.

**Grier** *See* GREER.

**Griselda** German and English name based on the Old German *gris* ('grey') and *hild* ('battle') and thus meaning 'grey warrior'. It was reasonably familiar among English speakers in medieval times. **Grizel** (or **Grizzel**) is a Scottish variant. **Grizzie** and ZELDA are shortened forms of the name.

**Grizel/Grizzel/Grizzie** *See* GRISELDA.

**Gudrun** German and Scandinavian name based on *guth* ('battle' or 'god') and *run* ('secret') and thus sometimes interpreted as meaning 'wily in battle'. It famously appeared as the name of the principal character in D. H. Lawrence's novels *The Rainbow* (1915) and *Women in Love* (1921).

**Guenevere** *See* GUINEVERE.

**Guinevere** French and English version of the Welsh Gwenhwyfar, itself from the Welsh *gwen* ('white' or 'fair') and *hwyfar* ('smooth' or 'soft'). The name was borne by King Arthur's faithless queen, but has been largely superseded now by the related JENNIFER. **Guenevere** is a variant form. Shortened to **Gwinny**. *See also* GAYNOR.

**Gunnhilda** *See* GUNNHILDE.

**Gunnhilde** Scandinavian name based on the Old Norse for 'strife war'. Also found as Gunnhilda.

**Gus/Gusta** *See* AUGUSTA.

**Gwen** Welsh name based on the Welsh *gweyn* ('white', 'fair' or 'blessed') or else as a shortened form of GWENDA, GWENDOLEN or GWYNETH. Although it still has strong Welsh connections, the name was taken up throughout the English-speaking world during the twentieth century.

**Gwenda** Welsh name based on the Welsh *gwen* ('white', 'fair' or 'blessed) and *da* ('good') that was taken up on an occasional basis by English speakers early in the twentieth century. Occasionally used as an informal version of GWENDOLEN. Shortened to GWEN.

**Gwendolen** Welsh name based on the Welsh *gwen* ('white', 'fair' or 'blessed') and *dolen* ('ring' or 'bow'), sometimes interpreted as meaning 'white circle' and thus a reference to the moon. Variant forms include Gwendolin, Gwendoline and Gwendolyn.

**Gwendolin/ Gwendoline/ Gwendolyn** *See* GWENDOLEN.

**Gweneth** *See* GWYNETH.

**Gwenllian** ('gwencleean') Welsh first name based on the Welsh *gwen* ('white', 'fair' or 'blessed') and *lliant* ('flood' or 'flow'). Sometimes interpreted to mean 'foamy white' and thus a reference to a pale complexion. Confined largely to Wales itself.

**Gwenneth/Gwenyth** *See* GWYNETH.

**Gwinny** *See* GUINEVERE.

**Gwladys** *See* GLADYS.

**Gwynedd** *See* GWYNETH.

**Gwyneth** Welsh name based on the Welsh *gwynaeth* ('luck' or 'happiness'). Variants include **Gwynedd, Gwynneth, Gwenyth, Gweneth** and **Gwenneth**. Shortened to GWEN.

**Gwynneth** *See* GWYNETH.

**Gypsy** English name based on the ordinary vocabulary word 'gypsy'. It was taken up by English speakers during the nineteenth century, both inside and outside the Romany community. Also found as **Gipsy**.

## GIRLS' NAMES

**Hadyn** *See* HAYDN.

**Hafwen** Welsh name based on *haf* ('summer') and *wen* ('fair') and meaning 'bright summer'.

**Hagar** Hebrew name meaning 'forsaken'. It appears in the Bible as the name of the servant of Abraham's wife Sarah who becomes the mother of Abraham's child Ishmael.

**Haidee** English name based on the Greek *aidoios* ('modest') or else treated as a variant form of HEIDI.

**Hailey/Haley** *See* HAYLEY.

**Halcyon** English name based on a Greek word meaning 'calm'. In Greek myth, Halcyon was the daughter of Aeolus who was turned into a kingfisher after she threw herself into the water. **Halcyone** is a variant form.

**Halcyone** *See* HALCYON.

**Halle** ('halley') English name that came into prominence in the 1990s through US film actress Halle Berry (b. 1968). She is said to have been named after the US department store Halle Brothers.

**Han/Hana** *See* HANNAH.

**Hani** Arabic name meaning 'happiness'.

**Hanna** *See* HANNAH.

**Hannah** Hebrew name meaning 'favour' or 'grace' and sometimes interpreted to mean 'God has favoured me'. It appears in the Bible and remains in frequent use. Also encountered as **Hanna** or **Hana**. Informal versions include **Han**, **Hannie** (or **Hanny**) and **Nancy**. *See also* ANNA.

**Hannie/Hanny** *See*
HANNAH.

**Happy** English name based
on the ordinary vocabulary
word 'happy'. It does not
appear to have been in use
prior to the twentieth century.

**Harmonia/Harmonie**
*See* HARMONY.

**Harmony** English name
based ultimately on the Greek
for 'concord' or 'unity'. A
relatively rare choice of first
name of twentieth-century
origin, it is occasionally found
in the variant forms **Harmonie**
or **Harmonia**.

**Harper** English name
denoting someone who plays
the harp. It is found chiefly in
the USA. Notable female
bearers of the name have
included US novelist Harper
Lee (b. 1926).

**Harrie** *See* HARRIET.

**Harriet** English name that
developed as a feminine
equivalent of HARRY. It was
taken up among English
speakers in the seventeenth
century. Variant forms include

Harriett, Harriette and
Harrietta. Commonly
shortened to **Harrie**, **Harry**,
**Hatty** or **Hattie**.

**Harriett/Harrietta/
Harriette/Harry** *See*
HARRIET.

**Hattie/Hatty** *See*
HARRIET; HENRIETTA.

**Hayden** *See* HAYDN.

**Haydn** ('haydun') Welsh
name of uncertain origin,
though possibly a variant of the
English surname Haddon,
meaning 'hill with heather', or
a Welsh version of AIDAN. As a
Germanic surname it had its
roots in the medieval *heiden*
('heathen'). It was initially an
exclusively masculine name,
but is today also bestowed
upon girls, possibly under the
influence of HEIDI. Also found
as **Hadyn**, **Hayden** or
**Haydon**.

**Haydon** *See* HAYDN.

**Hayley** English name that
originated as a place name
(Hailey in Oxfordshire) and
was taken up as a first name in
the 1940s. The original place

name means 'hay field'. Also found as **Haley**, **Hailey** or **Haylie**.

**Haylie** *See* HAYLEY.

**Haze** *See* HAZEL.

**Hazel** English name based on that of the tree but more often assumed to refer to the nut-brown colour of some people's eyes. It was one of many flower and plant names taken up by English speakers towards the end of the nineteenth century. Commonly shortened to **Haze**.

**Heather** English name based on the name of the moorland plant. It was taken up by English speakers towards the end of the nineteenth century, enjoying particular popularity in Scotland, and was at its most frequent around the middle of the twentieth century.

**Hebe** ('heebee') Greek name based on the Greek *hēbos* ('young') that made its first appearances among English speakers towards the end of the nineteenth century. The name is borne in Greek mythology by a daughter of Zeus.

**Hedda** Scandinavian name descended from the German Hedvig, itself based on the Old German words *hadu* ('contention' or 'struggle') and *wig* ('war'). The name is universally identified with the Henrik Ibsen play *Hedda Gabler* (1890).

**Heidi** ('highdee') Swiss name based on Adelheid (the German equivalent of ADELAIDE). It was taken up with some enthusiasm by English speakers in the 1960s in response to the televisation of the Swiss novelist Johanna Spyri's children's story *Heidi* (1881).

**Heledd** Welsh name of uncertain origin. It was borne by a legendary seventh-century Welsh princess. Also found as **Hyledd**.

**Helen** English name based on the Greek *hēlios* ('sun') and thus meaning 'shining one' or 'bright one'. The name is often linked with Helen of Troy, the beautiful daughter of Zeus over whom the ten-year Trojan War was fought. LALA is an informal version of the name. Variants in other languages include the French **Hélène**. *See also* EILEEN; ELAINE; ELEANOR; ELEN; ELLA; ELLEN; HELENA; NELL.

**Helena** English name that developed as a Latinized form of HELEN. This version of the name became popular among English speakers during the medieval period and has been in fairly regular use ever since. Variants include LENA and the Italian, Spanish and Portuguese **Elena**.

**Hélène** *See* HELEN.

**Helga** German and Scandinavian name based ultimately on the Old Norse *heill* ('hale' or 'hearty'), but later interpreted to mean 'blessed' or 'holy'. The name was in use among English speakers at the time of the Norman Conquest.

**Héloïse** ('heloeez') French name based either on the Old German Helewise or else sharing the same origins as LOUISE.

**Hen/Hennie/Henny** *See* HENRIETTA.

**Henrietta** English equivalent of the French **Henriette**, itself a feminine version of Henri (*see* HENRY). English speakers took up the name in the seventeenth century after it was introduced through Charles I's French wife Queen Henrietta Maria (Henriette-Marie; 1609–69). Variants include **Etta**, **Ettie** (or **Etty**), **Hen**, **Hennie** (or **Henny**), **Hattie** (or **Hatty**), **Hettie** (or **Hetty**) and **Netta** or **Nettie** (or **Netty**).

**Henriette** *See* HENRIETTA.

**Hephzibah** Hebrew name meaning 'in her is my delight'. It appears in the Bible and was consequently taken up by Puritans in the seventeenth century. A variant form is **Hepzibah**. Shortened forms of the name include **Eppie**, **Hepsie**, **Hepsey** and **Hepsy**.

**Hepsey/Hepsie/Hepsy/Hepzibah** *See* HEPHZIBAH.

**Hermia** English name that developed as a variant of HERMIONE. It was taken up by English speakers in medieval times and appeared in Shakespeare but is rare today.

**Hermione** ('hermiohnee')
Greek name that was adopted
as a feminine equivalent of
Hermes, the name of the
Greek messenger of the gods. It
may originally have derived
from the Greek for 'stone'.
The name appears in Greek
mythology as that of the
daughter of Menelaus and
Helen.

**Hero** Greek name of
uncertain meaning. It is most
familiar in ancient mythology
as the name of the lover of
LEANDER.

**Hesba** Greek name based on
the Greek *hespera* ('western').
It has made infrequent
appearances among English
speakers since the nineteenth
century.

**Hester** English name that
was adopted as a variant of
ESTHER in the seventeenth
century. Other versions of the
name include **Esta**, **Ester** and
**Hettie** (or **Hetty**).

**Hettie/Hetty** *See* ESTHER;
HENRIETTA; HESTER.

**Heulwen** Welsh name
meaning 'sunshine'.

**Hil** *See* HILARY.

**Hilary** English name
descended ultimately from the
Roman Hilarius, itself from the
Latin *hilaris* ('cheerful').
Originally a boys' name, it has
been applied to both sexes
since the nineteenth century.
**Hillary** is a variant spelling.
Shortened to **Hil** or **Hilly**.

**Hilda** German, Dutch,
Scandinavian and English name
based on the Old German *hild*
('battle'). The name appears
to have developed as an
abbreviated form of
HILDEGARD and other similar
names and was taken up by
English speakers during the
medieval period. A variant
form of the name is **Hylda**.

**Hildegard** German,
Scandinavian and English name
based on the Old German *hild*
('battle') and *gard* ('enclosure')
and interpreted to mean
'comrade in arms'. The
name has made occasional
appearances among English
speakers of German descent,
chiefly in the USA. Sometimes
shortened to HILDA. Also
found as **Hildegarde**.

**Hildegarde** *See* HILDEGARD.

**Hillary/Hilly** *See* HILARY.

**Hollie** *See* HOLLY.

**Hollis** English name meaning 'dweller in the holly grove'.

**Holly** English name that may have developed out of the ordinary vocabulary word 'holy' or else may have come from the name of the evergreen tree. It is often bestowed upon girls born in the Christmas season. Also found as **Hollie**.

**Honesta** *See* HONESTY.

**Honesty** English virtue name based on the ordinary vocabulary word 'honesty'. **Honesta** is a variant.

**Honey** English name based on the ordinary vocabulary word 'honey', which has been in use as a term of endearment since medieval times. It may also have developed as a variant of **Honoria** (*see* HONOR).

**Honor** English name based either on the Roman **Honoria** or else on the ordinary vocabulary word 'honour'. Recorded among English speakers as early as the Norman Conquest, it was among the virtue names approved by Puritans in the seventeenth century. It was formerly applied to boys as well as girls. Variants include **Honour**, **Honora**, **Honorine** and the French **Honore**. Sometimes shortened to NORA. *See also* HONEY.

**Honora/Honore/ Honoria/Honorine/ Honour** *See* HONOR.

**Hope** English virtue name that was taken up by English Puritans after the Reformation. It was sometimes given to sets of triplets alongside FAITH and CHARITY, occasionally to boys as well as girls. It is now reserved exclusively for girls and is more common in the USA than elsewhere.

**Horatia** Feminine version of HORATIO, which itself developed as a variant of HORACE under the influence of the Roman Horatius. It became well known through Horatia Nelson, the daughter of Admiral Lord (Horatio) Nelson (1758–1805).

**Hortense** French name descended from the Roman **Hortensia**, itself possibly based on the Latin *hortus* ('garden'). English speakers took up the name in the nineteenth century but it is now rare.

**Hortensia** *See* HORTENSE.

**Hosanna** English name based on the Hebrew *hosanna* ('save now' or 'save pray'). Because of its biblical associations it was taken up by English speakers early in the thirteenth century and was used initially for both sexes, although after the seventeenth century it appears to have been reserved for girls. Also found as **Hosannah**.

**Hosannah** *See* HOSANNA.

**Hy** *See* HYACINTH.

**Hyacinth** English name that was among the many flower names taken up by English speakers in the nineteenth century. It was borne in Roman legend by a youth accidentally killed by Apollo. It has been regarded as exclusively feminine since the late nineteenth century. Variants include **Hyacintha, Jacinda, Jacinta** and **Jacinth**. Shortened to **Hy** and, in Ireland, to **Sinty**.

**Hyacintha** *See* HYACINTH.

**Hylda** *See* HILDA.

**Hyledd** *See* HELEDD.

**Hypatia** Greek name based on the Greek *hupatos* ('highest'). It has made rare appearances as a first name among English speakers since the late nineteenth century. Sometimes shortened to **Patsy**.

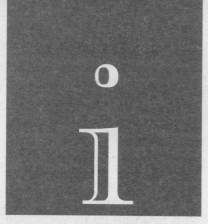

# GIRLS' NAMES

**Iantha** *See* IANTHE.

**Ianthe** ('ighanthee') Greek name based on *ion* ('violet') and *anthos* ('flower'). It was borne in Greek legend by a sea nymph, daughter of the sea god Oceanus. The name enjoyed some popularity as a literary name in the nineteenth century. Rare variants include **Iantha**, **Ianthina**, **Janthina** and **Janthine**. *See also* IOLANTHE.

**Ianthina** *See* IANTHE.

**Ib/Ibbie/Ibby** *See* ISABEL.

**Ida** ('ighda') English name based via Norman French on the Old Norse *id* ('labour' or 'work') or *itis* ('woman'). Some authorities link it with Mount

Ida in Crete, home of the infant Zeus. In Ireland it may be associated with the Gaelic **Ide** or **Ita**, based on *ita* ('thirsty'). Today the name is well known from Gilbert and Sullivan's opera *Princess Ida* (1884).

**Ide** *See* IDA.

**Idonea** English name based on the Old Norse *id* ('labour' or 'work'), and thus linked to the Norse goddess Iduna, or else possibly from the Latin *idoneus* ('suitable'). Also found as **Idonia** or **Idony**, it was fairly common among English speakers as early as the twelfth century.

**Idonia/Idony** *See* IDONEA.

**Iesha** *See* AISHA.

**Ila** *See* ISLA.

**Ilana** Jewish name based on the Hebrew for 'tree'. Also found as a Hungarian equivalent of HELEN, in which case it might also be encountered as **Ilona**.

**Ilayne** *See* ELAINE.

**Ilean/Ileen/Ileene/ Ilene** *See* EILEEN.

**Ilma** *See* WILHELMINA.

**Ilona** *See* ILANA.

**Ilsa/Ilse** *See* ELSA.

**Imelda** Spanish and Italian name descended from the Old German Irmhilde, itself from *irmin* or *ermin* ('whole' or 'entire') and *hild* ('battle'), thus meaning 'all-conquering'. It became popular among Roman Catholics in tribute to a fourteenth-century St Imelda. Famous bearers of the name include British actress Imelda Staunton (b. 1957).

**Immaculata** Irish name based via the Italian Immacolata on a title borne by the Virgin Mary, Maria Immacolata (a reference to the Immaculate Conception). It has made irregular appearances among Roman Catholics over the centuries.

**Immy** *See* IMOGEN.

**Imogen** English name that appears to have evolved through a mistaken reading of the Celtic Innogen, itself either from the Latin *innocens* ('innocent') or the Irish Gaelic *inghean* ('daughter', 'maiden' or 'girl'). The mistake seems to have been made when William Shakespeare's play *Cymbeline* (1609) was printed for the first time, the 'nn' becoming 'm'. Shortened to **Immy**.

**Ina** English and Scottish name that evolved as a variant of ENA and also as a shortened form of various longer names ending in '-ina', including CHRISTINA, EDWINA and GEORGINA. *See also* JAMIE.

**India** English name based on the name of the country, itself taken from that of the River Indus. The name was adopted by English speakers when India was the 'jewel of the British Empire'. It was made familiar to a wider audience as the name of a character in Margaret Mitchell's *Gone with the Wind* (1936).

**Indiana** English name of relatively recent invention that developed either as a variant of INDIA or else out of the name of the US state Indiana. When it made its first appearance in the early twentieth century it was reserved exclusively for girls. Commonly shortened to **Indy**.

**Indigo** English name based on the name of the deep blue dye obtained from the indigo plant.

**Indira** Indian name meaning 'beauty' or 'splendour'.

**Indy** *See* INDIANA.

**Inés** *See* INEZ.

**Inez** Spanish version of AGNES. Also found as **Inés**.

**Inga/Inge** *See* INGEBORG; INGRID.

**Ingeborg** Scandinavian name based on the Old Norse meaning 'fortification of Ing'. Shortened to **Inga** or **Inge**.

**Ingrid** Scandinavian and German name that resulted from the combination of Ing (the name of a Norse fertility god) and *frithr* ('fair' or 'beautiful') or *rida* ('to ride') and interpreted to mean 'Ing's ride'. It was not taken up on a significant scale in the English-

speaking world until around the middle of the nineteenth century. Shortened to **Inga** or **Inge**.

**Inness** *See* INNES.

**Iolanthe** English name based on the Greek *iola* ('violet') and *anthos* ('flower'). This appears to have been a relatively recent invention influenced by other flower names popular around the end of the nineteenth century. It was made more widely known through the Gilbert and Sullivan opera *Iolanthe* (1882). *See also* YOLANDA.

**Iona** English name based on that of the Scottish monastery island of Iona (originally Ioua, meaning 'yew-tree island', but supposedly altered to Iona by a misreading) or else possibly descended from the Greek *iola* ('violet'). As a first name, Iona has been in irregular use since the nineteenth century, chiefly among Scots.

**Ione** Greek name meaning 'violet'. It made irregular appearances among English speakers in the nineteenth century, apparently in the belief that it was an authentic ancient Greek coinage (although no classical records exist of the name).

**Iphigenia** Greek name meaning 'strong'. She appears in Greek legend as the daughter of Agamemnon and Clytemnestra who was selected for sacrifice to the goddess Artemis.

**Ira/Irena** *See* IRENE.

**Irene** ('ighreen' or 'ighreeny') English name based on the Greek *eirēnē* ('peace'). The name of a minor Greek goddess, it enjoyed a peak in popularity among English speakers in the 1920s. Variants in other languages include **Irena**. Variously shortened to **Ira**, **Rene** (pronounced 'reenee') or **Renie**.

**Iris** English, German and Dutch name based on that of the flower, although it may also have been inspired in part by the identical name of the Greek goddess of the rainbow. It was taken up by English speakers along with other flower names towards the end of the nineteenth century.

**Irma** German name meaning 'whole' that was taken up to a limited extent by English speakers towards the end of the nineteenth century. Its popularity in the USA was promoted by the films *My Friend Irma* (1949) and *Irma la Douce* (1963). Also found as **Erma**. *See also* EMMA.

**Isa** *See* ISABEL.

**Isabel** Spanish equivalent of ELIZABETH that was taken up by English speakers in the medieval period. It ranked among the most popular first names during the thirteenth and fourteenth centuries. Variant forms include **Ysabel** and the Scottish **Ishbel**, **Isbel** or **Isobel**. Informal versions include **Ib**, **Ibbie** (or **Ibby**), **Isa**, **Iz**, **Izzie**, **Izzy**, **Nib**, **Sib** and **Tibbie**. *See also* BELLA; ELLA; ISABELLA.

**Isabella** Italian version of ELIZABETH that made its first appearances among English speakers in the twelfth century. It began to appear more frequently in the English-speaking world towards the end of the nineteenth century, enjoying particular popularity in Scotland. Variant forms include the French **Isabelle**. *See also* ISABEL.

**Isabelle** *See* ISABELLA.

**Isadora** English name that developed as a feminine version of ISIDORE, meaning 'gift of Isis'. It made its first appearances among English speakers in the nineteenth century. The most celebrated bearer of the name to date has been the US dancer Isadora Duncan (1878–1927). Also found as **Isidora**. Familiar forms include **Issy**, **Iz**, **Izzie**, **Izzy** and DORA.

**Isbel** *See* ISABEL.

**Iseult** *See* ISOLDE.

**Ishbel** *See* ISABEL.

**Isidora/Isidore** *See* ISADORA.

**Isla** ('ighla') Scottish name of relatively recent invention, apparently unknown before the 1930s. It was based on a Scottish place name, that of the Scottish island of Islay, although it is sometimes considered to be a variant of ISABELLA. Also found as **Ila** or **Islay**.

**Islay** *See* ISLA.

**Isleen** *See* AISLING.

**Ismay** English name of uncertain origin. Recorded in use as early as the thirteenth century, it is sometimes linked with ESMÉ.

**Ismene** Greek name of unknown meaning. It is usually associated with the tragic myth of Oedipus, in which the name appears as that of a daughter of Oedipus and Jocasta.

**Isobel** *See* ISABEL.

**Isolda** *See* ISOLDE.

**Isolde** English and French name based on the Old French **Iseult** (or **Yseult**), itself from the Celtic for 'fair' or 'beautiful', or on the Old German Isvald, from the words for 'ice' and 'rule'. The name figures as that of an Irish princess in the tragic legend of Tristram and Isolde. Variants include **Isolda**, **Ysolde** and the Welsh **Essylt** or **Esyllt**.

**Issy** *See* ISADORA.

**Ita** *See* IDA.

**Ivah** Biblical name based on an Old Testament place name.

**Ivana** Feminine version of the Russian IVAN, itself an equivalent of JOHN. Variants include **Ivanka**.

**Ivanka** *See* IVANA.

**Ivoreen/Ivorie/Ivorine** *See* IVORY.

**Ivory** English name based on the ordinary vocabulary word. Variants include **Ivoreen**, **Ivorie** and **Ivorine**.

**Ivy** English plant name that was taken up as a first name alongside other plant and flower names towards the end of the nineteenth century. It enjoyed a peak in popularity in the 1920s.

**Iz/Izzie/Izzy** *See* ISABEL; ISADORA.

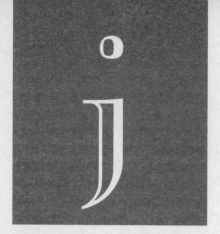

# GIRLS' NAMES

**Jacaline/Jacalyn** *See*
JACQUELINE.

**Jacey** English name based
either on the initials J. C. or
else based upon Jacinda (*see*
HYACINTH). Also found as
Jacy.

**Jacinda/Jacinta/
Jacinth/Jacintha** *See*
HYACINTH.

**Jackalyn/Jackey/Jacki/
Jackie/Jacklyn/Jacky/
Jaclyn** *See* JACQUELINE.

**Jacqueline** Feminine variant
of Jacques, the French
equivalent of the English JACK.
The name was recorded in use
in England in the thirteenth
century, but it was not until

the middle of the twentieth
century that it became widely
popular. Variants include
**Jacalyn, Jacaline, Jaclyn,
Jacklyn, Jackalyn, Jaqueline**
and **Jacquelyn**. Shortened to
**Jacki, Jackie, Jackey, Jacky,
Jakki, Jacqui** or **Jaqui**. *See also*
JACQUETTA.

**Jacquelyn** *See* JACQUELINE.

**Jacquetta** French variant of
JACQUELINE. The earliest
records of the name in use
among English speakers date
from medieval times.

**Jacqui** *See* JACQUELINE.

**Jacy** *See* JACEY.

**Jada** *See* JADE.

**Jade** English name based on
that of the semi-precious stone.
The name of the stone came
originally from the Spanish
*piedra de ijada* ('stone of the
bowels'), which referred to the
stone's supposed magical
influence upon intestinal
disorders. It was taken up by
English speakers towards the
end of the nineteenth century.
Variants include **Jada**.

**Jaden** *See* JAYDEN.

**Jaime** *See* JAMIE.

**Jakki** *See* JACQUELINE.

**Jameela** *See* JAMILA.

**Jamesina/Jami** *See* JAMIE.

**Jamie** Feminine equivalent of the masculine JAMES, itself a biblical name based on the Roman Iacomus or Jacomus and sharing the same roots as JACOB. Also found as **Jami** or **Jaime**. The Scottish variant **Jamesina** (sometimes shortened to INA) is rather more rare. *See also* JEMIMA.

**Jamila** Feminine equivalent of the Arabic and Indian JAMAL, itself based on the Arabic *jamal* ('beauty'). Variants include the Indian **Jameela**.

**Jan** English name that developed as a shortened form of various names, including JANET, JANICE and JANINE. Alternatively it may also be considered a variant of JANE, JEAN or JOAN. Since the early twentieth century it has been much more common as a name for girls than boys in the English-speaking world.

**Jancis** English name that appears to have resulted from the combination of JANE with FRANCES or CICELY. It made its first appearances in the 1920s and was possibly invented by novelist Mary Webb for a character in her book *Precious Bane* (1924).

**Jane** English name based via the French Jeanne or Jehane on the Roman Johanna (*see* JOANNA) and thus ultimately on JOHN. It was taken up by English speakers in the sixteenth century and gradually eclipsed the related JEAN and JOAN. Sometimes found as **Jayne** or used in combination with other names, as in **Sarah-Jane**. Familiar forms of the name include **Janey**, **Janie** and **Jaynie**. *See also* JANELLE; JANET; JANICE; JENNY; SHEENA; SIÂN; SIOBHAN.

**Janella** *See* JANELLE.

**Janelle** English name that developed as an elaboration of JANE. Variants include **Janella**.

**Janene** *See* JANINE.

**Janet** English name that evolved as a variant of JANE. It was in use among English speakers in medieval times but subsequently fell into disuse except in Scotland until its revival in the nineteenth century. **Janette** is a variant of French origin. Commonly shortened to JAN.

**Janette** *See* JANET; JEANETTE.

**Janey** *See* JANE.

**Janice** English name that evolved as a variant of JANE. It may have made its first appearance with the publication of Paul Leicester Ford's novel *Janice Meredith* (1899). Also found as **Janis** – as borne by US rock singer Janis Joplin (1943–70). Commonly shortened to JAN.

**Janie** *See* JANE.

**Janina** *See* JANINE.

**Janine** English version of the French Jeannine, itself an elaboration of the masculine name Jean (see JOHN). It enjoyed some popularity among English speakers in the 1930s and again in the late 1960s. Also found as **Jannine**, **Janene** and (rarely) **Janina**. Commonly shortened to JAN.

**Janis** *See* JANICE.

**Jannine** *See* JANINE.

**Janthina/Janthine** *See* IANTHE.

**Jaqueline/Jaqui** *See* JACQUELINE.

**Jas/Jasmin** *See* JASMINE.

**Jasmine** English name based on that of the flower jasmine (ultimately from the Persian *yasmin*). It was adopted by English speakers along with other flower names towards the end of the nineteenth century. Also found as **Jasmin**, **Yasmin**, **Yasmine** or **Yasmina** and more rarely as **Jessamine**, **Jessamyn** or **Jessamy**. Shortened to **Jas** or **Jaz**.

**Jaswinder** Indian name based on the Sanskrit *jasu* ('thunderbolt') and the god's name Indra, and thus meaning 'Indra of the thunderbolt'. Mostly confined to Sikh communities.

**Jay** English name that evolved as a shortened form of various names beginning with 'J', including JANE, although often assumed to relate to the bird of the same name or to be distantly descended from the Roman Gaius. It appears to have been applied to girls from the early twentieth century and is more frequent in Canada and the USA than elsewhere. Sometimes found as **Jaye**.

**Jayden** English name based on the Hebrew Jadon, which means 'Jehovah has heard'. It was taken up with some enthusiasm by English speakers in the early twenty-first century. Also found as **Jaden**.

**Jaye** *See* JAY.

**Jayne/Jaynie** *See* JANE.

**Jaz** *See* JASMINE.

**Jean** ('jeen') English name based – like JANE and JOAN – on the Old French Jehane, itself a feminine version of the masculine Jean (*see* JOHN). It became a favourite in Scotland in medieval times. **Jeanie** and **Jeannie** are familiar forms of the name with strong Scottish

associations. *See also* JEANETTE; SHEENA.

**Jeanette** ('jenet') English name that evolved from the French Jeanne. It was taken up in Scotland at a relatively early date but did not enter regular usage elsewhere in the English-speaking world until the twentieth century. Also found as **Jeannette**. A familiar form of the name in Scotland is **Jinty**.

**Jeanie** *See* JEAN.

**Jeannette** *See* JEANETTE.

**Jeannie** *See* JEAN.

**Jem** *See* JEMIMA.

**Jemima** Biblical name based on the Hebrew Yemimah, meaning 'wild dove' or possibly 'bright as day'. It was taken up by English Puritans in the seventeenth century and is sometimes considered to be a feminine equivalent of the masculine JAMES. **Jem**, **Jemmy** and **Mima** are familiar forms of the name.

**Jemma** *See* GEMMA.

**Jemmy** *See* JEMIMA.

**Jen** *See* JENNIFER; JENNY.

**Jena** Arabic name meaning 'small bird'.

**Jeni** *See* JENNY.

**Jenifer** *See* JENNIFER.

**Jenna** English name that developed as a variant of JENNY. It is a relatively recent adoption, making early appearances in the 1970s, when it was promoted through a character of the same name in the US television soap opera *Dallas*. Also found as **Jennai**.

**Jennai** *See* JENNA.

**Jenni/Jennie** *See* JENNY.

**Jennifer** English name that developed initially as a Cornish variant of GUINEVERE, meaning 'white ghost' – the name borne by King Arthur's unfaithful wife in Arthurian legend. It became established among English speakers in the eighteenth century. Also found as **Jenifer**. Shortened to **Jen**, **Jenni**, **Jennie** or JENNY.

**Jenny** English name that evolved as an informal variant

of JANE and JENNIFER. It seems to have made early appearances during medieval times as a variant of JEAN. Also found as **Jeni**, **Jenni** or **Jennie**. Commonly shortened to **Jen**. *See also* JENNA.

**Jerrie/Jerry** *See* GERALDINE.

**Jess** *See* JESSICA; JESSIE.

**Jessabel** *See* JEZEBEL.

**Jessamine/Jessamy/ Jessamyn** *See* JASMINE.

**Jessi** *See* JESSIE.

**Jessica** English name that appears to have been invented by William Shakespeare as the name of Shylock's daughter in his play *The Merchant of Venice* (1596). It seems Shakespeare modelled the name on the Hebrew Iscah or Jesca, meaning 'God beholds'. Commonly shortened to **Jess** or JESSIE.

**Jessie** English name that evolved as an informal variant of JESSICA but is now often considered a name in its own right. It was taken up by

English speakers, especially in Scotland, in the nineteenth century and was fairly common until the 1920s. Also found as **Jessi** or **Jessye**. A Gaelic form of the name is **Teasag**. Shortened to **Jess**.

**Jessye** *See* JESSIE.

**Jetta** English name based on the name of the black-coloured mineral jet. The name of the mineral came ultimately, via the Old French *jaiet*, from the Latin *gagates* ('stone from Gagai').

**Jewel** English name that was based on the ordinary vocabulary word 'jewel'. It was among the many words connected with gemstones that were taken up by English speakers as first names in the nineteenth century.

**Jezabel** *See* JEZEBEL.

**Jezebel** Hebrew name meaning 'pure'. Its use over the years has been restricted through its association with a biblical queen of Israel who was condemned by God for her immorality. Variant forms

include **Jessabel**, **Jezabel** and **Jezibelle**.

**Jezibelle** *See* JEZEBEL.

**Jill** English name that evolved as a shortened form of GILLIAN and is now often considered a name in its own right. Jill began to appear as an alternative to **Gill** as the usual shortened form of GILLIAN from the seventeenth century. **Jillie** and **Jilly** are informal variants.

**Jillian** *See* GILLIAN.

**Jillie/Jilly** *See* GILLIAN; JILL; JULIANA.

**Jinny** *See* VIRGINIA.

**Jinty** *See* JEANETTE.

**Jo** English name that developed as a shortened form of various longer names, including JOAN, JOANNA, JOANNE, JODY, JOELLE, JONI and JOSEPHINE. It is sometimes used in combination with other names, as in **Jobeth**.

**Joan** English name descended from the Roman **Johanna**, itself a feminine version of

Johannes (*see* JOHN). Records of the name's use among English speakers go back to the medieval period, when the name was imported from France in the form Jhone or Johan. *See also* JOANNA; JOANNE; JONI; SIOBHAN.

**Joani** *See* JONI.

**Joanna** English variant of JOAN based ultimately on the Roman Johannes (*see* JOHN). In medieval times the name was usually given in its Roman form as **Johanna** and it was not until the eighteenth century that the modern spelling became widely accepted. Commonly shortened to JO. *See also* JOANNE.

**Joanne** English name borrowed from Old French and, like JOAN, in origin a feminine equivalent of JOHN. It enjoyed a peak in popularity among English speakers in the 1970s but has since lost ground. Commonly shortened to JO. Also found as **Jo-Anne** or **Jo Anne**. See also JOANNA.

**Jobeth** *See* JO.

**Jobina** Feminine equivalent

of JOB, meaning 'persecuted' or 'afflicted'.

**Jocasta** Greek name of uncertain meaning. According to some authorities, the name comes from the mythical Io (understood to refer to the moon) combined with *kaustikos* ('burning') and thus meaning 'shining moon'. It is famous through the myth of Queen Jocasta of Thebes, who committed suicide after unknowingly marrying her own son, Oedipus.

**Jocelin** *See* JOCELYN.

**Jocelyn** English name based on the Old Norman Joscelin, which may have come from the name of a Germanic tribe or else from the Old German names Jodoc or Josse (meaning 'champion'). When bestowed upon girls, it is often considered to be a combination of JOYCE and LYNN. Variants include **Jocelin, Joseline, Joscelin, Josceline, Joselyn** and **Josslyn**. Shortened to **Jos** or **Joss**.

**Jodene/Jodi/Jodie** *See* JODY.

**Jody** English name that evolved as an informal variant of JO, JOSEPHINE, **Josie** and JUDITH. As a girls' name, it seems to date from the 1950s. Also found as **Jodi** or **Jodie**. Another variant is **Jodene**.

**Joella** See JOELLE.

**Joelle** Feminine version of JOEL, a biblical name meaning 'Yah is god' (Yah being another name for Jehovah, or God). Variants include **Joella** and **Joely**. Shortened to JO or JOEY.

**Joely** See JOELLE.

**Joey** Informal version of various names, including JOAN, JOANNA, JOANNE, JODY, JOELLE, JONI and JOSEPHINE, that is occasionally treated as a name in its own right.

**Johanna** See JOAN; JOANNA.

**Jojo** English name that resulted from the doubling of JO, the reduced form of JOAN, JOANNA, JOANNE, JODY, JOELLE, JONI; JOSEPHINE and other names.

**Jola/Jolana/Jolanda** See YOLANDA.

**Joleen** See JOLENE.

**Jolene** English name that probably resulted from the combination of JO and MARLENE or another name with a '-lene' ending. It appears to be of relatively recent coinage, becoming popular in the USA in the 1940s. Also found as **Joleen**.

**Jolie** English name that evolved as a variant of JULIA, JULIE or JULIANA. It appears to be a relatively recent introduction of the late twentieth-century.

**Joni** English name that developed via **Joani** as a variant of JOAN. Well-known bearers of the name have included Canadian singer-songwriter Joni Mitchell (Roberta Joan Anderson; b. 1943). Sometimes shortened to JO.

**Jonquil** English name based on the French *jonquille*, itself ultimately from the Latin *juncus* ('reed'). One of the less well-known of the flower names that were taken up by English speakers around the end of the nineteenth century, it was at its most popular in the 1940s and 1950s.

**Jordan** English name based on that of the sacred River Jordan, itself from the Hebrew *hayarden* ('flowing down'). It was formerly given to children baptized with water brought back from the River Jordan by pilgrims. Also found as **Jordana** or **Jordyn**.

**Jordana/Jordyn** *See* JORDAN.

**Jos** *See* JOCELYN.

**Josa** *See* JOSEPHINE.

**Joscelin/Josceline/ Joseline/Joselyn** *See* JOCELYN.

**Josepha/Josephina** *See* JOSEPHINE.

**Josephine** English equivalent of the French Joséphine, a feminine version of JOSEPH. Variants include **Josa**, **Josepha** and **Josephina**. Among familiar forms of the name are **Josette**, **Josie**, **Phenie** and **Pheeny**. Commonly

shortened to JO or JOEY. *See also* FIFI; JODY.

**Josette/Josie** *See* JOSEPHINE.

**Joss/Josslyn** *See* JOCELYN.

**Joy** English name based on the ordinary vocabulary word 'joy'. Also in use as a shortened version of JOYCE. It was in use in England as early as the twelfth century and was taken up by Puritans in the seventeenth century, who interpreted it as expressive of the 'joy' of religious faith.

**Joyce** English name descended from the Norman French Josce, meaning 'lord'. The name came to England with William the Conqueror in the eleventh century, although in those days it was treated as a masculine name. It reappeared (chiefly as a name for girls) around the seventeenth century. Sometimes shortened to JOY.

**Juanita** ('hwaneeta') Feminine version of JUAN, the Spanish equivalent of JOHN.

**Judi/Judie** *See* JUDITH.

**Judith** Biblical name based on the Hebrew Yehudhith, meaning 'Jewess' or 'woman of Judea'. It appears in the Bible and records of its use among English speakers go back beyond the Norman Conquest. It may also be found in use as an anglicization of the Gaelic SIOBHAN. Shortened to **Judi**, **Judie** or **Judy**. *See also* JODY.

**Judy** *See* JUDITH.

**Jules** *See* JULIA; JULIE; JULIET.

**Julia** Roman name that evolved as a feminine equivalent of JULIUS and was subsequently taken up by English speakers in the sixteenth century. Since 1900 it has lost ground to the French form of the name, JULIE. Shortened to **Jules**.

**Juliana** Feminine version of the Roman Julianus, a variant of JULIUS. It was taken up by English speakers as early as the twelfth century. Variant forms include **Julianna**, **Julianne**, **Julienne**, **Julie Ann** and the German **Juliane**. Occasionally shortened to **Jillie**, **Jilly** or, more rarely, LIANA.

**Juliane/Julianna** *See* JULIANA.

**Julianne** *See* JULIANA; LIANNE.

**Julie** French version of the Roman JULIA that was taken up on a wide basis among English speakers around the end of the nineteenth century. It gradually replaced Julia as the more common version of the name and remains in fairly regular use. Commonly shortened to **Jules**.

**Julie Ann/Julienne** *See* JULIANA.

**Juliet** English name based on the Italian Giulietta, itself an elaboration of the Italian Giulia, which was in turn descended from the Roman JULIA. Its use among English speakers was promoted by William Shakespeare's tragedy *Romeo and Juliet* (1595). Variants include the French **Juliette**. Shortened to JULIE or **Jules**.

**Juliette** *See* JULIET.

**June** English name based on the name of the month. Like

other first names based on months of the year, it appears to have been taken up by English speakers early in the twentieth century. Often bestowed upon girls born in June, it has become less common since the 1930s.

**Juniper** English name that was based on that of the plant, itself from the Latin *juniperus* (of unknown meaning). It appears in the Bible as a translation of the Hebrew *rothem* (the name of a desert shrub).

**Juno** Roman name taken from that of the goddess Juno, wife of Jupiter. It was subsequently taken up by the Irish, usually in the form UNA. Examples of its use in relatively modern times have included the Sean O'Casey play *Juno and the Paycock* (1924).

**Justie** *See* JUSTINE.

**Justine** French feminine equivalent of JUSTIN. Borne by a fourth-century Christian martyr of Padua, it was taken up by English speakers in the nineteenth century. Sometimes shortened to **Justie** or **Justy**.

**Justy** *See* JUSTINE.

# GIRLS' NAMES

**Kady** Irish name that may have evolved out of the Irish Gaelic *ceadach* ('first'). It is also sometimes treated as a variant of **Katie**.

**Kaleigh/Kaley** *See* KAYLEIGH.

**Kalypso** *See* CALYPSO.

**Kar** *See* KAREN.

**Kara** *See* CARA.

**Karen** Danish version of the English CATHERINE. It was adopted by English speakers in the USA in the 1920s. Variant forms include **Karin**, **Karyn**, **Carin**, **Caryn**, CARON, **Caronne**, CARINA, KEREN, **Karena** and **Karina**.

Occasionally shortened to **Kar** or **Kaz**. *See also* CARA.

**Karena** *See* KAREN.

**Karenza** *See* KERENZA.

**Karin** *See* KAREN.

**Karina** *See* CARINA; CATHERINE; KAREN.

**Karyn** *See* KAREN.

**Kasey** *See* CASEY.

**Kasia** *See* KEZIA.

**Kat** *See* CATHERINE; KATE; KATRINA.

**Kate** English name that developed as a shortened form of CATHERINE and related names such as KATHLEEN. It features twice in the plays of William Shakespeare and became increasingly popular towards the end of the nineteenth century. Also found as **Katie**, **Kati** and **Katy**.

**Kath/Katharine/ Katherine** *See* CATHERINE.

**Kathleen** English version of the Irish **Caitlin**, itself modelled on the English CATHERINE. The name was familiar on both sides of the Atlantic by the nineteenth century. Variant forms include **Cathleen** and **Kathlyn**. Commonly shortened to **Kath**, **Kathy**, **Kati**, **Katie** or **Katy**.

**Kathlyn** *See* KATHLEEN.

**Kathryn** *See* CATHERINE.

**Kathy** *See* CATHERINE; KATHLEEN.

**Kati/Katie** *See* KATE; KATHLEEN.

**Katrina** Scottish variant of CATHERINE, probably descended via CATRIONA from the Italian Caterina. Variants include **Katrine** and **Katriona**.

**Katrine/Katriona** *See* KATRINA.

**Katy** *See* CATHERINE; KATHLEEN.

**Katya** Russian equivalent of the English CATHERINE.

**Kay** English name that as a name for girls probably emerged initially as a simple

abbreviation for any longer name beginning with C or K, including CATHERINE and its many derivatives. Also found as **Kaye**.

**Kaye** *See* KAY.

**Kayla/Kaylee** *See* KAYLEIGH.

**Kayleigh** English and Irish first name that is thought to owe its modern popularity to the combination of KELLY or KYLIE and LEIGH or **Lee**. As **Kayley**, the ultimate source of the name was the Irish O Caollaidhe (meaning 'descendant of Caoladhe'), itself based on *caol* ('slender'). Also found as **Kaleigh**, **Kaylee**, **Kayly**, **Kayla** or **Cayla**.

**Kayley** *See* KAYLEIGH.

**Kaylin** Irish name meaning 'slender fair one'. An anglicization of the Irish Caoilfhinn or Caoilfhionn, it is also found as **Kayline** or **Keelan**.

**Kayline** *See* KAYLIN.

**Kayly** *See* KAYLEIGH.

**Kaz** *See* KAREN.

**Keelan** *See* KAYLIN.

**Keeleigh** *See* KEELEY.

**Keeley** English and Irish name that may have evolved as a variant of the Irish KEELIN. Well-known bearers of the name include the British actress Keeley Hawes (b. 1976). Also found as **Keely**, **Keeleigh** or KEIGHLEY.

**Keelin** Irish name that evolved as an anglicization of the Gaelic Caoilfhionn, itself based on *caol* ('slender') and *fionn* ('white'). *See also* KEELEY.

**Keely** *See* KEELEY.

**Keesha** *See* KEISHA.

**Keeva** *See* KEVA.

**Keighley** ('keethly') English name that originated as a place name in Yorkshire, or is otherwise treated as an altered form of KEELEY.

**Keira** *See* KIERA.

**Keisha** English name meaning 'dark-eyed'. Also found as **Keesha** or **Quisha**. *See also* LAKEISHA.

**Kelcey** *See* KELSEY.

**Kelley/Kellie** *See* KELLY.

**Kelly** Irish name that was taken up by English speakers as a first name for both sexes from the late 1950s. The Irish Gaelic form of the name is **Ceallagh**, meaning 'strife', 'war' or 'warlike'. Today it is usually reserved for girls. Also found as **Kelley** or **Kellie**.

**Kelsey** English name that evolved from the Old English Ceolsige, itself from the Old English *ceol* ('ship') and *sige* ('victory'). It has been used as a first name for both sexes since the 1870s. Also found as **Kelsie** or **Kelcey**.

**Kelsie** *See* KELSEY.

**Kena** *See* KENINA.

**Kendra** Feminine equivalent of the masculine KENDRICK, which means 'high summit'. Otherwise possibly the result of the combination of Ken and SANDRA.

**Kenia** *See* KENINA.

**Kenina** English name that developed as a feminine version of KENNETH. It was once fairly common in Scotland, but is rare today. Also found as **Kena**, **Kenna** or **Kenia**.

**Kenna** *See* KENINA.

**Kennedy** Irish, Scottish and English name that evolved as an anglicization of the Irish Gaelic Cinneidigh, derived from *ceann* ('head') and *eidigh* ('ugly') and thus meaning 'ugly head', and also as an anglicized version of the Scottish Gaelic Uarraig.

**Keren** English name that developed as a shortened form of the Hebrew **Kerenhappuch**, meaning 'container of kohl'. *See also* KAREN.

**Kerenhappuch** *See* KEREN.

**Kerensa** *See* KERENZA.

**Kerenza** Cornish name meaning 'love' or 'affection'. Variants include **Kerensa** and **Karenza**.

**Keri/Kerri/Kerrie** *See* KERRY.

**Kerry** English and Irish name probably taken from that of the Irish county of Kerry (meaning 'descendants of Ciar'). Since the 1960s it has been bestowed mainly on girls. Also found as **Kerrie**, **Kerri**, **Keri** or CERI.

**Kerstin** *See* KIRSTEN.

**Keshia** *See* KEZIA.

**Kestrel** English name based on the Old French *cressele* ('rattle'). Popularly associated with the bird of prey, it enjoyed a minor revival in the twentieth century.

**Keva** Anglicization of the Irish Caoimhe, which means 'beauty' or 'grace'. Also found as **Keeva**.

**Kez** *See* KEZIA.

**Kezia** Biblical name derived from the Hebrew Qetsiah, meaning 'cassia' (the name of the tree that produces cinnamon). It was among the biblical names adopted by Puritans in the seventeenth century. Also found as **Keziah**,

Keshia, **Cassia** or **Kasia**. Sometimes shortened to **Kez**, **Kiz**, **Kizzie**, **Kizzy**, **Kissie** or **Kissy**.

**Keziah** *See* KEZIA.

**Kiara** *See* KIERA.

**Kicki** *See* CHRISTINE.

**Kiera** Feminine equivalent of the masculine KIERAN, itself an English version of the Gaelic **Ciaran**, meaning 'little dark-haired one'. The name was largely confined to Ireland until the middle of the twentieth century. Also found as **Ciera**, **Ciara**, **Keira** or **Kiara**.

**Kilie** *See* KYLIE.

**Kim** English name that evolved as a shortened form of KIMBERLEY. Originally applied to both sexes, since the 1920s it has been used chiefly for girls. Sometimes found as **Kym**. Informal versions of the name include **Kimmy** and **Kimmie**.

**Kimberleigh** *See* KIMBERLEY.

**Kimberley** English name taken from that of the South African town of Kimberley. The town was named after British statesman John Wodehouse, 1st Earl of Kimberley, whose family came from Kimberley (meaning 'Cyneburga's wood') in England. It was taken up initially as a boys' name but later came to be used for girls. Also found as **Kimberleigh** or **Kimberly**.

**Kimberly** *See* KIMBERLEY.

**Kimmie/Kimmy** *See* KIM.

**Kirby** English name taken from a place name based on the Old Norse *kirkja* ('church'). Its history as a first name dates from the nineteenth century.

**Kirsten** Scandinavian version of CHRISTINE that was taken up as a first name among English speakers during the nineteenth century. Also encountered as **Kerstin** or **Kirstin**. Commonly shortened to KIRSTY.

**Kirstie** *See* KIRSTY.

**Kirstin** *See* KIRSTEN.

**Kirsty** English name that is

thought to have developed as a Scottish version of CHRISTINE. As **Kirstie** it appeared in the Robert Louis Stevenson novel *The Weir of Hermiston* (1896).

**Kissie/Kissy** *See* KEZIA.

**Kitty** English name that developed as an informal version of CATHERINE and related names such as KATHLEEN. It emerged among English speakers in the eighteenth century and has remained popular ever since (chiefly in the USA).

**Kiz/Kizzie/Kizzy** *See* KEZIA.

**Kodey/Kody** *See* CODY.

**Kora** *See* CORA.

**Kyle** English name that originated in a Scottish surname, itself taken from a place name from Ayrshire based on the Gaelic *caol* ('narrow'), as applied to narrow straits or channels. Initially applied to boys, it has been used increasingly for girls since the 1960s, often linked to KYLIE.

**Kyleigh** *See* KYLIE.

**Kylie** Australian name that has spread throughout the English-speaking world since the late 1970s. It probably evolved from KYLE or possibly KELLY. Its popularity in the 1980s was promoted by Australian television actress and pop singer Kylie Minogue (b. 1968). Occasionally found as **Kyly**, **Kilie** or **Kyleigh**.

**Kyly** *See* KYLIE.

**Kym** *See* KIM.

# GIRLS' NAMES

**Lacey** English name that originated in a surname based on a Norman place name, Lassy in Calvados. When used as a feminine name it is often assumed that there is a link with the ordinary vocabulary word 'lace'.

**Ladonna** French name meaning 'the lady'.

**Laelia** Roman name meaning 'cheerful' or 'chatty'. Also found as a variant of AURELIA. It was borne by a fifth-century Irish saint and taken up by English speakers in the nineteenth century. Also found as **Lelia** or **Lela**.

**Laetitia** *See* LETITIA.

**Laila/Lailah** *See* LEILA.

**Laine** *See* LANE.

**Lake** English name based on the ordinary vocabulary word. One of several nature-based names taken up in the late twentieth century.

**Lakeisha** English name of relatively recent coinage, probably the result of the addition of a La- prefix to the already existing KEISHA.

**Lakshmi** Indian name based on the Sanskrit *laksmi* ('mark' or 'sign'). According to Hindus, Lakshmi is the wife of Vishnu and represents beauty, good luck and wealth. It is often given to children with birthmarks.

**Lal** *See* LALAGE.

**Lala** Slavic name meaning 'tulip'. Also found as **Lalla**. *See also* HELEN; LALAGE.

**Lalage** ('lalagee') Greek name based on *lalagein* ('to chatter' or 'to babble'). It featured in the *Odes* of Horace and has appeared sporadically among English speakers since the nineteenth century. Shortened forms include **Lal**, LALA, **Lallie** and **Lally**.

**Lalita** Indian name based on the Sanskrit for 'playful'.

**Lalla/Lallie/Lally** *See* EULALIA; LALA; LALAGE.

**Lana** English name that developed out of ALANA, itself a feminine version of ALAN, meaning 'shining'. It seems to have made its first appearance, in the USA, in the 1920s and became well known in the 1940s through US actress Lana Turner (Julia Turner; 1920–95). Also used as a shortened form of SVETLANA.

**Lane** English name that originated as a surname based on the ordinary vocabulary word. Variants include **Laine**, **Laney** and **Layne**.

**Laney** *See* LANE.

**Lani** Hawaiian name meaning 'heaven' or 'sky'.

**Laoise** *See* LUCY.

**Lara** English name that emerged as a shortened form of the Russian **Larissa**, which was itself based on the name of an ancient Greek city (meaning 'citadel'), or else from the Latin for 'cheerful'. Also found as a variant of LAURA, the name was popularized by a character called Lara in Boris Pasternak's *Doctor Zhivago* (1957).

**Laraine** *See* LORRAINE.

**Larissa** See LARA.

**Lark** English name taken from the name of the songbird. It has made rare appearances among English speakers since the early twentieth century.

**Latasha** English name that apparently resulted from the combination of LATISHA and NATASHA. It established itself as a favourite within the black population of the USA in the early 1980s and is just one of several names created by adding the prefix 'La-' to existing names.

**Lateefa/Lateefah/ Lateifa/Lateiffa/Latifa** *See* LATIFAH.

**Latifah** Arabic name meaning 'gentle' or 'pleasant'.

Also found as **Lateefa**, **Lateefah**, **Lateifa**, **Lateiffa**, **Latifa** or **Latiffa**. It has become well-known through US rap singer Queen Latifah (Dana Elaine Owens; b. 1970).

**Latiffa** *See* LATIFAH.

**Latisha** English name of relatively recent invention, possibly influenced by LETITIA. Shortened to **Tisha**. *See also* LATASHA.

**Latoya** English name that was just one of several names created by adding the prefix 'La-' to existing names, making its first appearance in the USA in the 1970s.

**Laura** English, Spanish and Italian name based on the Latin *laurus* ('laurel' or 'bay'). In ancient Rome victorious emperors wore crowns of laurel leaves and the name thus became associated with 'victory' or 'triumph'. **Laurie**, **Lauri** (or **Lori**) and **Lolly** are familiar forms of the name. Variants include **Lora**, **Loreen**, **Laurena**, **Laureen**, **Laurene**, **Lorena**, **Laurice**, **Laurissa**, **Laurina**, **Laurinda**, **Lorelle**, **Lorinda** and **Lorita**. *See also* LAURABEL; LAUREN; LAURETTA.

**Laurabel** English name that resulted from the combination of LAURA and MABEL.

**Lauraine** *See* LORRAINE.

**Laureen** *See* LAURA.

**Laurel** English name based on the name of the tree. The early development of the name is thought to have been influenced by LAURA and it is sometimes considered to be a straightforward variant of that name. Also found as **Laurelle**. **Lauri** and **Laurie** are informal variants.

**Laurelle** *See* LAUREL.

**Lauren** English name that developed as a variant of LAURA. It appeared with increasing frequency among English speakers from the 1960s, having become familiar through US film actress Lauren Bacall (Betty Joan Perske; b. 1924). Also found as **Loren**.

**Laurena/Laurene** *See* LAURA.

**Lauretta** English name that developed from LAURA. It made its first appearances in medieval times. Sometimes shortened to **Lauri**, **Laurie** or **Lorrie**. Variants include **Loretta**, **Lorette** and **Laurette**.

**Laurette** *See* LAURETTA.

**Lauri** *See* LAURA; LAURETTA.

**Laurice** *See* LAURA.

**Laurie** *See* LAURA; LAURETTA.

**Laurina/Laurinda/ Laurissa** *See* LAURA.

**Lavena** *See* LAVINIA.

**Lavender** English name based on that of the scented plant. Like a number of other flower names it was taken up by English speakers towards the end of the nineteenth century but is rare today.

**Laverne** English name that resulted from the addition of the prefix 'La–' to the established **Verne**. This was one of a series of names that appeared by a similar process in the middle of the twentieth century, chiefly in the USA. The fact that there was an ancient Italian goddess of thieves called Laverna is almost certainly coincidental.

**Lavina** *See* LAVINIA.

**Lavinia** Roman name taken from that of the ancient Roman town of Lavinium (itself of unknown origin). According to legend, Lavinia was the name of the wife of Aeneas, and thus that of the mother of the Roman people. **Lavina** and **Lavena** are variant forms. Sometimes shortened to **Vinnie** or **Vinny**.

**Layla** Arabic name meaning 'wine' or 'intoxication'. The name became widely familiar throughout the Arabic world through the poetry of Qays ibn–al–Mulawwah (d. 688), whose works were often addressed to his cousin Layla. *See also* LEILA.

**Layne** *See* LANE.

**Lea** *See* LEAH; LEE.

**Leaf** English name based on the ordinary vocabulary word.

It enjoyed a vogue in the 1960s.

**Leah** Hebrew name meaning 'antelope', 'gazelle' or even 'cow' – although another derivation suggests it means 'languid' or 'weary'. It appears in the Bible as the name of Jacob's first wife. Variants include **Lea**, LEE and LIA.

**Leana/Leanna** *See* LIANA.

**Leanne** *See* LIANNE.

**Leanora/Leanore** *See* LEONORA.

**Lecia** *See* LETITIA.

**Leda** Greek name possibly based on the Lycian for 'woman'. The name is best known from the Greek myth of Leda and the swan, in which Leda is seduced by Zeus in the guise of a swan.

**Lee** English name that was based on the Old English *leah* ('wood', 'meadow' or 'clearing'). It has been employed as a first name for girls since the early twentieth century. Also found as **Lea** or **Leigh**. *See also* LEAH.

**Lee-Ann** *See* LIANNE.

**Leesa** *See* LISA.

**Leigh** *See* LEE.

**Leigh-Ann** *See* LIANNE.

**Leila** Arabic name meaning 'dark-haired', 'swarthy' or 'dark-eyed'. As **Leilah** it features in Persian legend. Lord Byron and Edward Bulwer-Lytton both made use of the name in their writings, promoting its use from the nineteenth century. Also found as **Laila**, **Lailah**, **Leilah**, **Lela** or **Lila**. *See also* LAYLA.

**Leilah** *See* LEILA.

**Lela** *See* LAEILA; LEILA.

**Lelia** *See* LAELIA.

**Lena** English, Scottish, German, Dutch and Scandinavian name that exists as a diminutive of various longer names ending '-lena' or '-lina', such as HELENA. It was taken up by English speakers in the middle of the nineteenth century. Also found as LINA.

**Lenda** *See* LINDA.

**Lenora** *See* LEONORA; ELEANOR.

**Lenore** *See* ELEANOR.

**Leona** Feminine equivalent of the masculine LEON, meaning 'lion'. **Leonie** is a variant form. **Liona** is a variant possibly influenced by FIONA.

**Leonie** *See* LEONA.

**Leonora** English name that developed via **Eleanora** as a variant of ELEANOR. It made its first appearances among English speakers in the nineteenth century. Variants include **Leanora**, **Leanore**, **Lenore** and **Lenora**. Sometimes shortened to NORA or **Norah**.

**Leontia** Feminine equivalent of the masculine LEO, meaning 'lion'.

**Leontine** ('leeonteen') English version of the French Léontine, itself based ultimately on the Roman Leontius, from the Latin *leo* ('lion'). Alternatively, the name may have resulted from the combination of LEONORA and Clementine. Also found as **Leontyne**.

**Leontyne** *See* LEONTINE.

**Les/Lesley** *See* LESLIE.

**Leslie** Scottish name derived from a place name (Lesslyn in Aberdeenshire) possibly based on the Gaelic *leas cuilinn* ('garden of hollies'). It was first recorded as a first name in the eighteenth century, promoted by the Robert Burns poem 'Bonnie Lesley'. The spelling **Lesley** is now chiefly reserved for girls. Commonly shortened to **Les**.

**Leta** English name based on the Latin *letus* ('glad').

**Leticia** *See* LETITIA.

**Letitia** English name based on the Latin *laetitia* ('gladness' or 'joy'). Also found as **Lecia**, **Laetitia** or **Leticia**, it was taken up by English speakers during the medieval period. Commonly shortened to **Lettie**, **Letty**, **Tish** or **Tisha**. *See also* LETTICE.

**Lettice** English name that developed out of LETITIA. It has medieval roots and was the more popular form of the name between the twelfth and seventeenth centuries but is now rare. Shortened to **Lettie** or **Letty**.

**Lettie/Letty** See ALETHEA; ARLETTE; LETITIA; LETTICE.

**Lexie** Feminine equivalent of the masculine LEX, which is thought to have evolved as a shortened form of ALEXANDER, influenced perhaps by REX. Also found as **Lexy**.

**Lexy** See LEXIE.

**Lia** Variant form of LEAH. Since the 1950s the name has also been encountered among English speakers as a shortening of various longer names, such as AMELIA and DELIA.

**Liadain** ('leeadan') Irish name that was probably based on the Irish Gaelic *liath* ('grey'). It appears in the Irish legend as the name of one of a pair of ill-fated lovers. Also found as **Líadan** or **Liadhain**.

**Líadan/Liadhain** See LIADAIN.

**Liana** French name that developed out of JULIANA or other names ending in '-liana'. It is rare among English speakers, who generally prefer the related name LIANNE. Also found as **Leana** or **Leanna**.

**Lianne** English name that evolved either out of the French JULIANNE or through the combination of LEE and ANNE. **Leanne** is a common variant form. **Lee-Ann** and **Leigh-Ann** are less common versions.

**Lib/Libby** See ELIZABETH; OLIVIA.

**Liddy** See LYDIA.

**Lil** See LILIAN; LILY.

**Lila** See LEILA; LILY.

**Lilac** English name based on that of the scented shrub. The name of the plant came ultimately via French and Spanish from the Arabic *lilak*, itself from the Persian *nilak* ('bluish').

**Lilian** English name that is thought to have developed from ELIZABETH or else through the combination of LILY and ANNE. It was first recorded among English speakers towards the end of the sixteenth century. Also found (especially in the USA) as **Lillian**. Shortened to **Lil** or LILY. Variants include the Scottish **Lilias** or **Lillias**.

**Lilias** *See* LILIAN.

**Lilith** Hebrew name variously interpreted to mean 'night monster', 'storm goddess' or 'screech owl'. In medieval times it was commonly believed that Adam had had a wife called Lilith before Eve but that she had been turned into a hideous demon for refusing to obey her husband. Also in use as a variant of LILY.

**Lilla/Lillah** *See* LILY.

**Lillian/Lillias** *See* LILIAN.

**Lillie/Lilly** *See* LILY.

**Lily** English name based on that of the flower, itself a symbol of purity. Also used as a shortened form of ELIZABETH. Familiar forms of the name include **Lil**, **Lilly** and **Lillie**. Other variants include **Lilla**, **Lillah**, **Lila** and **Tiger Lily** – borrowed from a character in J. M. Barrie's *Peter Pan* (1904). *See also* LILIAN.

**Lin** *See* LINDA; LINDSAY; LYNN.

**Lina** English name that developed as a shortened form of ADELINE, **Carolina** and other names ending '-lina' around the middle of the nineteenth century. It is sometimes also used as a variant of LENA.

**Linda** English name that appears to have developed in the late nineteenth century as a shortened form of BELINDA and other names with similar '-linda' endings. Occasionally found as **Lynda** or **Lenda**. **Lindie**, **Lyndi** and **Lindy** are familiar versions of the name. Shortened to **Lin**, LYNN or **Lynne**.

**Lindie** *See* LINDA.

**Lindsay** English name modelled on Lindsey in

Lincolnshire, a place name meaning 'island of Lincoln' or 'wetland belonging to Lincoln'. Also found as **Lindsey**, it was once reserved for males but has also been applied to girls since the 1930s. Also found as **Linsay**, **Linsey**, **Linzi**, **Lyndsay**, **Lynsay**, **Lindsie** or **Lynsey**. Shortened to **Lin** or **Lyn**.

**Lindsey/Lindsie** *See* LINDSAY.

**Lindy** *See* LINDA.

**Linette** *See* LYNETTE.

**Linnet** English name based on that of the songbird, or else used as a variant of LYNETTE or of the Welsh **Eiluned**. The bird name came ultimately from the Old French *linotte*, itself from *lin* ('flax'), the seeds of which are the bird's usual food.

**Linnette** *See* LYNETTE.

**Linsay/Linsey/Linzi** *See* LINDSAY.

**Liorah** Hebrew name meaning 'I have light'.

**Lis** *See* FELICITY.

**Lisa** English name that developed as a shortened form of ELIZABETH. It emerged as a popular first name in its own right in the 1960s. Also found as **Liza** and, rarely, **Leesa**. Familiar forms include **Liz**, **Lizzie**, **Lizzy**, **Lisette** and **Lysette**.

**Lisbet/Lisbeth** *See* ELIZABETH.

**Lisette** *See* ELIZABETH; LISA.

**Lisha** English name that developed as a shortened form of such names as DELICIA and FELICIA.

**Liss** *See* FELICITY.

**Lissa** *See* MELISSA.

**Lissie** *See* FELICITY.

**Lita** *See* LOLITA.

**Liv** Scandinavian name probably based on the Old Norse *hlif* ('defence' or 'protection') or linked to *liv* ('life').

**Livia** Roman name possibly

based on the Latin *lividus* ('leaden-coloured' or 'bluish'). It is also found as a familiar form of OLIVIA. It appears in William Shakespeare's *Romeo and Juliet* (1595). **Livy** and **Livvy** are familiar forms of the name.

**Livvy/Livy** *See* LIVIA.

**Liz/Liza** *See* ELIZABETH; LISA.

**Lizanne** English name that resulted from the combination of **Liz** and ANNE.

**Lizbeth** *See* ELIZABETH.

**Lizzie/Lizzy** *See* ELIZABETH; LISA.

**Lo** *See* LOIS; LOLA; LOLITA.

**Lois** ('lowiss') Biblical name possibly based on the Greek *loion* ('better' or 'good') but also in use as a variant of LOUISA or LOUISE. The name was taken up by English speakers in the seventeenth century. Shortened to **Lo**.

**Lola** Spanish and English name that developed alongside LOLITA as a variant of

DOLORES. Long established across the Spanish-speaking world, it has made occasional appearances among English speakers since the nineteenth century. Shortened to **Lo**. Variants include the rare **Lolicia**.

**Lolicia** *See* LOLA.

**Lolita** Spanish name that developed alongside LOLA as a variant of DOLORES. It first entered English-speaking use in the USA in the nineteenth century. Today it is closely associated with Vladimir Nabokov's novel *Lolita* (1955). Shortened to **Lo** or **Lita**.

**Lolly** *See* LAURA.

**Lora** *See* LAURA.

**Lorain/Loraine/ Lorayne** *See* LORRAINE.

**Loreen** *See* LAURA.

**Lorelei** German name meaning 'fairy cliff'. Lorelei is the name of a cliff on the Rhine where according to German legend a siren lured sailors to their death with her beautiful singing.

**Lorelle** *See* LAURA.

**Loren** *See* LAUREN.

**Lorena** *See* LAURA.

**Loreto** English and Irish name based ultimately upon an Italian place name. It was to Loreto in central Italy that angels supposedly carried the Holy House of the Virgin from Nazareth – hence the popularity of the name among Roman Catholics.

**Loretta/Lorette** *See* LAURETTA.

**Lori** *See* LAURA; LORRAINE.

**Lorinda** *See* LAURA.

**Loris** English name of obscure origins, but possibly a variant of LAURA. It seems to have made its first appearance in the latter half of the twentieth century, winning particular approval in Australia.

**Lorna** English name that is thought to have been invented by the British novelist R. D. Blackmore in his romantic novel *Lorna Doone* (1869). According to Blackmore, the name was based on the Scottish place name Lorn (in Argyll).

**Lorraine** English name based on a Scottish surname that may in turn have been borrowed from the eastern French province of Lorraine. It is often assumed to be a variant of LAURA. Also found as **Lauraine, Laraine, Lorain, Loraine** or **Lorayne**. **Lori** and **Lorri** are familiar forms of the name.

**Lorri** *See* LORRAINE.

**Lorrie** *See* LAURETTA.

**Lotta/Lottie/Lotty** *See* CHARLOTTE.

**Lotus** English name referring to the lotus fruit of Greek mythology, which was reputed to induce a state of indolent forgetfulness in those who ate it.

**Lou** *See* LOUISA; LOUISE.

**Louanne** *See* LUANNE.

**Louella** English name that resulted from the combination of Lou (from LOUISA or LOUISE) and the feminine suffix '-ella' (*see* ELLA). It was taken up by English speakers in the nineteenth century. Also found as **Luella**.

**Louie** *See* LOUISA; LOUISE.

**Louisa** Feminine form of LOUIS, itself from the Old German *hlut* ('famous') and *wig* ('warrior'). Adopted by English speakers in the eighteenth century, it has since been eclipsed by LOUISE. Also found as **Louiza** or **Luisa**. Shortened to **Lou** or **Louie**. LULU is a familiar form, of German origin. *See also* LOIS.

**Louise** Feminine variant of LOUIS that has largely replaced LOUISA among English speakers. This French version of the name seems to have made its first appearance among English speakers in the seventeenth century. **Luise** is a German variant. Shortened to **Lou** or **Louie** or occasionally LULU. *See also* HÉLOÏSE.

**Louiza** *See* LOUISA.

**Lourdes** Spanish name taken from that of a famous shrine in southern France where numerous miracles are claimed to have taken place since a French peasant girl had visions of the Virgin Mary there in the 1850s. Confined chiefly to the Roman Catholic community.

**Loveday** English name referring to the medieval 'lovedays' on which disputes were settled. First recorded in the thirteenth century, the name was usually reserved for children born on one of these days. Its modern use is largely confined to Cornwall (where it is also found as **Lowdy**).

**Lowdy** *See* LOVEDAY.

**Lowri** Welsh name representing a regional variant of LAURA. Also found as **Lowry**.

**Lowry** *See* LOWRI.

**Lu** *See* LULU.

**Luana/Luanna** *See* LUANNE.

**Luanne** English and Italian name apparently without any specific meaning. Also found as **Louanne** or **Luana** (or **Luanna**), it was taken up as a first name by English and

Italian speakers after it was used in the King Vidor film *The Bird of Paradise* (1932), for which it may have been invented.

**Lucasta** English name that was invented by the English poet Richard Lovelace (1618–57). Lovelace linked it to the Latin *lux casta* ('chaste light'). It is thought that the original Lucasta of Lovelace's poem 'Lucasta' (1649) was probably called LUCY or else bore the surname Lucas.

**Luce** *See* LUCIA; LUCY.

**Lucetta** English name that developed as a familiar variant of LUCIA or LUCY. It would appear to be of mainly historical interest, with records of its use among English speakers going back to the sixteenth century. A French variant is **Lucette**.

**Lucette** *See* LUCETTA.

**Lucia** ('loocheea' or 'loosia') Roman name that developed as a feminine version of LUCIUS, meaning 'light'. Because of its meaning it is thought that the name was originally reserved for children born at dawn.

Sometimes used as a variant of LUCY. Shortened to **Luce**.

**Lucie** *See* LUCY.

**Lucile/Lucilla** *See* LUCILLE.

**Lucille** French variant of the Roman Lucilla, itself based on LUCIA. Occasionally found as **Lucile** or **Lucilla**. Sometimes shortened to LUCY.

**Lucinda** English name that developed as a variant of LUCIA or LUCY. The earliest records of the name go back to Cervantes' classic work *Don Quixote* (1605). It became a popular choice of first name among English speakers in the eighteenth century. Sometimes shortened to LUCY or to CINDY, **Cindi** or **Sindy**.

**Lucky** English name that developed either as a nickname or else as a familiar version of such names as FELICITY or LUCY. It has made irregular appearances as a first name since the early twentieth century.

**Lucretia** Roman name that developed as a feminine form

of the masculine Lucretius, itself possibly based on LUCIUS but otherwise of unknown origin. Notable bearers of the name have included the notorious Lucretia Borgia (1480–1519).

**Lucy** English version of the Roman LUCIA. It also appears as a shortened form of LUCILLE or LUCINDA. Variants include LUCETTA, **Lucette**, the French **Lucie** and the Irish Gaelic **Laoise**. Among familiar forms are **Luce**, LUCKY and LULU.

**Ludmila** *See* LUDMILLA.

**Ludmilla** Russian name based on the Slavonic *lud* ('people') and *mil* ('grace'). Also found as **Ludmila**.

**Luella** *See* LOUELLA.

**Luisa** *See* LOUISA.

**Luise** *See* LOUISE.

**Lulu** German name that developed as a familiar form of Luise, the German version of LOUISE. Also found in use among English speakers as a familiar form of LUCY, it is a relatively recent introduction

to the English-speaking world, of twentieth-century origin. Sometimes shortened to **Lu**. *See also* LOUISA.

**Luned/Lunet** *See* ELUNED.

**Lydia** English name based ultimately on a Greek name meaning 'woman of Lydia' (a region in Asia Minor). It features in the Bible as the name of one of St Paul's converts. **Liddy** is a familiar form of the name.

**Lyn** *See* LINDSAY; LYNN.

**Lynda/Lyndi** *See* LINDA.

**Lyndsay** *See* LINDSAY.

**Lynette** English name that developed as a variant of LYNN. The addition of the '-ette' ending suggests a French influence. Also found as **Lynnette**, the name is popularly linked with the French *lune* ('moon') and the songbird called the linnet – hence such variants as LINNET, **Linette** and **Linnette**.

**Lynn** English name used as a shortened form of LINDSAY, LINDA and similar names. Also found as **Lin**, **Lyn** or **Lynne**, it made its first appearances in the nineteenth century.

**Lynne** *See* LYNN.

**Lynnette** *See* LYNETTE.

**Lynsay/Lynsey** *See* LINDSAY.

**Lyra** English name based on the Latin *lyra* ('lyre'). It has enjoyed renewed currency in the early twenty-first century through Lyra, one of the central characters in the *His Dark Materials* trilogy of books by Philip Pullman.

**Lysandra** Greek name meaning 'liberator of men'.

**Lysette** *See* LISA.

**Lyssa** *See* ALICIA.

## GIRLS' NAMES

**Mab** *See* MABEL; MAEVE.

**Mabel** English name based on the Old French *amabel* or *amable* ('lovely'). Also found as **Mable**, **Mabella** or **Mabelle** (linked to the French *ma belle*, meaning 'my lovely'). Other variants are **Maybelle** and **Maybelline**. Shortened to **Mab**, **Mabs** or MAY.

**Mabella/Mabelle/ Mable/Mabs** *See* MABEL.

**Mackenzie** Scottish name meaning 'son of Kenneth'. It is particularly associated with Canada, where it is understood to be a reference to the Mackenzie River.

**Macy** English name based ultimately on French and roughly meaning 'from Matthew's estate'.

**Mad/Maddie** *See* MADELEINE; MADISON; MADONNA.

**Maddison** *See* MADISON.

**Maddy** *See* MADELEINE; MADONNA.

**Madelaine** *See* MADELEINE.

**Madeleine** French and English name based on the Hebrew **Magdalene**, meaning 'of Magdala' (Magdala being a town on the Sea of Galilee). Mary Magdalene was the New Testament figure who supposedly washed Christ's feet with her tears. As **Magdalen**, **Madeline** or **Madlin**, the name was imported to England from France in the thirteenth century. Also found as **Madolina**, **Madoline**, **Madelaine** or **Madlyn**. Shortened to **Mad**, **Madge**, **Maddie**, **Maddy** or LENA. *See also* MAGDA.

**Madelina/Madeline** *See* MADELEINE.

**Madge** *See* MADELEINE; MARGARET.

**Madison** English name based either on **Magdalen** (*see* MADELEINE) or meaning 'son of Maud'. Also found as **Maddison**, it is largely confined to the USA, where it was promoted through James Madison (1751–1836), the country's fourth president. Shortened to **Mad** or **Maddie**.

**Madlin/Madlyn/ Madolina/Madoline** *See* MADELEINE.

**Madonna** English name based on the Italian title for the Virgin Mary, meaning 'my lady'. As a first name it appears to have been a twentieth-century introduction, promoted by American Italians. The name is famous as that of US pop singer and film actress Madonna (Madonna Louise Veronica Ciccone; b. 1958). Shortened to DONNA or **Maddy**.

**Mae** *See* MAY.

**Maev** *See* MAEVE.

**Maeve** ('mave') English version of the Irish **Meadhbh**, possibly from the Irish *meadhbhan* ('intoxication') and thus meaning 'she who intoxicates'. It is the name of a legendary queen of Connacht and is still largely confined to Ireland. Also found as **Maev**, **Mave**, **Meave**, **Meaveen**, **Medbh** or **Mab**.

**Magda** German and Scandinavian variant of the Hebrew **Magdalene**, meaning 'of Magdala' (Magdala being a town on the Sea of Galilee). Mary Magdalene was the New Testament figure who supposedly washed Christ's feet with her tears.

**Magdalen/Magdalene** *See* MADELEINE; MAGDA.

**Maggi/Maggie** *See* MARGARET.

**Magnolia** English flower name that like many other flower names made its first appearance among English speakers in the late nineteenth century.

**Mahala** *See* MAHALIA.

**Mahalia** English name

derived from the Hebrew for 'tenderness' (although other suggestions are that it was based on a musical term or on an ordinary vocabulary word meaning 'barren'). A biblical name, it was borne by US gospel singer Mahalia Jackson (1911–72). Variants include **Mahala**, **Mehala**, **Mehalah** and **Mehalia**.

**Mai** *See* MAY.

**Maia** *See* MAYA.

**Maidie** Scottish and Irish name apparently based on the ordinary vocabulary word 'maid', possibly influenced by MAISIE. It may also be found as an informal version of MARY (probably because the Virgin Mary is sometimes referred to as a 'maid of God'). Occasionally found as **Maidy**.

**Maidy** *See* MAIDIE.

**Mair/Maire** *See* MARY.

**Mairead** *See* MARGARET; MYRA.

**Mairi** *See* MARY.

**Mairin** *See* MAUREEN.

**Mairwen** Welsh name that resulted from the combination of MARY and *wen* ('white' or 'blessed').

**Maisie** Informal version of the Scottish **Mairead**, itself a variant of MARGARET. It came into fashion among English speakers in the late nineteenth century. Also found as **Mysie**.

**Maja** *See* MAYA.

**Malandra** English name that resulted from the combination of ALEXANDRA and MELANIE or similar names.

**Malia** ('maleea') Hawaiian name meaning 'perhaps' or 'probably'. It is sometimes also treated as a variant of MARY or MARIA. It became well known in 2009 as the name of one of the children of US President Barack Obama.

**Malinda** *See* MELINDA.

**Malise** Gaelic name meaning 'servant of Jesus'. In Scotland it is traditionally associated with the Gordon family.

**Mallory** *See* MALORY.

**Malory** English name that originated in a Norman French nickname meaning 'unfortunate', from the French *malheure* ('unhappy' or 'unlucky'). Also found as **Mallory** (the usual spelling when given to boys).

**Malvina** First name invented by the Scottish poet James Macpherson (1736–96) for a character in the celebrated poetry he claimed was the work of the legendary Gaelic bard Ossian. Macpherson may have based the name on the Gaelic *mala mhin* ('smooth brow').

**Mame** *See* MAMIE.

**Mamie** English name that developed as a variant of several different names, including MARGARET, MARY and MAY, although it is often assumed to be based on 'mammy' or 'mummy'. It made its first appearances in the USA during the nineteenth century. Also found as **Mame**.

**Mandy** *See* AMANDA; MIRANDA.

**Manette** *See* MARY.

**Manon** French name that evolved as a variant of MARIE.

**Manuela** Spanish name that developed as a feminine equivalent of MANUEL.

**Mara** Hebrew name supposedly meaning 'bitter', although it is often assumed to be a variant of MARY. The name appears in the Bible as the name Ruth's mother-in-law Naomi (meaning 'sweetness') gives herself when she complains that God has treated her badly. Also found as **Marah**.

**Marah** *See* MARA.

**Maralyn** *See* MARILYN.

**Marcella** Feminine equivalent of the Roman Marcellus, itself a variant of MARCUS. Occasionally found in its French form **Marcelle**, it has made sporadic appearances in English-speaking countries, especially Ireland.

**Marcelle** *See* MARCELLA.

**Marcia** Feminine equivalent of the Roman Marcius (or MARIUS) that became current in the English-speaking world in the late nineteenth century, notably in the USA (where the usual spelling since the 1920s has been **Marsha**). **Marcine** is a variant. Familiar forms include **Marcie** and **Marcy**.

**Marcie/Marcine/Marcy** *See* MARCIA.

**Mared** *See* MARGARET.

**Maredudd** *See* MEREDITH.

**Maree** *See* MARIE.

**Margaret** English and Scottish version of the Roman **Margarita**, itself descended from the Greek *margarités* ('pearl'). The name has been popular among English speakers since medieval times. Informal versions include **Madge**, **Maggie** (or **Maggi**), **Marge**, **Margi**, **Margie**, **Meg**, **Meggie**, **Megs** and **Moggy**. As well as Margarita, variants include **Mared**, **Margareta**, **Margaretta**, **Marghanita**, the Gaelic **Mairead** and the French **Marguerite**, **Marguerita** and MARGOT. *See also* DAISY; MAISIE; MARJORIE; MAY; MEGAN; PEARL; PEGGY; RITA.

**Margareta/Margaretta/ Margarita** *See* MARGARET.

**Margaux** *See* MARGOT.

**Marge** *See* MARGARET; MARJORIE.

**Margerie/Margery** *See* MARJORIE.

**Marghanita** *See* MARGARET.

**Margi/Margie** *See* MARGARET; MARJORIE.

**Margo** *See* MARGOT.

**Margot** ('margo') French variant of **Marguerite** (*see* MARGARET). It was adopted from the French by English speakers in medieval times but remained rare until the nineteenth century. Also found as **Margo**. The unusual spelling **Margaux** was invented by US actress Margaux Hemingway (Margot Hemingway; 1955–96).

**Marguerita/Marguerite** *See* MARGARET.

**Margy** *See* MARJORIE.

**Mari** *See* MARIE; MARY.

**Maria** Roman name descended from the Greek Mariam, itself based on the Hebrew Miryam. The original meaning may possibly have been 'to swell' (as in pregnancy). The usual pronunciation has changed since the nineteenth century from 'marigha' to 'mareea'. Variants include **Mariah**, **Mariel** (or **Marielle**), **Mariella**, **Marietta** (or **Mariette**) and the Irish **Moya**. *See also* MARIE; MARIKA; MARY; MIA; MIRIAM; MITZI; RIA.

**Mariah** *See* MARIA.

**Mariam/Mariamne** *See* MIRIAM.

**Marian** Feminine version of MARION, itself based on the French MARIE. It is sometimes also considered to be a combined form of MARY and ANN. The name was in use in England in medieval times. *See also* MARIANNE.

**Mariana/Mariane/ Marianna** *See* MARIANNE.

**Marianne** Variant of MARIAN, also assumed to be a combination of MARY and ANNE. It was first taken up by English speakers in the eighteenth century, when it existed alongside **Mary-Ann**. In France the name has been adopted for the symbolic woman representing the Republic itself. Also found as **Mariane**, **Maryanne**, **Mariana** and **Marianna**.

**Marie** French equivalent of MARY, based on the Roman MARIA. It was taken up by English speakers in the nineteenth century, initially in the USA. Also found as **Maree** or **Mari**. It may also appear in combination with other names, as in **Anne-Marie**. *See also* MIMI.

**Mariel** *See* MARIA; MURIEL.

**Mariella/Marielle/ Marietta/Mariette** *See* MARIA.

**Marigold** English flower name taken up by English speakers towards the end of the nineteenth century. The flower itself was originally named golde (after the precious metal, because of its colour) but was renamed in the medieval period in honour of the Virgin Mary. Sometimes shortened to GOLDIE.

**Marika** Slavonic name that emerged as a variant of MARIA.

**Marilene** *See* MARILYN.

**Marilyn** English name based on a combination of MARY and LYNN (or ELLEN), or simply an elaboration of Mary with the suffix '-lyn'. It became well known through US film actress Marilyn Monroe (Norma Jean Baker; 1926–62). Variants include **Maralyn, Marolyn, Marilene, Marylin, Marylyn, Merilyn** and **Merrilyn.**

**Marina** Feminine equivalent of the Roman family name Marinus, itself from MARIUS. Because of its similarity to the Latin *marinus* ('of the sea') it has always had maritime associations – as evidenced by Shakespeare's use of it for Pericles' daughter in *Pericles* (1607–8), with the explanation that she was born at sea. Sometimes shortened to **Rena.** *See also* MARNIE.

**Maris** English name of uncertain origin. It is thought that it may have had its roots in the Latin *stella maris* ('star of the sea').

**Marisa** Italian, Spanish and English name that evolved through the combination of MARIA or MARINA and LISA. Also found as **Marissa**, it is a relatively recent introduction to the English-speaking world, dating from the 1950s.

**Marissa** *See* MARISA.

**Marje/Marji** *See* MARJORIE.

**Marjorie** English version of the French **Marguerite** (*see* MARGARET), regarded as a separate name since at least the thirteenth century and sometimes linked to the herb marjoram. The earliest record of the name in England dates back to 1194, when it was given as **Margerie** or **Margery.** Shortened to **Marje, Marji, Marge, Margy, Margi** or **Margie.**

**Marla/Marleen/ Marlena** *See* MARLENE.

**Marlene** German variant of

Maria Magdalene. Its acceptance throughout the English-speaking world was a reflection of the international fame enjoyed by German-born US actress Marlene Dietrich (Maria Magdalene von Losch; 1904–92). Also found as **Marlena**, **Marleen** or **Marline**. Sometimes shortened to **Marla** or **Marley**.

**Marley/Marline** *See* MARLENE.

**Marna/Marni** *See* MARNIE.

**Marnie** English name of uncertain origin. Also found as **Marni**, it may have developed, via **Marna**, as a variant of MARINA. Alfred Hitchcock's film *Marnie* (1964) helped to promote the name, particularly in the USA.

**Marolyn** *See* MARILYN.

**Marsha** *See* MARCIA.

**Marshal** *See* MARSHALL.

**Marshall** English boys' name that has also been bestowed upon girls since the 1940s. The name is ultimately Germanic in origin, coming from *marah*

('horse') and *scalc* ('servant'), and was originally reserved for people connected with looking after horses. Also found as **Marshal**.

**Martha** English name based on the Aramaic for 'lady'. It was among the biblical names taken up by Puritans in the sixteenth century. Its popularity in the USA owes much to Martha Washington (1732–1802), wife of President George Washington. Shortened to **Marti**, **Martie**, **Marty**, **Mattie** or **Matty** as well as to **Patty** or **Pattie**.

**Marti/Martie** *See* MARTHA; MARTINA.

**Martina** Feminine equivalent of MARTIN, usually interpreted as meaning 'warlike', which was taken up by English speakers around the middle of the nineteenth century. Variants include **Martine**. Shortened to **Marti** or **Martie**.

**Martine** *See* MARTINA.

**Marty** *See* MARTHA.

**Mary** English version of the Roman MARIA, itself from the

Hebrew Miryam, which may have meant 'to swell', thus evoking pregnancy. The name of Christ's mother, Mary was bestowed upon around one-fifth of all female children born in England in the mid-eighteenth century. It also appears in combination with other names, as in **Mary-Ann**, **Mary-Jane** and **Marylou**. Variants include the Irish Gaelic **Maire**, the Scottish **Mairi** and the Welsh **Mair** and **Mari**. *See also* MAMIE; MAY; MIA; MIMI; MITZI; MOIRA; MOLLY; POLLY.

**Maryam** Arabic name that probably evolved as a variant of the Hebrew MIRIAM. Alternatively, it may have its root in a Syriac word meaning 'elevated'.

**Mary-Ann/Maryanne** *See* MARIANNE.

**Marylin** *See* MARILYN.

**Marylou** *See* MARY.

**Marylyn** *See* MARILYN.

**Mat** *See* MATILDA.

**Matilda** English name based via Norman French on the Old German Mahthildis, itself from *macht* ('might') and *hiltja* ('battle') and thus meaning 'mighty in battle'. It came to England with the Normans, being borne by William the Conqueror's wife Matilda (d. 1083). Shortened to **Mat**, **Mattie** (or **Matty**), **Pattie** (or **Patty**), **Tilda** or **Tilly**. *See also* MAUD.

**Mattie/Matty** *See* MARTHA; MATILDA.

**Maud** English, French, German and Dutch variant of MATILDA. It became well known through Henry I's daughter Maud or Matilda (1102–67). Also found as **Maude** or **Maudie**.

**Maude/Maudie** *See* MAUD.

**Maura** *See* MOIRA.

**Maureen** English version of the Irish **Mairin**, itself based on MARY and meaning 'little Mary'. It was taken up by English speakers towards the end of the nineteenth century and enjoyed a peak in popularity in the 1930s. Also found as **Maurene**, **Maurine** or **Moreen**. Shortened to **Mo** (or **Moe**).

**Maurene/Maurine** *See* MAUREEN.

**Mave** *See* MAEVE; MAVIS.

**Mavis** English and Scottish name based on a traditional name for the song thrush, itself originally from the Old French *mauvis*. It became popular among English speakers through the character Mavis Clare in the novel *The Sorrows of Satan* (1895) by Marie Corelli. **Mave** is a shortened form of the name.

**Mavourna** *See* MAVOURNEEN.

**Mavourneen** Irish name based on the Irish Gaelic for 'darling little one'. Also found in the form **Mavourna**.

**Max/Maxene/Maxie** *See* MAXINE.

**Maxine** Feminine version of the masculine MAXIMILIAN. It emerged as a popular girls' name among English speakers in the 1930s. Also found as

**Maxene**. Shortened to **Max**, **Maxie** (or **Maxy**) or **Micki** (or **Mickie**).

**Maxy** *See* MAXINE.

**May** Shortened form of MABEL, MARGARET and MARY that is now often treated as a name in its own right, invoking either the name of the plant and its blossom or else the name of the month. Also found as **Mai** or **Mae** – a variant popularized by US film actress Mae West (1892–1980).

**Maya** ('miya') English name of ancient Greek origin, possibly meaning 'nurse' or else based on the Latin *maior* ('greater'). It may also be linked to the Sanskrit for 'illusion'. Also found as **Maia**, **Maja** or **Mya**, it was borne in Greek mythology by the mother of Hermes by Zeus.

**Maybelle/Maybelline** *See* MABEL.

**Meadhbh** *See* MAEVE.

**Meagan/Meaghan** *See* MEGAN.

**Meave/Meaveen/ Medbh** *See* MAEVE.

**Medora** English name invented by the British poet George Gordon, Lord Byron (1788–1824) in his poem 'The Corsair'.

**Meena** Indian name based on the Sanskrit *mina* ('fish').

**Meg** *See* MARGARET; MEGAN.

**Megan** Welsh variant of MARGARET. It was largely confined to Wales until the late twentieth century. Commonly shortened to **Meg**, **Megs** or **Meggie** (or **Meggy**). Variants include **Meghan**, **Meaghan** and **Meagan** – forms that have been taken up in Australia and Canada in the mistaken belief that the name has Irish roots.

**Meggie/Meggy** *See* MARGARET; MEGAN.

**Meghan** *See* MEGAN.

**Megs** *See* MARGARET; MEGAN.

**Mehala/Mehalah/ Mehalia** *See* MAHALIA.

**Meinwen** Welsh name meaning 'white' or 'fair'.

**Mel** *See* IMELDA; MELANIE; MELINDA; MELISSA; MELVINA.

**Melanie** French, English and Dutch name adapted via Old French from the Roman Melania, itself from the Greek *melas* ('black' or 'dark'). The name was originally reserved for children with dark hair, dark eyes or a swarthy complexion. Shortened to **Mel**. Variants include **Melany**, **Mellony** and the French **Mélanie**.

**Melany** *See* MELANIE.

**Melba** English name of Australian origin. The name appears to have been taken up initially in tribute to the Australian opera singer Dame Nellie Melba (Helen Mitchell; 1861–1931), who adopted the name from her home city, Melbourne.

**Melesina/Melicent** *See* MILLICENT.

**Melina** Variant form of several different names, such as EMMELINE, MELINDA and

MELISSA. It has made rare appearances among English speakers since the nineteenth century.

**Melinda** English name that is thought to have developed out of BELINDA and other similar names. A link with the Latin *mel* ('honey') has been suggested. Also found as **Malinda**, it was first taken up by English speakers in the eighteenth century. Shortened to **Mel**.

**Meliora** English name based on the Latin *melior* ('better'). It has made rare appearances in Britain since medieval times, confined chiefly to Cornwall.

**Melisent** *See* MILLICENT.

**Melissa** Greek name based on *melissa* ('bee'), itself from *meli* ('honey'). It has been in use among English speakers since the sixteenth century. Occasionally shortened to **Mel**, **Missie** or **Lissa**.

**Mellony** *See* MELANIE.

**Melodie** *See* MELODY.

**Melody** English name based

on the ordinary vocabulary word 'melody', itself descended from the Greek *melodia* ('singing of songs'). It made its first appearances among English speakers in the late eighteenth century. Also found as **Melodie**.

**Melva** English name of uncertain origin that may have developed from a Celtic word for 'chief'. Sometimes treated as a shortened form of MELVINA.

**Melvina** Feminine version of the Scottish MELVIN, which may be linked to the Old English *wine* ('friend') or else with the Gaelic for 'smooth brow'. Shortened to **Mel**.

**Meraud** English name of uncertain origin, though often assumed to be linked with the word 'emerald'. Alternatively, it may have evolved from an earlier Celtic name, perhaps based on *mur* ('the sea'). It is confined largely to Cornwall.

**Mercedes** Spanish and French name based on the Spanish *merced* ('mercy'), itself descended from the Latin *mercedes* ('wages' or 'ransom').

Christ's crucifixion was sometimes interpreted as a form of ransom for the sins of mankind and it was this notion that linked 'ransom' with 'mercy'. *See also* MERCY; SADIE.

**Mercia** *See* MERCY.

**Mercy** English virtue name that is also in use as shortened form of MERCEDES. It was one of the many virtue names adopted by English Puritans in the seventeenth century, and has long since fallen from favour. MERRY is a familiar form of the name. A rare Latinate variant is **Mercia**.

**Meredith** English version of the Welsh **Maredudd** or **Meredydd**, meaning 'great chief'. The Welsh form of the name is little known outside Wales itself, although the English form can be found across the English-speaking world. Sometimes shortened to MERRY.

**Meredydd** *See* MEREDITH.

**Meriel** *See* MURIEL.

**Merilyn** *See* MARILYN.

**Merle** English name that

probably developed initially as a variant of MERYL or MURIEL but is also often linked to the French *merle* ('blackbird'). As a first name for girls it was taken up towards the end of the nineteenth century.

**Merlyn** Feminine equivalent of MERLIN, itself an English version of the Welsh Myrddin, meaning 'sea-hill fort'.

**Merrill** *See* MURIEL.

**Merrilyn** *See* MARILYN.

**Merry** English name that exists as a shortened form of various other names, including MARY, MERCY and MEREDITH. In the USA it is also employed as a variant of Mary, from which it is almost indistiguishable in US pronunciation.

**Meryl** English name that developed out of MURIEL. The most well-known bearer of the name to date has been the US film actress Meryl Streep (Mary Louise Streep; b. 1949).

**Mia** Italian and Spanish name that may have come from the Italian and Spanish *mia* ('mine') but is also often treated as a diminutive form of MARIA. The most famous bearer of the name to date has been US film actress Mia Farrow (b. 1945).

**Michaela** ('mikayla') Feminine equivalent of MICHAEL, itself based on the Hebrew for 'who is like God?' Also found as **Mikaela**. Shortened to **Mick** or **Mickey** (or **Micky**).

**Michèle/Micheline** *See* MICHELLE.

**Michelle** English version of the French **Michèle**, itself a feminine equivalent of Michel (*see* MICHAEL). The French Michèle was taken up by English speakers in the 1940s, but was soon eclipsed by its anglicized form Michelle. Often shortened to **Chelle**, **Shell** or SHELLEY. **Micheline** and **Michelline** are rare variant forms.

**Michelline** *See* MICHELLE.

**Mick/Mickey** *See* MICHAELA.

**Micki/Mickie** *See* MAXINE.

**Mikaela** *See* MICHAELA.

**Milan/Milana** *See* MILENA.

**Milborough** English name based on the Old English *milde* ('mild') and *burg* ('borough' or 'fortress'). The name of a seventh-century English saint, it has made occasional reappearances among English speakers since medieval times.

**Milcah** Hebrew name meaning 'queen'. It appears in the Bible as the name of a niece of Abraham.

**Mildred** English name based on the Old English Mildthryth, itself from *milde* ('mild') and *thryth* ('strength') and thus meaning 'gentle strength'. It was borne by a seventh-century saint and was revived by English speakers in the seventeenth century. Shortened to **Millie** or **Milly**.

**Milena** Czech name based on the word *mil* ('grace'). In Italy, where it is also popular, it is treated as a combined form of the names MARIA and Elena (*see* HELEN). Variants include **Milan** or **Milana**.

**Millicent** English version of the French Mélisande, itself based on the Old German for 'hard worker'. It came to England from France in the late twelfth century (initially as Melisende or Melisenda). Shortened to **Millie** or **Milly**. Variants include **Melicent**, **Melisent** and **Melesina**.

**Millie/Milly** *See* AMELIA; CAMILLA; EMILY; MILDRED; MILLICENT.

**Mima** *See* JEMIMA.

**Mimi** Italian name that developed as a variant of MARIE. Its use among English speakers was promoted through the appearance of the name in Giacomo Puccini's opera *La Bohème* (1896).

**Mimosa** English name based on that of the tropical shrub.

**Mina** *See* WILHELMINA.

**Mindy** English name that appears to have developed under the influence of **Mandy** (*see* AMANDA) and CINDY.

**Minerva** Roman name borne by the goddess of wisdom and possibly based on the Latin *mens* ('mind') or else

on an unknown Etruscan source. Records of its use as a first name date from the Renaissance. Sometimes shortened to **Minnie**.

**Minna** English name based either on the Old German *minna* ('memory' or 'love') or else on the Old German *min* ('small'). Also found as a shortened form of WILHELMINA. Its use among English speakers was for many years confined largely to Scotland.

**Minnie** *See* MINERVA; WILHELMINA.

**Minta/Minty** *See* ARAMINTA.

**Mira** *See* MIRANDA; MYRA.

**Mirabel** English name based on the Latin *mirabilis* ('wonderful'). It was taken up by English speakers in the twelfth century and was also employed as a masculine name until the eighteenth century. Also found as **Mirabelle** or **Mirabella**.

**Mirabella/Mirabelle** *See* MIRABEL.

**Miranda** English name based
on the Latin *mirari* ('to wonder
at') and thus meaning
'adorable' or 'fit to be loved'.
The name was invented by
William Shakespeare for
Prospero's daughter in his play
*The Tempest* (1611). Sometimes
shortened to **Mira**, **Mandy**,
**Randa** or **Randy**.

**Miriam** Hebrew name
meaning 'good' or 'full' and
possibly descended from an
unknown Egyptian root.
Closely related to MARY, the
name features in the Bible and
has always been a favourite
within the Jewish community.
Also found as **Myriam**,
**Mariam** or **Mariamne**. *See also*
MARYAM; MITZI.

**Missie** *See* MELISSA.

**Misty** English name based
on the ordinary English
vocabulary word. The name
made its debut among English
speakers in the 1970s, inspired
by the Clint Eastwood film
*Play Misty For Me* (1971) –
'Misty' being the name of a
song (1954) that features
centrally in the plot.

**Mitzi** English name that

developed as an informal
version of various other names,
including MARIA, MARY and
MIRIAM.

**Mo** *See* MAUREEN.

**Modest** *See* MODESTY.

**Modesty** English virtue
name that may be a modern
equivalent of the Late Latin
name Modestus, which had
much the same meaning.
Occasionally found as **Modest**.

**Modwen** Welsh name based
on *morwyn* ('maiden').

**Moe** *See* MAUREEN.

**Moggy** *See* MARGARET.

**Moina** Irish and Scottish
name possibly based on the
Gaelic for 'girl of the peat-
moss'.

**Moira** English version of the
Irish **Maire**, itself a variant of
MARY. It probably evolved
through the usual
pronunciation of Mary in Irish.
As **Maura**, the name was borne
by a fifth-century martyr.
English speakers took up Moira
in the nineteenth century, and

it became a particular favourite in Scotland. Also found in the USA as **Moyra**.

**Moll/Mollie** *See* MOLLY.

**Molly** English name that emerged as an informal version of MARY. The change of 'r' to 'll' is a standard evolution shared with several other names. Also found as **Moll**, best known from Daniel Defoe's novel *Moll Flanders* (1722), and **Mollie**.

**Mona** English version of the Irish Muadhnait, itself from *muadh* ('noble' or 'good'). Occasionally also in use as a variant of MONICA. It took root initially in Ireland and was taken up by English speakers elsewhere towards the end of the nineteenth century, when Irish names were in vogue. Also found as **Moyna**.

**Monday** English name that is usually reserved for girls born on a Monday. Little used since medieval times.

**Monica** English name of uncertain origin. Attempts have been made to trace it back to the Greek *monos* ('alone') or

the Latin *monere* ('to warn' or 'to advise'). Sometimes shortened to MONA. Variant forms include the French **Monique**, the German **Monika** and the familiar form **Monny**.

**Monika/Monique/ Monny** *See* MONICA.

**Montana** English name based on the Latin for 'mountain'. It is largely confined to the USA, where it is also the name of a state.

**Mor** Scottish and Irish name based on the Gaelic for 'large' or 'great'. In late medieval times this was the most popular of all Irish girls' names and it has remained in regular use in Scotland and Ireland into modern times. Variants include MORAG and **Moreen**.

**Morag** Scottish name based on the Gaelic *mor* ('great'). Another derivation suggests it comes from the Gaelic for 'sun'. Some authorities have also described it as a Scottish equivalent of MARY or SARAH. It is still thought of as a predominantly Scottish name.

**Morann** *See* MUIREANN.

**Morcant** *See* MORGAN.

**Moreen** *See* MAUREEN; MOR.

**Morgan** English name based on the Welsh **Morcant**, which may have come from the words *mor* ('sea') and *cant* ('circle' or 'edge') but is otherwise of unknown origin. It is sometimes suggested that the name means 'sea-bright'. Its use as a girls' name was promoted by Arthurian legend, in which it is borne by Morgan le Fay. **Morgana** is a variant form.

**Morgana** *See* MORGAN.

**Morna** *See* MYRNA.

**Morven** English name of uncertain Scottish derivation. It may have come from the Morvern district in north Argyll, Scotland, itself based on the Gaelic for 'great gap', or else from the Gaelic *mor bheinn* ('great peak'). As a first name it was promoted by its identification as Fingal's kingdom in the Ossianic poems of James Macpherson published in the eighteenth century.

**Morwen** *See* MORWENNA.

**Morwenna** Cornish and Welsh name based either on the Welsh *morwyn* ('maiden') or else on the Welsh *mor* ('sea') and *gwaneg* ('wave'). Several Cornish churches are named after the Celtic St Morwenna, who lived in the fifth century. Also found as **Morwen**.

**Moya** *See* MARIA.

**Moyna** *See* MONA.

**Moyra** *See* MOIRA.

**Muireann** Irish name based on the Irish Gaelic *muir* ('sea') and *fionn* ('white' or 'fair'). Also found as **Muirinn** or **Morann** and frequently equated with MAUREEN.

**Muirinn** *See* MUIREANN.

**Muirne** *See* MYRNA.

**Muriel** English version of the Irish Gaelic Muirgheal and the Scottish Gaelic Muireall, meaning 'sea-bright'. The earliest records of the name come from Brittany, Scotland and Ireland, although it also appears to have been in use in England by medieval times. Also found as **Mariel**, **Meriel** or **Merrill**. *See also* MERYL.

**Murphy** Irish name based on the Irish Gaelic for 'sea hound'. More often used for boys, its use as a girls' name is largely confined to the USA.

**Mya** *See* MAYA.

**Myf** *See* MYFANWY.

**Myfanwy** ('muvanwee') Welsh name based on the Welsh *my* ('my dear') and *manwy* ('fine' or 'precious') and thus meaning 'my fine one' or 'my dear precious one'. Alternatively, the name may have developed from *menyw* ('woman'). It is largely confined to Wales. Shortened to **Myf**, **Myfi** or FANNY.

**Myfi** *See* MYFANWY.

**Myra** English name that was possibly based on the Greek *muron* ('myrrh') or the Latin *mirari* ('to wonder at'), or else developed as an anagram of MARY or as a variant of

MOIRA. In Scotland it is sometimes used as an anglicization of **Mairead**. The name appears to have been invented by the English poet Fulke Greville (1554–1628) for the subject of his love poems. Also found as **Mira**.

**Myriam** *See* MIRIAM.

**Myrna** English version of the Irish **Muirne**, a name based on the Gaelic *muirne* ('affection' or 'tenderness'). The name of the mother of the legendary Irish hero Fion Mac Cumhaill, it was taken up by English speakers in the nineteenth century. Also found as **Morna**.

**Myrtill/Myrtilla** *See* MYRTLE.

**Myrtle** English plant name based on the name of the garden shrub, which was a symbol of victory in ancient Greece. Like many other flower names, it was adopted as a first name among English speakers in the middle of the nineteenth century. Variants of the name include **Myrtill** and **Myrtilla**.

**Mysie** *See* MAISIE.

# GIRLS' NAMES

**Nadia** Shortened form of the Russian Nadezhda, meaning 'hope' (or, alternatively, from Arabic words meaning 'moist with dew'). The name became popular among English and French speakers in the early twentieth century. Variants include the French **Nadine**.

**Nadine** *See* NADIA.

**Nairne** Gaelic name meaning 'from the river'.

**Nan** *See* ANN; NANCY; NANETTE.

**Nana** *See* ANNA; HANNAH.

**Nance** *See* NANCY.

**Nancy** English name that probably evolved as a familiar form of ANN. Notable bearers of the name have included a character in Charles Dickens' *Oliver Twist* (1837–8). Shortened forms include **Nan** and **Nance**.

**Nanette** English and French name that probably evolved from ANN, via **Nan**. Its popularity was much promoted by the success of Vincent Youman's operetta *No, No, Nanette* (1925).

**Nanny** *See* ANN; NANCY.

**Naomi** ('nayohmee') Hebrew name meaning 'pleasantness', 'pleasure' or 'my delight'. In the Old Testament Book of Ruth, Naomi is Ruth's mother-in-law. It was among the biblical names adopted by Puritans in the seventeenth century.

**Narelle** Australian name of obscure meaning. A relatively recent introduction, it ranked among the most popular girls' names in Australia in the 1970s.

**Nat** *See* NATALIE; NATASHA.

**Natalia** *See* NATALIE.

**Natalie** English and French name based on the Russian **Natalya**, itself from the Latin *natale domini* ('birthday of the Lord'). The name is often given to girls born on or near Christmas Day. **Nat** and **Tally** are shortened forms. *See also* NATASHA.

**Natalya** *See* NATALIE; NATASHA.

**Natasha** Russian name that evolved initially as a familiar variant of **Natalya** (*see* NATALIE). Notable instances of the name in literature have included Natasha Rostova in Leo Tolstoy's *War and Peace* (1863–9). Shortened forms include **Nat** and **Tasha**.

**Neala** Irish feminine equivalent of NEIL, which is generally understood to mean 'champion'.

**Neassa** Irish Gaelic name of uncertain but undoubtedly ancient origin. It was borne by the mother of King Conchobar of Ulster.

**Nell** English name that evolved as an informal version of various girls' names,

including ELEANOR, ELLEN and HELEN. The initial 'N' was probably adopted through the repeated use of such everyday phrases as 'mine Ell'. Variants include **Nellie** and **Nelly**.

**Nella** *See* FENELLA.

**Nellie/Nelly** *See* FENELLA; NELL.

**Nena** *See* NINA.

**Nerissa** English name that probably developed out of the Greek *nereis* ('sea-nymph'). It is thought to have been coined by William Shakespeare as a name for Portia's sharp-witted maidservant in *The Merchant of Venice* (1596–8).

**Nerys** Welsh name of uncertain derivation but possibly meaning 'lady' (based on the Welsh *ner*, meaning 'lord'). Alternatively, it may be a development of NERISSA. A relatively modern invention, it is little heard outside Wales.

**Nessa** *See* AGNES; VANESSA.

**Nessie/Nesta** *See* AGNES.

**Netta/Nettie/Netty** *See*
ANNETTE; HENRIETTA;
JEANETTE.

**Ngaio** ('nayo' or 'nigh-o')
New Zealand Maori name
taken either from the name of
a tree or from the Maori for
'clever'. The most famous
bearer of the name to date has
been the New Zealand crime
novelist Dame Ngaio Marsh
(1899–1982).

**Nia** *See* NIAMH.

**Niamh** ('neev' or 'neeav')
Irish name meaning 'radiance'
or 'brightness'. The name of a
pagan goddess, it is rare outside
Ireland. Sometimes shortened
to **Nia** in Wales.

**Nib** *See* ISABEL.

**Nichola/Nick/Nickie/
Nicky** *See* NICOLA.

**Nicola** English and Italian
name representing a feminine
equivalent of NICHOLAS. It is
fairly common in English-
speaking countries and, as
**Nicole**, in France. Variants
include **Nichola**. Commonly
shortened to **Nick**, **Nickie**,
**Nicky** or **Nikki**.

**Nicole** *See* NICOLA.

**Nigelia** *See* NIGELLA.

**Nigella** English equivalent of
NIGEL, a name that is thought
to have been adopted as the
Latin version of NEIL soon after
the Norman Conquest. Also
found as **Nigelia**.

**Nikita** Russian name that
evolved out of the Greek
Aniketos, meaning
'unconquerable'. It has made
infrequent appearances in the
English-speaking world in
recent years.

**Nikki** *See* NICOLA.

**Nina** Russian name that may
have evolved from ANN or as a
shortened form of various
longer Russian names ending
in -nina, such as Antonina.
Alternatively, it may be linked
to the Spanish for 'little girl'.
Variant forms include **Nena**,
**Ninette** and **Ninita**.

**Ninette/Ninita** *See* NINA.

**Nita** *See* ANITA.

**Noele** French and English
name based on the French *Noël*

('Christmas'). Variously given with or without the diaeresis, the name has been reserved traditionally for children born on Christmas Day or during the Christmas period. Variants include **Noelle** and **Noelene** (or **Noeleen**).

**Noeleen/Noelene/ Noelle** *See* NOELE.

**Nola** *See* FENELLA.

**Nonie** *See* NORA.

**Nora** Irish name based on HONOR, which has since been adopted in England, Scotland and elsewhere. Also found as **Norah**, it is sometimes assumed to be a shortened form of ELEANOR or LEONORA or a feminine version of NORMAN.

Variants include **Nonie** and **Noreen**.

**Norah/Noreen** *See* NORA.

**Norma** English and Italian name possibly derived from the Latin *norma* ('rule', 'pattern' or 'standard'). It is often assumed (especially in Scotland) to be a feminine version of NORMAN.

**Nornie** *See* LEONORA.

**Nuala** *See* FENELLA.

**Nyree** Anglicized version of the Maori name **Ngaire** (of unknown origin). The popularity of New Zealand-born actress Nyree Dawn Porter (1940–2001) in the television series *The Forsyte Saga* promoted use of the name in the 1970s.

# GIRLS' NAMES

**Ocean** English name based on the ordinary vocabulary word 'ocean'. Oceanus was the name of a Greek sea-god. Also found as **Oceana**.

**Oceana** *See* OCEAN.

**Octavia** Roman name based on the Latin *octavus* ('eighth'). Originally reserved for eighth-born children, it was adopted in the English-speaking world from the nineteenth century. **Ottavia** is a variant form. Sometimes shortened to **Tavia**.

**Odelia/Odella/Odelyn** *See* ODILE.

**Odessa** Greek name meaning 'long journey'.

**Odetta** *See* ODETTE.

**Odette** French name that developed via the Old French masculine name Oda from the Old German *od* ('riches'). It is best known through Second World War French Resistance heroine Odette Churchill (1912–95). **Odetta** is a variant form.

**Odile** ('ohdeel') French name that may have been developed from the German OTTO, meaning 'riches', or from the Old German *othal* ('fatherland'). It may also be a feminine version of ODELL. **Odelia, Odella, Odelyn** and **Odilia** are variant forms.

**Odilia** *See* ODILE.

**Ofra** *See* OPRAH.

**Oighrig** *See* ERICA

**Ola** Scandinavian name meaning 'descendant'.

**Olanda** Italian name based on the Italian name for Holland.

**Oleta/Olethea** *See* ALETHEA.

**Olga** Russian variant of the Scandinavian HELGA. The name was adopted in England in the late nineteenth century. Also found as **Olya**.

**Olimpia** See OLYMPIA.

**Olinda** Italian name from the Latin meaning 'fragrant herb'. Also found as **Olynda**.

**Oliva** See OLIVE.

**Olive** English name based on the Latin *oliva* ('olive tree'). As **Oliva**, it was first adopted by English speakers in the thirteenth century. It was revived in the nineteenth century, probably inspired by the olive's reputation as a symbol of peace. Variants include **Olivette**.

**Olivette** See OLIVE.

**Olivia** English and Italian name based ultimately on the Latin *oliva* ('olive tree'). It became popular among English speakers in imitation of William Shakespeare's Olivia in *Twelfth Night* (1601). Shortened forms include **Libby** and **Livvy**.

**Olwen** Welsh name based on the Welsh *ol* ('footprint') and *wen* ('white' or 'blessed'). In Welsh legend, Olwen was a beautiful woman whose footprints sprouted white clover. Also found as **Olwin** and **Olwyn**.

**Olwin/Olwyn** See OLWEN.

**Olya** See OLGA.

**Olympia** Greek name based on Olympus (the home of the gods in ancient Greek mythology). It is best known as the title of a frankly realistic portrait of a reclining nude woman painted by Edouard Manet in 1865. Also found as **Olimpia**.

**Olynda** See OLINDA.

**Omega** Greek name taken from the last letter of the Greek alphabet. It has tended to be reserved for last-born children, just as ALPHA has been employed on occasion for the first-born.

**Ona** See UNA.

**Ondina/Ondine** See UNDINE.

**Onora** *See* HONOR.

**Oona/Oonagh** *See* UNA.

**Opal** Indian name based on the Sanskrit for 'precious stone'. It was traditionally given to girls born in October (opal being the birthstone for that month). Variants include the rare **Opaline**.

**Opaline** *See* OPAL.

**Ophelia** English and Italian name based on the Greek Ophelos, meaning 'help' or 'profit'. It is closely associated with the doomed heroine in William Shakespeare's tragedy *Hamlet* (1599).

**Ophrah** *See* OPRAH.

**Oprah** Hebrew name of obscure meaning (possibly 'fawn'). Made famous through US chat show host Oprah Winfrey (b. 1954), it is also found as **Ofra** or **Ophrah**.

**Ora** English name of obscure origin, possibly based on the Latin *orare* ('to pray'). It may also have developed as a shortened form of CORA or DORA.

**Oralee** *See* ORALIE.

**Oralie** English name of obscure origin, sometimes assumed to be a variant of AURELIA or else from the Hebrew meaning 'my light'. Also found as **Oralee**, **Orli** or **Orly**.

**Orea** Greek name meaning 'of the mountains'.

**Oriana** English name based on the Latin *oriri* ('to rise') and thus meaning 'dawn' or 'sunrise'. It was among the poetic names bestowed by admirers upon Elizabeth I. Variant forms include **Ariane**, **Oriane** and **Orianna**.

**Oriane/Orianna** *See* ORIANA.

**Oriel** English name based on the Old German for 'battle heat'. Introduced to Britain by the Normans in the eleventh century, it has never been very common. Variants include **Auriel** and **Oriole**.

**Orin** Irish name meaning 'dark-haired'.

**Orinda** *See* ORINTHIA.

**Orinthia** Greek name based on the Greek verb *orinein* ('to excite'). In the variant form **Orinda**, it was well known as the pen-name of English writer Katherine Philips (1631–64), called 'The Matchless Orinda'.

**Oriole** *See* ORIEL.

**Orla** Irish name based on the Gaelic for 'golden princess'. Also found as **Orlagh** or **Orlaidh**.

**Orlagh/Orlaidh** *See* ORLA.

**Orlanda** Feminine equivalent of the masculine ORLANDO, which means 'famous land'.

**Orli/Orly** *See* ORALIE.

**Orna** Irish name based on the Gaelic for 'dark-haired'. Also found as **Ornah**.

**Ornah** *See* ORNA.

**Orsina** English and French feminine equivalent of the masculine ORSON, itself based, via Old French *ourson* ('bearcub'), on the Latin *ursus* ('bear'). *See also* URSULA.

**Ottavia** *See* OCTAVIA.

**Ottilie** French and German name equivalent to ODILE. A variant form is **Ottoline**, as borne by British literary figure Lady Ottoline Morrell (1873–1938).

**Ottoline** *See* OTTILIE.

**Owena** Feminine equivalent of the Welsh masculine name OWEN, thus meaning 'well-born', or else 'lamb'.

# P

## GIRLS' NAMES

**Pacifica** *See* PEACE.

**Paddy** *See* PATRICIA.

**Page/Paget** *See* PAIGE.

**Paige** English name meaning 'page' or 'servant'. Medieval pages were young men serving in the households of the rich noble families of England and were always male, although the name is now reserved exclusively for girls. Also found as **Page** or **Paget**.

**Paloma** Spanish name based on the Latin *palumba* ('dove').

**Pam/Pamala** *See* PAMELA.

**Pamela** English name that was invented by the English soldier-poet Sir Philip Sidney in *Arcadia* (1590). Sidney (who stressed the second syllable) derived the name from the Greek *pan* ('all') and *meli* ('honey'), thus creating a name meaning 'all sweetness'. Variants include **Pamala**, **Pamelia** and **Pamella**. Commonly shortened to **Pam** or, in Australia, **Pammy**.

**Pamelia/Pamella/ Pammy** *See* PAMELA.

**Pandora** English and Greek name based on the Greek words *pan* ('all') and *dōron* ('gift') and thus meaning 'all-gifted' or 'many-gifted'. In Greek legend, Pandora disobeyed instructions not to open a mysterious box and thus released all the woes that mankind has been subject to ever since. All that remained in the box was hope.

**Pansy** English flower name that was first introduced in the nineteenth century. It is sometimes linked to the French *pensée* ('thought'). Notable bearers of the name have included Pansy Osmond in *The Portrait of a Lady* (1881) by Henry James.

**Paris** Greek name borne by the son of King Priam of Troy, a central character in the story of the Trojan War. Traditionally a boys' name, in recent years it has also been employed for girls.

**Parthenia** Greek name based on the Greek *parthenos* ('virgin'). Popularly associated with the Parthenon in Athens, which was dedicated to the goddess Athena Parthenos (Athena the Maid), the name has been adopted by English speakers since the nineteenth century.

**Parthenope** ('parthenopee') Greek name based on the Greek *parthenos* ('virgin') and *ops* ('face') and thus meaning 'maiden-faced'. In Greek legend, Parthenope was a siren who drowned herself in despair after she failed to lure Odysseus with her singing.

**Pascale** French feminine equivalent of the masculine PASCAL, which was based on the Latin *Paschalis* ('of Easter'). It was taken up as a first name by the early Christians, originally being reserved for boys born in the Easter season.

**Pat** *See* PATIENCE; PATRICIA.

**Patience** English 'virtue' name based ultimately on the Latin *pati* ('to suffer'). It was popular with early Christians and was later revived by the Puritans. At first it was given to both sexes but it has long since been reserved exclusively for females. Sometimes shortened to **Pat** or **Patty**.

**Patricia** Feminine version of PATRICK, based on the Latin *patricius* ('nobleman'). The name was introduced in written records of the Romans to distinguish female members of noble families from males. Shortened forms of the name include **Pat**, **Patsy**, **Patty**, **Patti**, **Pattie**, **Paddy**, **Tricia** and **Trisha**.

**Patsy** *See* PATRICIA.

**Patti/Pattie/Patty** *See* MARTHA; PATIENCE; PATRICIA.

**Paula** Feminine equivalent of PAUL, which was itself based on the Latin *paulus* ('little' or 'small'). It was first taken up by English speakers in medieval times but only emerged as a significantly popular choice from the 1950s. POLLY is sometimes treated as a familiar variant of the name.

**Paulanne/Pauleen/ Paulene** *See* PAULINE.

**Pauletta** *See* PAULETTE.

**Paulette** French feminine version of PAUL, itself based on the Latin *paulus* ('little' or 'small'). Famous bearers of the name have included the US actress Paulette Goddard (Pauline Marion Goddard Levy; 1911–90). Also found as **Pauletta**.

**Paulina** *See* PAULINE.

**Pauline** French feminine version of PAUL, itself based on the Latin *paulus* ('little' or 'small'). Although **Paulina**, the original Roman version of the name, became the traditional English version, the French spelling is now more common. Also found as **Paulene**, **Pauleen** or **Paulanne**. *See also* PAULETTE.

**Payton** *See* PEYTON.

**Peace** English name that was among the names celebrating a variety of abstract qualities favoured by Puritans on both sides of the Atlantic in the seventeenth century. It is now found only infrequently. **Pacifica** is a rare variant.

**Peaches** English name based on the name of the fruit. Previously a nickname or term of endearment, it became well-known through Peaches Honeyblossom Michelle Charlotte Angel Vanessa Geldof (b. 1989), daughter of Irish rock star Bob Geldof.

**Pearl** English jewel name, which was first adopted as a first name among English speakers in the late nineteenth century. It is also found occasionally as a variant of MARGARET, which was itself based on the Greek for 'pearl'. Also found as **Pearle**. Familiar forms include **Pearlie**, **Pearly** and **Perlie**.

**Pearle/Pearlie/Pearly** *See* PEARL.

**Peg** *See* PEGGY.

**Pegeen** Irish name that evolved, via **Peg** (*see* PEGGY),

as a shortened form of
MARGARET. There is a
character of the name in J. M.
Synge's *The Playboy of the
Western World* (1907).

**Peggie** *See* PEGGY.

**Peggy** English name that
developed as a variant of
MARGARET. Also found as **Peg**
or **Peggie**, this has long been
treated as an independent name
in its own right. It probably
arose originally as a rhyming
version of **Meggy**. Famous
bearers of the name have
included British actress Peggy
Ashcroft (1907–91).

**Pelagia** Greek name
meaning 'mermaid'.

**Pen** *See* PENELOPE.

**Penelope** English name of
uncertain origin, probably
based on the Greek *pene*
('thread' or 'bobbin'), or else
on the Greek *penelops* (the
name of a species of duck). In
Greek legend, Penelope was
the faithful wife of the hero
Odysseus. In Ireland the name
is an anglicization of
Fionnghuala (*see* FENELLA).
Shortened to **Pen** or **Penny**.

**Penina** *See* PENINAH.

**Peninah** Hebrew name
meaning 'pearl'. Also found as
Penina.

**Penny** *See* PENELOPE.

**Peony** English flower name
that made its debut as a first
name in the nineteenth
century. The flower may have
got its original (Greek) name
from Palon, physician to the
gods.

**Pepper** English name based
on the name of the spice on
the model of SAFFRON and
other related names.

**Peppi** *See* PERPETUA.

**Perdita** English name based
on the Latin *perditus* ('lost').
William Shakespeare is thought
to have invented the name for
the castaway heroine in his play
*The Winter's Tale* (1611).
**Purdie** (or **Purdy**) is an
accepted shortened form.

**Perlie** *See* PEARL.

**Peronel/Peronelle** *See*
PETRONELLA.

**Perpetua** Roman name based on the Latin *perpetuus* ('perpetual'). The name was borne by a third-century Christian martyr and since then has been largely confined to the Roman Catholic community. Sometimes shortened to **Peppi**.

**Perrine** Feminine version of the masculine PETER, which means 'rock'.

**Persephone** ('persefonee') Greek name based on the Greek *pherein* ('to bring') and *phonē* ('death') and thus meaning 'bringing death'. In Greek legend, Persephone was the beautiful daughter of Zeus and Demeter who was carried off to the underworld by Hades.

**Pet** *See* PETRA; PETRONELLA; PETULA.

**Peta** Feminine version, apparently of Australian origin, of the masculine PETER, which means 'rock'. Sometimes extended to **Petena**.

**Petal** English name based on the ordinary vocabulary word 'petal', commonly used as a term of endearment.

**Peterina** Feminine version of the masculine PETER, which means 'rock'. Variants include **Peternella**.

**Peternella** *See* PETERINA.

**Petra** Feminine equivalent of the boys' name PETER, based on the Latin *petros* ('rock'). The appeal of the name was bolstered in 1812 by the discovery of the romantic ruins of the ancient Jordanian city of Petra. Variants include **Petrina** and **Petrona**.

**Petranella** *See* PETRONELLA.

**Petrina/Petrona** *See* PETRA.

**Petronel** *See* PETRONELLA.

**Petronella** Roman family name (originally Petronius) of uncertain meaning that has been used as a first name by English speakers since the twelfth century. Also found as **Petranella**, **Petronilla**, **Petronel**, **Peronel** or **Peronelle**, it is treated sometimes as a feminine version of PETER. Shortened to **Pet**.

**Petronilla** *See* PETRONELLA.

**Petula** English name of uncertain origin, though possibly inspired by the flower name petunia. Apparently a twentieth-century invention, it is often assumed to be a feminine equivalent of PETER. Notable bearers of the name have included British pop singer Petula Clark (Sally Owen; b. 1932). Shortened to **Pet**.

**Peyton** English name based on a place name meaning 'farm of Paega'. The name, used for boys and girls, is more frequent in the USA than elsewhere, promoted perhaps by the US television drama series *Peyton Place* in the 1960s. Also found as **Payton**.

**Phamie** *See* EUPHEMIA.

**Phebe** *See* PHOEBE.

**Phedra** Greek name meaning 'bright'.

**Pheeny** *See* JOSEPHINE.

**Phemie** *See* EUPHEMIA.

**Phenie** *See* JOSEPHINE.

**Pheobe** *See* PHOEBE.

**Phil** *See* FELICITY; PHILIPPA; PHILOMENA; PHYLLIDA; PHYLLIS.

**Philadelphia** Greek name meaning 'brotherly love'. The name was borne by an ancient city in Asia Minor and was subsequently adopted by the Puritans. It is popular chiefly in the USA, influenced by the city of Philadelphia, Pennsylvania.

**Philipa** *See* PHILIPPA.

**Philippa** Feminine version of PHILIP, meaning 'lover of horses'. It was introduced originally for use in medieval written records to distinguish male and female bearers of the name Philip. Also found as **Phillipa** or **Philipa**. *See also* PHILIPPINA; PIPPA.

**Philippina** English and German name that developed out of PHILIPPA. In medieval times it was suggested that the name came from the Greek words *philein* ('to love') and *poinē* ('pain') and referred to the Christian practices of self-flagellation.

**Philis/Phillice** *See* PHYLLIS.

**Phillida** *See* PHYLLIDA.

**Phillie** *See* PHILOMENA; PHYLLIDA; PHYLLIS.

**Phillipa** *See* PHILIPPA.

**Phillis** *See* PHYLLIS.

**Philly** *See* PHILOMENA; PHYLLIDA; PHYLLIS.

**Philomel** *See* PHILOMELA.

**Philomela** Greek name based on the Greek words *philos* ('dear' or 'sweet') and *melos* ('song'), and thus meaning 'sweet singer'. Another derivation suggests the word means 'nightingale'. Also found as **Philomel**.

**Philomena** English and German name based on the Greek words *philein* ('to love') and *menos* ('strength') and thus meaning 'strongly beloved' or 'strength-loving'. Variants

include **Philomene**, **Philomina** and **Filomena**. Shortened to **Phil** or **Phillie** (or **Philly**).

**Philomene/Philomina** *See* PHILOMENA.

**Phoebe** ('feebee') Roman version of a Greek name based on the Greek *phoibē* ('bright' or 'shining'). In Greek legend, Phoebe was a daughter of Uranus and Gaia. The name also features in Shakespeare, as that of a shepherdess. Sometimes found as **Phebe** or **Pheobe** and occasionally as a shortened form of EUPHEMIA.

**Phoenix** ('feenix') English name that alludes to the legendary bird of Arabian mythology, which was believed to burst periodically into flames and rise renewed from its own ashes.

**Phyliss** *See* PHYLLIS.

**Phyllida** Variant form of PHYLLIS, which emerged as a distinct name in its own right in the fifteenth century. Also found as **Phillida**, it was popular among English speakers in the seventeenth century. Sometimes shortened to **Phil** or **Phillie** (or **Philly**).

**Phyllis** English and German name based on the Greek *phullis* ('green branch'). In Greek legend, Phyllis was a beautiful country girl who hanged herself when disappointed in love. The gods then transformed her into an almond tree. Variants include **Felis, Phillice, Phillis, Philis** and **Phyliss**. Shortened to **Phil** or **Phillie** (or **Philly**). *See also* PHYLLIDA.

**Pia** Italian name based on the Latin *pia* ('pious', 'dutiful' or 'godly'), a feminine equivalent of the masculine Pius.

**Piety** English 'virtue' name that was adopted by the Puritans in the seventeenth century. Piety was one of the characters representing different virtues depicted in John Bunyan's *The Pilgrim's Progress* (1678, 1684).

**Pilar** ('peelar') Spanish name based on the phrase *Nuestra Señora del Pilar* ('Our Lady of the Pillar'), inspired by visions of the Virgin Mary on a pillar at Saragossa.

**Pip** *See* PIPPA.

**Piper** English name meaning 'one who plays the pipes'.

**Pippa** Shortened version of PHILIPPA, now also used as a name in its own right. It became popular with English speakers after the publication of Robert Browning's poetic drama *Pippa Passes* (1841). Sometimes shortened to **Pip**.

**Pleasance** English name based on the Old French *plaisance* ('pleasure'). The name was introduced to England by the Normans. **Pleasant** is a rare variant – as borne by Pleasant Riderhood in Charles Dickens' novel *Our Mutual Friend* (1865).

**Pleasant** *See* PLEASANCE.

**Pol/Poll/Pollie** *See* POLLY.

**Polly** Variant form of MARY, influenced by MOLLY. This familiar form of Mary has been known for several centuries, as illustrated by its use in 'Polly put the kettle on'. Notable bearers of the name include Polly Peachum in John Gay's *The Beggar's Opera* (1728). Also found as **Pollie**. Shortened to Pol or **Poll**.

**Pollyanna** English name combining POLLY and ANNA, popular chiefly in the USA. It appears to have been invented by Eleanor Hodgman Porter in her novel *Pollyanna* (1913).

**Pomona** Italian name based on the Latin for 'fruitful'.

**Poppy** English flower name based on the Old English *popaeg*. The name was popular in Edwardian England and reached a peak in the 1920s, despite or because of the association between the flower and the dead of World War One.

**Portia** ('porsha') Anglicization of the Roman Porcia, a feminine form of the family name Porcius, itself probably from the Latin *porcus* ('hog' or 'pig'). Other theories suggest it could mean 'gift' or 'safe harbour'. It is famous as the name of the heroine in William Shakespeare's *The Merchant of Venice* (1598).

**Posie** *See* POSY.

**Posy** English flower name

that seems to have made its first appearance among English speakers in the 1920s. Sometimes assumed to be a shortened form of JOSEPHINE. Also found as **Posie**.

**Precious** English name based on the ordinary vocabulary word, commonly used as a term of endearment.

**Prima** Feminine equivalent of the masculine PRIMO, meaning 'first-born'.

**Primrose** English flower name based ultimately on the Latin *prima rosa* ('first rose'). It made its debut as a first name towards the end of the nineteenth century and reached a peak in popularity during the 1920s.

**Primula** English flower name based ultimately on the Latin *primus* ('first'). It made its debut as a first name towards the end of the nineteenth century.

**Princess** Feminine equivalent of the boys' name PRINCE. Similarly modelled on the royal title, it tends to be used more often as an informal term of endearment rather than as a formal first name.

**Pris** *See* PRISCILLA.

**Priscilla** ('prisilla') Roman name based on the Latin *priscus* ('ancient' or 'old'). The intention behind the name seems to have been to suggest that the bearer will enjoy a long life. Shortened forms include CILLA – as borne by British singer Cilla Black (Priscilla White; b. 1943) – and the less common **Pris**, **Prissy** and **Scilla**.

**Prissy** *See* PRISCILLA.

**Proserpine** Roman version of the Greek PERSEPHONE. It has been suggested that the name may be linked to the Latin *proserpere* ('to creep forth'), evoking the idea of spring flowers emerging after winter. Shortened to **Pross** or **Prossy**.

**Pross/Prossy** *See* PROSERPINE.

**Pru** *See* PRUDENCE; PRUNELLA.

**Prudence** English 'virtue' name based on the Roman

Prudentia, itself from the Latin *prudens* ('provident'). It was among the most popular 'virtue' names adopted by Puritans in the seventeenth century. Shortened to **Pru**, **Prue** or **Purdy** (or **Purdie**).

**Prue** *See* PRUDENCE; PRUNELLA.

**Prunella** English name probably based ultimately on the Latin *pruna* ('little plum'). The word also referred to a smooth woollen silk, to the wild flower selfheal (*Prunella vulgaris*) and to the hedge sparrow or dunnock. Famous bearers of the name include the British actress Prunella Scales (b. 1932). Shortened to **Pru** or **Prue**.

**Psyche** ('sighkee') Greek name based on the Greek *psukhē* ('soul'). In Greek myth, Psyche represented the human soul, falling in love with Eros (or Cupid).

**Purdie/Purdy** *See* PERDITA; PRUDENCE.

**Purity** English 'virtue' name that has been in use as a first name since medieval times.

# GIRLS' NAMES

**Queenie** English name
either from REGINA ('queen' in
Latin) or from the Old English
*cwene* ('woman'). Sometimes
used as a nickname for anyone
called VICTORIA (a reference to
Queen Victoria). Also found as
**Queeny**.

**Queeny** *See* QUEENIE.

**Quisha** *See* KEISHA.

# GIRLS' NAMES

**Rach/Rachael** *See* RACHEL.

**Rachel** Hebrew name meaning 'ewe' (symbolizing innocence and gentleness). As **Rahel** it appears in the Old Testament as the name of Jacob's second wife, the mother of Joseph and Benjamin. Also found as **Rachael** (and occasionally **Rachelle**) or **Raquel**. Shortened to **Rach**, **Rachie**, RAE or **Ray**. *See also* ROCHELLE; SHELLEY.

**Rachelle/Rachie** *See* RACHEL.

**Radcliffe** Feminine version of the masculine RADCLIFF, which means 'red cliff'.

**Radclyffe** is a variant form, as borne by British novelist Marguerite Radclyffe Hall (1886–1943), author of the notorious *The Well of Loneliness* (1928).

**Radclyffe** *See* RADCLIFFE.

**Rae** Scottish name possibly based on the Gaelic *rath* ('grace'). *See also* RACHEL.

**Raelene** Australian compound name combining RAE (from RACHEL) with the feminine suffix -line. A relatively recent Australian introduction dating from the middle of the twentieth century, it was probably inspired by such parallel names as DARLENE.

**Rahel** *See* RACHEL.

**Raina** *See* REGINA.

**Rainbow** English name based on the ordinary vocabulary word.

**Raine** *See* REGINA.

**Raisa** ('ryeesa') Greek name meaning 'tolerant'.

**Ramona** Feminine version of RAYMOND, meaning 'well-advised protector'. Of Spanish origin, it became popular in Canada and the USA after the publication of Helen Hunt Jackson's novel *Ramona* in 1884.

**Randa/Randy** *See* MIRANDA.

**Raquel/Ray** *See* RACHEL.

**Reagan** *See* REGAN.

**Reanna** English name of obscure origins. A recent introduction, it may have evolved from RHEA and was probably influenced by DEANNA and the Welsh RHIANNON. Also found as **Reanne** or **Rheanna**.

**Reanne** *See* REANNA.

**Reba** *See* REBECCA.

**Rebecca** Hebrew name possibly meaning 'heifer' or, according to another theory, 'binding', 'knotted cord' or 'noose' (perhaps in reference to the marriage bond). It appears (as **Rebekah**) in the Old Testament. Commonly shortened to **Becky**, **Becca** or, less frequently, **Reba**.

**Rebekah/Rebekar** *See* REBECCA.

**Reenie** English name based on the French masculine RENÉ, itself ultimately from the Latin *renatus* ('reborn'). Also found as **Renée**, with or without an accent. Other variants are **Rena** (or **Rina**) and **Renata**. *See also* DOREEN; MAUREEN.

**Regan** English name of unknown origin, though possibly a variant of REGINA. It may be linked with the Irish surname Regan or Reagan and appeared as the name of one of the king's three daughters in William Shakespeare's tragedy *King Lear* (1605). Also found as **Reagan**.

**Reggie** *See* REGINA.

**Regina** ('rejeena') English name based on the Latin *regina* ('queen'). Regina was a popular choice of girls' name in medieval times, when it was also found as **Reina**, an anglicization of the French Reine. Other variants include **Raine** and **Raina**. Sometimes

shortened to **Reggie**. *See also*
GINA; QUEENIE; REGAN.

**Reina** *See* REGINA.

**Rena/Renata** *See* REENIE.

**Rene** *See* IRENE.

**Renée** *See* REENIE.

**Renie** *See* IRENE.

**Rexanne** Feminine
equivalent of REX, probably
influenced by **Roxanne**.

**Rhea** Greek name meaning
'flow', originally borne by an
earth goddess identified as the
mother of Zeus. Another
legend names Rhea Silva as the
mother of Romulus and
Remus, founders of Rome.
Also found as RIA.

**Rheanna** *See* REANNA.

**Rhian** Welsh name meaning
'maiden'. This appears to be a
modern innovation. A variant
is **Rhianu**.

**Rhianna** *See* RHIANNON.

**Rhiannon** Welsh name
meaning 'nymph' or 'goddess',

probably based on *rigantona*, a
Celtic royal title meaning 'great
queen'. The name is thought
to have been borne by a Celtic
goddess associated with horses
and was later carried by the
legendary Celtic Princess
Rhiannon. Also found as
**Riannon** or **Rhianna**.

**Rhianu** *See* RHIAN.

**Rhoda** Hebrew name based
on the Greek *rhodon* ('rose'), or
alternatively possibly meaning
'a woman from Rhodes'. It
appears in the New Testament
as the name of a servant girl in
the house of Mary, mother of
John. In Scotland the name is
often treated as a feminine
equivalent of RODERICK.

**Rhona** Scottish name that
developed either from a place
name (from Rona, an island in
the Hebrides) or as a feminine
variant of RONALD or
Raghnaid. Also found as **Rona**.
Its use is still largely confined
to Scotland. *See also* ROWENA.

**Rhonda** Welsh name based
on the Welsh *rhon* ('pike' or
'lance') and *da* ('good'). It was
probably influenced by RHODA
and RONA and acquired extra

significance through the link with the Rhondda valley (named after a local river) in South Wales.

**Rhonwen** *See* ROWENA.

**Ria** Shortened version of MARIA, VICTORIA and other names ending in -ria. *See also* RHEA.

**Riannon** *See* RHIANNON.

**Rica** *See* ERICA; FREDERICA.

**Richmal** English name that resulted from the combination of MICHAEL and RICHARD. A relatively recent introduction, it is known chiefly from British children's author Richmal Crompton (1890–1969), writer of the *Just William* stories.

**Rickie/Ricky** *See* FREDERICA.

**Rina** *See* REENIE.

**Riona** *See* CATRIONA.

**Rita** English name that developed originally as an Italian and Spanish variant of **Margarita** (*see* MARGARET) and is now considered to exist as a name in its own right. Its popularity was boosted by US film star Rita Hayworth (Margarita Carmen Cansino; 1918–87).

**Robena** *See* ROBIN.

**Roberta** Feminine equivalent of ROBERT. It was introduced in the 1870s and became especially popular in Scotland and the USA, where it was further promoted by the Jerome Kern musical *Roberta* (1933). **Robertina** is a rare variant form. Shortened to BOBBIE or **Berta**.

**Robertina** *See* ROBERTA.

**Robin** English name that developed out of ROBERT and has long had its own independent existence. The name came to England from France in medieval times and was bestowed originally only on boys. It has been used for girls since the 1950s. Variants include **Robyn**, **Robynne** and **Robina** (also found as **Robena** and **Robinia**).

**Robina/Robinia/ Robyn/Robynne** *See* ROBIN.

**Rochelle** French name that developed either as a feminine form of the French Roch, as a variant of RACHEL, or else was inspired by a place name (the French port of La Rochelle) meaning 'little rock'.

**Rohanna** Feminine equivalent of the masculine ROHAN, possibly from the Irish Gaelic for 'red'.

**Roisin** See ROSE.

**Roma** Roman name based on that of the city of Rome. The Emperor Hadrian built a temple in Rome to the goddess Roma and she was worshipped throughout Roman territories. It has appeared sporadically as a first name since the nineteenth century.

**Romaine** French name meaning 'Roman woman'. The feminine equivalent of ROMAN, it was first adopted by English speakers in the nineteenth century. Variants include **Romayne** and the Latinate **Romana**.

**Romana/Romayne** See ROMAINE.

**Romey** See ROSEMARY.

**Romola** Italian name meaning 'woman of Rome', a feminine version of the masculine Romulus. George Eliot's novel *Romola* (1863) promoted familiarity with the name.

**Romy** English name variously linked to the Latin for 'sea dew' or to the names ROSE and MARY. See ROSEMARY.

**Ron** See RONALDA; ROWENA; VERONICA.

**Rona** See RHONA; ROWENA.

**Ronalda** Feminine equivalent of RONALD, which itself developed out of the Old Norse Rognvaldr. Variants include **Ronna** and **Ronnette**. Shortened to **Ron** or **Ronnie** (or **Ronni**).

**Ronna/Ronnette** See RONALDA.

**Ronni/Ronnie** See RONALDA; ROWENA; VERONICA.

**Roo** See RUE; RUTH.

**Ros** *See* ROSALIND; ROSAMUND.

**Rosa/Rosabel/ Rosabella** *See* ROSE.

**Rosaleen** *See* ROSALIND.

**Rosalia** *See* ROSALIE.

**Rosalie** French name that developed from the older Latin **Rosalia**, the name of a Roman festival in which people decorated the tombs of the dead with garlands of roses. The success of the Hollywood musical *Rosalie* in the 1930s, starring Nelson Eddy, did much to popularize the name in the mid-twentieth century.

**Rosalin** *See* ROSALIND.

**Rosalind** English name linked to the Old German Roslindis, itself based on *hros* ('horse') and either *lind* ('tender' or 'soft') or *linta* ('lime'), in which case it means 'horse shield made of lime wood'. The Spanish linked it to *rosa* and *linda*, giving it the meaning 'pretty rose'. Variants include **Rosalyn, Rosalynne, Rosalin, Rosalinda, Roseline, Roselyn, Roslyn, Rosslyn** and

**Rosaleen**. Shortened to **Ros** or **Roz**.

**Rosalinda/Rosaline/ Rosalyn/Rosalynne** *See* ROSALIND.

**Rosamond** *See* ROSAMUND.

**Rosamund** English name combining the Old German *hros* ('horse') and *mund* ('protection'), although a more popular derivation of medieval origin links it to the Latin *rosa mundi* ('rose of the world') or *rosa munda* ('pure rose'). Also found as **Rosamond**. Sometimes shortened to **Ros** or **Roz**.

**Rosanna** English name combining ROSE and ANNA. It also appears as **Roseanna, Rosanne, Rozanne** or **Roseanne. Rosannah**, meanwhile, suggests a combination of ROSE with HANNAH.

**Rosannah/Rosanne** *See* ROSANNA.

**Rosario** Spanish name that originated in the phrase *Nuestra Señora del Rosario* ('Our Lady of the Rosary'). In Spain it is given to boys and girls, but it is reserved for girls in the English-speaking world.

**Roschana** *See* ROXANA.

**Rose** English name based on the Old German *hros* ('horse') or *hrod* ('fame') but now associated universally with the flower, from the Latin *rosa*. **Rosie** and **Rosy** are informal versions. Other variants include **Rosa**, **Rosabel** and **Rosabella** ('beautiful rose'), **Roselle**, **Rosetta** ('little rose'), **Rosette** and the Spanish **Rosita**. An Irish variant, meaning 'little rose', is **Roisin** or **Rosheen** (reflecting its pronunciation). Also used as a shortening of ROSEMARY and other names beginning with Rose-.

**Roseanna/Roseanne** *See* ROSANNA.

**Roseline** *See* ROSALIND.

**Roselle** *See* ROSE.

**Roselyn** *See* ROSALIND.

**Rosemarie** *See* ROSEMARY.

**Rosemary** English flower name based on the Latin *ros*

*marinus* ('sea dew'), a reference to the plant's blue-green foliage. It is sometimes also considered to be a combined form of ROSE and MARY. Also found as **Rosemarie**. Shortened forms include ROSE, **Rosie** and the rare **Romey** (or ROMY).

**Rosetta/Rosette/ Rosheen** *See* ROSE.

**Rosie** *See* ROSE; ROSEMARY.

**Rosita** *See* ROSE.

**Roslyn/Rosslyn** *See* ROSALIND.

**Rosy** *See* ROSE.

**Rowan** English version of the Irish Gaelic **Ruadhan**, meaning 'little red-haired one'. It is sometimes linked instead to the alternate name of the mountain ash, which bears red berries. Once an exclusively boys' name, it is now used for both sexes. A variant applied to girls only is **Rowanne**.

**Rowanne** *See* ROWAN.

**Rowena** English name based on the Old English *hrod*

('fame') and *wynn* ('joy') or, alternatively, a Celtic name linked to the Welsh **Rhonwen**, itself from *rhon* ('pike' or 'lance') and *gwen* ('white' or 'fair') and thus meaning 'slender and fair'. Sometimes found as **Rowina**. Shortened to **Ron**, **Ronnie**, **Rona** or RHONA.

**Rowina** *See* ROWENA.

**Roxana** Latinized version of the Persian first name **Roschana**, meaning 'dawn' or 'light'. The most famous Persian bearer of the name was Roxana, Persian wife of Alexander the Great. **Roxane** or **Roxanne** are common English and French versions of the name. Commonly shortened to **Roxie** or **Roxy**.

**Roxane/Roxanne/ Roxie/Roxy** *See* ROXANA.

**Roz** *See* ROSALIND; ROSAMUND.

**Rozanne** *See* ROSANNA.

**Ruadhan** *See* ROWAN.

**Rube/Rubie/Rubina** *See* RUBY.

**Ruby** English jewel name based on the Latin *rubeus* ('red'). Notable bearers of the name include US television comedienne Ruby Wax (b. 1953). Variants include **Rube**, **Rubie** and **Rubina**.

**Rue** English name inspired by the plant rue, but also sometimes considered to be a variant of RUTH. Also found as **Roo**.

**Ruth** Hebrew name of uncertain origin, variously interpreted as meaning 'companion', 'friend' or 'vision of beauty'. It was among the biblical names taken up by Puritans after the Reformation. **Roo** and **Ruthie** are informal variants.

**Ruthie** *See* RUTH.

# GIRLS' NAMES

**Sabella** English name that is thought to have developed from ISABELLA. This is a relatively recent introduction, of twentieth-century invention.

**Sabia** Irish name that developed as a Latinized version of the Gaelic SADHBH. The earliest records of the name go back to the medieval period.

**Sabina/Sabine** *See* SADHBH.

**Sabrina** Welsh name that has been in occasional use among English speakers since the nineteenth century. The name features in Welsh legend as that of an illegitimate daughter of King Locrine who was drowned in the River Severn (subsequently named after her) on the orders of Locrine's widow Gwendolen. Also found as **Zabrina**.

**Sadhbh** ('sorv') Irish name based on the Gaelic for 'sweet'. It was commonly given to girls in medieval Ireland. Today it is more likely to be found in such anglicized forms as SABIA, **Sabina**, and **Sabine**.

**Sadie** English name that developed as a familiar form of SARAH. It emerged from the shadow of Sarah in the late nineteenth century and enjoyed a peak in popularity in the 1970s. It is also in use as a familiar form of MERCEDES.

**Saffie/Saffrey** *See* SAFFRON.

**Saffron** English name that has been in occasional use among English speakers since the 1960s. The origin of the name lies in the golden-yellow crocus stigmas long used as a spice. Informal versions include **Saffie** and **Saffrey**.

**Sahara** English name taken from that of the Sahara desert in Africa. A relatively recent introduction as a first name.

**Sal** *See* SALLY; SARAH.

**Salena/Salina** *See* SELINA.

**Salley/Sallie** *See* SALLY.

**Sally** English name that began life as a diminutive form of SARAH. The process by which the 'r' in the name became 'll' is fairly standard among English first names. Also found as **Sallie** or **Salley**. Commonly shortened to **Sal**. The name may also be combined with other names, as in **Sallyann** (or **Sally-Anne**) and **Sally-Jane**.

**Sallyann/Sally-Anne/ Sally-Jane** *See* SALLY.

**Salome** ('salohmee') Greek version of an Aramaic name of unknown meaning, possibly linked to the Hebrew *shalom* ('peace'). The name's association with Herod's daughter, whose demand for the head of John the Baptist brought about his execution, has stopped it becoming a popular choice.

**Sam** *See* SAMANTHA.

**Samantha** Feminine equivalent of SAMUEL. It appears to have first entered use in the southern USA, perhaps under the influence of ANTHEA, during the eighteenth century. Its popularity was boosted in 1956 by the Cole Porter song 'I love you, Samantha' from the film *High Society*. Shortened to **Sam** or **Sammy** (or **Sammie**).

**Sammie/Sammy** *See* SAMANTHA.

**Sandie** *See* SANDRA.

**Sandra** English name based on the Italian Alessandra (*see* ALEXANDRA). Variants include **Zandra**, **Sandrine**, the Scottish **Saundra** and the chiefly US **Sondra**. **Sandy** and **Sandie** are familiar forms of the name. *See also* CASSANDRA.

**Sandrine/Sandy** *See* SANDRA.

**Sanna** *See* SUSANNAH.

**Saoirse** ('sairsha') Irish name meaning 'freedom'.

**Sapphira** *See* SAPPHIRE.

**Sapphire** English jewel name based on the Hebrew *sappir* ('sapphire' or 'lapis lazuli'). It was first taken up by English speakers along with other jewel names in the nineteenth century. A variant of the name, in which form it may be found in the New Testament, is **Sapphira**.

**Sara** *See* SARAH.

**Sarah** Hebrew name meaning 'princess'. It appears in the Bible as the name of the ninety-year-old wife of Abraham. Also found as **Sara** and, in former times, as **Sarey** or **Sarra**, as well as in combination with other names, as in **Sarah-Jane**. Among rarer variants are **Sarina** and **Sarita**. In Ireland the name is sometimes linked with **Saraid** (meaning 'excellent') and SORCHA. Familiar forms include SALLY, **Sal** and **Sassie**. *See also* SADIE; ZARA.

**Sarah-Jane** *See* SARAH.

**Saraid** *See* SARAH.

**Saranna** English name that resulted from the combination of SARAH and ANNA. It seems to have made its first appearance among English speakers in the eighteenth century.

**Sarey/Sarina/Sarita/ Sarra** *See* SARAH.

**Sasha** Familiar form of ALEXANDRA, of Russian origin.

**Saskia** Dutch name of obscure origin that was taken up by English speakers in the 1950s. Recorded in use among the Dutch in medieval times, it may have evolved from the Old German *sachs* ('Saxon').

**Sassie** *See* SARAH.

**Saundra** *See* SANDRA.

**Savanna** English name based on the Spanish *zavana* ('grassland' or 'plain'). Also found as **Savannah** or **Zavanna**.

**Savannah** *See* SAVANNA.

**Scarlet** *See* SCARLETT.

**Scarlett** English name that was originally reserved for (chiefly male) dealers in scarlet cloth or for people wearing scarlet-coloured clothing. As a girls' name it was popularized by US novelist Margaret Mitchell, who created Scarlett O'Hara in *Gone With the Wind* (1936). Also found as **Scarlet**. *See also* ASHLEY; RHETT.

**Scilla** *See* PRISCILLA.

**Seirian** ('sighreean') Welsh name meaning 'bright one'.

**Selena** *See* SELINA.

**Selima** Arabic name meaning 'peace', also sometimes treated as a variant of SELINA. *See also* SELMA.

**Selina** English version of the Greek Selene, based either on the Greek *selēnē* ('moon') or possibly on the Latin *caelum* ('heaven'). **Salena**, **Selena** and **Salina** are variant forms. *See also* CÉLINE.

**Selma** English name of uncertain origin. It is sometimes presumed to be a contracted form of SELIMA that emerged in the eighteenth century under the influence of THELMA. Also found as **Zelma**.

**Senga** Scottish name that probably evolved from the Gaelic *seang* ('slender'). Another theory links the name with AGNES, which it spells when read backwards.

**Serafina** *See* SERAPHINA.

**Seraphina** Latin name derived from the Hebrew *seraphim* ('fiery' or 'burning ones'). In the Bible the name is borne by an order of angels. Sometimes found as **Serafina** and shortened to **Fina**.

**Serena** English name based on the Latin *serenus* ('calm' or 'serene'). It is sometimes considered to be an aristocratic name and in recent times has become a royal name, as borne by Serena Stanhope, Viscountess Linley (b. 1970). Rare variant forms include **Serina**, **Serenah** and **Serenna**.

**Serenah** *See* SERENA.

**Serendipity** *See* SERENITY.

**Serenna** *See* SERENA.

**Serenity** English name based on the ordinary vocabulary word. Not unrelated is the

equally recent introduction,
**Serendipity**.

**Serina** *See* SERENA.

**Shakira** Arabic name
meaning 'grateful'.

**Shana** *See* SIÂN.

**Shane** *See* SHAUNA.

**Shani** *See* SHAUNA.

**Shania** ('shanigha') English
name borrowed from a Native
American original, meaning
'on my way', or else a variant
of **Shane** (*see* SHAUNA). It has
become widely familiar
through Canadian pop singer
Shania Twain (b. 1965).

**Shanna/Shannah** *See*
SUSANNAH.

**Shannon** English name that
probably developed as a
combination of **Shane** and
SHARON, although it is often
assumed that it comes from the
name – meaning 'the old one'
– of the Irish river (despite the
fact that the name is little used
in Ireland).

**Shantel/Shantelle** *See*
CHANTAL.

**Shari** *See* SHARON.

**Sharlene** *See* CHARLENE.

**Sharlott** *See* CHARLOTTE.

**Sharmain/Sharmaine**
*See* CHARMAINE.

**Sharon** English name based
ultimately on the Hebrew
Saron, from *sar* ('to sing' or
'singer'). The name features in
the Bible as the name of a
valley in Palestine, famed for its
natural beauty. Variant forms
include **Sharron**, **Sharona** (or
**Sherona**), **Sharonda** and
**Sharyn**. Sometimes shortened
to **Shari**.

**Sharona/Sharonda/
Sharron/Sharyn** *See*
SHARON.

**Shauna** Feminine equivalent
of the Irish SEAN, itself a
version of JOHN. Variants
include **Shane** (which is
particularly popular in
Australia) and **Shani**.

**Sheba** *See* BATHSHEBA.

**Sheela/Sheelah** *See* SHEILA.

**Sheena** English version of the Scottish and Irish Gaelic Sìne, itself an equivalent of the English JANE or JEAN. It was taken up by English speakers in the 1930s, chiefly in Scotland. Also found as **Shena**, **Sheenagh**, **Sheona** or SHONA.

**Sheenagh** *See* SHEENA.

**Sheila** English version of the Irish Gaelic Sile, an equivalent of the English CELIA. It reached a peak in the UK in the 1930s, by which time it was no longer thought of as distinctly Irish. Also found as **Sheela**, **Sheelah** or **Shelagh**.

**Shelagh** *See* SHEILA.

**Shell** *See* MICHELLE.

**Shelley** English name that originated as a place name meaning 'wood on a slope'. It may also be used as a familiar form of MICHELLE or RACHEL. As a first name it emerged in the mid-nineteenth century under the influence of the English poet Percy Bysshe Shelley (1792–1822). Like SHIRLEY it is now reserved chiefly for girls. Also found as **Shelly**.

**Shelly** *See* SHELLEY.

**Shena/Sheona** *See* SHEENA.

**Sheree/Sheri/Sherie** *See* CHERIE.

**Sherill/Sherilyn** *See* CHERYL.

**Sherley** *See* SHIRLEY.

**Sherona** *See* SHARON.

**Sherri/Sherry** *See* CHERIE; SHIRLEY.

**Sheryl** *See* CHERYL.

**Shevaun** *See* SIOBHAN.

**Shirl/Shirlee** *See* SHIRLEY.

**Shirley** English name that originated as a place name based on the Old English *scir* ('county' or 'bright') and *leah* ('wood' or 'clearing'). Formerly reserved for boys, it was transferred to girls after the publication of Charlotte Brontë's novel *Shirley* (1849).

Variants include **Sherley** and **Shirlee**. SHELLEY, **Sherry**, **Sherri** and **Shirl** are familiar forms of the name.

**Shona** Scottish Gaelic feminine equivalent of JOHN. It is also in use as a variant of SHEENA.

**Shula** Familiar form of the Jewish **Shulamit**, based ultimately on *shalom* ('peace'). As Shulamit it features in the biblical Song of Solomon and is today a common Hebrew name.

**Shulamit** *See* SHULA.

**Shyanne** *See* CHEYENNE.

**Siân** ('sharn') Welsh version of JANE, also in existence as a feminine variant of SEAN. It was taken up in Wales in the 1940s and may appear with or without the accent. **Siana** (or **Shana**) is a familiar form of the name.

**Siana** *See* SIÂN.

**Sib** *See* ISABEL; SYBIL.

**Sibb/Sibbie/Sibby** *See* SYBIL.

**Sibyl** *See* SYBIL.

**Sid** *See* SIDNEY.

**Sidney** English name that may have begun as a Norman French place name, Saint-Denis, or, more likely, came from the Old English *sidan* ('wide') and *eg* ('river island' or 'wide island'). Also found as **Sydney**. Commonly shortened to **Syd** or **Sid**.

**Sidonie** French version of the Roman Sidonia (meaning 'of Sidon', Sidon being the capital of Phoenicia). Another derivation suggests it comes from the Greek *sindon* ('linen'), probably in reference to the linen shroud of Jesus Christ. Also found as **Sidony**.

**Sidony** *See* SIDONIE.

**Siena** *See* SIENNA.

**Sienna** Italian name derived from that of the city. As a first name it appears to have made its debut in the nineteenth century. Well-known bearers of the name include US film actress Sienna Miller (b. 1981). Also found as **Siena**.

**Sierra** Spanish name meaning 'mountain range'. Its history as a first name among English speakers is a relatively recent phenomenon.

**Sigourney** English name that may be Scandinavian in origin, with the meaning 'conqueror'. It was popularized by US novelist F. Scott Fitzgerald in *The Great Gatsby* (1925). Notable bearers of the name include US film actress Sigourney Weaver (Susan Alexandra Weaver; b. 1949).

**Sigrid** Scandinavian name based on the Old Norse meaning 'fair and victorious'. Sometimes shortened to **Siri**.

**Silvia** Italian and English name based on the Roman Silvius, from the Latin *silva* ('wood'). In Roman legend, Rhea Silvia was the mother of Romulus and Remus, the founders of Rome. The variant form **Sylvia** is now the more common spelling of the name. **Sylvie** is a French version. Shortened to **Syl**.

**Simona** *See* SIMONE.

**Simone** French variant of

SIMON that was first taken up in the English-speaking world in the 1940s. Celebrated bearers of the name have included the French writer Simone de Beauvoir (1908–86). Also found in the form **Simona**.

**Sindy** *See* CINDY.

**Síne** *See* SHEENA.

**Sinead** ('shinnayd') Irish version of the English JANET. It retains its identification as an essentially Irish name. Famous bearers of the name have included the Irish actress Sinead Cusack (b. 1948) and Irish singer-songwriter Sinead O'Connor (b. 1966).

**Siobhan** ('shivorn') Irish version of the English JOAN. The name is more common in Ireland than elsewhere. Notable bearers of the name have included the Irish actress Siobhan McKenna (1923–86). Also found as **Shevaun** and the modern form **Chevonne**.

**Siri** *See* SIGRID.

**Sis/Sissy** *See* CECILIA; CISSIE.

**Skeeter** English name that began as a nickname for any small or energetic person. It may have come from 'mosquito' or else from 'skeets' or 'scoots'. It is a twentieth-century introduction of US origin. A well-known bearer of the name is US country singer Skeeter Davis (Mary Frances Penick; b. 1931).

**Sky** *See* SKYE.

**Skye** English name based either upon the ordinary vocabulary word or else intended as a reference to the Scottish island of Skye. Also found as **Sky**. Other variants include **Skyla**.

**Skyla** *See* SKYE.

**Sofia/Sofie** *See* SOPHIA.

**Sondra** *See* SANDRA.

**Sonia** ('sonya') Russian variant of Sofiya, an equivalent of the English SOPHIA. It was taken up by English speakers in the early twentieth century and now exists as an independent name. Also found as **Sonya** or **Sonja**.

**Sonja/Sonya** *See* SONIA.

**Sophia** Greek name meaning 'wisdom'. The original St Sophia was probably not a real person but the result of a misinterpretation of the phrase *hagia sophia* ('holy wisdom'). Variants include **Sofia** and **Sophie**, a French version of the name (also found as **Sofie** or **Sophy**), that is now the more common form. *See also* SONIA.

**Sophie** *See* SOPHIA; SOPHRONIA.

**Sophronia** Greek name based on *sōphrōn* ('prudent' or 'sensible'). The name was taken up by English speakers in the nineteenth century. Sometimes shortened to **Sophie** or **Sophy**.

**Sophy** *See* SOPHIA; SOPHRONIA.

**Sorcha** ('sorka') Irish and Scottish Gaelic name meaning 'brightness'. In Ireland it is often treated as a Gaelic variant of SARAH. In Scotland it is sometimes linked to CLARA.

**Sorel/Sorell** *See* SORREL.

**Sorrel** English plant name that was adopted as a first name in the 1940s. The plant name is thought to have come originally from the German *sur* ('sour'), a reference to the sour taste of its leaves. Also found as **Sorrell**, **Sorell** and **Sorel**.

**Sorrell** *See* SORREL.

**Spring** English name based either on the name of the season or a reference to natural springs or wells. A nineteenth-century introduction, it remains relatively rare.

**Stace** *See* STACEY.

**Stacey** English name that evolved as a feminine equivalent of STACY. It may also be found as a variant of ANASTASIA. Also found as **Stacy**, **Stacie** or **Staci**. Commonly shortened to **Stace**.

**Staci/Stacie/Stacy** *See* STACEY.

**Star** *See* STELLA.

**Stef/Stefanie/Steffany/ Steffie** *See* STEPHANIE.

**Stella** English name based on the Latin *stella* ('star'). The name was first used as a title for the Virgin Mary, *Stella Maris* ('star of the sea'). Modern variants of the name include **Star**. *See also* ESTELLE.

**Steph** *See* STEPHANIE.

**Stephanie** English version of the French Stéphanie, itself based on the Roman Stephania or Stephana, and equivalent to the English STEPHEN. Also found as **Stefanie** or **Steffany**. Familiar forms include **Steph**, **Stef**, **Steffie**, **Stevi** and **Stevie**.

**Stevi/Stevie** *See* STEPHANIE.

**Storm** English name based on the ordinary vocabulary word, suggesting a passionate, lively nature. The name does not seem to have been used before the late nineteenth century.

**Su/Sue** *See* SUSAN; SUSANNAH.

**Sukie/Suky** *See* SUSAN.

**Summer** English name inspired by the name of the season.

**Sunday** English name taken from that of the day of the week. Never common, this appears to be a twentieth-century invention, confined to children born on a Sunday.

**Susan** English name that developed out of SUSANNAH. It made its first appearances in the seventeenth century. Occasionally found as **Suzan**. Familiar forms include **Sue** and **Su** as well as **Susie** (or **Suzie**), **Suzy** and **Sukie** (or **Suky**).

**Susanna** *See* SUSANNAH.

**Susannah** English version of the Hebrew Shushannah, derived from *shoshan* ('lily'). Later eclipsed by SUSAN, it has also appeared as **Susanna** or **Suzanna**. Other variants include **Suzanne** and **Suzette** (both originally French) as well as **Susanne**. **Sue** (or **Su**), **Susie**, **Suzie** (or **Suzy**) and the more unusual **Sanna** and **Shanna** (or **Shannah**) are familiar forms of the name.

**Susanne** *See* SUSANNAH.

**Susie** *See* SUSAN; SUSANNAH.

**Suzan** *See* SUSAN.

**Suzanna/Suzanne/ Suzette** *See* SUSANNAH.

**Suzie/Suzy** *See* SUSAN; SUSANNAH.

**Svetlana** Russian name based on the Slavonic *svet* ('light'). Sometimes shortened to LANA.

**Sybil** English version of the Roman Sibilla, Sibylla, Sybella or Sybilla, based ultimately on the Greek for 'prophetess'. Benjamin Disraeli's novel *Sybil* (1845) did much to revive the name in the nineteenth century. Variants include **Sibyl**, **Sybille** and **Cybill**. Shortened to **Sib** (or **Sibb**) and **Sibbie** (or **Sibby**).

**Sybille** *See* SYBIL.

**Syd/Sydney** *See* SIDNEY.

**Syl/Sylvia/Sylvie** *See* SILVIA.

**Symphony** English name based on the ordinary vocabulary word. A relatively recent introduction as a first name.

# GIRLS' NAMES

**Tabatha/Tabbie/Tabby** *See* TABITHA.

**Tabitha** Aramaic name meaning 'doe' or 'gazelle'. The biblical Tabitha, a worthy Christian woman of Joppa, was brought back to life by the prayers of St Peter. Also found as **Tabatha**. Often shortened to **Tabbie** or **Tabby**. *See also* DORCAS.

**Tace** *See* TACEY.

**Tacey** English name based on the Latin *tacere* ('to be silent'). The Puritans adopted the name in the form **Tace** (meaning 'hush'). Variant forms include **Tacy** and **Tacita**.

**Tacita/Tacy** *See* TACEY.

**Talitha** Aramaic name meaning 'maiden'. It appears in the New Testament as the name of a young girl raised from the dead by Jesus.

**Tallula** *See* TALLULAH.

**Tallulah** Native American name meaning 'running water'. The celebrated US actress and wit Tallulah Bankhead (1903–68) inherited the name from her grandmother. It may also be used as a variant of the Irish Gaelic **Tallula**, from words meaning 'abundance' and 'lady' or 'princess'.

**Tally** *See* NATALIE.

**Tamar** *See* TAMARA.

**Tamara** Russian version of the Hebrew **Tamar**, meaning 'palm tree' or 'date palm'. In the Bible, Absalom's daughter Tamar was praised for her 'fair countenance'. *See also* TAMMY.

**Tammi/Tammie** *See* TAMMY.

**Tammy** English name that evolved out of TAMARA and TAMSIN and is now considered a name in its own right. Well-known bearers of the name have included US country singer Tammy Wynette (Virginia Wynette Pugh; 1942–98). Also found as **Tammi** or **Tammie**.

**Tamsin** Cornish version of the medieval **Thomasin**, **Thomasina** or **Thomasine** (a feminine form of THOMAS) that has been popular since the 1950s. **Tasmin** is a modern variant of the name. Commonly shortened to TAMMY.

**Tanesha** *See* TANISHA.

**Tania** *See* TANYA.

**Tanisha** English name based on the Hausa for 'born on Monday'. Also found as **Tanesha** or **Tenesha**.

**Tansy** English name taken from that of the strongly perfumed, colourful yellow garden flower. The original source of the plant name is the Greek *athanasia* ('immortality'). Also found as a shortened form of ANASTASIA.

**Tanya** Anglicization of the Russian TATIANA, which has

emerged as a name in its own right since the 1940s. Also found as **Tania** or **Tonya**.

**Tara** ('tahra') English name that was originally an Irish place name meaning 'hill'. It may also be linked to the earth goddess Temair, whose name means 'dark one'. The castle on the hill of Tara in County Meath features prominently in Irish legend. It is also a popular Indian name, whose meanings include 'shining'.

**Taryn** English name resulting from the combination of TARA and **Karyn** (*see* KAREN).

**Tasha** *See* NATASHA.

**Tasmin** *See* TAMSIN.

**Tatiana** Russian name that may have Asian roots or else come from the Roman family name Tatius or from the Greek *tattō* ('I arrange'). Shortened versions of the name include TANYA.

**Tatum** English name meaning 'cheerful bringer of joy'. Famous bearers of the name include US actress Tatum O'Neal (b. 1963).

**Tavia** *See* OCTAVIA.

**Tawney** *See* TAWNY.

**Tawny** English name based on the Old French *tané* ('tanned'). Like GINGER and Sandy it was traditionally reserved for people with a certain hair colour – in this case brown. Also found as Tawney.

**Tayla/Tayler** *See* TAYLOR.

**Taylor** English name based on a surname originally reserved for those engaged in the business of tailoring. It was formerly given only to boys but is now more common among girls. Also found as Tayla or Tayler.

**Tea/Teah** *See* TIA.

**Teal** English name based on that of the teal duck. It is recorded in use in Britain as early as the fourteenth century. Also found as Teale.

**Teale** *See* TEAL.

**Teasag** *See* JESSIE.

**Teena** *See* TINA.

**Tegan** *See* TEGWEN.

**Tegwen** Welsh name combining words meaning 'beautiful' and 'fair' or 'holy'. It appears to be a relatively modern invention. Also found as Tegan.

**Tekla** *See* THEKLA.

**Temperance** English name that was among the 'virtue' names adopted by the Puritans in the seventeenth century. It has become rare since the late nineteenth century.

**Tempest** English name that was based on the ordinary vocabulary word meaning 'severe storm'.

**Tenesha** *See* TANISHA.

**Teresa** English, Italian and Spanish name based on Greek words meaning 'reaper' or 'harvester' and 'guarding' or 'watching' or else taken from the name of the Greek island of Thera. Also spelt Theresa, it spread throughout the Roman Catholic world through two saints bearing the name. Thérèse is the French equivalent. Often shortened to Teri, Terri,

TERRY, **Tess, Tessie, Tessy** or TESSA. *See also* TRACY.

**Teri/Terri** *See* TERESA; TERRY.

**Terry** English name that evolved as a shortening of TERESA. Variant spellings of the name include **Terri** and **Teri**.

**Tertia** ('tersha') Roman name based on the Latin *tertius* ('three') and thus traditionally reserved for third-born daughters.

**Tess** *See* TERESA; TESSA.

**Tessa** English name that exists both as an informal version of TERESA and as an independent name of obscure European origins. Notable bearers of the name and its variant forms **Tess** and **Tessie** have included the heroine of Thomas Hardy's novel *Tess of the D'Urbervilles* (1891).

**Tessy** *See* TERESA.

**Tetty** *See* ELIZABETH.

**Thea** *See* DOROTHY; THEODORA.

**Thecla** *See* THEKLA.

**Theda** *See* THEODORA.

**Thekla** English version of the Greek Theokleia, itself based on the Greek *theos* ('god') and *kleia* ('glory'). Also found as **Tekla** or **Thecla**.

**Thel** *See* ETHEL; THELMA.

**Thelma** English name invented by the British novelist Marie Corelli (1855–1924) for the Norwegian central character in her novel *Thelma* (1887). Corelli may have based the name on the Greek *thelema* ('will' or 'wish'). Sometimes shortened to **Thel**.

**Theo** *See* THEODORA.

**Theodora** Feminine version of THEODORE, based on the Greek for 'God's gift'. It shares the same roots as **Dorothea**, with the two parts of the name put in reverse order. **Fedora** is a variant form. Sometimes shortened to **Thea**, DORA or **Theda**.

**Theresa/Thérèse** *See* TERESA.

**Thirsa** See THIRZA.

**Thirza** English name descended from the Hebrew Tirzah, which may have had its origins in a place name or else in Hebrew words meaning 'acceptance' or 'pleasantness'. Also found as **Thirsa**.

**Thomasin/Thomasina/ Thomasine** See TAMSIN.

**Thora** Scandinavian name based on that of Thor, the Norse god of thunder. In Britain it became widely familiar through the film and television actress Thora Hird (1913–2003). Variants include **Thyra** and **Tyra**.

**Thyra** See THORA.

**Tia** English name that evolved as a shortened form of various longer names, such as LETITIA. Variants include **Tea** and **Teah**.

**Tiara** Greek name meaning 'crowned'.

**Tibbie** See ISABEL.

**Tiff** See TIFFANY.

**Tiffany** English name based on the Greek Theophania (meaning 'manifestation of God') via the French variant Tifainé. It was traditionally reserved for girls born on the feast of Epiphany (6 January). Tiffany's is the name of a select jewellery store in New York. Sometimes shortened to **Tiff**, **Tiffie** or **Tiffy**.

**Tiffie/Tiffy** See TIFFANY.

**Tiger Lily** See LILY.

**Tilda/Tilly** See MATILDA.

**Tina** English name that evolved from CHRISTINA and other names with a similar ending. Famous bearers of the name have included US rock singer Tina Turner (Annie Mae Bullock; b. 1939). Occasionally found as **Teena**.

**Tisha** See LETITIA.

**Titania** ('titahneea') Greek first name meaning 'giant'. It is strongly associated with the queen of the fairies in William Shakespeare's comedy *A Midsummer Night's Dream* (1595–6).

**Titty** *See* LETITIA.

**Toinette** *See* ANTOINETTE.

**Toni** *See* ANTOINETTE; ANTONIA.

**Tonya** *See* ANTONIA; TANYA.

**Topaz** English jewel name that has made occasional appearances since the late nineteenth century. During medieval times the name was sometimes treated as a variant of the boys' name Tobias (*see* TOBY). Also found as **Topaze**.

**Topaze** *See* TOPAZ.

**Topsy** English name of obscure origin. It may have evolved from the word 'topsail' and thus became associated with black slaves brought to the Americas in sailing ships. It was used by Harriet Beecher Stowe for the black orphan slave girl in her novel *Uncle Tom's Cabin* (1852).

**Tori/Toria/Tory** *See* VICTORIA.

**Totty** *See* CHARLOTTE.

**Toyah** English name of obscure origins, possibly from the Scandinavian for 'toy' or possibly on the model of the Jewish Tovah. It is best known through British pop singer and actress Toyah Willcox (b. 1958).

**Trace/Tracey/Tracie** *See* TRACY.

**Tracy** English and French name that was originally a Greek place name meaning 'place of Thracius', although it is also treated as a shortening of TERESA. It was formerly given to boys as well as girls. The films *The Philadelphia Story* (1940) and *High Society* (1956) both featured heiress Tracy Samantha Lord. Also found as **Tracey** or **Tracie** and shortened to **Trace**.

**Trafford** English first name of Germanic origin meaning 'dweller beyond the ford'.

**Treena** *See* CATHERINE.

**Tricia** *See* PATRICIA.

**Trina** *See* CATRIONA.

**Trini/Trinidad/**

**Trinita/Trinitee/ Trinitey** *See* TRINITY.

**Trinity** English name inspired by the Holy Trinity of the Christian faith. Variant forms include **Trini**, **Trinidad**, **Trinita**, **Trinitee** and **Trinitey**.

**Tris** *See* BEATRICE.

**Trish/Trisha** *See* PATRICIA.

**Triss/Trix/Trixie** *See* BEATRICE; BEATRIX.

**Trudi/Trudie** *See* TRUDY.

**Trudy** English name that developed as a shortened form of GERTRUDE, meaning 'ruler of the spear', or alternatively of ERMINTRUDE, meaning 'wholly beloved'. Also found as **Trudi** or **Trudie**.

**Truly** English name based on the ordinary vocabulary word meaning 'honestly'.

**Tryphena** English name based on the Greek for 'daintiness' or 'delicacy'. It features in the New Testament and has made occasional appearances among English speakers since the Reformation.

**Tuesday** English name usually reserved for children born on a Tuesday.

**Tyra** *See* THORA.

# GIRLS' NAMES

**Uda** ('ooda'/'oodel') English name meaning 'thriving woman'. **Udele** and **Udell** are variant forms.

**Udele/Udell** *See* UDA.

**Ula** ('oolah') Celtic name meaning 'jewel of the sea'. Also found as **Oola**. *See also* EULALIA.

**Ulanda** African name meaning 'confident'. Also encountered as **Ulandah** or **Ulande**.

**Ulandah/Ulande** *See* ULANDA.

**Ulrica** Scandinavian name that developed as a feminine version of Ulric, itself from the Norse Wulfric ('wolf ruler'). Also found as **Ulrika**.

**Ulrika** *See* ULRICA.

**Ulyana** ('ulyahner') Russian name that may have evolved as a variant of YELENA, meaning 'friendly'.

**Uma** ('oomer') English name that was probably invented in the late nineteenth century by Scottish novelist Robert Louis Stevenson in his story 'The Beach of Falesa'.

**Umber** English name from that of the colour umber, which is reddish brown.

**Una** ('ooner' or 'yooner') Irish and Scottish name possibly from the Irish *uan* ('lamb') or else from the Latin *unus* ('one'). Also found as **Ona, Oonagh** or **Oona**.

**Undine** ('undeen') Roman name meaning 'of the waves'. Undine was a water-sprite who experienced mortality by bearing a child by a human husband. **Ondina** and **Ondine** are variant forms.

**Unice** *See* EUNICE.

**Unity** English name from the Latin *unus* ('one'). It was among the 'virtue' names enthusiastically taken up by English Puritans in the sixteenth and seventeenth centuries.

**Urania** Greek name meaning 'heavenly'. It was the name of the muse of astronomy in classical Greek mythology.

**Urbaine** English feminine equivalent of the Roman URBAN, meaning 'citizen'.

**Urse/Ursie** *See* URSULA.

**Ursula** English, German and Scandinavian name from the Latin *ursa* ('she-bear') and meaning 'little she-bear'. The fourth-century Cornish St Ursula led an ill-fated all-female Crusade. **Ursuline** is a variant. Shortened forms include **Urse** and **Ursie**.

**Ursuline** *See* URSULA.

**Usha** ('oosher') Indian name from the Sanskrit for 'dawn'. It appears in the *Rig-Veda* as the name of the beautiful daughter of heaven.

**Utopia** English name meaning 'idealistic'. The original Utopia was a harmonious fictional land invented by Sir Thomas More in 1516 in a book with the same name.

## GIRLS' NAMES

**Val** *See* VALENTINA; VALERIE.

**Valda** Cornish name meaning 'flower'. It is also in use among German speakers, based on the Old German *vald* ('power').

**Valentina** English and French name derived ultimately from the Latin *valens* ('strong' or 'healthy'). The link with St Valentine's Day (14 February) has long given the name romantic associations. Commonly shortened to **Val**.

**Valerie** English and French version of the Roman Valeria (from the Latin for 'strong' or 'healthy'). Commonly shortened to **Val**.

**Valma** *See* VALMAI.

**Valmai** Cornish and Welsh, possibly from words which combine to mean 'mayflower'. Also found as **Valma**.

**Vanda** *See* WANDA.

**Vanessa** English name invented by the poet and satirist Jonathan Swift (1667–1745). Swift made up the name when writing to his friend Esther Vanhomrigh, taking 'Van' from Vanhomrigh and 'Essa' from Esther. Commonly shortened to **Nessa** or **Nessie**.

**Vashti** Name of probable Persian origin, meaning 'beautiful'. It appears in the Bible and was first introduced to the English-speaking world by Puritans in the seventeenth century.

**Vaughan** ('vorn') English and Welsh name, from the Welsh *fychan* ('little one'). Also found as **Vaughn**, it is used as a name for both boys and girls.

**Vaughn** *See* VAUGHAN.

**Velma** English name of

uncertain origin, possibly inspired by such similar names as SELMA and THELMA. *See also* WILHELMINA.

**Velvet** English name inspired by the luxurious soft cloth of the same name.

**Venetia** ('veneesha') English name based on the Latin title for the city of Venice. The name became popular after the publication of the novel *Venetia* (1837) by Benjamin Disraeli.

**Venus** Roman name for the goddess of love. Famous bearers of the name in modern times have included US tennis player Venus Williams (b. 1980).

**Vera** English name based either on the Russian *viera* ('faith') or else on the Latin *verus* ('true'). Sometimes treated as a shortened form of VERONICA, it was first taken up in the English-speaking world in the nineteenth century.

**Verena** Swiss name of unknown meaning, though possibly sharing the same roots as VERA. Its use among English

speakers was promoted by its appearance in the Henry James novel *The Bostonians* (1886).

**Verily** *See* VERITY.

**Verity** English name based on the Latin *verus* ('truth'). It was among the 'virtue' names adopted by English Puritans in the seventeenth century. A relatively rare variant is **Verily** (meaning 'truly').

**Verna** English first name of uncertain origin. It may have evolved as a feminine version of VERNON or else out of the Latin *vernus* ('spring').

**Verona** English name derived from that of the Italian city (itself of uncertain origin). It is sometimes considered to be a variant of VERONICA.

**Veronica** English name probably based on the Latin *vera icon* ('true image'), or on the Greek Pherenike ('victory bringer'). St Veronica wiped Christ's face on his way to be crucified. VERONA and the French **Veronique** are variants. **Ron, Ronnie** and VERA are shortened forms.

**Veronique** *See* VERONICA.

**Vesta** English name based on that of the Roman goddess of the hearth and fire, itself from the Greek *hestia* ('hearth'). It was adapted as a first name in the English-speaking world in the nineteenth century.

**Veva** *See* GENEVIEVE.

**Vi** *See* VIOLET.

**Vic/Vickie/Vicky** *See* VICTORIA.

**Victoria** English and Spanish name based on the Latin *victoria* ('victory'). It became popular among English speakers with the accession of Queen Victoria (1819–1901) in 1837. Shortened forms include **Tori**, **Toria**, **Tory**, **Vic**, **Vickie**, **Vicky**, **Vikki** and **Viti**. *See also* QUEENIE; VITA.

**Vida** *See* DAVINA.

**Vikki** *See* VICTORIA.

**Vilma** *See* WILHELMINA.

**Vina** *See* DAVINA.

**Vinnie/Vinny** *See* LAVINIA; VIRGINIA.

**Viola** English name derived from the Latin *viola* ('violet'). The popularity of the name in the English-speaking world was largely the result of the influence of the character Viola in William Shakespeare's *Twelfth Night* (1601). *See also* YOLANDA.

**Violet** English name derived from the Latin plant name (a traditional symbol of modesty). It was introduced to Britain in medieval times, sometimes in the form Violante. Variants include **Violetta** and **Violette**. A shortened form is **Vi**.

**Violetta/Violette** *See* VIOLET.

**Virginia** English version of the Roman Verginius, itself from the Latin for 'maiden'. In legend Verginius was a beautiful girl murdered by her father to save her from an unsuitable match. Shortened forms include GINGER, **Ginny**, **Jinny**, **Vinnie** and **Vinny**.

**Vita** ('veeta') English and Scandinavian name based on

the Latin *vitus* ('life'), or alternatively on the Sanskrit for 'desire' or 'wish'. It is also sometimes found as a shortened form of VICTORIA.

**Viti** *See* VICTORIA.

**Viv** *See* VIVIAN.

**Viva** English name based on the Latin *vivus* ('alive' or 'lively'). Also found as **Vivia**.

**Vivia** *See* VIVA.

**Vivian** English name based on the Latin *vivus* ('alive' or 'lively'). Borne by the fifth-century martyr St Vivianus, it was originally reserved for males. Variants include **Viviana, Vivianne, Vivien, Vivienne** and **Viviette**. Commonly shortened to **Viv**.

**Viviana/Vivianne/ Vivien/Vivienne/ Viviette** *See* VIVIAN.

**Vonda** *See* WANDA.

**Vonnie** *See* YVONNE.

# GIRLS' NAMES

**Wallis** Feminine equivalent of the masculine WALLACE, variously meaning 'Welsh' or (from Old French *waleis*) simply 'foreign' or 'stranger'. It is particularly associated with Wallis Simpson (1896–1986), for whom Edward VIII abdicated in 1936.

**Wanda** English name of obscure origin, possibly from the Old German for 'young shoot'. It is sometimes treated as a variant of WENDY and is also found in such variant forms as **Vanda**, **Vonda** and **Wenda**.

**Wanetta** English name based on the Old English for 'pale one'. **Wanette** is a variant form.

**Wanette** *See* WANETTA.

**Wenda** *See* WANDA.

**Wendy** Name invented by the Scottish playwright J. M. Barrie in his children's story *Peter Pan* (1904). It was inspired by a young girl who called Barrie her 'fwendy-wendy' but may have been in use before as a shortening of GWENDA or GWENDOLEN.

**Wenonah** *See* WINONA.

**Whitney** English name taken from a place name meaning 'at the white island'. Originally a surname, it has been used for both sexes since the early twentieth century. Notable bearers of the name include US film actress Whitney Houston (b. 1964).

**Whoopi** English name of obscure meaning. It is best known through US comedienne and actress Whoopi Goldberg (Caryn Johnson; b. 1955).

**Wilhelmina** German name that was taken up as a feminine equivalent of Wilhelm, the German form of WILLIAM. Also found as **Wilhelmine** or **Williamina**. Shortened forms include ELMA, **Ilma**, **Mina**, MINNA, **Minnie**, VELMA, **Vilma**, **Willa** and **Wilma**.

## **Wilhelmine/Willa/ Williamina** See WILHELMINA.

**Willow** English name based on that of the tree. Its use as a first name is a relatively recent phenomenon, possibly promoted by the 1988 film *Willow*.

**Wilma** See WILHELMINA.

**Wilona** English name based on the Old English for 'gracious friend'.

**Win** See WINIFRED.

**Winifred** English and Welsh name derived from the Old English *wynn* ('joy') and *frith* ('peace'). Also found as **Winifrid** or **Winnifred**, it became common from the

sixteenth century. Shortened forms include **Win**, **Winn** and **Winnie**.

## **Winifrid/Winn/ Winnie/Winnifred** See WINIFRED.

**Winona** Sioux Indian name meaning 'eldest daughter'. Borne by a legendary American Indian princess, it is best known today through US film actress Winona Ryder (b. 1971). Variants include **Wenonah**, **Winonah** and **Wynona**.

**Winonah** See WINONA.

**Wren** English name based on that of the small songbird.

**Wynne** Feminine equivalent of the masculine WYNN and thus variously based on the Welsh *wyn* ('white' or 'blessed') or else on an Old English surname meaning 'friend'.

**Wynona** See WINONA.

# GIRLS' NAMES

**Xandra** ('zandra') Greek name meaning 'protective'. Also found as **Zandra**.

**Xanthe** ('zanthee') Greek name from *xanthos* ('golden' or 'yellow'). It appears several times as the name of minor characters in Greek mythology.

**Xara** *See* ZARA.

**Xaverine** *See* XAVIA.

**Xavia** ('zayveea' or 'zavveea') Feminine equivalent of the masculine XAVIER, from the Arabic word for 'bright' or 'shining', or else from the Basque for 'new house'. Variants include **Xaviera** and **Xaverine**.

**Xaviera** *See* XAVIA.

**Xena** *See* XENIA.

**Xenia** ('zeenya') English name from the Greek *xenia* ('hospitable'). Sometimes encountered as **Xena**, **Zenia** or **Zina**. *See also* ZENA.

**Ximena** ('zimeena') Greek name meaning 'from the woods'. **Xyline** and **Xylona** are variants.

**Xyline/Xylona** *See* XIMENA.

## GIRLS' NAMES

**Yalinda** *See* YOLANDA.

**Yana** Slavic name meaning 'lovely'. Also found as **Yanah** or **Yanny**.

**Yanah** *See* YANA.

**Yannette** English name that probably developed as a variant of ANNETTE.

**Yanny** *See* YANA.

**Yasmin/Yasmina/ Yasmine** *See* JASMINE.

**Yelena** Russian name meaning 'friendly'.

**Yola** *See* YOLANDA.

**Yolanda** French name of Germanic origin, from the Greek for 'violet flower'. Alternatively, it may have developed from VIOLA. Also found as **Yolande**, **Yolette**, **Jolanda**, **Jolana** or **Yalinda**. **Jola** and **Yola** are shortened forms. *See also* IOLANTHE.

**Yolande/Yolette** *See* YOLANDA.

**Ysabel** *See* ISABEL.

**Ysanne** ('eezan') English name possibly resulting from the combination of ISABEL and ANNE.

**Yseult/Ysolde** *See* ISOLDE.

**Yvette** ('eevet') English name of French origin that probably developed out of the older YVONNE.

**Yvonne** ('eevon') English name of French origin that was originally taken up as a feminine equivalent of YVES, itself from the Old Norse *yr* ('yew'). Variants include **Evonne**. An informal version is **Vonnie**. *See also* YVETTE.

# GIRLS' NAMES

**Zabrina** *See* SABRINA.

**Zandra** *See* ALEXANDRA; SANDRA; XANDRA.

**Zara** Arabic name meaning 'flower', also in use as a variant of SARAH. Also found as **Xara**.

**Zavanna** *See* SAVANNA.

**Zaynab** Arabic name possibly based on that of a flower. It was borne by one of the daughters of the prophet Muhammad.

**Zelda** English name possibly from the Yiddish for 'happiness' but otherwise a shortened form of the Germanic GRISELDA.

**Zelie** French name meaning 'ardent'.

**Zelma** *See* SELMA.

**Zena** Persian name meaning 'woman'. Also found as **Zina**, it may have developed as a familiar form of **Zinaida**, but is also found as a variant of Rosina or XENIA.

**Zenia** *See* XENIA.

**Zenobia** Greek name meaning 'power of Zeus' or 'life from Zeus'. Since the sixteenth century it has been particularly associated with Cornwall and south-western Britain.

**Zeta** *See* ZITA.

**Zilla** *See* ZILLAH.

**Zillah** Hebrew name meaning 'shade' or 'shadow'. Appearing in the Bible as **Zilla**, it remains a traditional choice of name among Romany families.

**Zilpah** Hebrew name meaning 'sprinkling'. It appears in the Old Testament as the name of Leah's maid. **Zilpha** is a variant form.

**Zilpha** *See* ZILPAH.

**Zina** *See* XENIA; ZENA.

**Zinaida** *See* ZENA.

**Zinnia** English flower name that appears to have been first taken up as a first name in the twentieth century.

**Zipporah** Jewish name meaning 'bird'. It appears in the Bible as the name of the wife of Moses.

**Zita** ('zeeta') English and Italian name derived from the medieval Tuscan *zita* ('little girl'). Also found as **Zeta**, as in the case of Welsh film actress Catherine Zeta Jones (b. 1969).

**Zoe** ('zoey') Greek name meaning 'life'. It became popular after it appeared in Greek translations of the Bible as the nearest equivalent to the Hebrew EVE. Variant forms include **Zoë** and **Zoey**.

**Zoë/Zoey** *See* ZOE.

**Zola** English name based on an Italian surname or else a variant of ZOE. Notable bearers of the name in modern times have included South African runner Zola Budd (b. 1966).

**Zora** Arabic name meaning 'dawn'. Also found as **Zorah**.

**Zorah** *See* ZORA.

**Zuleika** ('zooleeka'/ 'zoolika') Persian name meaning 'brilliant beauty'. It is well-known from the Max Beerbohm novel *Zuleika Dobson* (1911) about a young woman whose beauty drives her lovers to kill themselves.

# BOYS

# BOYS' NAMES

**Aaron** Biblical name of obscure origin, possibly Egyptian or else descended from the Hebrew Aharon, variously interpreted as meaning 'bright' or 'high mountain'. It appears in the Bible as the name of the brother of Moses. Also encountered as **Arn**.

**Ab** *See* ABNER.

**Abbot** English name meaning 'father of the abbey'. Also found as **Abbott**.

**Abbott** *See* ABBOT.

**Abdul** *See* ABDULLAH.

**Abdullah** Arabic name meaning 'servant of Allah'. It

has special significance in the Islamic world as the name of Muhammad's father. Shortened to **Abdul**.

**Abe** *See* ABEL; ABNER; ABRAHAM.

**Abel** Biblical name that may have evolved from the Hebrew Hebel, itself based on *hevel* ('breath' or 'vapour'), or from the Assyrian for 'son'. It appears in the Bible as the name of Adam and Eve's younger son. Shortened to **Abe**.

**Abner** Biblical name based on the Hebrew for 'father of light'. It appears in the Bible as the name of Saul's cousin. Shortened to **Ab** or **Abe**.

**Abraham** Biblical name based on the Hebrew *av hamon* ('father of a multitude' or 'father of many nations'). It appears in the Bible as the name of the father of the Hebrew nation. **Abram** is a variant. Shortened to **Abe**, **Ham** or **Bram**.

**Abram** *See* ABRAHAM.

**Absalom** Biblical name

based on the Hebrew Abshalom, meaning 'father of peace'. It appears in the Bible as the name of King David's favourite son. *See also* AXEL.

**Achille** *See* ACHILLES.

**Achilles** Greek name supposedly based on the Greek *a-* ('without') and *kheilea* ('lips'), thus meaning 'lipless', or else based on the name of the River Akheloos. It was borne in Greek mythology by the hero Achilles, whose name reflected the tradition that he was never suckled. Also found as **Achille**.

**Acke** *See* AXEL.

**Adair** Irish name meaning 'dweller by the oak wood'. A reference to the druids who attended sacred oaks in Celtic folklore, it also appears in Scotland as a variant of EDGAR.

**Adam** Biblical name based on the Hebrew *adama* ('earth') and meaning 'human being' or 'man'. It may be linked to the Hebrew for 'red' (a reference to the colour of human skin or to the red clay from which God fashioned the first man).

Variants include the Scottish **Adie** and the Irish **Adamnan**, which means 'little Adam'.

**Adamnan** *See* ADAM.

**Adan** *See* AIDAN.

**Addie/Ade** *See* ADRIAN.

**Aden** *See* AIDAN.

**Adie** *See* ADAM; ADRIAN; AIDAN.

**Adlai** Biblical name descended via Aramaic from the Hebrew Adaliah, meaning 'God is just' or alternatively 'my ornament'. It appears in the Bible and was taken up by English speakers in the nineteenth century.

**Adolf** *See* ADOLPH.

**Adolph** German name descended from the Old German Adalwolf, itself from the Old German *adal* ('noble') and *wolf* ('wolf'). It replaced the Old English equivalent Aethulwulf but was dropped when it became identified with the German Nazi dictator Adolf Hitler (1889–1945) –

**Adolf** being the modern German form of the name.

**Adonis** Greek name based on the Phoenician *adon* ('lord'). It appears in Greek mythology as the name of a beautiful youth who captivated Aphrodite.

**Adrian** English name descended from the Roman **Hadrian**, itself from the Latin for 'man of Adria' (a reference to a town in northern Italy). **Ade**, **Addie** and **Adie** are shortened forms of the name.

**Aed** ('aigh') Scottish and Irish name meaning 'fiery one'. It was borne by several early Irish kings.

**Aelwyn** Welsh name meaning 'fair-browed'.

**Ahmad** *See* AHMED.

**Ahmed** Arabic name based on the Arabic *hamida* ('to praise') and thus meaning 'more praiseworthy'. Also encountered as **Ahmad** or **Ahmet**.

**Ahmet** *See* AHMED.

**Aidan** English version of the Irish Aodan, itself a variant of **Aodh** (the name of a Celtic sun god, meaning 'fire'). The anglicized form succeeded the Irish form in Ireland early in the twentieth century. Occasionally also encountered as **Adan**, **Aden** or **Edan**. **Adie** is an informal version. *See also* HAYDN.

**Ailean** *See* ALAN.

**Ainslee** *See* AINSLEY.

**Ainsley** English name that originated as a place name (common to Nottinghamshire and Warwickshire) based on the Old English *an* ('one') and *leah* ('clearing' or 'wood') and meaning 'lonely clearing' or 'my meadow'. Occasionally spelled **Ainslee** or **Ainslie**.

**Ainslie** *See* AINSLEY.

**Ajay** Indian name based on the Sanskrit for 'unconquerable'.

**Akash** Indian name based on the Sanskrit for 'sky'.

**Al** Shortened form of such names as ALAN, ALASTAIR, ALBERT, ALEXANDER, ALFRED and ALVIN. Famous bearers of the name have included US singer and film actor Al Jolson (Asa Yoelson; 1886–1950) and US film actor Al Pacino (b. 1939).

**Alain** *See* ALAN.

**Alan** English and Scottish name of Celtic origin, supposedly from the Celtic *alun* ('concord' or 'harmony') or otherwise interpreted as meaning 'rock'. It was introduced to England by the Normans in the eleventh century. Variants include **Allan**, **Allen**, the French **Alain**, the Welsh **Alun** and the Scottish Gaelic **Ailean**. Shortened to AL.

**Alasdair** *See* ALASTAIR.

**Alastair** English name modelled on the Scottish Gaelic **Alasdair**, itself a variant of ALEXANDER. Having established itself among the Scots, it began to appear more widely among English speakers during the nineteenth century. Also encountered as **Alistair** or **Alister**. Shortened to **Aly**.

**Alban** English name possibly based on the Roman place name Alba Longa (a district of Rome), itself from the Latin *albus* ('white'), or else on the Celtic *alp* ('rock' or 'crag'), and interpreted as meaning 'white hill'. Also found as **Albany** or **Albin**. Shortened to **Albie** or **Alby**.

**Albany** *See* ALBAN.

**Albert** English and French name based on the Old German Adalbert, itself from the Old German *adal* ('noble') and *beraht* ('bright' or 'famous') and thus meaning 'nobly famous'. It was promoted through Queen Victoria's German-born husband Prince Albert of Saxe-Coburg and Gotha (1819–61). Shortened to AL or BERT (or BERTIE).

**Albie/Albin/Alby** *See* ALBAN.

**Alden** English name that originated as a surname meaning 'trustworthy friend'.

**Aldis** English name that originated as a surname meaning 'old house'.

**Aldo** *See* ALDOUS.

**Aldous** English name apparently based on the Old German **Aldo**, itself from the Old German *ald* ('old'). It was a fairly frequent choice in eastern England during the thirteenth century. Famous bearers of the name have included British novelist Aldous Huxley (1894–1963). **Aldus** is a variant.

**Aldus** *See* ALDOUS.

**Alec** English name that developed as a shortened form of ALEXANDER. It proved especially popular in Scotland but has become less frequent in recent years, in part due to the rise of ALEX. Variants include **Alic**, **Alick** and **Aleck**. Shortened to **Lec**.

**Aleck** *See* ALEC.

**Aled** Welsh name meaning 'offspring'. It enjoyed considerable exposure outside Wales from the 1980s through Welsh singer Aled Jones (b. 1971).

**Alex** English name that developed as a shortened form of ALEXANDER. It appears to have been an early twentieth-century introduction. Also encountered as **Alix**. LEX and **Lexie** are familiar forms of the name. *See also* ALEC.

**Alexander** Greek name based on the Greek *alexein* ('to defend') and *aner* ('man') and thus meaning 'defender of men'. Famous as the name of the Alexander the Great, King of Macedon (356–323 BC), it proved especially popular in Scotland. Shortened forms include ALEC, ALEX, **Sandy**, SASHA; **Xan** and **Xander**. *See also* ALASTAIR.

**Alexis** English and Russian name descended from the Greek Alexios, itself like ALEXANDER based on the Greek *alexein* ('to defend'). Shortened to **Lexie** or **Lexy**.

**Alf** *See* ALFRED.

**Alfa** *See* ALPHA.

**Alfie** *See* ALFRED.

**Alfonso** *See* ALPHONSE.

**Alfred** English name descended from the Old English Aelfraed, itself based on the Old English *aelf* ('elf') and

*raed* ('counsel') and meaning
'inspired advice'. Another
derivation links it with the Old
English Ealdfrith, meaning 'old
peace'. It became widely
known through Alfred the
Great, King of Wessex
(849–99). Shortened to AL, **Alf**,
**Alfie** or FRED. *See also* AVERY.

**Algar** *See* ALGER.

**Alger** ('aljer') English name
descended ultimately from the
Old English Aelfgar, itself from
the Old English *aelf* ('elf') and
*gar* ('spear'). As **Algar**, it was
fairly common during the
medieval period. Alger Hiss
(1904–96) was a US
government official accused of
being a Soviet spy.

**Algernon** English name
based on the Norman French
*als gernons* ('with whiskers'). It
was employed originally as a
nickname for anyone with a
moustache or whiskers.
Shortened to **Algie** or **Algy**.

**Algie/Algy** *See* ALGERNON.

**Ali** Arabic name meaning
'elevated' or 'sublime'. As the
name of Muhammad's cousin
and the first Islamic convert, it

is a traditional favourite
throughout the Islamic world.

**Alic/Alick** *See* ALEC.

**Alistair/Alister** *See*
ALASTAIR.

**Alix** *See* ALEX.

**Allan/Allen** *See* ALAN.

**Alonso/Alonzo** *See*
ALPHONSE.

**Aloysius** ('alohwishus')
English, German, French and
Dutch name representing a
fanciful Latinized variant of
LOUIS. It was in common
currency in medieval Italy and
subsequently became a
favourite choice among
Roman Catholics.

**Alpha** English name based on
the first letter of the Greek
alphabet and thus suggesting
excellence or prime
importance. Its use as a first
name in the English-speaking
world goes back to the
nineteenth century. Also
spelled **Alfa**.

**Alphonse** French name
based on the Old German *adal*

('noble') and *funs* ('ready' or 'prompt'), or else *ala* ('all') and *hadu* ('struggle') or *hild* ('battle'). Variants include the Spanish **Alfonso** or **Alonso** (or **Alonzo**). **Fonsie** and **Fonzie** are informal versions.

**Alun** *See* ALAN.

**Alva** English name based on the Hebrew Alvah, meaning 'height' or 'exalted'. Famous bearers of the name have included US scientist and inventor Thomas Alva Edison (1847–1931). Also found as **Alvah**.

**Alvah** *See* ALVA.

**Alvar** English name descended from the Old English Aelfhere, itself based on *aelf* ('elf') and *here* ('army' or 'warrior'), but also occasionally encountered in use as an anglicized form of the Spanish Alvaro. Records of its use among English speakers go back to the Norman Conquest.

**Alvie** *See* ALVIN.

**Alvin** English name descended from the Old English Aelfwine, itself based

on the Old English *aelf* ('elf') and *wine* ('friend') and thus meaning 'elf friend'. **Alwyn** and **Aylwin** are variant forms. Shortened to AL or **Alvie**.

**Alwyn** *See* ALVIN.

**Aly** *See* ALASTAIR.

**Ambrose** English name descended from the Roman Ambrosius, itself from the Greek *ambrosios* ('immortal' or 'divine'). It has been in regular use among English speakers since at least the eleventh century, particularly among Irish Roman Catholics. *See also* EMRYS.

**Amery** *See* AMORY.

**Amias** *See* AMYAS.

**Amory** English name of Germanic origin meaning 'famous ruler'. Also spelled **Amery**, **Emery** or **Emmery**.

**Amos** Hebrew name possibly meaning 'borne' or 'carried' and usually interpreted as meaning 'borne by God'. Another derivation suggests it comes from the Hebrew for 'strong' or 'courageous'. It appears in the Bible as the name of an Old Testament prophet.

**Amyas** English name descended either from the Roman Amatus, from the Latin for 'loved', or alternatively from a French surname meaning 'person from Amiens'. It has made occasional appearances among English speakers since the sixteenth century. Also spelled **Amias**.

**Anatole** French name descended from the Roman Anatolius, itself based on the Greek *anatole* ('sunrise' or 'east'). It was a popular choice among early Christians.

**Anders** *See* ANDREW.

**Anderson** English name that originated as a surname meaning 'son of Andrew'.

**Andi/Andie/André** *See* ANDREW.

**Andrew** English, Russian and Greek name descended from the Greek Andreas, itself from the Greek *andreia* ('manliness') and thus meaning 'manly' or 'brave'. It appears in the Bible as the name of one of the apostles. Variants include the French **André** and the Scandinavian **Anders**. Shortened to **Andy**, **Andie**, **Andi**, **Randi** (or **Randy**) or the Scottish DREW. *See also* DANDY.

**Andy** *See* ANDREW.

**Aneirin** *See* ANEURIN.

**Aneurin** ('anighrin') Welsh name of obscure origin, possibly based on the Welsh *an* ('all') and *eur* ('gold') and interpreted as 'precious one'. Attempts have also been made to trace it back to the Roman Honorius, meaning 'honourable'. It was in use in Wales by the medieval period. Also spelled **Aneirin**. Shortened to **Nye**.

**Angel** English name descended via Latin from the Greek *angelos* ('messenger') and meaning 'messenger of God' or simply 'angel'. Famous bearers of the name have included Angel Clare in the Thomas Hardy novel *Tess of the D'Urbervilles* (1891). **Angelo** is an Italian and Spanish variant.

**Angelo** *See* ANGEL.

**Angus** English version of the Scottish Gaelic Aonghas (or Aonghus), itself based on the Gaelic *aon* ('one') and *ghus* ('choice') and thus meaning 'sole choice'. The name's history in Scotland goes back to at least the fifteenth century. Shortened to GUS.

**Ansel/Ansell** *See* ANSELM.

**Anselm** English name descended from the Old German Anshelm, itself from the Old German *ans* ('god') and *helm* ('helmet') and thus meaning 'protected by God'. It has made occasional appearances among English Roman Catholics over the centuries. **Ansel** and **Ansell** are variants.

**Anson** English name that originated as a surname meaning 'son of Agnes' or 'son of Anne'.

**Anthony** English name descended from the Roman Antonius, popularly linked with the Greek *anthos* ('flower') but possibly of Etruscan origin. It was borne by several early saints and was in use among English speakers by the twelfth century. Also found as **Antony**, in the Italian form **Antonio** or in the German and Russian form **Anton**. Shortened to **Tony**.

**Anton/Antonio/ Antony** *See* ANTHONY.

**Aodh** *See* AIDAN; EGAN; EUGENE; HUGH; IAGAN; MADOC.

**Archer** English name that originated as a surname meaning 'bowman'.

**Archibald** English name that evolved from the Norman French Archambault, itself from the Old German *ercan* ('genuine') and *bald* ('bold') and thus interpreted as 'truly brave'. In Scotland it may be considered an anglicized form of GILLESPIE. Shortened to **Archie** (or **Archy**) or **Baldie**.

**Archie/Archy** *See* ARCHIBALD.

**Ardal** Irish name meaning 'high valour'.

**Ardan** Irish name based on the Irish Gaelic word for 'pride'. It appears in Irish mythology as the name of the brother of Deirdre's lover Naoise.

**Arden** English name that originated in a place name variously meaning 'dwelling place' or 'gravel'.

**Ariel** Jewish name based on the Hebrew for 'lion of God'. It appears in the Bible but is more famous today as the name of the sprite in William Shakespeare's last play, *The Tempest* (1611).

**Arlan** Cornish name that may have evolved out of Allen or Elwin. It was borne by a saint in early Cornish legend.

**Arlo** Spanish name meaning 'barberry tree'. Sometimes encountered as a variant of CHARLES. Notable bearers of the name have included US folk singer Arlo Guthrie (b. 1947).

**Armani** English name that probably developed out of the German Herman. It is popularly associated with

Italian fashion designer Giorgio Armani (b. 1934).

**Armstrong** English name that originated as a surname meaning 'strong in the arm'.

**Arn** *See* AARON; ARNOLD.

**Arnie** *See* ARNOLD.

**Arnold** English and German name descended from the Old German Arinwalt, itself from the Old German *arn* ('eagle') and *wald* ('ruler') and thus meaning 'eagle ruler'. It was brought to England by the Normans. Shortened to **Arn** or **Arnie**.

**Art** English name that evolved as a shortened form of ARTHUR. It has become particularly associated with the jazz world, being borne by pianist Art Tatum (1909–56) and saxophonist Art Pepper (1925–82) among others.

**Artair** *See* ARTHUR.

**Artemus** Greek name that is thought to have evolved from the feminine Artemis, the name of the Greek goddess of the moon and the hunt. It appears in the New Testament and was taken up by English Puritans in the seventeenth century.

**Arthur** English name of obscure Celtic origin, possibly based on the Celtic *artos* ('bear') or the Irish *art* ('stone') or else descended from the Roman clan name Artorius. It is famous as the name of the legendary English King Arthur. Variants include the Scottish Gaelic **Artair**. Shortened to ART.

**Asa** Jewish name based on the Hebrew for 'healer' or 'doctor'. It appears in the Bible as the name of a king of Judah.

**Ash** See ASHLEY; ASHTON.

**Asher** Jewish name based on the Hebrew for 'fortunate' or 'happy'. It appears in the Bible as the name of one of Jacob's sons.

**Ashley** English name that originated as a place name based on the Old English *aesc* ('ash') and *leah* ('clearing' or 'wood'). It enjoyed a considerable boost following the success of the film *Gone*

*with the Wind* (1939), based on the novel by Margaret Mitchell, in which the name appears. Shortened to **Ash**.

**Ashton** English name that originated as a place name meaning 'ash tree town'. Shortened to **Ash**.

**Athelstan** English name descended from the Old English Aethelstan, itself based on the Old English *aethel* ('noble') and *stan* ('stone') and thus meaning 'nobly strong'.

**Aub** See AUBREY.

**Auberon** English name of obscure origin, possibly a variant of AUBREY. It is sometimes associated with **Oberon**, the name borne by the king of the fairies in Shakespeare's *A Midsummer Night's Dream* (1595–6). Shortened to **Bron**.

**Aubrey** English and French name descended from the Old German Alberic, itself from the Old German *alb* ('elf') and *richi* ('riches' or 'power') and thus meaning 'elf ruler' or 'supernaturally powerful'.

Shortened to **Aub**. *See also*
AUBERON.

**Augie** *See* AUGUSTUS.

**Augustine** English name
descended from the Roman
Augustinus, a variant of
AUGUSTUS. Famous as the
name of St Augustine of Hippo
(354–430) and of St Augustine
(d. 604), the first Archbishop of
Canterbury. Shortened to GUS
or **Gussie**. *See also* AUSTIN.

**Augustus** Roman name
based on the Latin *augustus*
('august', 'great' or
'magnificent'). It was first
adopted as a title by the
Roman Emperor Octavian in
27 BC and was later introduced
to Britain from Germany at the
time of the accession of the
Hanoverian George I.
Shortened to GUS, **Gussie** or
**Augie**. *See also* AUGUSTINE;
AUSTIN.

**Aulay** *See* OLAF.

**Austen** *See* AUSTIN.

**Austin** English name that
evolved as a variant of
AUGUSTINE. It was taken up
by English speakers in the

medieval period. Also
encountered as **Austen**.

**Avery** English name that
evolved from ALFRED in
medieval times.

**Avice** *See* AVIS.

**Avis** English name possibly
related to the German Hedwig
(meaning 'struggle') or else
based on the Latin *avis* ('bird').
Also found as **Avice**.

**Axel** Scandinavian variant of
ABSALOM that has also been in
occasional use among English
speakers – chiefly in the USA,
where it was introduced by
Scandinavian immigrants. **Acke**
is a familiar form of the name.

**Aylmer** English name
descended from the Old
English Aethelmaer, itself based
on the Old English *aethel*
('noble') and *maere* ('famous')
and thus meaning 'nobly
famous'. The Old English form
of the name was in use before
the Norman Conquest. *See also*
ELMER.

**Aylwin** *See* ALVIN.

**Azaria** Biblical name

descended from the Hebrew Azaryah, meaning 'helped by God'. It appears in the Bible and has consequently been in occasional use as a first name among English speakers since the seventeenth century. Also spelled **Azariah**.

**Azariah** *See* AZARIA.

## BOYS' NAMES

**Baileigh** *See* BAILEY.

**Bailey** English name variously meaning 'berry clearing', 'bailiff' or 'town fortification'. Also found as **Baileigh** or **Bayleigh**.

**Baird** Scottish name that originated as a surname meaning 'minstrel' or 'bard'. Also found as **Bard**.

**Baldie** *See* ARCHIBALD.

**Baldric** English name based on the Old German *balda* ('bold') and *ricja* ('rule'). It came to England with the Normans in the eleventh century. Also found as **Baldrick**.

**Baldrick** *See* BALDRIC.

**Baldwin** English name based on the Old German *bald* ('bold' or 'brave') and *wine* ('friend') and thus meaning 'brave friend'. It was introduced as a first name from Flanders around the twelfth century. Variants include the Welsh MALDWYN.

**Balfour** Scottish name that originated as a place name meaning 'village with pasture'.

**Balthasar** *See* BALTHAZAR.

**Balthazar** English version of the biblical Belshazzar, which was itself based on the Babylonian Belsharrausur (meaning 'Baal protect the king'). The name appears in the Bible as that of one of the Three Wise Men. Also encountered as **Balthasar**.

**Baptist** English name based ultimately on the Greek *baptistēs* ('baptist'). Because of its biblical associations with John the Baptist the name has a long history in the Christian world. Also found as **Baptiste**.

**Baptiste** *See* BAPTIST.

**Barack** African name descended from the Hebrew **Baruch**, the meaning of which is 'blessed'. It came to public attention in 2008 with the election of Barack Obama (b. 1961) as US president.

**Barclay** *See* BERKELEY.

**Bard** *See* BAIRD.

**Barnabas** English name based ultimately on the Aramaic for 'son of consolation'. It appears in the Bible as the name of one of St Paul's companions and was taken up by English speakers during the medieval period. It was eventually eclipsed by BARNABY. **Barney** (or **Barny**) is a shortened form.

**Barnaby** English name that developed as a variant of BARNABAS and established itself as the dominant form of the name in the nineteenth century. Often shortened to **Barney**.

**Barnard** *See* BERNARD.

**Barney** *See* BARNABAS; BARNABY.

**Barny** *See* BARNABAS.

**Baron** English name that originated as a surname based on the Old German *baro* ('free man'). Also found as **Barron**.

**Barr** Scottish name meaning 'crest' or 'supreme'.

**Barratt** *See* BARRETT.

**Barrett** English name that originated as a surname based either on the Old German *bera* ('bear') and *wald* ('rule') or Middle English *baret* ('dispute'). Also found as **Barratt**.

**Barrie** *See* BARRY.

**Barron** *See* BARON.

**Barry** English name based either upon the Gaelic *bearach* ('spear') or else upon the Irish Barra, a shortened form of Fionnbarr (*see* FINBAR). The variant form **Barrie** did not emerge until the 1920s. **Bas**, **Baz** and **Bazza** are informal versions of the name.

**Bart** *See* BARTHOLOMEW.

**Bartholomew** Biblical name based on the Aramaic for

'son of Talmai' (Talmai meaning 'abounding in furrows'). It appears in the New Testament as a name borne by one of the apostles (possibly Nathaniel). Shortened to **Bart** or **Barty** and less commonly to **Bat** or **Tolly**.

**Bartram** See BERTRAM.

**Barty** See BARTHOLOMEW.

**Baruch** See BARACK.

**Bas** See BARRY; BASIL.

**Basil** English name based on the Greek *basileus* ('king') and thus meaning 'royal'. It made occasional appearances among English speakers in medieval times, having been imported with returning Crusaders. Shortened to **Bas** (or **Baz**).

**Bastian** See SEBASTIAN.

**Bat** See BARTHOLOMEW.

**Baxter** English name that originated as a surname based on the Old English for 'baker'.

**Bayleigh** See BAILEY.

**Baz** See BARRY; BASIL; SEBASTIAN.

**Bazza** See BARRY; SEBASTIAN.

**Beau** English name based on the French *beau* ('handsome'). Notable bearers of the name in recent times have included US film actor Beau Bridges (b. 1941).

**Beavis** See BEVIS.

**Bellamy** English name that originated as a surname based on the Old French for 'handsome friend'.

**Ben** English name that developed as a shortened form of BENEDICT or BENJAMIN. Records of this shortened form go back as far as the medieval period.

**Benedick** See BENEDICT.

**Benedict** English name based on the Latin *benedictus* ('blessed'). Borne by the sixth-century St Benedict who founded the Benedictine order of monks, it became a popular choice among English Roman Catholics. Variants include

**Benedick** and **Bennet** (or
**Bennett**). Shortened to BEN.
*See also* BENITO.

**Benito** Italian and Spanish
equivalent of BENEDICT. It is
perhaps best known as the
name of Italian dictator Benito
Mussolini (1883–1945).

**Benjamin** English name
based on a Hebrew name
variously interpreted as
meaning 'son of the right
hand', 'son of the south' or
'son of my old age' but often
interpreted as meaning
'favourite'. It appears in the
Bible as the name of the
youngest of the sons of Jacob
and Rachel. Shortened to BEN,
BENNY or **Benjie**, **Benji** (or
**Benjy**).

**Benji/Benjie/Benjy** *See*
BENJAMIN.

**Bennet/Bennett** *See*
BENEDICT.

**Bennie** *See* BENNY.

**Benny** English name that
developed as a shortened form
of BENJAMIN. Also encountered
as **Bennie**. *See also* BEN.

**Benson** English name that
originated as a surname
meaning 'son of Ben'.

**Bentley** English name that
originated as a place name
(occurring in several counties
of England) based on the Old
English *beonet* ('bent grass') and
*leah* ('wood' or 'clearing') and
thus interpreted as meaning
'place of coarse grass'.

**Beppe** ('beppay' or 'beppee')
Informal version of the Italian
GIUSEPPE, itself an equivalent
of JOSEPH. **Beppo** is a variant.

**Beppo** *See* BEPPE.

**Berkeley** ('barklee' or
'burklee') English name that
originated as a place name
(from Gloucestershire) based
on the Old English *beorc*
('birch') and *leah* ('wood').
Variants of the name include
**Barclay** and **Berkley**.

**Berkley** *See* BERKELEY.

**Bernard** English and French
name based either upon the
Old English *beorn* ('man' or
'warrior') and *heard* ('brave'), or
else upon the Old German *ber*
('bear') and *hart* ('bold') and

thus meaning 'brave as a bear'.
Also encountered as **Barnard**.
Commonly abbreviated to
**Bernie** and, less frequently, to
**Bunny**.

**Bernie** *See* BERNARD.

**Bert** English name that
developed as a shortened form
of such names as ALBERT,
BERTRAM, CUTHBERT and
HERBERT. Also encountered as
**Burt**. *See also* BERTIE.

**Bertie** English name that
developed as a shortened form
of such names as ALBERT and
BERTRAM (*see also* BERT). It
was in regular use until the
1940s, since when it has largely
fallen out of favour.

**Bertram** English name based
on the Old German *beraht*
('bright' or 'famous') and *hramn*
('raven') and thus meaning
'famous raven' or – because
ravens were symbols of wisdom
in Germanic mythology – 'wise
person'. Variants include
**Bartram** and **Bertrand**,
although this can also be traced
back to the Old German for
'bright shield'.

**Bertrand** *See* BERTRAM.

**Beuno** ('bighnoh') Welsh
name of obscure meaning. It
was borne by a seventh-
century Welsh saint.

**Bev** *See* BEVAN; BEVERLEY.

**Bevan** Welsh name based on
the Welsh *ap Evan* ('son of
Evan'). Commonly abbreviated
to **Bev**.

**Beverley** English name that
originated as a place name
(from Humberside) based on
the Old English *beofor* ('beaver')
and *leac* ('stream'). It has
become rare since the 1950s.
Commonly abbreviated to
**Bev**.

**Bevis** English name possibly
based on the French *beau fils*
('handsome son'), or else on
the French place name
Beauvais. The name came to
England with the Normans.
Variants include **Beavis**.

**Bijay** *See* VIJAY.

**Bill/Billy** *See* WILLIAM.

**Bing** English name of obscure
origin. It may have been
adopted originally as an
abbreviated form of **Bingo**, the

name of a well-known cartoon character, and subsequently enjoyed a boost through US singer and film actor Bing Crosby (Harry Lillis Crosby; 1901–77).

**Bingo** *See* BING.

**Birch** English name that originated as a surname based on the name of the birch tree, but also sometimes interpreted as meaning 'bright' or 'shining'. Birk is a variant.

**Birk** *See* BIRCH.

**Bjarne** *See* BJÖRN.

**Björn** Swedish name based on the Old Norse for 'bear'. Also found as **Bjørn** or **Bjarne**.

**Black** English name based on the ordinary vocabulary word 'black' and usually reserved for boys with dark hair or complexion.

**Blaine** Scottish name of obscure origin that has been in occasional use among English speakers since the early twentieth century. It would appear to be a modern

reworking of the much older **Blane**.

**Blair** Scottish name that originated as a place name based on the Gaelic *blar* ('field' or 'plain'). It has enjoyed a modest revival since the middle of the twentieth century, chiefly in Canada and the USA.

**Blaise** English and French name descended from the Roman Blasius, itself from the Latin *blaesus* ('lisping' or 'stammering'). Also encountered as **Blase** or **Blaze**.

**Blake** English name based either on the Old English *blaec* ('black') or conversely *blac* ('pale' or 'white').

**Blane** *See* BLAINE.

**Blase/Blaze** *See* BLAISE.

**Bligh** English name based on the Old English for 'bliss'. Also found as BLY.

**Bly** English name based on a surname of Irish Gaelic or Old Norse origin, usually interpreted as meaning 'descendant of Blighe'. *See also* BLIGH.

**Bo** English and Scandinavian name, variously considered a shortened form of ROBERT and other names.

**Boas** *See* BOAZ.

**Boaz** Hebrew name of uncertain origin, possibly meaning 'swiftness' or perhaps 'man of strength'. It appears in the Bible as the name of Ruth's husband. Also spelled **Boas**.

**Bob** English name that developed as a shortened form of ROBERT. This form of the name was in use among English speakers by at least the early eighteenth century. *See also* BOBBY.

**Bobby** English name that developed as a shortened form of ROBERT. Sometimes encountered in combination with other names, as in **Bobby Joe**. *See also* BOB.

**Bonar** English name based on the Old French for 'courteous'.

**Boniface** English name based ultimately on the Latin *bonum* ('good') and *fatum* ('fate') or alternatively *bonum* ('good') and *facere* ('to do') and thus meaning either 'good fate' or 'well-doer'. **Bono** is an informal variant.

**Bono** *See* BONIFACE.

**Booth** English name that originated as a surname originally based on the Old Norse for 'hut' or 'shed'.

**Boris** Russian name based either on the Old Slavonic *bor* ('fight' or 'struggle') or more likely on the Tartar nickname Bogoris, meaning 'small'. It was taken up by English speakers in the nineteenth century.

**Bourn/Bourne** *See* BYRNE.

**Bowen** Welsh name that originated as a surname meaning 'son of Owen'.

**Boyce** English name based on the French *bois* ('wood'). It has made occasional appearances as a first name since the early twentieth century.

**Boyd** Scottish name based on the Gaelic *buidhe* ('yellow'). Its history as a first name among the Scots goes back several hundred years, having been reserved initially for people with blond hair (although another derivation suggests it evolved as a reference to people from the island of Bute).

**Brad** *See* BRADFORD; BRADLEY.

**Bradford** English name that originated as a place name (from northern England) based on the Old English *brad* ('broad') and *ford* ('ford'). Shortened to **Brad**.

**Bradley** English name that originated as a place name based on the Old English *brad* ('broad') and *leah* ('wood' or 'clearing'). Its modern use is largely confined to the USA. Shortened to **Brad** – as borne by US film actor Brad Pitt (b. 1965).

**Brady** Irish name possibly based ultimately on the Gaelic *bragha* ('chest' or 'throat'), and thus meaning 'large-chested'.

**Bram** *See* ABRAHAM.

**Bramwell** English name that originated as a place name (from Derbyshire) meaning 'place of brambles'. Variants include **Branwell** – as borne by Patrick Branwell Brontë (1817–48), the artist brother of the celebrated Brontë sisters.

**Bran** Celtic name meaning 'crow' or 'raven' and originally the name of a Celtic god. It is also in use as a shortened form of BRANDON.

**Brand** English name based on the ordinary vocabulary word 'firebrand'.

**Brandan** *See* BRENDAN.

**Brandon** English name that originated as a place name based on the Old English *brom* ('broom' or 'gorse') and *dun* ('hill'). It was taken up as a first name in the nineteenth century, chiefly in the USA, apparently under the influence of the Irish BRENDAN. Variants include **Branton**. Sometimes abbreviated to BRAN or **Brandy**.

**Brandy/Branton** *See* BRANDON.

**Branwell** *See* BRAMWELL.

**Breandan** *See* BRENDAN.

**Brendan** Irish name descended from the Gaelic Breanainn, meaning 'prince' – although alternative derivations suggest it means 'stinking hair' or 'dweller by the beacon'. It had become one of the top fifty names in Australia by the 1970s. Variants include **Brandan**, BRANDON and the Irish Gaelic **Breandan**.

**Brent** English name that originated as a place name (from Devon and Somerset) apparently based on the Old English word for 'hill'. Popular chiefly in Canada and the USA, it enjoyed a peak in popularity in the 1970s and 1980s.

**Bret** *See* BRETT.

**Brett** English name originally bestowed upon Breton settlers in medieval England that has been in increasing use as a first name since the middle of the twentieth century, chiefly in the USA. Also encountered as **Bret**.

**Bri** *See* BRIAN.

**Brian** English and Irish name based ultimately on the Irish Gaelic *brigh* ('strength' or 'power'). It appears in Irish mythology as the name of the tenth-century king Brian Boru but came to England with the Bretons who arrived with William the Conqueror. Also encountered as **Brien** or **Bryan**. Shortened to **Bri**.

**Brice** *See* BRYCE.

**Brick** English name that originated as a nickname for a strong person.

**Brien** *See* BRIAN.

**Brigham** English name that originated as a place name (from Cumbria and north Yorkshire) based on the Old English *brycg* ('bridge') and *ham* ('homestead'). In the USA the name is usually associated with the US Mormon leader Brigham Young (1801–77).

**Brin** *See* BRYN.

**Brock** English name that originated as a surname meaning 'badger-like'.

**Broderic** *See* BRODERICK.

**Broderick** English name meaning 'son of Roderick', probably influenced by RODERICK. Also found as **Broderic**.

**Brodie** Scottish name based on the Scots Gaelic for 'ditch'. Also encountered as **Brody**.

**Brody** *See* BRODIE.

**Bron** *See* AUBERON.

**Brook** English name based on the ordinary vocabulary word 'brook'. It was adopted initially by black Americans in the USA but has since made sporadic appearances throughout the English-speaking world.

**Brooklyn** English name based upon that of the Brooklyn district of New York City. It enjoyed a significant boost in 1999 when it was chosen by English footballer David Beckham and pop singer Victoria Beckham for their newborn son.

**Brough** ('bruff') English name that originated as a surname meaning 'dweller at the tower fortress'.

**Bruce** Scottish name that was originally imported as the Norman French baronial name de Brus, itself from an unidentified place name in northern France. The name has largely lost its uniquely Scottish character and today ranks among the most popular names in Australia. **Brucie** is an informal version of the name.

**Brucie** *See* BRUCE.

**Bruno** English and German name based on the Old German *brun* ('brown') and originally usually reserved for people with brown hair, brown eyes or a swarthy complexion.

**Bryan** *See* BRIAN.

**Bryce** English name of obscure Celtic origin. Also encountered as **Brice**.

**Bryn** Welsh name based on the Welsh *bryn* ('hill') but also

in use as a shortened form of
BRYNMOR. Also encountered
as **Brin**.

**Brynmor** Welsh name that
originated as a place name
(from Gwynedd) based on the
Welsh *bryn* ('hill') and *mawr*
('large'). Sometimes
abbreviated to BRYN.

**Buck** English name based on
the ordinary vocabulary word
'buck' (denoting a male deer or
rabbit) and thus suggesting a
lively, spirited young man. It
emerged as a popular choice of
name in the USA in the early
twentieth century.

**Bud** *See* BUDDY.

**Buddy** English name that
developed as a nickname
meaning 'friend' or 'pal',
possibly originally a variant of
'brother'. It has been in fairly
regular use in the USA since
the early twentieth century.
Shortened to **Bud**.

**Bunny** *See* BERNARD.

**Burl** English name based on
the Germanic for 'cup bearer'.
Confined chiefly to the USA,
it became well known through

US singer and actor Burl Ives
(1909–95).

**Burn/Burne** *See* BYRNE.

**Burt** *See* BERT.

**Buster** English name that
developed as a nickname,
presumably based on the verb
'bust' and thus suggesting a
person given to breaking or
smashing things. It was taken
up by English speakers in the
USA towards the end of the
nineteenth century. Famous
bearers of the name have
included US silent film
comedian Buster Keaton
(Joseph Francis Keaton;
1895–1966).

**Byrne** English name that
originated as a surname
meaning 'brook' or 'stream'.
Also found as **Bourn**, **Bourne**,
**Burn** or **Burne**.

**Byron** English name based
on the Old English *aet thaem
byrum* ('at the byres') that has
made rare appearances as a first
name in relatively recent times.
The name is usually associated
with the British poet Lord
Byron (George Gordon, 6th
Baron Byron; 1784–1824).

# BOYS' NAMES

**Cabbot** *See* CABOT.

**Cabot** English name of French origin, possibly meaning 'to sail'. Also found as **Cabbot**, it is sometimes bestowed in tribute to the Italian-born English explorer John Cabot (c. 1450–98).

**Cadan** Irish Gaelic name meaning 'wild goose'. It appeared in legend as the name of a mythical hero.

**Cade** English name based ultimately on a traditional nickname meaning 'round'. It enjoyed some popularity among English speakers after appearing in Margaret Mitchell's novel *Gone with the Wind* (1936).

**Cadel** *See* CADELL.

**Cadell** Welsh name based on the Old Welsh *cad* ('battle'). Also encountered as **Cadel**.

**Cadfael** ('cadfyle') Welsh name meaning 'battle metal'. It was popularized in the late twentieth century through the medieval mystery novels of Ellis Peters featuring the detective monk Brother Cadfael.

**Cadwalader** Welsh name derived from the Welsh *cad* ('battle') and *gwaladr* ('disposer') and thus interpreted as 'general' or 'commander'. Borne by a seventh-century saint who died fighting the Saxons and by several other Welsh kings and princes, it remains a uniquely Welsh name. Also spelled **Cadwallader** or **Cadwaladr**.

**Cadwaladr/ Cadwallader** *See* CADWALADER.

**Caerwyn** Welsh name based on *caer* ('fort') and *wyn* ('white'). Also spelled CARWYN.

**Caesar** Roman name

possibly based on the Latin *caesares* ('head of hair') or otherwise from *caedere* ('to cut'). It has made occasional appearances as a first name among English speakers since the eighteenth century. Variants include **Cesar**.

**Cahal** *See* CAROL; CATHAL.

**Cai** *See* CAIUS.

**Caius** Roman name based on the Latin for 'rejoice'. Shortened to **Cai**, although this form of the name can also be traced as a Welsh name (*see* KAY). Also found as **Gaius**.

**Cal** *See* CALUM; CALVIN; CATHAL.

**Calder** Scottish name that originated as a place name based on the Scots Gaelic for 'stream by the hazels'.

**Caldwell** Scottish name that originated as a surname meaning 'cold stream'.

**Cale** *See* CALEB.

**Caleb** Biblical name based on the Hebrew Kaleb, variously interpreted as meaning 'intrepid', 'bold' or 'dog' (suggesting a doglike devotion to God). It appears in the Bible as the name of one of Moses' companions. Shortened to **Cale**.

**Caley** *See* CALUM.

**Calhoun** Irish name that originated as a surname meaning 'from the forest'.

**Callan** Irish name descended from the Irish Gaelic Culann.

**Callum/Cally** *See* CALUM.

**Calum** Scottish name that developed from the Roman Columba, meaning 'dove'. Although it has a long history as a Scottish name, it has enjoyed increasing acceptance among English speakers since the middle of the twentieth century. Also spelled **Callum**. Shortened to **Cal**, **Cally** or **Caley**.

**Calvin** French name descended via the Old French *chauve* from the Latin *calvus* ('bald'), and thus meaning 'little bald one'. It was taken up in the sixteenth century in tribute to the French Protestant theologian Jean Calvin (1509–64) and became especially popular among Protestants in the USA. Shortened to **Cal**.

**Cameron** Scottish name based on the Gaelic *cam shron* ('crooked nose'). It has retained its strong Scottish connections, being well known as a clan name.

**Campbell** Scottish name based on the Gaelic *cam beul* ('crooked mouth') that has been in occasional use over the centuries, chiefly in Scotland. It is best known as the surname of one of the Scottish clans, historically the sworn enemies of the MacDonalds.

**Caradoc** Welsh name based on the Welsh *car* ('love') and thus meaning 'amiable'. As Caradog or Caractacus, it was borne by a famous first-century British chieftain who led the resistance against the Romans. It has been in irregular use among the Welsh since the medieval period.

**Cardew** English name based on the Welsh for 'black fort'.

**Carey** English name that developed as a variant of CARY in the nineteenth century. In Irish use it may have evolved from the Gaelic O Ciardha ('descendant of the dark one'). The Welsh may trace it back to the place name Carew.

**Carl** English name based on the Old English *ceorl* ('man'), or otherwise encountered as a shortened form of CARLTON. It was taken up by English speakers around the middle of the nineteenth century. Sometimes encountered in the German form **Karl**. *See also* CHARLES.

**Carleton** *See* CARLTON.

**Carlo** Italian equivalent of CHARLES.

**Carlos** Spanish equivalent of CHARLES.

**Carlton** English name that originated as a place name based on the Old English *ceorl* ('man') and *tun* ('settlement'). Also spelled **Carleton**. Commonly shortened to CARL. *See also* CHARLTON.

**Carlyle** English name that

originated as a surname and place name (Carlisle in Cumbria) meaning 'fort of Luguvalium'.

**Carol** English name that as a name for boys is (now rarely) used as an anglicized form of the Roman Carolus. Variants include **Carroll** and the Irish **Cahal** or CATHAL (meaning 'battle-mighty').

**Carr** English name that originated as a surname based on the Old Norse for 'overgrown marsh'.

**Carrick** English name based on the Gaelic for 'rock' or 'crag'.

**Carroll** See CAROL; CEARBHALL.

**Carson** English name that may have been based on an unidentified place name. As a first name, it is associated primarily with people with Irish or Scottish connections.

**Carter** English name denoting a person who transports goods by cart. In Scotland it is sometimes treated as an anglicization of the Gaelic

Mac Artair, meaning 'son of Artair'.

**Carver** English name based on the Cornish Gaelic for 'great rock'. It appears in R. D. Blackmore's classic romance *Lorna Doone* (1869).

**Carwyn** Welsh name based on the Welsh *car* ('love') and *gwyn* ('white' or 'blessed'). *See also* CAERWYN.

**Cary** English name that originated as a place name (the River Cary in the counties of Devon and Somerset). It enjoyed a peak in popularity in the 1940s and 1950s when it became well known through British-born US film star Cary Grant (Alexander Archibald Leach; 1904–86). *See also* CAREY.

**Casey** English name that can be traced back to an Irish surname meaning 'vigilant in war'. It is often associated with the US folk hero Casey Jones (John Luther Jones; 1863–1900), who died saving his passengers on the 'Cannonball Express' and who was himself named after his birthplace, Cayce, in Kentucky. Also spelled **Kasey**.

**Cash** *See* CASSIUS.

**Caspar** English version of the Dutch JASPER that was adopted by English speakers in the nineteenth century. Traditionally identified as the name of one of the biblical Three Wise Men (who are not actually named in the Bible), it may also be spelled **Casper**.

**Casper** *See* CASPAR.

**Caspian** English name of uncertain origin, possibly modelled on the Caspian Sea situated between Russia and Asia. It became widely known through a character of the name in the *Chronicles of Narnia* by C. S. Lewis (1898–1963).

**Cass** *See* CASSIUS.

**Cassidy** English name based on the Irish O Caiside. A relatively recent introduction, it is confined largely to the USA.

**Cassie** *See* CASSIUS.

**Cassius** Roman name of uncertain meaning, possibly based on the Latin *cassus* ('empty'). Well-known bearers of the name in modern times have included the US boxer Muhammad Ali (Cassius Clay; b. 1942). Shortened to **Cass**, **Cash** or **Cassie**.

**Cat** English name that evolved initially as a nickname for anyone with a tempestuous character. It has appeared in generally informal use among English speakers since the early twentieth century, enjoying particular popularity among jazz musicians.

**Cathal** Irish name based on the Gaelic *cath* ('battle') and *val* ('rule'). Notable bearers of the name have included a seventh-century Irish saint. Also found as **Cahal**. Shortened to **Cal**.

**Cavan** Irish name based on that of the Irish county, itself from the Gaelic *cabhan* ('grassy hill'). Also found as **Kavan**.

**Ceallagh** *See* KELLY.

**Cearbhall** ('keerval' or 'kurval') Irish name of uncertain meaning, possibly from the Gaelic *cearbh* ('hacking'). It was fairly frequent in Ireland during the medieval period and later became widely known through Irish President Cearbhall O Dalaigh (1911–78). Sometimes anglicized as **Carroll** or CHARLES.

**Cecil** English name descended either from the Roman Caecilius, itself from the Latin *caecus* ('blind'), or else from the Welsh Seissylt, ultimately from the Latin *sextus* ('sixth'). It became well known in England through the powerful Cecil family.

**Cedric** English name based on the Old English Cerdic, itself of uncertain meaning, or alternatively on the Welsh Cedrych, from *ced* ('bounty'). Although Scottish novelist Sir Walter Scott may have had the Welsh form of the name in mind, it is traditionally believed that the modern name resulted from an inaccurate rendering of the Old English name in his historical novel *Ivanhoe* (1819).

**Cenydd** See KENNETH.

**Cesar** See CAESAR.

**Chad** English name descended from the Old English Ceadda, itself possibly based on the Celtic *cad* ('battle' or 'warrior'). Borne by the seventh-century St Chad, Archbishop of York, it enjoyed a modest peak in popularity as a first name during the 1970s, chiefly in the USA.

**Chae** See CHARLES.

**Chaim** ('hyim') Jewish name descended from the Hebrew Hyam, itself from the Hebrew *hayyim* ('life'). It is in fairly common use within Jewish communities around the world, especially in the USA.

**Chance** English name based on the ordinary vocabulary word denoting fortune or luck.

**Chancellor** English name that originated as a surname based on the Old French for 'counsellor'.

**Chancey** See CHAUNCEY.

**Chandler** English name that originated as a surname denoting a maker of candles. It enjoyed a boost in the late 1990s as the name of one of the flatmates in the popular US television series *Friends*.

**Chandra** Indian name based on the Sanskrit for 'moon'.

**Chapman** English name that originated as a surname denoting a merchant or pedlar. Notable bearers of the name have included British journalist and novelist Chapman Pincher (Henry Chapman Pincher; b. 1914).

**Charles** English and French name based ultimately on the Old German *karl* ('free man'). Also encountered in Ireland as an anglicization of CEARBHALL. It became popular after Mary Queen of Scots gave the name to her son Charles James Stuart. Variants in other languages include the Scottish **Chae** or **Chay**. Among familiar forms of the name are **Charlie**, **Chas**, **Chaz**, CHUCK and CHICK.

**Charleton** *See* CHARLTON.

**Charlie** *See* CHARLES.

**Charlton** English name that originated as a place name based on the Old English *ceorl* ('free man') and *tun*

('settlement'), and thus meaning 'settlement of free men'. The most famous bearer of the name to date has been the US film actor Charlton Heston (John Charlton Carter; b. 1924). Also found as **Charleton**. *See also* CARLTON.

**Chas** *See* CHARLES.

**Chase** English name that is popular chiefly in the USA. It came originally from the ordinary vocabulary word 'chase' and was in use in medieval times as a nickname for a hunter.

**Chauncey** English name of uncertain Norman French origin that has been in occasional use among English speakers since the thirteenth century. Today it is found chiefly in the USA. Also found as **Chancey** or **Chauncy**.

**Chauncy** *See* CHAUNCEY.

**Chay** *See* CHARLES.

**Chaz** *See* CHARLES.

**Ches** *See* CHESNEY.

**Chesney** English name

meaning 'camp' that has been in occasional use as a first name since the beginning of the twentieth century. Commonly shortened to **Ches** or **Chet** – as borne by US jazz musician Chet Baker (Chesney Baker; 1929–88).

**Chester** English name that originated as a place name (the city of Chester in Cheshire), itself from the Latin *castra* ('camp' or 'fort'). Sometimes abbreviated to **Chet**.

**Chet** *See* CHESNEY; CHESTER.

**Chick** English name that is sometimes regarded as an informal version of CHARLES or otherwise as a nickname for a youth or person of small build. It appeared with increasing frequency among English speakers from the nineteenth century, mainly in the USA.

**Chip** *See* CHRISTOPHER.

**Chris** Shortened version of various longer names, including CHRISTOPHER and CHRISTIAN. Sometimes spelled **Kris**.

**Christian** English name descended from the Roman Christianus, itself from the Latin for 'Christian'. Its adoption as a first name was promoted through Christian, the allegorical central character in John Bunyan's *The Pilgrim's Progress* (1678, 1684). Sometimes abbreviated to CHRIS.

**Christmas** English name, based on the name of the festival, that has made rare appearances as a first name since the thirteenth century, usually reserved for children born on Christmas Day itself. *See also* NOEL.

**Christopher** English name descended from the Greek Khristophoros, itself from the Greek *Khristos* ('Christ') and *pherein* ('to bear') and thus meaning 'bearing Christ' – a reference to the legend of St Christopher, who carried the boy Jesus over a stream and thus became the patron saint of travellers. Familiar forms include CHRIS, **Christy**, **Kit** and **Chip**. *See also* KESTER.

**Christy** *See* CHRISTOPHER.

**Chuck** Shortened form of CHARLES that is also used informally as a term of endearment. It can be traced back to the Old English *chukken* (to cluck). Variants include **Chuckie**.

**Chuckie** *See* CHUCK.

**Churchill** English name that originated as a place name meaning 'church on a hill'.

**Ciabhan** ('keevan') Irish name based on the Irish Gaelic for 'full-haired'. It is sometimes anglicized as **Keevan**.

**Cian** ('kain' or 'kee-ern') Irish name based on the Gaelic for 'ancient'. It appears in Irish mythology as the name of the son-in-law of Brian Boru. Also encountered as KEAN or **Keane** or, in Ireland, **Kian**.

**Ciaran** *See* KIERAN.

**Cillian** *See* KILLIAN.

**Claiborne** *See* CLAYBORNE.

**Clancey** *See* CLANCY.

**Clancy** English and Irish name that developed variously from the Irish surname Mac Fhlannchaidh ('son of Flannchadh') or else as a variant of CLARENCE. It was taken up by English speakers in the nineteenth century, chiefly in the USA. Also spelled **Clancey**.

**Clarence** English name meaning 'of Clare' that was adopted in the fourteenth century as a ducal title and appeared as a first name from the nineteenth century. Its use among English speakers owed much to Edward VII's son Albert Victor, Duke of Clarence (1864–92), whose premature death attracted public sympathy. Shortened to **Clarrie** or CLANCY. *See also* SINCLAIR.

**Clark** English name that originated as a surname denoting a clerk or secretary. Well-known bearers of the name have included US film actor Clark Gable (William Clark Gable; 1901–60). Also spelled **Clarke**.

**Clarke** *See* CLARK.

**Clarrie** *See* CLARENCE.

**Claud** *See* CLAUDE.

**Claude** English and French name descended from the Roman Claudius, itself based on the Latin *claudus* ('lame'). It was taken up by English speakers during the sixteenth century. Also spelled **Claud**.

**Claus** ('klowce' or 'klorz') German name that evolved from Niklaus, the German equivalent of NICHOLAS.

**Clay** *See* CLAYBORNE; CLAYTON.

**Clayborne** English name that originated as a surname meaning 'dweller in a place with clay soil near a brook'. Also found as **Claiborne**. Sometimes shortened to **Clay**.

**Clayton** English name that originated as a place name (from north and central England) based on the Old English *claeg* ('clay') and *tun* ('settlement'). **Clay** is a shortened form.

**Cledwyn** Welsh name based on the Welsh *caled* ('hard' or 'rough') and *gwyn* ('white' or 'blessed').

**Clem/Clemence/ Clemens** *See* CLEMENT.

**Clement** English name based on the Latin *clemens* ('merciful'). It was in common currency among English speakers during the medieval period. Variants include **Clemence** and **Clemens**. Shortened to **Clem**.

**Cliff** Shortened form of CLIFFORD or CLIFTON. It enjoyed a peak in popularity in the late 1950s and 1960s in response to the chart success of British pop singer Cliff Richard (Harold Webb; b. 1940).

**Clifford** English name that originated as a place name (common to the counties of Gloucestershire, Herefordshire and Yorkshire) based on the Old English *clif* ('cliff' or 'riverbank') and *ford* ('ford') and thus meaning 'ford by a slope'. Commonly abbreviated to CLIFF.

**Clifton** English name that originated as a place name (common to several English counties) based on the Old English *clif* ('cliff' or 'riverbank') and *tun* ('settlement') and thus meaning 'town on a cliff'. Sometimes abbreviated to CLIFF.

**Clint** Shortened version of CLINTON. Today it is usually identified with the US film actor and director Clint Eastwood (b. 1930), whose popularity in the 'spaghetti westerns' of the 1960s and 1970s brought the name new exposure.

**Clinton** English name that originated, like CLIFTON, as a place name based on the Old English *clif* ('cliff' or 'riverbank') and *tun* ('settlement') and thus meaning 'town on a cliff'. It was adopted initially by English speakers in the USA in tribute to the Clinton family, which produced two governors of New York. *See also* CLINT.

**Clitus** English name descended from the Greek Kleitos, which may itself have come from the Greek *kleos* ('glory'). Borne by one of Alexander the Great's generals, it has made occasional appearances as a first name in modern times, chiefly in the USA.

**Clive** English name that originated as a place name (common to several English counties) based on the Old English *clif* ('cliff' or 'riverbank'). Perhaps the earliest bearer of the name was Clive Newcome in William Makepeace Thackeray's novel *The Newcomes* (1853–5), who was apparently named after the British soldier and administrator Robert Clive (1725–74).

**Clovis** English name that was taken up as a Latinized version of the French LOUIS in the nineteenth century. It enjoyed renewed exposure through the collection of short stories entitled *The Chronicles of Clovis* (1911), written by the British author Saki (Hector Hugh Monro; 1870–1916).

**Clyde** Scottish name based on that of the River Clyde in south-west Scotland, which can be interpreted as meaning 'the washer'. It established itself early on as a popular choice among black Americans (perhaps because many US plantation owners were of Scottish descent).

**Codey** *See* CODY.

**Cody** English name that is thought to have evolved from an Irish surname meaning 'descendant of a helpful person'. Although rare in the UK, it has enjoyed some popularity in the USA and elsewhere, perhaps through association with the celebrated Wild West hero Buffalo Bill Cody (William Frederick Cody; 1846–1917). Also spelled **Codey** or **Kody**.

**Coinneach** ('kooinock') Scottish name based on the Gaelic for 'handsome' or 'fair'. It continues in occasional use in Scotland but elsewhere has given way to KENNETH.

**Col/Colan** *See* COLIN.

**Colbert** English name based on the Old German *col* (of uncertain meaning) and *berht* ('bright' or 'famous'). It was in common use during the medieval period.

**Colby** English name based on the Norse for 'from the dark country'.

**Cole** English name of uncertain origin that may have evolved originally from the Old English *cola* ('swarthy') or else as a variant of NICHOLAS or as an abbreviated form of **Coleman** (*see* COLMAN). It is best known today as the name of the celebrated US songwriter Cole Porter (1891–1964).

**Coleman** *See* COLMAN.

**Colin** English name that developed, via the medieval Col, from NICHOLAS but is now widely regarded as an independent name. In Scotland it is sometimes considered to be an anglicization of the Gaelic Cailean, meaning 'puppy' or 'whelp'. Variants include **Collin**, **Colyn**, the Welsh **Collwyn** and the Irish **Colan**. Shortened to **Col** or COLL.

**Coll** Scottish name based on the Gaelic Colla, itself from the Old Celtic for 'high'. Sometimes found as a shortened form of COLIN.

**Colley** Irish name meaning 'swarthy'. Famous bearers of the name have included the

English actor and playwright Colley Cibber (1671–1757).

**Collier** English name that originated as a surname meaning 'charcoal burner'. Also found as **Collyer** or **Colyer**.

**Collin/Collwyn** *See* COLIN.

**Collyer** *See* COLLIER.

**Colm** *See* COLUM.

**Colman** Irish name that developed like COLUM out of the Roman Columba, itself from the Latin for 'dove'. It was borne by several early Irish saints. Also found as **Coleman**.

**Colom** *See* COLUM.

**Coltrane** English name meaning 'young horse' or 'frisky'.

**Colum** Irish name based on the Roman Columba, itself from the Latin for 'dove'. Its popularity in Ireland can be traced back to St Columba (521–97), who is often credited with bringing Christianity to the country. Variants include **Colm** and **Colom**.

**Colyer** *See* COLLIER.

**Colyn** *See* COLIN.

**Comfort** English name based on the ordinary vocabulary word 'comfort'. It enjoyed some popularity among English speakers after the Reformation and continued to make rare appearances among both sexes into the nineteenth century.

**Comhnall** *See* CONAL.

**Con** *See* CONNOR; CONRAD; CONSTANT.

**Conal** Irish name based on the Irish Gaelic for 'wolf' and 'strong' or otherwise meaning 'high mighty'. Notable bearers of the name have included several famous Irish warriors and chieftains. Also spelled **Conall** or, in Scotland, **Comhnall**.

**Conall** *See* CONAL.

**Conan** ('kohnan' or, in Ireland, 'konnan') Irish name based on the Irish Gaelic *cu* ('hound' or 'wolf', or otherwise 'high') that was fairly common among English speakers between the twelfth and fifteenth centuries.

**Conn** *See* CONNOR.

**Connor** Irish name based on the Gaelic Conchobar or Conchobhar, itself thought to mean 'hound lover' or 'wolf lover' and thus usually bestowed originally upon hunters. It appears in mythology as the name of a legendary Irish king. **Conor** is a modern variant. Shortened to **Con** or **Conn**.

**Conor** *See* CONNOR.

**Conrad** English version of the German Konrad, itself based on the Old German *kuon* ('bold') and *rad* ('counsel') and thus meaning 'bold counsel'. It was taken up by English speakers during the medieval period. Shortened to **Con**.

**Conroy** English name based on the Gaelic for 'wise'.

**Constant** English and French name descended from the Roman Constans, itself from the Latin *constans* ('constant' or 'steadfast'). Recorded in use during medieval times, it was among the 'virtue' names taken up by Puritans after the Reformation. Shortened to **Con**.

**Constantine** English and French version of the Roman Constantinus, itself from the Latin *constans* ('constant' or 'steadfast'). It was taken up by English speakers in the nineteenth century in response to renewed interest in classical history.

**Coop** *See* COOPER.

**Cooper** English name meaning 'barrel maker'. Shortened to **Coop**.

**Corbin** English name based on the Old French for 'black-haired' or 'raucous'.

**Corey** English name of uncertain origin that has made occasional appearances since the 1960s, chiefly within the black community in the USA. Also found as **Cory**, **Korey**, **Korrie** and **Korey**.

**Corin** French name

descended from the Roman Quirinus, which may have evolved ultimately from the Sabine *quiris* ('spear'). It was borne by a number of early Christian martyrs.

**Cormac** Irish name based on the Gaelic *corb* ('defilement') and *mac* ('son') or otherwise interpreted as meaning 'charioteer'. It was borne by many notable figures in early Irish history. Variants include **Cormack**, **Cormick** and the Scottish **Cormag**.

**Cormack/Cormag/ Cormick** *See* CORMAC.

**Cornel** *See* CORNELL.

**Cornelius** Biblical name of uncertain origin, possibly based on the Latin *cornu* ('horn'). It appears in the Bible and was imported to the English-speaking world from the Netherlands around the fifteenth century. Familiar forms include **Cornie**, **Corney** and **Corny**.

**Cornell** English name that has been in occasional use since the nineteenth century, chiefly in the USA. It is thought that it

may have begun originally as a medieval shortening of CORNELIUS. **Cornel** is a variant form.

**Corney/Cornie/Corny** *See* CORNELIUS.

**Cory** *See* COREY.

**Cosimo** *See* COSMO.

**Cosmo** English, German and Italian name descended from the Greek Kosmas, itself from the Greek *kosmos* ('order', 'harmony' or 'beauty'). It was introduced to the English-speaking world by the Scottish dukes of Gordon in the eighteenth century, who encountered it in Tuscany in the Italian form **Cosimo**.

**Courtenay/Courteney** *See* COURTNEY.

**Courtney** English name that originated as the Norman French place name Courtenay (meaning 'domain of Curtius'), although it was also in use as a nickname based on the French *court nez* ('short nose'). Variants include **Courtenay** and **Courteney**.

**Coy** English name of uncertain origin, possibly taken from the ordinary vocabulary word 'coy'. Mostly confined to the USA.

**Craig** Scottish name that originated as a place name based on the Gaelic *creag* ('crag'). It has largely lost its uniquely Scottish character.

**Crawford** Scottish name that originated as a place name meaning 'ford where the crows gather'.

**Creighton** ('cryton') Scottish name that originated as a place name based on the Gaelic *crioch* ('border' or 'boundary') and the Old English *tun* ('settlement').

**Crispin** English version of the Roman Crispinus, meaning 'curly-haired'. It was taken up by English speakers in the seventeenth century.

**Crosbie** *See* CROSBY.

**Crosby** English name of Scandinavian origin, meaning 'at the cross'. Variants include Crosbie.

**Cuba** English name based on the name of the Caribbean island of Cuba. It became well known through US actor Cuba Gooding Junior (b. 1968).

**Cuddie/Cuddy** *See* CUTHBERT.

**Cullan** Scottish and Irish name based on the Gaelic for 'at the back of the river'. Also spelled **Cullen**.

**Cullen** *See* CULLAN.

**Curt** *See* CURTIS; KURT.

**Curtis** English name based on the Old French *curteis* ('courteous') that has been in use as an occasional first name since the eleventh century, when it was borne by the eldest son of William the Conqueror. Early in its history it acquired a new derivation, from the Middle English *curt* ('short') and *hose* ('leggings'). Shortened to **Curt**.

**Cuthbert** English name descended from the Old English Cuthbeorht, itself from *cuth* ('known') and *beorht* ('bright' or 'famous') and thus meaning 'well known'. It became famous as the name of the seventh-century English St Cuthbert, Bishop of Lindisfarne. **Cuddie** or **Cuddy** are informal Scottish variants. Shortened to BERT.

**Cy** *See* CYRUS.

**Cyprian** Roman name based on the Latin for 'from Cyprus'. Variants include **Cypriano**.

**Cypriano** *See* CYPRIAN.

**Cyril** English name descended from the Greek Kyrillos, itself based on the Greek *kurios* ('lord'). It was borne by several early saints.

**Cyrus** Biblical name descended from the Greek Kyros, which may have evolved from the Greek *kurios* ('lord'), although it may equally have come from Persian words meaning 'sun' or 'throne'. Shortened to **Cy** or **Sy**, chiefly in the USA.

## BOYS' NAMES

**Dacre** ('dayker') English name that originated as a place name (from Cumbria) meaning 'trickling stream'. A strongly aristocratic name, it is now rare.

**Dafydd** *See* DAVID.

**Dag** Scandinavian name based on the Old Norse *dagr* ('day').

**Dai** ('digh') Welsh first name based on the Old Celtic *dei* ('to shine') but often considered to be a shortened form of DAVID. Since the nineteenth century it has become established as one of the most characteristic of all Welsh names.

**Daibhidh** *See* DAVID.

**Dale** English name that originated as a surname originally borne by people living in a dale or valley. Confined chiefly to the USA, it has been given to both sexes since the first decade of the twentieth century.

**Daley** Irish name based on the Gaelic for 'descendant of Dalach'. Sometimes encountered as **Daly**.

**Dallas** English name that originated as a place name meaning 'dweller in the dale'. Its use in the USA has been promoted through association with Dallas, Texas.

**Dalton** English name meaning 'valley town'. It is more common in the USA than elsewhere.

**Daly** *See* DALEY.

**Dalziel** ('deeyel') Scottish name that originated as a place name meaning 'field of the sun gleam'.

**Damian** English name descended from the Greek Damianos, itself from the Greek *daman* ('to subdue' or 'to rule') and thus meaning 'tamer'. It was known among English speakers as early as the thirteenth century. Also found as **Damien** (a French version of the name). *See also* DAMON.

**Damien** *See* DAMIAN.

**Damon** English variant of DAMIAN that emerged around the middle of the nineteenth century. It features in Greek mythology in the legend of the two devoted friends Damon and Pythias.

**Dan** English name based on the Hebrew for 'judge', but more often in use today as a shortened form of DANIEL or similar names. It appears in the Bible as the name of a son of Jacob. *See also* DANNY.

**Dana** English name that evolved as a shortened form of DANIEL in the nineteenth century. Today it is more often bestowed upon girls, linked to such names as DANIELLE.

**Dandie** *See* DANDY.

**Dandy** English name based on the ordinary vocabulary word 'dandy', but also in use as

a familiar form of such names as DANIEL. It has made occasional appearances in both sexes since the early twentieth century. Also found as **Dandie**.

**Dane** English name that is thought to have developed as a variant of DEAN. It has appeared with increasing frequency since the early twentieth century, but is rare outside the USA.

**Daniel** English, French and German name based on the Hebrew for 'God is my judge' or 'God has judged'. In Ireland it is also regarded as an anglicized form of Domhnall. In Wales it may be an anglicization of **Deiniol**, meaning 'attractive' or 'charming'. It appears in the Bible as the name of an Old Testament prophet. Shortened to DAN or DANNY (or **Dannie**). *See also* DANA.

**Dannie** *See* DANIEL; DANNY.

**Danny** English name that was taken up as an informal version of DANIEL early in the twentieth century. Like Daniel, it has strong Irish associations, as celebrated in the song

'Danny Boy' (1913). Also encountered as **Dannie**. Shortened to DAN.

**Dante** ('dantay' or 'dontay') Italian name based on the Latin *durare* ('to endure') and thus meaning 'enduring' or 'steadfast'. It is famous as the name of the Italian poet Dante Alighieri (1265–1321).

**Dara** Irish name that developed out of the Gaelic Mac Dara. It appears in the Old Testament. Also encountered as **Darach**.

**Darach** *See* DARA.

**Darby** English name that originated in the place name Derby, itself based on the Old Norse *diur* ('deer') and *byr* ('settlement'), thus meaning 'deer park'. Sometimes used in Ireland as an anglicization of DERMOT. Also found as **Derby**.

**Darcy** English name borrowed from the name of the town of Arcy in France. The popularity of the name among English speakers was promoted by the stern but handsome aristocrat Fitzwilliam

Darcy in the Jane Austen novel *Pride and Prejudice* (1813). Also spelled **D'Arcy**.

**D'Arcy** *See* DARCY.

**Darel/Darell** *See* DARRYL.

**Dario** Italian name descended from the Roman DARIUS.

**Darius** Roman name based on the Persian *daraya* ('to hold' or 'to possess') and *vahu* ('good' or 'well') and thus meaning 'protector' or 'wealthy'. It has continued to make appearances into modern times. *See also* DARIO.

**Darnell** English name that originated as a surname based on the Old English for 'hidden nook'.

**Darran** *See* DARREN.

**Darrell** *See* DARRYL.

**Darren** English name that is thought to have developed as a variant of DARRYL. It seems to have made its first appearance among English speakers in the USA in the 1920s. Also found as **Darran** or **Darrin**.

**Darrin** *See* DARREN.

**Darryl** English name that originated in the Norman baronial surname d'Airelle (referring to Airelle in Calvados). An alternative derivation traces the name back to the Old English *deorling* ('darling'). Also found as **Daryl**, **Darel**, **Darell** or **Darrell**.

**Daryl** *See* DARRYL.

**Dave/Davey** *See* DAVID.

**David** English name based on the Hebrew for 'favourite', 'beloved' or 'darling'. It appears in the Bible as the name of the greatest of the kings of the Israelites and later became especially well established in Wales and Scotland. **Dave**, **Davie**, **Davey** and **Davy** are informal versions. Among variants in other languages are the Gaelic **Daibhidh** and the Welsh **Dafydd** or DEWI. *See also* DAI; TAFFY.

**Davie** *See* DAVID.

**Davis** English name meaning 'David's son'.

**Davy** *See* DAVID.

**Dayton** English name meaning 'Day's settlement' or 'David's settlement'. It is more common in the USA than elsewhere.

**Deacon** English name that originated as a surname meaning 'dusty one', 'servant' or 'messenger'. Variants include **Deakin**. Shortened to **Deke**.

**Deakin** *See* DEACON.

**Dean** English name that can be traced back either to the Old English *denu* ('valley') or to the ecclesiastical rank 'dean'. It seems to have made its debut as a first name in the USA. Variant forms are **Deane** and **Dene**. *See also* DINO.

**Deane** *See* DEAN.

**Decimus** Roman name based on the Latin for 'ten'.

**Declan** English version of the Irish Deaglan, of uncertain meaning. It became popular as a first name among the Irish in the 1940s.

**Deepak** *See* DIPAK.

**Deforest** English name that

has made occasional appearances since the nineteenth century, chiefly in the USA, sometimes in reference to US novelist John DeForest (1826–1906). Also found as **Deforrest** or **DeForrest**.

**Deforrest/DeForrest** *See* DEFOREST.

**Deiniol** *See* DANIEL.

**Deke** *See* DEACON.

**Del** *See* DELBERT; DELROY; DEREK.

**Delainey/Delainie** *See* DELANEY.

**Delaney** English name drawing on Irish Gaelic and Old French origins and variously meaning 'dark challenger' or 'from the elder grove' or else based on a reference to the Slaney river. Variants include **Delainey**, **Delanie** and **Delany**.

**Delany** *See* DELANEY.

**Delbert** English name that is thought to have evolved in parallel with DELMAR and

DELROY and other similar names. Shortened to **Del**.

**Delmar** English name of uncertain origin, possibly a variant of ELMER. It has enjoyed some popularity in the USA since the middle of the twentieth century.

**Delroy** English name that is thought to have evolved as a variant of LEROY. It has enjoyed some popularity in the UK since the middle of the twentieth century. Shortened to **Del**.

**Dempsey** English name based on the Gaelic for 'proud descendant'.

**Dempster** English name that originated as a surname meaning 'judge'.

**Den** *See* DENNIS.

**Dene** *See* DEAN.

**Denham** *See* DENHOLM.

**Denholm** English name that originated as a place name based on the Old English *denu* ('valley') and *holm* ('island'). Famous bearers of the name have included the British actor Denholm Elliott (1922–92). Variants include **Denham**, meaning 'home in a valley'.

**Denis** *See* DENNIS.

**Denison** *See* DENNISON.

**Denley** English name that originated as a surname meaning 'wood or clearing in a valley'.

**Dennis** English name descended from the Greek Dionysios, denoting a devotee of the Greek god of wine Dionysos. Also rendered as **Denys** or **Denis** (the French spelling of the name). Shortened to **Den** or, more rarely, **Denny**.

**Dennison** English name meaning 'son of Dennis'. Also found as **Denison** or **Tennyson**.

**Denny** *See* DENNIS.

**Denton** English name that originated as a place name based on the Old English *denu* ('valley') and *tun* ('settlement').

**Denver** English name that

originated as a surname meaning 'Danes' crossing'.

**Denys** *See* DENNIS.

**Denzel** *See* DENZIL.

**Denzil** English name that originated in the Cornish place name Denzell, alternatively interpreted as meaning 'fort' or 'fertile upland'. Records of its use go back to the sixteenth century, when it was borne by the English statesman Denzil Holles (1599–1680). Also found as **Denzel** or **Denzyl**.

**Denzyl** *See* DENZIL.

**Derby** *See* DARBY.

**Derek** English name descended from the Old German Theodoric, meaning 'ruler of the people'. It is thought to have come to England with Flemish immigrants in the fifteenth century. Also rendered as **Derrick**, **Deryck** or **Deryk**. Variants in other languages include the Dutch **Dirk**. **Del** and **Derry** are informal versions. *See also* DIETRICH.

**Dermid** *See* DERMOT.

**Dermot** English version of the Irish **Diarmaid** or **Diarmuid**, possibly based on the Gaelic *di* ('without') and *airmait* ('envy'). As Diarmaid it was the name of a legendary king of Tara. As Dermot, it made its first appearances in Ireland in the nineteenth century. Variants include **Diarmid**, **Dermid** and the Scottish **Diarmad**.

**Derrick/Derry** *See* DEREK.

**Derwent** English name that originated as a place name meaning 'river that flows through oak woods'.

**Deryck/Deryk** *See* DEREK.

**Des/Desi** *See* DESMOND.

**Desmond** English name based on the Irish Gaelic surname Deas-Mhumhan, meaning 'someone from south Munster'. It appears to have assumed its present form under the influence of ESMOND. Shortened to **Des** or **Desi** (also rendered as **Desy** or **Dezi**).

**Desy** *See* DESMOND.

**Deverell** Celtic name that

originated as a place name meaning 'fertile river bank'. Also spelled **Deverill**.

**Devereux** English name based on the French *de Evreux* ('of Evreux'). Its modern use as a first name is confined chiefly to the USA.

**Deverill** *See* DEVERELL.

**Devlin** Irish name based on the Irish Gaelic for 'fiercely brave'.

**Devon** English name based on that of the county of Devon. It has made rare appearances, chiefly in the USA, since the middle of the twentieth century.

**Dewey** *See* DEWI.

**Dewi** Welsh variant of DAVID. Of ancient origins, it enjoyed a revival in Wales in the twentieth century. **Dewey** is a variant of the name in the USA.

**Dex** *See* DEXTER.

**Dexter** English name based on the Old English *deag* ('dye') and thus meaning 'dyer'. It is sometimes associated with the Latin *dexter*, meaning 'right-handed' or 'auspicious'. Shortened to **Dex**.

**Dezi** *See* DESMOND.

**Diarmad/Diarmaid/ Diarmid/Diarmuid** *See* DERMOT.

**Dick** Informal variant of RICHARD. It has been suggested that the name evolved via **Rick** as a result of the difficulty English speakers experienced in pronouncing the initial 'R' in the rolled Norman French manner. Also found as **Dickie** or **Dicky**.

**Dickie** *See* DICK.

**Dickson** *See* DIXON.

**Dicky** *See* DICK.

**Didi** *See* DIDIER.

**Didier** French name descended from the Roman Desiderius, itself based on the Latin *desiderium* ('longing'). Sometimes shortened to **Didi**.

**Diego** Spanish name of uncertain origin, possibly based

on the Greek *didakh* ('teaching'). It is sometimes assumed to be a variant of SANTIAGO.

**Dieter** ('deeter') German name based on the Old German *theuth* ('people' or 'race') and *hari* ('army' or 'warrior').

**Dietrich** German equivalent of DEREK. Sometimes shortened to **Till**.

**Digby** English name that originated as a place name (Digby in Lincolnshire) itself based on the Old Norse *diki* ('ditch') and *byr* ('settlement') and thus meaning 'farm by a ditch'. Its use as a first name dates from the nineteenth century.

**Diggory** English name of uncertain origin, but possibly based on the French *l'esgaré* ('the lost one' or 'astray'). The name may have been popularized by the fourteenth-century romance *Sir Degaré* and emerged as a favourite choice in Cornwall. Also found as **Digory**.

**Digory** *See* DIGGORY.

**Dilip** Indian name possibly based on the Sanskrit *dili* ('Delhi') and *pa* ('protecting'). Also found as **Duleep**.

**Dillon** *See* DYLAN.

**Dimitri** *See* DMITRI.

**Dino** ('deenoh') Italian and Spanish name that evolved as a shortened form of Bernardino and various other names with a similar '-dino' ending. Also found as an informal variant of DEAN.

**Dinsdale** English name that originated as a place name meaning 'settlement by a moat'.

**Dion** English name descended via the Roman Dionysius from the Greek Dionysios or some other similar Greek source.

**Dipak** Indian name based on the Sanskrit *dipa* ('light' or 'lamp') and *ka* ('little' or 'like'). Also found as **Deepak**.

**Dirk** *See* DEREK.

**Dixon** English name that originated as a surname meaning 'son of Richard'. Also found as **Dickson**.

**Django** Romany name meaning 'I awake'. It is famous as the nickname of Belgian jazz guitarist Jean 'Django' Reinhardt (1910–53).

**Dmitri** Russian name descended from the Roman Demetrius, itself ultimately from the Greek *de* ('earth') and *meter* ('mother'). Also found as **Dimitri**. **Mitya** is a familiar form.

**Dod** Scottish variant of GEORGE. Also found as **Doddy**.

**Doddy** *See* DOD.

**Dolan** *See* DOOLAN.

**Dom** *See* DOMINIC.

**Domenick/Domingo** *See* DOMINIC.

**Dominic** English name descended from the Roman Dominicus, itself based on the Latin *dominus* ('lord'). Borne in the thirteenth century by St Dominic, founder of the Dominican order of monks, it became a favourite choice of Roman Catholics. In Ireland it is sometimes treated as an anglicization of Domhnall. Also found as **Domenick** or **Domingo** (a Spanish version). Shortened to **Dom**.

**Don** Shortened form of DONALD and DONOVAN. It won acceptance as a name in its own right from the nineteenth century. **Donny** is a variant.

**Donal** *See* DONALD.

**Donald** English version of the Gaelic Domhnall, itself from the Celtic *dubno* ('world') and *val* ('rule' or 'mighty') and thus meaning 'world mighty' or 'world ruler'. The final 'd' came either through attempts by English speakers to pronounce the Gaelic name in an authentic manner or through the influence of such Germanic names as RONALD. **Donal** is an Irish form. Shortened to DON or **Donny**.

**Donny** *See* DON; DONALD; DONOVAN.

**Donovan** Irish name based on the Gaelic *donn* ('brown')

and *dubh* ('black' or 'dark'), and thus meaning 'dark brown' (referring to the colour of a person's hair, eyes or complexion). Shortened to DON or **Donny**.

**Doolan** Irish name that originated as a surname meaning 'black defiance'. Also found as **Dolan**.

**Doran** English name based on an Irish Gaelic surname meaning 'descendant of Deoradhan' (Deoradhan itself meaning 'exile' or 'wanderer').

**Dorian** English name descended from the Greek Dorieus, meaning 'person from Doris' (Doris being a region in ancient Greece). It is well known from the Oscar Wilde novel *The Picture of Dorian Gray* (1891), in which it may have made its first appearance. **Dorien** and **Dorrien** are variant forms.

**Dorien/Dorrien** *See* DORIAN.

**Doug** *See* DOUGAL; DOUGLAS.

**Dougal** English version of

the Irish Gaelic Dubhgall or Dughall, derived from the Gaelic *dubh* ('black') and *gall* ('stranger'). It was applied originally to the dark-haired Danes who settled in Ireland early in that country's history. Variants include **Dugald** and **Doyle**. Shortened to **Doug** (or **Dug**) or **Dougie** (or **Duggy**).

**Dougie** *See* DOUGAL; DOUGLAS.

**Douglas** Scottish name that originated as a place name based on the Gaelic *dubh* ('black') and *glas* ('stream'). Well known in Scotland from the earls of Douglas, it has been reserved for boys since the seventeenth century. Shortened to **Doug** (or **Dug**) or **Dougie** (or **Duggie**).

**Doyle** *See* DOUGAL.

**Drake** English name meaning 'dragon'.

**Drew** English name that evolved as a shortened form of ANDREW or else out of DROGO. It established itself in Scotland before winning acceptance elsewhere from the

1940s, usually as a name for boys.

**Driscol** *See* DRISCOLL.

**Driscoll** English name based on the Irish Gaelic for 'interpreter'. Also spelled **Driscol**.

**Drogo** English name of uncertain meaning, possibly based on the Old Saxon *drog* ('ghost') or Old German *tragan* ('to bear' or 'to carry') or, more likely, from the Slavonic *dorogo* ('dear'). It was brought to England by the Normans. *See also* DREW.

**Drummond** Scottish name that originated as a place name. Still largely confined to Scotland.

**Duane** English version of the Gaelic Dubhan, itself based on *dubh* ('black') and meaning 'little dark one'. It became popular among English speakers in the 1940s and 1950s. Also spelled **Dwayne** or **Dwane**.

**Dud** *See* DUDLEY.

**Dudley** English name that

originated as a place name based on the Old English for 'wood or clearing of Dudda'. It is also encountered in Ireland as an anglicization of Dubhdara or DARA. It became well known as the surname of Elizabeth I's favourite Robert Dudley, Earl of Leicester (c. 1532–88). Shortened to **Dud**.

**Duff** Scottish name based on the Gaelic *dubh* ('dark' or 'black') and originally bestowed upon people with dark hair or complexion.

**Dug** *See* DOUGAL; DOUGLAS.

**Dugald** *See* DOUGAL.

**Duggie** *See* DOUGAL; DOUGLAS.

**Duke** English name based either on the title 'duke' or else a shortened form of MARMADUKE. It was taken up by English speakers early in the twentieth century, chiefly in the USA.

**Duleep** *See* DILIP.

**Duncan** English version of the Gaelic Donnchadh, based on the Old Celtic *donn* ('dark')

and *cath* ('battle') and thus meaning 'dark warrior'. It has a long history as a Scottish name, having been borne by three eleventh-century Scottish kings. Shortened to **Dunk**, **Dunkie** or **Dunky**.

**Dunk/Dunkie/Dunky** *See* DUNCAN.

**Dunstan** English name that originated as a place name based on the Old English *dun* ('hill') and *stan* ('stone') and meaning 'stony hill'. It is best known as the name of the tenth-century English St Dunstan, Archbishop of Canterbury.

**Durand** French and English name based on the Latin *durans* ('enduring'). It came to England with the Normans and has made rare reappearances in succeeding centuries. Also found as **Durant**.

**Durant** *See* DURAND.

**Dustin** English name of uncertain origin that may have evolved as a Norman version of the Old Norse Thurstan, meaning 'Thor's stone', or else from the Old German for 'brave fighter'. Famous bearers of the name include US actor Dustin Hoffman (b. 1937). *See also* DUSTY.

**Dusty** English name linked either to DUSTIN or else a borrowing of the ordinary vocabulary word 'dusty' (referring to the colour of a person's hair or complexion). It has made occasional appearances as a first name since the 1950s.

**Dwane/Dwayne** *See* DUANE.

**Dwight** English name possibly based on the medieval French Diot and perhaps ultimately on the Roman Dionysius (*see* DENNIS). Its popularity in the USA reflects the fame of US President Dwight D. Eisenhower (1890–1969).

**Dylan** Welsh name that may have evolved via the Welsh *dylif* ('flood') from the Celtic word for 'sea'. Attempts to interpret the name more exactly have included 'son of the wave' and 'influence'. Famous bearers of the name have included Welsh poet Dylan Thomas (1914–53). **Dillon** is a variant spelling.

# BOYS' NAMES

**Eachann** ('yachan') Scottish name based on the Gaelic *each* ('horse') and *donn* ('brown'). Sometimes considered to be a Gaelic equivalent of HECTOR. Also found as **Eacheann**.

**Eacheann** *See* EACHANN.

**Eamon** ('aimon') Irish equivalent of the English EDMUND. Also found as **Eamonn**.

**Eamonn** *See* EAMON.

**Earl** English name based on the aristocratic rank, itself from the Old English *eorl* ('nobleman' or 'chieftain'). It was often bestowed upon those who worked as servants in the households of English earls.

Also found as **Earle** or **Erle**. *See also* DUKE; ERROL; KING; PRINCE.

**Earle** *See* EARL.

**Earnest** *See* ERNEST.

**Easter** English name based on the name of the Christian festival of Easter, itself a reference to the Germanic spring goddess Eostre.

**Eb/Eben** *See* EBENEZER.

**Ebenezer** English name based on the Hebrew *ebenhaezer* ('stone of help'). It appears in the Bible and was consequently taken up as a first name by Puritans in the seventeenth century. Shortened to **Eb** or **Eben**.

**Ed** English name that developed as a shortened form of such names as EDGAR, EDMUND, EDWARD and EDWIN. **Eddie** and **Eddy** are informal forms of the same names that emerged at much the same time.

**Edan** *See* AIDAN.

**Eddie/Eddy** *See* ED.

**Eden** English name based either on the Old English Edun or Edon, which came in turn from the Old English *ead* ('riches') and *hun* ('bearcub'), or on the name of the biblical paradise, itself from the Hebrew *eden* ('delight' or 'paradise'). It was taken up as a first name by Puritans in the seventeenth century.

**Edgar** English name descended from the Old English Eadgar, itself based on the Old English *ead* ('riches') and *gar* ('spear') and thus meaning 'rich in spears' or 'owner of many spears'. Variants include **Adair**. Shortened to ED or **Eddie**.

**Edmé** *See* ESMÉ.

**Edmond** *See* EDMUND.

**Edmund** English name descended from the Old English Eadmund, itself based on the Old English *ead* ('riches') and *mund* ('protector') and thus meaning 'protector of wealth' or 'happy protection'. Variants include the French **Edmond** and the Spanish and Portuguese **Edmundo**. Shortened to ED, **Eddie** (or Eddy), **Ned**, **Neddie** (or **Neddy**), **Ted** or **Teddie** (or **Teddy**). *See also* EAMON.

**Edmundo** *See* EDMUND.

**Edom** Scottish variant of ADAM.

**Edric** English name meaning 'fortunate ruler'.

**Edryd** Welsh name meaning 'restoring'.

**Edsel** English equivalent of the German Etzel, based either on the Old German *adal* ('noble') or on the nickname *Atta* ('father'). The most famous bearer of the name to date has been Edsel Ford (1893–1943), son of the US industrialist Henry Ford.

**Eduardo** *See* EDWARD.

**Edward** English name descended from the Old English Eadweard, itself from the Old English *ead* ('riches') and *weard* ('guard') and thus meaning 'guardian of riches', 'fortunate guardian' or 'wealth guardian'. Famous bearers of the name have included eight kings of England. Variants include the Spanish **Eduardo**. Shortened to ED, **Eddie**, **Eddy**, **Ned**, **Neddie**, **Neddy**, **Ted**, **Teddie** or **Teddy**.

**Edwin** English name descended from the Old English Eadwine, itself based on the Old English *ead* ('riches') and *wine* ('friend') and thus meaning 'friend of riches' or 'rich friend'. It was in fairly regular use among English speakers during the medieval period. ED and **Eddie** are common diminutives of the name.

**Edwy** English name meaning 'richly beloved'.

**Effie** *See* EPHRAIM.

**Egan** Irish name based on the Gaelic Aogan, itself a variant of Aodh, meaning 'fire'.

**Egbert** English name based on the Old English Ecgbeorht, from the Old English *ecg* ('edge') and *beorht* ('bright' or 'famous') and thus meaning 'bright sword' or 'famed swordsman'. It was common in Anglo-Saxon England prior to the Norman Conquest.

**Egon** German name based on the Old German *ek* ('edge') and thus meaning 'swordpoint'.

**Elden** *See* ELDON.

**Eldon** English name that originated as a place name (from County Durham) based on the personal name Ella and the Old English *dun* ('hill'). **Elden** is a variant form.

**Eldred** English name based on the Old English Ealdred, itself from the Old English *eald* ('old') and *raed* ('counsel') and thus meaning 'long-established counsel'.

**Elgar** English name meaning 'noble spearman'.

**Eli** ('eeligh') Hebrew name meaning 'high', 'elevated' or 'exalted'. It appears in the Bible and was consequently adopted as a first name by English speakers in the seventeenth century. **Ely** is a variant form.

**Elias** Greek version of the biblical ELIJAH. It was taken up by English Puritans in the seventeenth century. Variants include **Ellis**.

**Elihu** Hebrew name meaning 'God is he' or 'the Lord is Yah'. It appears in the Old Testament and was consequently taken up by English speakers after the Reformation.

**Elijah** Biblical name based on the Hebrew Eliyahu, meaning 'God is Yah' (Yah being another name for Jehovah). It was the name of a biblical prophet and was also borne by John the Baptist. *See also* ELIAS.

**Eliot/Eliott** *See* ELLIOTT.

**Elisha** Hebrew name based on *el* ('God') and *sha* ('to help' or 'to save') and thus meaning 'God is salvation'. It appears in the Bible as the name of a revered Old Testament prophet.

**Elkanah** Hebrew name meaning 'God has created' or 'the Lord is possessing'. It appears in the Bible and was taken up by English speakers in the seventeenth century.

**Ellar** Scottish name that developed as an anglicization of the Gaelic Eallair, itself from the Latin *cella* ('cellar'). The name was originally borne by butlers or stewards in monasteries.

**Ellerie** *See* ELLERY.

**Ellery** English name that has made occasional appearances since the early twentieth century. Occasionally found as **Ellerie**.

**Elliot** *See* ELLIOTT.

**Elliott** English name that came originally from a Norman French variant of ELIAS. Also encountered as **Eliot**. Other variants include **Eliott** and **Elliot**.

**Ellis** *See* ELIAS.

**Elm** *See* ELMER.

**Elmer** English name based on the Old English *aethel* ('noble') and *maer* ('famous'). The name's popularity in the USA may be traced back to the brothers Ebenezer and Jonathan Elmer, who were prominent figures during the American War of Independence. **Elm** and **Elmy** are familiar forms of the name. *See also* AYLMER.

**Elmo** Italian name based ultimately on the Old German *helm* ('helmet' or 'protection'). Also found as a familiar form of ERASMUS.

**Elmore** English name that originated as a place name meaning 'river banks with elms'.

**Elmy** *See* ELMER.

**Elroy** English name that developed as a variant of LEROY. It has proved particularly popular among black Americans since the nineteenth century.

**Elsdon** English name that originated as a place name (from Northumbria) based on the Old English for 'Elli's valley'.

**Elton** English name that originated as a place name based on the Old English for 'Ella's settlement'. It made its debut as a first name in the twentieth century.

**Elvis** English name that is thought to have evolved from the surname Elwes, which had its origins in ÉLOISE, or alternatively from the Irish Ailbhe. Today it is universally associated with the US rock and roll singer Elvis Presley (1935–77), who inherited the name from his father Vernon Elvis Presley.

**Elwin** *See* ELWYN.

**Elwyn** Welsh name that is thought to have evolved from the Welsh for 'fair brow' or 'elf friend'. It has also been suggested that it may have come about as a variant of ALVIN. Other versions of the name include **Elwin**.

**Ely** *See* ELI.

**Emanuel** Biblical name based on the Hebrew Immanuel, meaning 'God with us'. It appears in the Bible and was consequently taken up by English speakers in the seventeenth century. Often spelled **Emmanuel** or found, in the USA, in the Spanish variant MANUEL. Familiar forms of the name include **Man** and **Manny**.

**Emerson** English name meaning 'son of Emery' that has made occasional appearances as a first name in relatively recent times. **Emmerson** is a rare variant.

**Emery** English name based on the Old German Emmerich or Amalric, itself from the Old German *amal* ('labour') and *ric* ('ruler') and meaning 'powerful noble'. It came to England with the Normans and until the eighteenth century was borne by both sexes. Occasionally encountered as **Emory**.

**Emil** *See* EMILE.

**Emile** French name descended ultimately from the Roman Aemilius, itself from the Latin for 'striving' or 'eager'. Usually rendered in France as **Émile**, it has made irregular appearances among English speakers since the middle of the nineteenth century. **Emilio** is an Italian, Spanish and Portuguese variant.

**Émile/Emilio** *See* EMILE.

**Emlyn** Welsh name that is sometimes traced back to the Roman Aemilius, itself from the Latin for 'striving' or 'eager', or else from unknown

Celtic roots. It has retained its strong Welsh associations.

**Emmanuel** *See* EMANUEL.

**Emmerson** *See* EMERSON.

**Emmet** English name that developed from EMMA. It is sometimes bestowed in Ireland in honour of the Irish rebel Robert Emmet (1778–1803).

**Emo** German name sometimes variously given the meaning 'serious' or 'mother' or otherwise linked to the Irish Emagh.

**Emory** *See* EMERY.

**Emrys** Welsh name that developed as a variant of AMBROSE. Apparently a twentieth-century introduction, it is still largely confined to Wales.

**Enda** Irish Gaelic name based on the Gaelic *éan* ('bird').

**Engelbert** German name based on the Old German *Angil* ('Angle') and *berht* ('famous' or 'bright'). Also found as **Englebert** – as borne by British singer Englebert

Humperdinck (Arnold George Dorsey; b. 1936).

**Englebert** *See* ENGELBERT.

**Enoch** English name based on the Hebrew Hanok, thought to mean 'dedicated', 'trained' or 'experienced'. It appears in the Bible and was consequently taken up by English Puritans in the seventeenth century.

**Enos** Biblical name based on the Hebrew for 'mankind'. It is sometimes encountered in Ireland as an anglicization of the Gaelic Aonghus (*see* ANGUS).

**Enzo** Italian name possibly based on the Old German *ent* ('giant'). Also used as a shortened form of Lorenzo.

**Eoan** *See* EUGENE.

**Eochaidh** ('yochee') Irish name based on the the Irish Gaelic *each* ('horse'). It appears in Irish legend as the name of a sun-god. Also found as **Eochy**.

**Eochy** *See* EOCHAIDH.

**Eoghan** ('owan') Irish and

Scottish name of uncertain origin. It may have evolved from the Gaelic words for 'yew' and 'born' and may mean 'born of the yew'. It is sometimes encountered in Ireland as an anglicization of EUGENE or OWEN and in Scotland of EWAN, EVAN or HUGH.

**Eph** *See* EPHRAIM.

**Ephraim** Biblical name based on the Hebrew Ephrayim, meaning 'fruitful'. It appears in the Bible as the name of Joseph's second son. **Effie** and **Eph** are familiar forms of the name.

**Erasmus** English name based via Latin on the Greek Erasmos, itself from *eran* ('to love') and thus meaning 'beloved', 'desired' or 'longed for'. *See also* ELMO.

**Erastus** English name descended from the Greek Erastos, meaning 'beloved' or 'dear one'. Today it is equally familiar in its diminutive form **Rastus**.

**Eric** English name based on the Old Norse Eyrekr, itself

from *ei* ('ever' or 'always') or *einn* ('one') and *rikr* ('ruler') and thus meaning 'ever-ruling' or possibly 'island ruler'. It would appear that the name came to England with Danish settlers before the Norman Conquest. Variants include **Rick** and **Ricky** (or **Rikki**).

**Erle** *See* EARL.

**Ern** *See* ERNEST.

**Ernan** *See* IARNAN.

**Ernest** English name based on the Old German *eornost* ('earnestness' or 'seriousness'). It made its first appearances among English speakers at the time of accession of the Hanoverian George I. Occasionally found as **Earnest** through confusion with the ordinary vocabulary word. Shortened to **Ern** or **Ernie**.

**Ernie** *See* ERNEST.

**Errol** Scottish name that originated as a place name. Sometimes associated with EARL, from which it may have evolved, or HAROLD, it proved especially popular among black Americans in the twentieth century.

**Erskine** Scottish name taken from a place name (Erskine near Glasgow) that was subsequently taken up among English speakers from the nineteenth century.

**Erwin** *See* IRWIN.

**Esau** ('eesor') Biblical name based upon the Hebrew Esaw, meaning 'hairy'. It appears in the Bible as the name of one of Isaac and Rebecca's twin sons, who was born covered with red hair.

**Esmond** English name based on the Old German *est* ('favour' or 'grace') and *mund* ('protection') and thus meaning 'favoured protector'. Occasionally found as **Esmund**.

**Esmund** *See* ESMOND.

**Etan** *See* ETHAN.

**Ethan** Biblical name descended from the Hebrew Eythan, meaning 'constant', 'firm', 'strong' or alternatively 'long-lived'. It appears in the Bible and was taken up by

Puritans from the seventeenth century. **Etan** is a Jewish variant.

**Ethelbert** English name based on the Old English *aethele* ('noble') and *beorht* ('bright'). Borne by the brother of Alfred the Great, it continued in irregular use after the Norman Conquest. *See also* ALBERT.

**Ethelred** English name based on the Old English *aethele* ('noble') and *raed* ('counsel') and thus meaning 'noble counsel'. It was common in England before the Norman Conquest.

**Étienne** French name that evolved as a variant of STEPHEN.

**Euan** *See* EWAN.

**Eugene** English name descended via French from the Greek Eugenios, meaning 'noble' or 'well-born'. It was borne by several early Christian saints and popes. In Ireland it became accepted as an anglicization of **Aodh**, EOGHAN or **Eoan**. Shortened

to GENE. *See also* EWAN; OWEN.

**Eustace** English name descended via French from the Greek Eustakhios, from the Greek *eu* ('good') and *stakhus* ('ear of corn' or 'grapes') and thus interpreted as meaning 'fruitful'. *See also* STACY.

**Evan** Welsh name based on **Iefan** or **Ieuan**, a variant of the English JOHN. It seems to have made its first appearance among the Welsh around 1500. Also found as **Ifan**.

**Evander** Roman name based on the Greek Euandros, from the Greek *eu* ('good') and *aner* ('man'). It appears in Roman legend as the name of a hero who founded a city on the site of modern Rome. It has proved popular among Scots, who sometimes treat it as an anglicization of the Gaelic Iomhair.

**Evelyn** English name bestowed upon both sexes. As a masculine name it appears to have made its first appearance early in the twentieth century. Notable bearers of the name have included British novelist Evelyn Waugh (1903–66).

**Everard** English name based on the Old German *eber* ('boar') and *hart* ('brave' or 'strong') and thus meaning 'fierce as a boar'.

**Everett** English name that is thought to have evolved as a variant of EVERARD. Also encountered as **Everitt**.

**Everitt** *See* EVERETT.

**Ewan** ('yoowan') English version of the Gaelic EOGHAN (also the source of OWEN). It has retained its strong Scottish associations. Also spelled **Euan** or **Ewen**.

**Ewart** English name that developed out of EDWARD or else from a place name in Northumbria. The name

enjoyed modest popularity among English speakers in tribute to Prime Minister William Ewart Gladstone (1809–98).

**Ewen** *See* EWAN.

**Ewing** English name meaning 'law friend'. Also found as **Ewin** or **Ewynn**.

**Ezekiel** Biblical name based on the Hebrew Yehezqel, meaning 'God will strengthen'. It appears in the Bible and was consequently taken up by English Puritans in the seventeenth century. Shortened to **Zeke**.

**Ezra** Hebrew name meaning 'help'. It appears in the Bible as the name of a prophet and was consequently taken up by Puritans in the seventeenth century.

# BOYS' NAMES

**Fabian** English name descended from the Roman Fabianus, itself based on the Latin *faba* ('bean') and thus signifying a grower of beans. It is thought to have been introduced to England by the Normans. Variants include the French **Fabien** and the Italian, Spanish and Portuguese **Fabio**.

**Fabien/Fabio** *See* FABIAN.

**Fachtna** ('fokna') Irish name of uncertain origin, though possibly based on the Gaelic for 'malicious' or 'hostile'.

**Faisal** Arabic name meaning 'judge'. Also found as **Faysal** or **Feisal**.

**Farley** English name that originated as a surname meaning 'fair meadow'.

**Faron** *See* FARRAN.

**Farouk** *See* FARUQ.

**Farquhar** ('farkwah') Scottish name that developed as an anglicized form of the Scottish Gaelic Fearchar, itself based on the Gaelic for 'man' and 'dear' and thus meaning 'dear one'.

**Farran** English name that may have been based on the Old French for 'pilferer' or 'ferret' or else developed as a medieval variant of FERDINAND. Other forms of the name include **Farren** and **Faron**.

**Farrell** Irish name based on the Irish Gaelic for 'warrior'.

**Farren** *See* FARRAN.

**Farrer** English name that was based ultimately on the Latin for 'iron'.

**Faruq** Arabic name meaning 'person who can tell right from wrong'. **Farouk** is a variant spelling.

**Faulkner** English name that originated as a surname itself descended from the Roman Falco, meaning 'falconer'.

**Faysal** *See* FAISAL.

**Fearghal** *See* FERGAL.

**Fearghas/Feargus** *See* FERGUS.

**Fedele** *See* FIDEL.

**Feichin** ('fayhin') Irish name based on the Irish Gaelic *fiach* ('raven').

**Feisal** *See* FAISAL.

**Feliciano** *See* FELIX.

**Felix** Roman name based on the Latin *felix* ('happy' or 'lucky'). It appears in the Bible and has enjoyed a marked resurgence in popularity since the 1990s. Variants in other languages include **Feliciano** and the Irish PHELIM.

**Fenn** English name that originated as a surname meaning 'marsh-dweller'.

**Fenton** English name that originated as a place name from northern England. The original place name was based on the Old English *fenn* ('marsh' or 'fen') and *tun* ('settlement').

**Ferd/Ferdie** *See* FERDINAND.

**Ferdinand** German, French and English name based on the Old German *fridu* ('peace') and *nand* ('bravery') and thus meaning 'peace through bravery'. Another derivation suggests the name developed out of the Old German *farth* ('journey') and *nand* ('prepared'). Variants include the Spanish **Fernando**. Shortened to **Ferd**, **Ferdie**, **Ferdy** or **Nandy**.

**Ferdy** *See* FERDINAND.

**Fergal** Anglicized form of the Irish **Fearghal**, itself based on the Gaelic *fear* ('man') and *gal* ('valour') and thus meaning 'man of valour'.

**Fergie** *See* FERGUS.

**Fergus** English version of the Gaelic **Fearghas**, based on *fear* ('man') and *gus* ('force' or 'strength') and thus meaning 'man of force'. Borne by a legendary Irish hero of Ulster, the name has retained its strong Scottish and Irish associations. Variants include **Feargus**. Shortened to **Fergie** or **Fergy**.

**Fergy** *See* FERGUS.

**Fernando** *See* FERDINAND.

**Fernley** Cornish first name of unknown meaning.

**Ferrer** Spanish name that originated as a Catalan surname meaning 'blacksmith'. It became popular in tribute to St Vicente Ferrer (d. 1418).

**Fester** German variant of SYLVESTER. The name became familiar to English speakers through a character of the name in the popular 1960s US television series (later filmed) *The Addams Family*.

**Festus** Roman name meaning either 'festive' or else 'steadfast'. It appears in the Bible and has appeared among English speakers on an occasional basis since the medieval period.

**Fiachna** *See* FIACHRA.

**Fiachra** Irish name based on the Gaelic *fiach* ('raven'). It was borne by a seventh-century French saint, the patron saint of gardeners. Also found as **Fiachna**, a variant revived in the twentieth century.

**Fidel** Spanish name descended from the Roman Fidelis, itself from the Latin *fidelis* ('faithful'). **Fedele** is an Italian variant.

**Fielding** English name that originated in a surname meaning 'field'.

**Fife** Scottish name that originated as a place name based on the name of the legendary Pictish hero Fib. Largely confined to people with strong Scottish associations, it also appears in the variant form **Fyfe**.

**Finbar** Anglicized form of the Irish **Fionnbarr** (or **Fionbharr**), itself based on the Gaelic *fionn* ('fair' or 'white') and *barr* ('head'). It was borne by several early Irish saints. Also found as **Finnbar**.

**Findlay** *See* FINLAY.

**Fingal** Anglicized form of
the Scottish Fionnghall, itself
based on *fionn* ('fair' or 'white')
and *gall* ('stranger') and thus
meaning 'pale stranger'.
Initially it was borne chiefly by
Norse immigrants in Scotland.
Also found as **Fingall**.

**Fingall** *See* FINGAL.

**Finian** *See* FINNIAN.

**Finlay** Scottish name
descended from the Gaelic
Fionnlagh, itself based on the
Gaelic *fionn* ('fair' or 'white')
and *laogh* ('warrior') and thus
meaning 'fair hero'. Also found
as **Findlay** or **Finley**.

**Finley** *See* FINLAY.

**Finn** Irish name based on the
Gaelic *fionn* ('fair' or 'white').
Also found as **Fionn**, it was
borne by the celebrated
legendary hero Finn MacCool.

**Finnian** Irish name based on
the Gaelic *fionn* ('fair' or
'white'). Also found as **Finian**.

**Finnbar** *See* FINBAR.

**Fintan** Irish name based on
the Irish Gaelic *fionn* ('white'

or 'fair') and another word
variously meaning 'ancient' or
'fire'. The name was borne by
several Celtic saints.

**Fionbharr** *See* FINBAR.

**Fionn** *See* FINN.

**Fionnbarr** *See* FINBAR.

**Fisher** English name that
originated as a surname
meaning 'fisherman'.

**Fitz** *See* FITZGERALD;
FITZROY.

**Fitzgerald** English name
meaning 'son of Gerald'.
Ultimately of Old French
origin, it is often shortened to
**Fitz**.

**Fitzroy** English name
meaning 'son of the king'. It
was used initially as a nickname
for illegitimate sons of English
monarchs. Shortened to **Fitz**.

**Flann** Irish name that
developed as a shortened form
of **Flannan**, itself based on the
Gaelic *flann* ('red' or 'ruddy').
Famous bearers of the name
have included the Irish novelist

Flann O'Brien (Brian O'Nolan; 1911–66).

**Flannan** *See* FLANN.

**Fleming** English name that originated in a surname meaning 'man of Flanders'.

**Fletcher** English name that originated as a surname denoting a maker of arrows, originally based on the Old French *fleche* ('arrow'). It is perhaps best known through Fletcher Christian (c. 1764–94), leader of the infamous 1789 *Bounty* mutiny.

**Flinn** *See* FLYNN.

**Flint** English name meaning 'stream'.

**Flip** *See* PHILIP.

**Florian** English and German name descended from the Roman Florianus, itself based on the Latin *flos* ('flower'). It has made irregular appearances among English speakers since medieval times.

**Floyd** English name based on the Welsh LLOYD. It has been in use as a first name since the

nineteenth century, chiefly in the USA.

**Fluellen** *See* LLEWELLYN.

**Flynn** Scottish name based on the Scots Gaelic for 'son of the red-haired one'. Also found as **Flinn**.

**Fonsie** *See* ALPHONSE.

**Forbes** Scottish name based on the Gaelic *forba* ('field' or 'district').

**Ford** English name that originated as a surname denoting a person living close to a river crossing.

**Forest** *See* FORREST.

**Forrest** English name based on the ordinary vocabulary word 'forest'. Its popularity in the USA can be traced back to the fame of Confederate commander Nathan Bedford Forrest (1821–77). Also found as **Forest**.

**Forrester** English name meaning 'forester'. Ultimately of Old French origin, it may also be found as **Forster**.

**Forster** *See* FORRESTER.

**Foster** English name of obscure origin, variously interpreted as meaning 'foster-parent', 'forester', 'shearer' or 'saddle-tree maker'. Famous bearers of the name have included US statesman John Foster Dulles (1888–1959).

**France** English name based either on the name of the country or else a variant of FRANCIS.

**Francesco** Italian equivalent of FRANCIS. Sometimes shortened to **Franco**.

**Francis** English name descended from the Roman Franciscus, itself from the Latin for 'Frenchman'. The name is supposed to have had its origin in St Francis of Assisi (1182–1226), who was renamed by his father following his return from France. Shortened to FRANK or **Frankie**. *See also* PACO.

**Francisco** Spanish equivalent of FRANCIS. Sometimes shortened to **Franco**.

**Franco** *See* FRANCESCO; FRANCISCO.

**François** ('fronswa') French name descended ultimately from the Roman Franciscus. Notable bearers of the name have include two sixteenth-century kings of France.

**Frank** English name that developed as a shortened form of FRANCIS or FRANKLIN but is now frequently considered to be a name in its own right. The name became increasingly common among English speakers from the middle of the nineteenth century. An informal version is **Frankie**.

**Frankie** *See* FRANCIS; FRANK; FRANKLIN.

**Franklin** English name based on the Middle English *frankeleyn* ('freeman'). In medieval times the word was used to describe a person who owned land but who was not of noble rank. Also found as **Franklyn**. Shortened to FRANK or **Frankie**.

**Franklyn** *See* FRANKLIN.

**Fraser** Scottish name that has

been in occasional use as a first name among English speakers since the 1930s. Ultimately derived from a Norman place name of uncertain meaning, it has retained its strong Scottish links. Also found as **Frazer** or **Frazier**.

**Frazer/Frazier** *See* FRASER.

**Fred** English name that developed as a shortened form of FREDERICK and which is occasionally considered a name in its own right. Variants include **Freddie** and **Freddy**. *See also* ALFRED.

**Freddie/Freddy/ Frederic** *See* FRED; FREDERICK.

**Frederick** English name based on the Old German *fridu* ('peace') and *ric* ('ruler' or 'power') and usually interpreted to mean 'peaceful ruler'. It came to England with the Normans in the eleventh century but it was not until the eighteenth century that the name became widespread. Also found as **Frederic** or **Fredric**. Variants in other languages include the German **Friedrich**. Shortened to FRED, **Freddie** or **Freddy**. *See also* FRITZ.

**Fredric** *See* FREDERICK.

**Freeman** English name meaning 'free man'.

**Friedrich** *See* FREDERICK.

**Fritz** German equivalent of FREDERICK.

**Fulton** Scottish name, possibly based upon a Scottish place name, that has been in occasional use as a first name since the end of the nineteenth century.

**Fyfe** *See* FIFE.

**Fyodor** *See* THEODORE.

# BOYS' NAMES

**Gab/Gabby** *See* GABRIEL.

**Gabriel** Hebrew name meaning 'my strength is God' or 'man of God'. It appears in the Bible as the name of the Archangel Gabriel and was consequently taken up by English speakers during the medieval period. Shortened to **Gab** or **Gabby**.

**Galahad** English name of uncertain origin. It would seem to have been invented by early compilers of Arthurian legend as the name of the most virtuous of King Arthur's knights. Attempts have been made to link the name with the Hebrew Gilead.

**Gallagher** Irish name that originated as an Irish Gaelic surname meaning 'foreign helper'.

**Galloway** Irish name that originated as an Irish Gaelic surname meaning 'stranger'.

**Galvin** English name variously taken up as a variant of GAWAIN or else developed as an Irish Gaelic name based on *geal* ('white') and *fionn* ('bright') or *gealbhan* ('sparrow').

**Gamaliel** Biblical name descended from the Hebrew Gamliel, meaning 'my reward is God' or 'recompense of God'. It appears in the Bible as the name of a teacher of St Paul. It was the middle name of US President Warren G. Harding (1865–1923).

**Garcia** Spanish and Portuguese name of uncertain origin. Recorded in medieval times as Garsea, it may be linked to the Basque *artz* ('bear').

**Gareth** Welsh name that developed out of GERAINT, although it has also been linked with such names as GARTH,

GARY and GERARD and is often interpreted as meaning 'gentle'. Having established itself in Wales, it made its first appearance in England as early as the sixteenth century. Shortened to **Gaz**.

**Garey** *See* GARY.

**Garfield** English name based on the Old English *gar* ('spear-shaped area' or 'triangle of land') and *feld* ('open country'). It has been in occasional use as a first name, chiefly in the USA, since the end of the nineteenth century. Shortened to **Garry** or GARY.

**Garnet** English name that was taken up in the nineteenth century at a time when many other jewel names came into fashion.

**Garret** Irish and English name that was adopted as an occasional first name from the seventeenth century, becoming particularly popular in Ireland. The name itself seems to have been based on GERALD or GERARD. Also found as **Garrett**. **Garry** and GARY are shortened forms of the name. *See also* GARRISON.

**Garrett** *See* GARRET.

**Garrick** English name based on the Old English *gar* ('spear') and *ric* ('ruler'). Its initial popularity may have been promoted by the fame of the eighteenth-century British actor David Garrick (1717–79).

**Garrison** English name that originated as a place name (Garriston in North Yorkshire). Another possibility is that the name evolved simply as 'Garrett's son'. The name was boosted in the USA through admiration for William Lloyd Garrison (1805–79), a noted campaigner against slavery.

**Garry** *See* GARFIELD; GARRET; GARY.

**Garth** English name based on the Old Norse *garthr* ('enclosure'). Sometimes treated as a variant of GARETH, it enjoyed a peak in popularity in the 1940s. Notable bearers of the name have included US country singer Garth Brooks (b. 1962).

**Garve** Scottish name that originated as a place name meaning 'rough place'.

**Gary** English name that was probably of Norman French origin, perhaps from the Germanic *gar* ('spear'). Often linked to the Welsh GARETH, it became well known through US film actor Gary Cooper (Frank James Cooper; 1901–61), who took his pseudonym from Gary, Indiana, where his agent lived. Also found as **Garry** or **Garey**. Sometime shortened to **Gaz**. *See also* GARFIELD; GARRET.

**Gaston** French name based on the German for 'stranger' or 'guest'.

**Gavin** Scottish and English form of the Welsh GAWAIN. It enjoyed a peak in popularity in the 1970s and 1980s.

**Gawain** Welsh name possibly based on the Welsh *gwalch* ('hawk'). It is often associated with Sir Gawain, one of the knights of the Round Table in Arthurian legend. Since the sixteenth century it has largely been replaced by GAVIN. *See also* GALVIN.

**Gayelord** *See* GAYLORD.

**Gaylord** English name based on the French *gaillard* ('dandy'). It has become rare since the middle of the twentieth century. **Gayelord** is a variant form.

**Gaz** *See* GARETH; GARY.

**Gene** English name that developed as a shortened form of EUGENE. It was particularly popular in the USA in the first half of the twentieth century.

**Geoff** *See* GEOFFREY.

**Geoffrey** English name based on the Old German *gavja* ('territory') and *fridu* ('peace') and thus meaning 'peaceful ruler'. Another derivation suggests that it may have evolved from GODFREY. Commonly shortened to **Geoff**. Variants include **Jeffrey** (or **Jeffery**) and its abbreviated form **Jeff**.

**Geordie** *See* GEORGE.

**George** English name based via the Roman Georgius on the Greek Georgios, itself from *geōrgos* ('farmer'). The name of the patron saint of England, it became popular after the accession of George I in 1714. Variants in other languages include **Giorgio** and **Jorge**. Among informal versions are **Georgie**, **Georgy** and **Geordie**.

**Georgie/Georgy** *See* GEORGE.

**Ger** *See* GERALD; GERARD.

**Geraint** ('gerighnt') Welsh name of uncertain meaning, possibly based via the Roman Gerontius on the Greek *gerontos* ('old man'). The name features in Arthurian legend as that of one of the knights of the Round Table.

**Gerald** English and Irish name based on the Old German *ger* ('spear') and *wald* ('rule') and thus meaning 'spear rule'. The name came to England with the Normans and later acquired a reputation as an aristocratic name. **Jerrold** is a variant of largely historical interest. Variants in other languages include the Welsh **Gerallt**. Shortened to **Ger** or GERRY. *See also* GARRET.

**Gerallt** *See* GERALD.

**Gerard** English, Irish and Dutch name descended from the Old German *ger* ('spear') and *hardu* ('brave' or 'hardy') and thus meaning 'brave with the spear'. Commonly shortened to **Ger** or GERRY. Variants include **Gerhard**, **Gerrard** and **Jerrard**. *See also* GARRET.

**Gerhard** *See* GERARD.

**Germain/Germaine** *See* JERMAINE.

**Gerrard** *See* GERARD.

**Gerrie** *See* GERRY.

**Gerry** English name that evolved as a variant of such names as GERALD and GERARD. Also found as **Gerrie** or JERRY.

**Gervaise** *See* GERVASE.

**Gervase** English name descended from the Roman Gervasius, itself from the Greek *geras* ('old age'), or else on the Old German *ger* ('spear') and *vas* ('servant') and thus meaning 'spear servant'. The name of a first-century saint, it was taken up by English Roman

Catholics in the sixteenth century. Also found as **Gervaise** or JARVIS.

**Gerwen** *See* GERWYN.

**Gerwyn** Welsh name meaning 'fair love'. Also spelled **Gerwen**.

**Gethin** Welsh name meaning 'dark-skinned'.

**Gian/Gianni** *See* GIOVANNI.

**Gib/Gibbie** *See* GILBERT.

**Gid** *See* GIDEON.

**Gideon** Hebrew name meaning 'hewer' or 'one who cuts down' or alternatively 'having a stump for a hand' or 'great warrior'. It appears in the Bible and was consequently taken up by English speakers in the seventeenth century. Today it is more common in the USA than elsewhere. Shortened to **Gid**.

**Gil** *See* GILBERT; GILCHRIST.

**Gilbert** English name based via French on the Old German *gisil* ('pledge' or 'hostage') and

*berht* ('bright' or 'famous') and meaning 'bright pledge'. In Scotland it is also treated as an anglicized form of the Gaelic Gilbride, meaning 'servant of St Bridget'. Shortened to **Gib**, **Gibbie**, **Gil**, **Gilly**, BERT or BERTIE.

**Gilchrist** English name based on the Gaelic for 'servant of Christ'. It has a long history but seems to have disappeared from use since the nineteenth century.

**Giles** English name based via French on the Greek Aigidios, itself from the Greek *aigidion* ('kid' or 'young goat'). The name was moderately common among English speakers of both sexes in medieval times, especially in Scotland, but is now reserved for males. **Gyles** is a variant form.

**Gillespie** Anglicized form of the Scottish Gaelic Gilleasbaig, meaning 'servant of the bishop'.

**Gilly** *See* GILBERT.

**Gilroy** Irish and Scottish name based on the Gaelic for 'son of the red-haired lad'.

**Ginger** English name that developed as a nickname for anyone with red hair or a tempestuous character.

**Gino** ('jeenoh') Italian name that developed as a shortened form of various longer names with a '-gino' ending but is now often considered a name in its own right.

**Giorgio** *See* GEORGE.

**Giovanni** Italian version of JOHN. Shortened to **Gian** or **Gianni**.

**Giuseppe** ('jusepee') Italian version of JOSEPH. *See also* BEPPE.

**Gladstone** Scottish name that originated as a place name based on the Old English *glaed* ('kite') and *stan* ('rock'). It has made irregular appearances as a first name since the late nineteenth century, sometimes in tribute to British prime minister William Gladstone (1809–98).

**Glanville** English name based either on a Norman French place name or else on the Old English for 'clean field'. Variants include **Glenvil** and **Glenville**.

**Glen** *See* GLENN.

**Glendower** Welsh name that originated as a place name based on the Welsh *glyn* ('valley') and *dwr* ('water'). Its adoption as a first name was inspired by admiration for the Welsh hero Owen Glendower (c. 1359–1416). Also found as **Glyndwr**.

**Glenn** Scottish and English name based on the Gaelic *gleann* ('valley'). It was taken up as a first name for boys towards the end of the nineteenth century. **Glen** is a variant form. *See also* GLYN.

**Glenvil/Glenville** *See* GLANVILLE.

**Glyn** Welsh name based on the Welsh *glyn* ('valley'). Its early development in the early twentieth century may have been influenced by the similar GLENN and GWYN. Having established itself in Wales it began to make appearances elsewhere in the English-speaking world. Also found as **Glynn**.

**Glyndwr** *See* GLENDOWER.

**Glynn** *See* GLYN.

**Goddard** English name that originated in a surname based on the Old English *god* ('god') and *heard* ('brave' or 'hardy'). Variants in other languages include the German **Gotthard**.

**Godfrey** English name based on the Old German *god* ('god') and *fridu* ('peace') and thus meaning 'god's peace'. It came to England with the Normans and was a popular choice of name through medieval times and beyond. Variants in other languages include the German **Gottfried**.

**Goldwin** English name that originated as a surname descended from the Old English Godwine, itself from *gold* ('gold') and *wine* ('friend'). **Goldwyn** is a variant form.

**Goldwyn** *See* GOLDWIN.

**Gomer** Hebrew name meaning 'complete'. It appears in the Bible and was consequently taken up by Puritans in the seventeenth century. It appears in Welsh legend as the name of the mythical founder of the Welsh people.

**Gomez** Spanish name that originated as a surname meaning 'man'.

**Gopal** Indian name based on the Sanskrit for 'protector of cows'.

**Gordon** Scottish name that originated as a place name possibly based on the Celtic for 'spacious fort'. The name retains its strong Scottish associations, being a famous clan name.

**Goronwy** Welsh name of uncertain meaning. It appears in the *Mabinogion* and as a consequence has been taken up on an occasional basis over succeeding centuries. Shortened to **Gron**.

**Gottfried** *See* GODFREY.

**Gotthard** *See* GODDARD.

**Grady** Irish name meaning 'noble'.

**Graeme** *See* GRAHAM.

**Graham** English and Scottish name of twelfth-century origin, thought to have come from an English place name (Grantham in Lincolnshire), which itself was based on the Old English *grand* ('gravel') and *ham* ('homestead'), thus meaning 'gravelly place' or alternatively 'Granta's homestead'. Also found as **Gram**, **Graeme** or **Grahame**.

**Grahame/Gram** *See* GRAHAM.

**Granger** English name meaning 'farmer' or 'bailiff'.

**Grant** Scottish name that originated as a surname probably based on the Norman French *grand* ('large' or 'tall'). As a first name it has enjoyed particular popularity in Canada and the USA, where it was promoted through US President Ulysses S. Grant (1822–85).

**Granville** English name based on a Norman baronial surname, itself modelled on a place name based on *grand* ('large') and *ville* ('settlement'). Also found as **Grenville**.

**Gray** English name based on the ordinary vocabulary word 'grey'. Also found as **Grey**.

**Grayson** English name that was originally applied to the children of grey-haired men. Also found as **Greyson**.

**Greg/Gregg/Gregor** *See* GREGORY.

**Gregory** English name based via the Roman Gregorius on the Greek Gregorios, itself from *gregorein* ('to watch' or 'be vigilant'). Because St Peter bade his followers to 'be vigilant' the name was taken up with some enthusiasm by early Christians. Variants include the Scottish **Gregor** and the Welsh **Grigor**. Shortened to **Greg**, **Gregg** or **Greig**.

**Greig** *See* GREGORY.

**Grenville** *See* GRANVILLE.

**Gresham** English name that originated as a place name based on the Old English for 'grazing' and 'hamlet'.

**Greville** English name that originated as a surname based on a Norman French place name. The name has strong aristocratic associations, having been borne as a surname by the Earls of Warwick.

**Grey** *See* GRAY.

**Greyson** *See* GRAYSON.

**Griff** *See* GRIFFITH.

**Griffin** Welsh name descended from the Roman Griffinus but also treated as a variant of GRIFFITH.

**Griffith** English version of the Welsh **Gruffudd** or **Gruffydd**, itself based on the Welsh for 'lord' or 'prince'. Records of its use in Wales go back to at least the sixteenth century. Shortened to **Griff**. *See also* GRIFFIN.

**Grigor** *See* GREGORY.

**Gron** *See* GORONWY.

**Grover** English name that originated as a place name based on the Old English *graf* ('grove'). As a first name it is confined largely to the USA, sometimes used in tribute to US President Stephen Grover Cleveland (1837–1908).

**Gruffudd/Gruffydd** *See* GRIFFITH.

**Guido** *See* GUY.

**Gunnar/Gunter** *See* GÜNTHER.

**Günther** German name based on the Old German *gund* ('strife') and *heri* ('army'). It was taken up by English speakers in medieval times but has never been common. Also found as **Gunter** or **Gunnar**.

**Gus** English name that evolved as a shortened form of such names as ANGUS and AUGUSTUS. **Gussie** is a familiar form. *See also* GUSTAV.

**Gussie** *See* GUS.

**Gustaf** *See* GUSTAV.

**Gustav** Swedish name descended from Gotstaf, itself from *got* ('god') and *stafr* ('staff') and thus meaning 'staff of the gods'. Notable bearers of the name have included British composer Gustav Holst (1874–1934), whose parents were Swedish. Variants include the Swedish **Gustaf** and the

French **Gustave**. Shortened to GUS.

**Gustave** *See* GUSTAV.

**Guthrie** Scottish name that originated as a surname based on the Scottish Gaelic for 'windy'.

**Guy** English name based via French on the Old German Wido, from *wit* ('wide') or *witu* ('wood'). It came to England with the Normans in the eleventh century and subsequently became popular through the medieval romance *Guy of Warwick*. Variants in other languages include the Italian **Guido**.

**Gwilym** *See* WILLIAM.

**Gwyn** Welsh name based on the Welsh *gwyn* ('white', 'fair' or 'blessed'). It has retained its strong Welsh associations although it has made occasional appearances elsewhere in the English-speaking world since the early twentieth century. Also found as **Gwynn**. *See also* WYNN.

**Gwynfor** Welsh name based on the Welsh *gwyn* ('white', 'fair' or 'blessed') and *mawr* ('great' or 'large') and interpreted to mean 'fair lord' or 'fair place'. Apparently an early twentieth-century introduction. **Wynfor** is a variant.

**Gwynn** *See* GWYN.

**Gyles** *See* GILES.

# BOYS' NAMES

**Hackett** English name that originated as a surname meaning 'little woodcutter' in Old Norse.

**Hadley** English name based on a place name meaning 'heathery hill'.

**Hadrian** *See* ADRIAN.

**Hadyn** *See* HAYDN.

**Haig** English name that originated as a surname meaning 'one who lives in an enclosure'.

**Hal** *See* HARRY; HENRY.

**Haldan** *See* HALDANE.

**Haldane** English name that originated as a surname meaning 'half Dane'. Variants include **Haldan**, **Halden** and **Haldin**.

**Halden/Haldin** *See* HALDANE.

**Hale** English name based on a place name meaning 'nook' or 'recess'.

**Hall** English name based on the ordinary vocabulary word 'hall' that has made occasional appearances as a first name over the centuries. The name was given originally to servants in the halls of great manor houses.

**Hallam** English name based on a place name meaning 'nook' or 'stone'.

**Ham** *See* ABRAHAM.

**Hamilton** English name that originated as a place name, used chiefly in Scotland and the USA. The original place name referred to the (lost) village of Hamilton or Hameldune in Leicestershire, which itself took its name from the Old English *hamel* ('flat-topped') and *dun* ('hill').

**Hamish** Scottish name descended from the Gaelic Sheumais, itself a version of **Seumas** (*see* SEAMUS). It has retained its Scottish links but is today encountered across the English-speaking world (usually where the population have Scottish connections).

**Hammond** Scottish name based on the Old German *heim* ('house' or 'home') that has been in occasional use among English speakers since the nineteenth century. Notable bearers of the name have included British novelist Hammond Innes (Ralph Hammond Innes; 1913–98).

**Hanford** English name that originated as a place name meaning 'rocky ford'.

**Hank** English name that developed as an informal version of JOHN. Originally Hankin, it is also often linked to HENRY. It established itself during the nineteenth century, chiefly in the USA.

**Hannibal** Phoenician name based on *hann* ('grace') and Baal (the name of a god) and thus meaning 'grace of Baal'. It is famous as the name of the third-century BC Carthaginian general who led his army over the Alps to launch a surprise attack on Rome.

**Hans** German equivalent of JOHN.

**Hansel** Scandinavian name meaning 'gift from God'. Best known from the fairytale of Hansel and Gretel.

**Harcourt** English name that may have originated as an Old French place name meaning 'from a fortified court' or else from the Old English for 'falconer's cottage'.

**Harding** English name based on the Old English *heard* ('brave' or 'strong').

**Hardy** English name of uncertain meaning that has been in occasional use as a first name since the early twentieth century. It is possible that the name was based originally on the ordinary vocabulary word 'hardy'.

**Hari** Indian name based on the Sanskrit for 'yellow-brown'.

**Harlan** English name that originated as a place name based on the Old English *hara* ('hare') and *land* ('land'). It is confined largely to the USA, where its initial popularity was promoted by US judge John Marshall Harlan (1833–1911), a staunch defender of civil rights. **Harland** is a variant.

**Harland** *See* HARLAN.

**Harley** English name that originated as a place name that may have meant 'hare meadow', 'long field' or 'rocky meadow'.

**Harold** English name descended from the Old English Hereweald, itself from *here* ('army') and *wealdan* ('to rule') and thus meaning 'general'. It was borne by the Saxon King Harold II, whose death at the Battle of Hastings in 1066 signalled the beginning of the Norman Conquest. Shortened to HARRY. *See also* ERROL.

**Harper** English name denoting someone who plays the harp. It is found chiefly in the USA.

**Harris** English name that originated as a surname meaning 'son of Harry'. *See also* HARRISON.

**Harrison** English name meaning 'son of Harry' that has been in regular use as a first name since the nineteenth century. Its relative popularity in the USA may have been influenced by the two presidents with the surname Harrison. Other notable bearers of the name have included US film actor Harrison Ford (b. 1942). Shortened to HARRY. *See also* HARRIS.

**Harry** English name that developed as an informal version of HENRY or HAROLD but is now frequently treated as a name in its own right. It was established among English speakers by medieval times and enjoyed another peak in popularity in the nineteenth century. **Hal** is a shortened form. *See also* HARRISON.

**Hartley** English name that originated as a place name (found in several counties of England), itself usually linked to the Old English *heorot* ('hart') and *leah* ('clearing'). Another derivation suggests it means 'stony meadow'.

**Harv/Harve** *See* HARVEY.

**Harvey** English name that originated as a surname of Breton origin, from *haer* ('battle') and *vy* ('worthy'). It came to England with the Normans and was revived in the nineteenth century. Occasionally found as **Hervey**. Shortened to **Harv** or **Harve**.

**Hasan** *See* HUSSEIN.

**Havelock** ('haverlok') English and Welsh name that has made infrequent appearances as a first name since the nineteenth century. It is usually thought to have arisen as a Welsh equivalent of OLIVER.

**Hayden** *See* HAYDN.

**Haydn** Welsh name of uncertain origin, though possibly a variant of the English surname Haddon, meaning 'hill with heather'. It may also have evolved as a Welsh version of the Celtic AIDAN. As a Germanic surname it had its roots in the medieval *heiden* ('heathen'). Also found as **Hadyn**, **Hayden** or **Haydon**.

**Haydon** *See* HAYDN.

**Headley** *See* HEDLEY.

**Heath** English name based on the ordinary vocabulary word 'heath'. Notable bearers of the name have included British cartoonist William Heath Robinson (1872–1944) and Australian film actor Heath Ledger (1979–2008).

**Heathcliff** English name meaning 'dweller by the heather cliff'. Also found as **Heathcliffe**, it is well known through the brooding Heathcliff of Emily Brontë's novel *Wuthering Heights* (1847).

**Heathcliffe** *See* HEATHCLIFF.

**Heber** Hebrew name meaning 'enclave' or 'fellowship'. A biblical name, it is also used in Ireland as an anglicized form of the Gaelic Eibhear.

**Heck/Heckie** *See* HECTOR.

**Hector** Greek name based on *ekhein* ('to hold' or 'to resist') and usually interpreted as meaning 'holding fast'. It was famous in Greek mythology as the name of the Trojan warrior killed by Achilles. In Scotland it is sometimes connected with the Gaelic EACHANN. **Heck** and **Heckie** are shortened Scottish forms.

**Heddwyn** Welsh name based on *hedd* ('peace') and *wyn* ('white' or 'blessed'). The name enjoyed some popularity among Welsh speakers in tribute to the poet Ellis Humphrey Evans, who wrote under the name Hedd Wyn until his death in the First World War.

**Hedley** English name that originated as a place name (from several locations in northern England) based on the Old English *haeth* ('heather') and *leah* ('clearing'). Also found in the variant form **Headley**.

**Heilyn** Welsh name based on *heilio* ('to prepare'). The name, which appears twice in the *Mabinogion*, was originally reserved for servants who worked as stewards or wine-pourers in big houses.

**Heinrich/Hendrik/Henri** *See* HENRY.

**Henry** English name descended from the German Heinrich, itself from *heim* ('house' or 'home') and *ric* ('ruler' or 'owner') and thus meaning 'house owner' or 'lord of the manor'. It was taken up by English speakers in the medieval period and became firmly established as a royal name, although HARRY was the more common form before the seventeenth century. **Heinrich** is a German version of the name, while **Hendrik** is Dutch and **Henri** is French. Shortened to **Hal**. *See also* HANK.

**Herb** *See* HERBERT.

**Herbert** English, German and French name based on the Old German *heri* or *hari* ('army') and *berht* ('bright') and interpreted as meaning 'famous army'. The name was relatively common among English speakers during the medieval period. Shortened forms of the name include **Herb** and **Herbie**. *See also* BERT.

**Herbie** *See* HERBERT.

**Hercules** Roman equivalent of the Greek Heracles or Herakles that resulted from the combination of the name of the Greek goddess Hera and *kleos* ('glory'), thus meaning 'glory of Hera'. It is sometimes found in Scotland as an anglicization of the Gaelic Athairne and in the Shetlands as an equivalent of the Norse Hacon. **Herk** and **Herkie** are shortened forms of the name.

**Hereward** English name based on the Old English *here* ('army') and *weard* ('protection'). It became famous through the Anglo-Saxon leader Hereward the Wake, who rebelled against Norman rule in the eleventh century.

**Herk/Herkie** *See* HERCULES.

**Herman** English name descended from the Old German Hariman, itself from *hari* ('army') and *man* ('man') and thus meaning 'soldier' or 'warrior'. It was taken up by English speakers around the middle of the nineteenth century, chiefly among German immigrants in the USA.

**Hervey** *See* HARVEY.

**Hesketh** English name that originated as a place name (from northern England) based on the Old Norse *hestr* ('horse') and *skeithr* ('racecourse'). It was probably inspired by the long-established tradition of horse-racing in Scandinavia.

**Hew/Hewie** *See* HUGH.

**Hezekiah** Biblical name based on the Hebrew Hizqiyah, meaning 'my strength is Yah' or 'Yah is strength' (Yah being an alternative name of Jehovah or God). It appears in the Bible and was subsequently taken up by English speakers in the seventeenth century.

**Hi** *See* HIRAM.

**Hieronymus** *See* JEROME.

**Hil** *See* HILARY.

**Hilary** English name
descended ultimately from the
Roman Hilarius, itself based on
the Latin *hilaris* ('cheerful'). It
was taken up by English
speakers during the medieval
period as a name chiefly for
boys. Also found as **Hillary**.
Variants in other languages
include the Welsh **Ilar**.
Shortened to **Hil** or **Hilly**. *See
also* ELLERY.

**Hildebrand** German name
based on the Old German *hild*
('battle') and *brand* ('sword'). It
fell out of use among English
speakers around the end of the
medieval period but enjoyed a
minor revival in the nineteenth
century.

**Hillary/Hilly** *See* HILARY.

**Hilton** English name that
originated as a place name
meaning 'from the hill farm'.
Also found as **Hylton**.

**Hiram** Hebrew name
possibly descended from
Ahiram, meaning 'my brother
is exalted', or else of unknown
Phoenician origin. It appears in
the Bible as the name of a king
of Tyre and was subsequently
taken up by Puritans in the

seventeenth century. It is now
confined largely to the USA.
Also found as **Hyram**.
Shortened to **Hi**.

**Hob** *See* ROBERT.

**Hobart** *See* HUBERT.

**Hodge** *See* ROGER.

**Hogan** Irish name based on
the Irish Gaelic for 'youthful'.

**Holden** English name that
originated as a place name
meaning 'hollow valley'. As a
first name its history goes back
as far as the nineteenth century.
Today it is best known through
Holden Caulfield, the central
character in J. D. Salinger's
novel *The Catcher in the Rye*
(1951).

**Hollis** English name meaning
'dweller in the holly grove'.

**Homer** Greek name possibly
based on the Greek *homeros*
('hostage'). The name is
universally associated with the
eighth-century BC Greek poet,
author of the *Iliad* and the
*Odyssey*. Particularly popular in
the USA, it also provided the

name of cartoon character Homer Simpson.

**Hopcyn** *See* HOPKIN.

**Hopkin** English and Welsh name based in medieval times via **Hob** on ROBERT. **Hopcyn** is a Welsh variant.

**Horace** English and French name descended from the Roman Horatius, itself possibly from the Latin *hora* ('hour' or 'time'). Celebrated as the name of the Roman poet Horace (Quintus Horatius Flaccus; 65–8 BC), it was adopted by English speakers in the eighteenth century but is now rare. Occasionally shortened to **Horry**. *See also* HORATIO.

**Horatio** English name that developed as a variant of HORACE under the influence of the Roman Horatius. It became well-known through Admiral Lord (Horatio) Nelson (1758–1805).

**Horry** *See* HORACE.

**Horst** German name meaning 'wood' or else based on *horsa* ('horse').

**Howard** English name that may have its origins in a similar Scandinavian name based on *ha* ('high') and *ward* ('guardian'). Other suggestions link the name with the Old German Huguard, from *hugu* ('heart') and *vardu* ('protection'), or with the Old French Houard, meaning 'worker with a hoe', or else with the Old English for 'hog-warden'. **Howie** is an informal version.

**Howel** *See* HOWELL.

**Howell** English name that was based either on an English surname or else on the Welsh HYWEL. It made its first appearances among English speakers around the middle of the nineteenth century. Also found as **Howel**.

**Howie** *See* HOWARD.

**Hubert** English, French and German name based on the Old German Hugibert, meaning 'bright spirit' or 'inspiration'. It came to England with the Normans in the eleventh century. Variants include **Hobart**. Shortened to BERT.

**Hudson** English name meaning 'son of Hudd' or 'son of Hugh'. Its popularity in Canada and the USA is a reflection of the early exploration of the area by the English adventurer Henry Hudson (d. 1611), after whom Hudson Bay was named.

**Huey** *See* HUGH.

**Huffie** *See* HUMPHREY.

**Hugh** English and Welsh name based ultimately on the Old German *hug* ('heart' or 'mind') or used as an anglicization of various Gaelic names, including the Scottish UISDEAN. Also found as **Hew** or, in Wales, **Huw**. Informal versions include **Hughie** and **Hewie** (or **Huey**) and, in Scotland, **Shug** or **Shuggie**. *See also* HUGO.

**Hughie** *See* HUGH.

**Hugo** English name that developed as a variant of HUGH. It emerged as an alternative Latinized form of Hugh around the middle of the nineteenth century.

**Hum** *See* HUMBERT.

**Humbert** English, French and German name based on the Old German *hun* ('bear-cub' or 'Hun') and *beraht* ('bright' or 'famous'). It became well known through the fictional Humbert Humbert in the Vladimir Nabokov novel *Lolita* (1955). Sometimes shortened to **Hum**.

**Hump/Humph** *See* HUMPHREY.

**Humphrey** English name descended from the Old German Hunfred, itself from *hun* ('bear-cub' or 'Hun') and *fridu* ('peace') and thus meaning 'peaceful Hun'. It was relatively frequent through the medieval period and beyond, although it is less common today. Also found as **Humphry**. Shortened to **Hump, Humph** or **Huffie**.

**Humphry** *See* HUMPHREY.

**Hunter** English and Scottish name that originated as a surname based on the ordinary vocabulary word 'hunter'.

**Husain/Husayn/ Hussain** *See* HUSSEIN.

**Hussein** Arabic name based on *hasan* ('good' or 'beautiful'). It was borne by a grandson of Muhammad who became the founder of the Shi'ite sect. Also found as **Hasan, Husain, Hussain** or **Husayn.**

**Huw** *See* HUGH.

**Hy/Hyam** *See* HYMAN.

**Hylton** *See* HILTON.

**Hyman** Jewish name based via **Hyam** on the Hebrew *hayyim* ('life'). Sometimes shortened to **Hy**. **Hymie** and **Chaim** are familiar forms of the name.

**Hymie** *See* HYMAN.

**Hyram** *See* HIRAM.

**Hywel** Welsh name meaning 'eminent' or 'conspicuous'. It remains rare outside Wales itself. *See also* HOWELL.

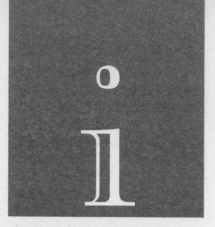

## BOYS' NAMES

**Iagan** Scottish name representing a Gaelic version of Aodhagan, itself based on Aodh, meaning 'fire'.

**Iago** Welsh and Spanish equivalent of JAMES, based on the Roman Jacobus. Its identification with the villainous Iago of William Shakespeare's *Othello* (1604) may have hindered its spread as a popular choice of name over the centuries.

**Iain** *See* IAN.

**Ian** Scottish name that developed as a variant of the English JOHN. It emerged as a distinct name in Scotland in the nineteenth century and quickly made the transition to other parts of the English-speaking world. A variant largely confined to Scotland is the Gaelic **Iain**.

**Iarlaith** ('yarla') Irish name meaning 'knight'. Sometimes found in the anglicized form JARLATH.

**Iarnan** ('yarnan') Irish and Scottish name meaning 'iron man'. Sometimes anglicized as **Ernan**.

**Ibraheem** *See* IBRAHIM.

**Ibrahim** Arabic version of ABRAHAM. A revered name in Islamic tradition, it was borne by the father of Ismail, from whom all Muslims claim descent. Also found as **Ebrahim** or **Ibraheem**, it remains one of the most popular names in the Arab world today.

**Ichabod** ('ikabod') Biblical name based on the Hebrew Ikhabhodh, meaning 'no glory' or 'where is the glory?' It was taken up by Puritans in the seventeenth century, and became well known through Ichabod Crane in Washington Irving's short story 'The

Legend of Sleepy Hollow' (1820).

**Idris** Welsh name based on *iud* ('lord') and *ris* ('ardent', 'fiery' or 'impulsive') and thus meaning 'ardent ruler' or 'fiery lord'. The name appears in Welsh mythology as that of the sorcerer Idris after whom Cader Idris, the second highest mountain in Wales, was named.

**Idwal** Welsh name based on *iud* ('lord' or 'master') and *wal* ('wall').

**Iefan** *See* EVAN.

**Iestyn** *See* JUSTIN.

**Ieuan/Ifan** *See* EVAN.

**Ifor** Welsh name of uncertain origin, possibly derived from *iôr* ('lord'). The name was borne by several important figures in Welsh legend and history. It is often confused with IVOR, although the names do not come from the same source.

**Iggy** *See* IGOR.

**Ignatius** Spanish, Russian and English name descended from the Roman family name Egnatius, the origins of which are obscure – although it later came to be associated with the Latin *ignis* ('fire'). It became popular among Roman Catholics in tribute to St Ignatius Loyola (1491–1556), the Spanish founder of the Jesuits. *See also* INIGO.

**Igor** Russian name based either on IVOR or else on the Scandinavian Ingvarr, which resulted from the combination of Ing (the name of the Norse god of peace and fertility) and *varr* ('careful'), thus meaning 'cared for by Ing'. It has made irregular appearances among English speakers since the nineteenth century. **Iggy** is an informal version.

**Ike** *See* ISAAC.

**Illtud** *See* ILLTYD.

**Illtyd** ('illtood') Welsh name based on *il* ('multitude') and *tud* ('land'), thus meaning 'land of the people'. It was borne by a sixth-century Welsh saint. Also found as **Illtud**.

**Imran** Arabic name meaning 'family of Imran'.

**Inderjit** Indian name based on the Sanskrit for 'conqueror of Indra'.

**Indiana** English name of relatively recent invention that developed either as a variant of INDIA or else from the name of the US state Indiana. The appearance of the name in the *Indiana Jones* movies of the 1980s promoted it as a boys' name. Shortened to **Indy**.

**Indra** Indian name based on the Sanskrit for 'possessing drops (of rain)'. It is borne in Hindu mythology by the supreme god of the atmosphere and sky, hence also the lord of rain.

**Indy** *See* INDIANA.

**Ingmar** Scandinavian name that resulted from the combination of the name of the Norse fertility god Ing with *maerr* ('famous').

**Ingram** English name that is thought to have developed from the Norman Ingelram or Engelram, itself from the Germanic name Ingilrammus, from Engel and *hramn* ('raven'). It was in fairly common use among English speakers from medieval times until the seventeenth century.

**Inigo** Spanish version of IGNATIUS, which was subsequently taken up by English speakers. Records of the name in use in England go back to at least the sixteenth century, when it was borne by the celebrated English architect Inigo Jones (1573–1652).

**Innes** ('innis') Scottish name that developed as an anglicization of the Gaelic Aonghas (*see* ANGUS). Also found as **Inness**.

**Inness** *See* INNES.

**Ioan** Welsh equivalent of JOHN.

**Iolo** Welsh name that developed as an informal variant of IORWERTH, although it is often considered to be a variant of JULIUS. Welsh speakers had taken up the name by the eighteenth century. A variant form is **Iolyn**.

**Iolyn** *See* IOLO.

**Iomhar** *See* IVOR.

**Iorwerth** Welsh name based on the Welsh *iôr* ('lord') and *berth* ('beautiful' or 'handsome'), thus meaning 'handsome lord'. The name appeared in the *Mabinogion* and remains confined to Wales, where it is sometimes considered a variant of the English EDWARD. **Yorath** is a variant form.

**Ira** Hebrew name meaning 'watchful'. It appears in the Bible and in the seventeenth century was taken up by English Puritans. Famous bearers of the name have included US lyricist Ira Gershwin (1896–1983).

**Irial** Irish name of unknown Gaelic origin.

**Irv/Irvin/Irvine** *See* IRVING.

**Irving** Scottish name that came originally from a place name in Dumfriesshire. Notable bearers of the name have included Russian-born US songwriter Irving Berlin

(Israel Baline; 1888–1989). Variants include **Irvin** and **Irvine**. Shortened to **Irv**.

**Irwin** English name based on the Old English *eofor* ('boar') and *wine* ('friend'), thus meaning 'boar friend', that has made infrequent appearances among English speakers since the middle of the nineteenth century. Also found as **Erwin**.

**Isaac** Biblical name based on the Hebrew Yitschaq, possibly meaning 'he laughs' or 'laughter'. It appears in the Bible as the name of the son of Abraham and Sarah, whose birth brought delight to his elderly parents. It remains chiefly a Jewish name, also spelt **Izaak**. Shortened to **Ike**, **Zac**, **Zack**, **Zak** or **Zakki**.

**Isaiah** Biblical name based on the Hebrew Yeshayah, meaning 'salvation of Yah' (Yah being another name for Jehovah, or God). It features in the Bible as the name of an Old Testament prophet but is rarely encountered outside Jewish communities. Also found as **Isiah**.

**Ishmael** Biblical name based

on the Hebrew Yishmael, meaning 'God will hearken'. It appears in the Bible as the name of Abraham's son. **Ismail** is a popular Arabic form of the name.

**Isiah** *See* ISAIAH.

**Isidore** English name based on the Greek Isidoros, itself from the Egyptian Isis (the name of an Egyptian goddess) and the Greek *dōron* ('gift'), thus meaning 'gift of Isis'. In ancient times it was sometimes treated as a Christian equivalent of the Jewish ISAIAH. Shortened to **Izzie** or **Izzy**.

**Islwyn** ('ighlwin') Welsh name based on that of a mountain in Gwent, itself from the Welsh *is* ('below') and *llwyn* ('grove').

**Ismail** *See* ISHMAEL.

**Israel** Biblical name based on the Hebrew Yisrael, from *sarah* ('to struggle') and *el* ('God'), thus meaning 'he who struggles with God' or alternatively 'may God prevail'. It features in the Bible as the collective name borne by Jacob's descendants. Shortened to **Issy**, **Izzie** or **Izzy**.

**Issy** *See* ISRAEL.

**Ithel** Welsh name meaning 'generous lord'.

**Ivan** Russian equivalent of the English JOHN that has been in occasional use among English speakers since the end of the nineteenth century. Commonly shortened to **Van**.

**Ives** ('eevs') Cornish equivalent of the French YVES, based ultimately on the Old Norse *yr* ('yew').

**Ivor** English version of the Scandinavian Ivarr, based on *ur* ('yew' or 'bow') and *arr* ('warrior') and thus meaning 'bowman'. Today it is commonly associated with the Welsh IFOR. A Scottish Gaelic variant is **Iomhar**.

**Izaak** *See* ISAAC.

**Izzie/Izzy** *See* ISIDORE; ISRAEL.

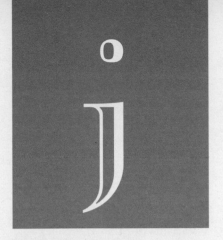

# J

## BOYS' NAMES

**Jack** English name that evolved as an informal version of JOHN. It emerged as Jackin before arriving at its modern form, and became increasingly common from around the middle of the nineteenth century. By the beginning of the twenty-first century it was securely established as the most popular of all boys' names. Also found as **Jak** or **Jax**. *See also* JACKIE; JACKSON; JACQUES; JAKE; JOCK.

**Jackie** Informal variant of JACK. Also found as **Jacky**, it became increasingly common from the end of the nineteenth century.

**Jackson** English name meaning 'son of Jack'. Its popularity in the USA was promoted through President Andrew Jackson (1767–1845) and Confederate general Thomas 'Stonewall' Jackson (1824–63). Shortened to JACK or **Jacky**.

**Jacky** *See* JACKIE; JACKSON.

**Jacob** Biblical name based via the Roman Jacobus on the Hebrew Yaakov, meaning 'May God protect'. It was in occasional use as a clerical name among English speakers before the Norman Conquest and was taken up with new enthusiasm by Puritans in the seventeenth century. *See also* JAKE; JAMES.

**Jacques** French equivalent of JACK.

**Jaden** *See* JAYDEN.

**Jael** Jewish name based on the Hebrew **Yael**, itself taken from the Hebrew name for a female wild goat.

**Jago** English name that evolved as a Cornish version of JAMES. It enjoyed a minor revival in popularity in the twentieth century.

**Jaikie** *See* JAKE.

**Jaimal** *See* JAMAL.

**Jak** *See* JACK.

**Jake** English name that developed as a variant of JACK and JACOB but is now often regarded as a name in its own right. It has appeared with increasing frequency since the beginning of the twentieth century. Informal versions include **Jakey**, **Jakie** and **Jaikie**.

**Jakey/Jakie** *See* JAKE.

**Jamal** Arabic and Indian name derived from the Arabic *jamal* ('beauty'). Although not one of the older traditional names of the Islamic world, it is nevertheless popular in many countries of the Middle East. Also found as **Gamal**, **Gamil**, **Jaimal** or **Jamil** and in India as **Jameel**.

**Jameel** *See* JAMAL.

**James** Biblical name based on the Roman Iacomus or Jacomus and sharing the same roots as JACOB. It was the name of two of Christ's disciples and was taken up by English speakers in the twelfth century. It remains one of the most enduring of all English first names. Commonly shortened to JIM, **Jimmy** or **Jimmie** and more rarely to JEM or **Jemmy**. Jamie is another variant (originally Scottish). Variants in other languages include the Irish SEAMUS. *See also* HAMISH; JAGO.

**Jamie** *See* JAMES.

**Jamil** *See* JAMAL.

**Jan** ('yan') Dutch and Scandinavian equivalent of JOHN. It was in use among English speakers in medieval times, but since the early twentieth century it has become much more common as a girls' name.

**Japheth** ('jayfeth') Biblical name based on the Hebrew Yepheth, meaning 'enlargement' or 'expansion'. It appears in the Bible as the name of Noah's eldest son and was among the biblical names taken up by Puritans in the seventeenth century. Shortened to **Japhy**.

**Japhy** *See* JAPHETH.

**Jared** Biblical name based on the Hebrew *yeredh* ('descended' or 'descent', or possibly 'rose'). It features in the Bible as the name of one of Adam's descendants and was consequently taken up by Puritans in the seventeenth century. Also found as **Jarred**, **Jarod** or **Jarrod**.

**Jarlath** English version of the Irish Gaelic IARLAITH. The name is rarely found outside Galway, where it was borne by a local saint.

**Jarod/Jarred/Jarrod** *See* JARED.

**Jarvis** English name based on GERVASE and in use as a first name since the nineteenth century. There is a character of the name in Charles Dickens' novel *A Tale of Two Cities* (1859). Also found as **Jervis**.

**Jason** English name based on the Greek Iason, itself probably from the Greek *iasthai* ('to heal'). Familiar in Greek legend from the story of Jason and the Argonauts, it also appears in the Bible and in this instance may

represent a variant of JOSHUA. It was taken up by English speakers in the seventeenth century.

**Jasper** English name that may have its origins in the Persian for 'treasurer', although it is usually assumed that it relates to the gemstone jasper. Jasper (or CASPAR) is popularly supposed to have been the name of one of the Three Wise Men. In Victorian times it was a favourite name for the villains of melodrama and pantomime.

**Javier** *See* XAVIER.

**Jax** *See* JACK.

**Jay** English name that evolved as a shortened form of various names beginning with 'J', including JAMES, although it is often assumed that it relates to the bird of the same name or that it is distantly descended from the Roman Gaius. It is more frequent in Canada and the USA than elsewhere. Sometimes found as **Jaye**.

**Jayden** English name based on the Hebrew Jadon, which means 'Jehovah has heard'. It was taken up with some enthusiasm by English speakers in the early twenty-first century. Also found as **Jaden**.

**Jaye** *See* JAY.

**Jean** *See* JOHN.

**Jed** *See* JEDIDIAH.

**Jedidiah** Biblical name meaning 'beloved of God' or 'friend of Yah' ('Yah' being another name for Jehovah, or God). It features in the Bible and was consequently among the names taken up by English Puritans in the seventeenth century. Today it is more likely to be encountered in its abbreviated form **Jed**.

**Jeff** *See* GEOFFREY; JEFFERSON.

**Jefferson** English name meaning 'son of Jeffrey'. The name was adopted by many people in the USA in tribute to US President Thomas Jefferson (1743–1826) and Confederate President Jefferson Davis (1808–89). Shortened to **Jeff**.

**Jeffery/Jeffrey** *See* GEOFFREY.

**Jem** English name that evolved as a shortened form of JAMES, although it is now often associated with JEREMY. It was taken up by English speakers in the nineteenth century. Also found as **Jemmy**. *See also* JEREMIAH.

**Jemmy** *See* JEM.

**Jenkin** English and Welsh name that is thought to have evolved from the same medieval roots as JACK. It has a strong Welsh flavour, largely because the surname Jenkins is particular common among the Welsh.

**Jep** *See* JEPSON.

**Jephtha** *See* JEPHTHAH.

**Jephthah** Biblical name based on the Hebrew Yiphtah, meaning 'God opens'. It appears in the Bible and was revived by English speakers in the nineteenth century. Also found as **Jephtha** or **Jeptha**.

**Jepson** English name that evolved as a medieval variant of GEOFFREY. Sometimes shortened to **Jep**.

**Jeptha** *See* JEPHTHAH.

**Jeremiah** Biblical name based on the Hebrew Yirmeyah, meaning 'appointed by God' or 'exalted by Yah' (Yah being an alternative for Jehovah, or God). It appears in the Bible and was taken up by Puritans in the seventeenth century. It is also used in Ireland as a variant of **Diarmaid**. Shortened to **Jerrie**, JERRY or JEM. *See also* JEREMY.

**Jeremy** English name that evolved from the biblical JEREMIAH. It was in use during the medieval period and remained in currency even after the Puritans revived the biblical Jeremiah in the seventeenth century. Shortened to **Jerrie** or JERRY or JEM.

**Jermain** *See* JERMAINE.

**Jermaine** English name based on the French **Germain**, variously meaning 'German' or 'brotherly'. It is best known through US singer Jermaine Jackson (b. 1954). Variants include **Germaine**, **Jermain**, **Jermane**, **Jermayne**, **Jermin** and **Jermyn**.

**Jermane/Jermayne/ Jermin/Jermyn** *See* JERMAINE.

**Jerome** English name descended via **Hieronymus** from the Greek Hieronymos, itself based on *hieros* ('holy') and *onoma* ('name') and thus meaning 'one who bears a holy name'. Often confused with the otherwise unconnected JEREMY, it made appearances among English speakers as early as the twelfth century. Shortened to **Jerrie** or JERRY.

**Jerrard** *See* GERARD.

**Jerrie** *See* GERRY; JEREMIAH; JEREMY; JEROME; JERRY.

**Jerrold** *See* GERALD.

**Jerry** English name that developed as a shortened form of JEREMIAH, JEREMY and JEROME. Also found as **Jerrie**, it appears to have made its debut among English speakers in the eighteenth century and has remained in wide circulation ever since. *See also* GERRY.

**Jervis** *See* JARVIS.

**Jess** *See* JESSE.

**Jesse** ('jessee') English name based on the Hebrew Yishay, meaning 'Jehovah exists' or 'gift of Jehovah'. It features in the Bible as the name of King David's father and was taken up by English speakers in the eighteenth century, becoming particularly popular in the USA. Variants include **Jess** and **Jessie**.

**Jessie** *See* JESSE.

**Jesus** Variant of JOSHUA, meaning 'saviour' or 'Jehovah saves'. As the name of Jesus Christ, it is rare in English-speaking countries, being considered too holy for secular use. It is more common, however, in Spanish- and Portuguese-speaking countries.

**Jethro** English name based on the Hebrew Yitro or Ithra, meaning 'abundance' or 'excellence'. It appears in the Bible as the name of the father-in-law of Moses and was consequently taken up by English Puritans in the sixteenth century. It remained fairly common until the end of the nineteenth century.

**Jim** English name that evolved as a shortened form of JAMES and is now often considered to be a name in its own right. Medieval in origin, it was greatly promoted by Robert Louis Stevenson's Jim Hawkins, the hero of his novel *Treasure Island* (1883). **Jimmy**, **Jimmie** and **Jimi** are variants.

**Jimi/Jimmie/Jimmy** *See* JIM.

**Jo** *See* JOE; JOJO; JOSEPH.

**Joab** Hebrew name meaning 'praise Jehovah'.

**Joachim** ('yoakim') Hebrew name meaning 'exalted by God'. Also found in the Spanish form **Joaquin**.

**Joaquin** *See* JOACHIM.

**Job** Biblical name based on the Hebrew Iyyobh, meaning 'persecuted' or 'afflicted'. The biblical Job demonstrated his faithfulness to God through a series of trials and misfortunes, as told in the Book of Job. **Joby** and **Jobie** are familiar forms of the name.

**Jobie/Joby** *See* JOB.

**Jocelyn** English name based on the Old Norman Joscelin, itself possibly taken from that of a Germanic tribe or else from the Old German names Jodoc or Josse (meaning 'champion'). The name was in regular use in England through the medieval period and was revived in the nineteenth century. Commonly shortened to **Jos** or **Joss**.

**Jock** Scottish variant of JACK or JOSEPH. It remains strongly associated with Scotland, although it is not in fact much used as a name in Scotland itself. **Jocky** (or **Jockey**) is a familiar form of the name.

**Jockey/Jocky** *See* JOCK.

**Jody** English name that evolved as a variant of GEORGE, JUDE and JOE. As a boys' name, it was heard with increasing frequency among English speakers during the nineteenth century.

**Joe** English name that evolved as a shortened form of such names as JOSEPH, JOHN, JONATHAN and JOSHUA. It became common among English speakers in the nineteenth century. Also found as **Jo** or **Joey**. *See also* JODY.

**Joel** Biblical name based on the Hebrew YOEL, meaning 'Yah is god' (Yah being another name for Jehovah, or God). It appears around a dozen times in the Bible and was in use in medieval England. It is also popular among Jews.

**Joey** *See* JOE; JOSEPH; JOSHUA.

**John** English name based via the Roman Johannes on the Hebrew Yohanan or Johanan, meaning 'Yah is gracious' or 'Yah is merciful' (Yah being another name for Jehovah, or God). It features in the Bible as the name of John the Baptist, among others, and ranks among the most popular of all first names. Familiar forms include JACK, HANK, **Jon** and **Jonny** (also found as **Johnnie** or **Johnny**). Variants in other languages include the French **Jean**. *See also* EVAN; HANS; IAN; IOAN; SEAN.

**Johnathan/Johnathon** *See* JONATHAN.

**Johnnie/Johnny** *See* JOHN.

**Jojo** English name that resulted from the doubling of Jo, the reduced form of JOSEPH and other names.

**Jolyon** *See* JULIAN.

**Jon** *See* JOHN; JONATHAN.

**Jonah** Biblical name based on the Hebrew Yonah, meaning 'dove'. It appears in the Bible as the name of a prophet who is swallowed by a whale but its later popularity was hindered by its reputation as an unlucky name. *See also* JONAS.

**Jonas** English name based on the Greek Ionas, an equivalent of JONAH. It has been in use among English speakers since the nineteenth century or earlier and, because it does not carry the same association with misfortune, came to eclipse Jonah. **Joney** is a familiar form of the name.

**Jonathan** English name based on the Hebrew Yahonathan, meaning 'Yah has given' or 'Yah's gift' (Yah being another name for Jehovah, or God). It appears in the Bible and was taken up by English speakers as early as the thirteenth century. Also found as **Jonathon** and occasionally as **Johnathan** or **Johnathon**. Shortened to **Jon**, **Jonny** or, more rarely, **Jonty**.

**Jonathon** *See* JONATHAN.

**Joney** *See* JONAS.

**Jonny** *See* JOHN; JONATHAN.

**Jonty** *See* JONATHAN.

**Jools** *See* JULES.

**Jordan** English name taken from that of the sacred River Jordan – itself from the Hebrew *hayarden* ('flowing down'). It was formerly given to children baptized with water brought back from the River Jordan by pilgrims. **Judd** is a variant.

**Jorge** *See* GEORGE.

**Jos** *See* JOCELYN; JOSEPH; JOSIAH.

**José** ('hozay') Spanish equivalent of JOSEPH that is also occasionally encountered among English speakers, chiefly in the USA. *See also* PEPE.

**Joseph** English and French name based on the Hebrew Yoseph, meaning 'Yah may add' or 'Yah added' (in other words, 'God gave this son'). The name appears in the Bible as that of Mary's husband and became increasingly popular among English speakers after the Reformation. **Jo**, JOE, **Joey** and **Jos** are shortened forms.

**Josh** *See* JOSHUA; JOSIAH.

**Joshua** Biblical name based on the Hebrew Yehoshua or Hosea, meaning 'Yah saves' or 'Yah is salvation' (Yah being another name for Jehovah, or God). It appears in the Bible as the name of the man who succeeded Moses as the leader of the Israelites. JOE, **Joey** and **Josh** are shortened forms.

**Josiah** Biblical name based on the Hebrew Yoshiyah, meaning 'Yah supports' or 'Yah heals' (Yah being another name for Jehovah, or God). It appears in the Bible and was taken up by English speakers in the seventeenth century. Shortened to **Jos** or **Josh**.

**Joss** *See* JOCELYN.

**Jotham** Hebrew name meaning 'Jehovah is perfect'. It appears in the Bible as the name of Gideon's youngest son. Also found as **Jothan**.

**Jothan** *See* JOTHAM.

**Joyce** English name descended from the Norman French Josce, meaning 'lord'. The name came to England with William the Conqueror in the eleventh century, when it was treated as a masculine name. Now reserved almost exclusively for girls.

**Juan** ('hwarn' or 'jooan') Spanish equivalent of JOHN. It is one of the most common names found within Spanish-speaking communities of the USA and elsewhere.

**Judah** Biblical name based on the Hebrew Yehudhah or Yehuda, meaning 'praised' or 'he who is praised'. It appears in the Bible and was consequently taken up by English speakers in the seventeenth century. **Yehudi** is a variant form. *See also* JUDE.

**Judas** *See* JUDE.

**Judd** *See* JORDAN.

**Jude** English variant of the biblical **Judas**. The name is sometimes applied to the apostle Judas Thaddaeus (the patron saint of lost causes) to distinguish him from the treacherous Judas Iscariot, whose version of the name is little used today. Also well known through the Thomas Hardy novel *Jude the Obscure* (1895).

**Jules** French name based either on JULIAN or JULIUS. It was taken up by English speakers towards the end of the nineteenth century. A variant of relatively recent invention is **Jools** – as borne by British keyboard player Jools Holland (Julian Holland, b. 1958).

**Julian** English name based on the Roman Julianus, a variant of JULIUS. It made early appearances in medieval times. **Jolyon** and **Julyan** are rare variants. Sometimes shortened to JULES.

**Julius** Roman family name of uncertain origin that was taken up by English speakers during the nineteenth century. According to legend, the first bearer of the name was Iulus, the son of Aeneas. The name may come from the Greek for 'downy' or 'hairy' – a reference to the first growth of beard in young men. Occasionally shortened to JULES.

**Julyan** *See* JULIAN.

**Junior** English name that developed initially as a nickname for any young person, derived from the Latin for 'younger'. Long used to distinguish a son from a father with the same name, it is rare outside the USA.

**Justie** *See* JUSTIN.

**Justin** English name descended from the Roman Justinus, itself a variant of Justus. Borne by several early saints and two Byzantine emperors, it appeared with increasing frequency among English speakers from the 1970s. Variants include **Justyn** and the Welsh **Iestyn**. **Justie** and **Justy** are familiar forms.

**Justy/Justyn** *See* JUSTIN.

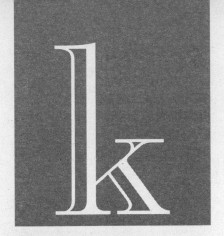

# BOYS' NAMES

**Kai** ('kay') Scandinavian name that may be linked to the Old Norse *katha* ('chicken') or else with the Roman CAIUS.

**Kamal** Arabic and Indian name variously based on the Arabic *kamal* ('perfection') and the Sanskrit *kamala* ('pale red'). Also found as **Kamil**.

**Kamil** See KAMAL.

**Kane** English equivalent of the Gaelic Cathán, itself from the Irish *cath* ('battle' or 'fighter'). It may also be linked to a Welsh word meaning 'beautiful'. It is today more common in Australia and the USA than it is in the UK. *See also* KEAN.

**Karim** ('kareem') Arabic name meaning 'noble' or 'generous'.

**Karl** See CARL.

**Karr** See KERR.

**Kasey** See CASEY.

**Kavan** See CAVAN.

**Kay** English name that as a name for boys probably developed ultimately out of the Roman Gaius (of uncertain meaning). It features in Arthurian legend as the name of Sir Kay, King Arthur's steward.

**Kean** Irish name that developed as an anglicization of the Gaelic CIAN, meaning 'vast', or of the Gaelic *cean* ('head'). It was once common in Ireland, where it was particularly associated with the O'Hara family. Also rendered as **Keane** or KANE.

**Keane** See KEANE.

**Keanu** ('keeahnoo') Hawaiian name meaning 'cool breeze from the mountains'. It has become widely familiar through US film actor Keanu Reeves (b. 1964).

**Keefe** Irish name meaning 'noble'.

**Keefer** *See* KIEFER.

**Keegan** *See* KEGAN.

**Keenan** Irish name based on the Irish Gaelic for 'little ancient one'.

**Kegan** Irish name meaning 'son of Egan' or alternatively 'little fiery one'. Sometimes considered an Irish equivalent of HUGH. Also found as **Keegan**.

**Keir** Scottish name of uncertain origin, possibly from the Gaelic for 'swarthy'. Largely confined to Scotland, it became widely known through British trade unionist and politician Keir Hardie (James Keir Hardie; 1856–1915).

**Keiran** *See* KIERAN.

**Keith** Scottish name that was originally a Scottish place name in East Lothian, itself possibly from the Celtic word for 'wood' or 'windy place'. As a

first name, it made its debut in the nineteenth century.

**Kelan** Irish name representing an anglicization of the Gaelic Caolan, itself based on *caol* ('slender').

**Kelcey** *See* KELSEY.

**Kelly** Irish name that was taken up by English speakers as a first name for both sexes from the late 1950s. The usual Irish Gaelic form of the name is **Ceallagh**, meaning 'strife', 'war' or 'warlike'.

**Kelsey** English name based on the Old English Ceolsige, itself from the Old English *ceol* ('ship') and *sige* ('victory'). It has appeared as a first name for both sexes since the 1870s. **Kelcey** is a variant.

**Kelvin** English name that made its debut in the 1920s, possibly under the influence of such names as CALVIN and MELVIN. It may have had its roots ultimately in the Old English words for 'ship' and 'friend'.

**Kemp** English name that was originally a surname based on the Middle English word *kempe* ('athlete' or 'wrestler'), itself descended from the Old English *kempa* ('warrior' or 'champion').

**Ken** *See* KENDALL; KENNETH; KENTON; KENYON.

**Kendal** *See* KENDALL.

**Kendall** English name taken from Kendal in Cumbria and meaning 'valley of the River Kent'. It is also possible that it evolved from the place name Kendale (in Humberside), itself from the Old Norse *keld* ('spring'), or else from the Old Welsh name Cynnddelw. Also found as **Kendal** and commonly shortened to **Ken**.

**Kendrick** Welsh and Scottish name that probably developed out of the Old Welsh Cynwrig, itself possibly from the Old Celtic for 'high summit'. It may also be linked with the Old English Ceneric or Cyneric, itself from *cene* ('keen' or 'bold') and *ric* ('power').

**Kenelm** English name descended from the Old English Cenelm, itself based on *cene* ('bold' or 'keen') and *helm* ('helmet' or 'protection') and thus meaning 'bold defender'. It was fairly common in England during the medieval period.

**Kennard** English name based ultimately upon the Old English words *cene* ('keen' or 'bold') or *cyne* ('royal') and *weard* ('guard') or *heard* ('brave' or 'hardy'). A historical variant is **Kenward**.

**Kennedy** Irish, Scottish and English name that evolved as an anglicization of the Irish Gaelic Cinneidigh, based on *ceann* ('head') and *eidigh* ('ugly') and thus meaning 'ugly head', and also as an anglicized version of the Scottish Gaelic Uarraig.

**Kenneth** Scottish and English name that is thought to have evolved out of the Gaelic names Cinead (meaning 'born of fire') and Cainneach (meaning 'handsome one') and thus meaning 'fair and fiery'. Commonly shortened to **Ken** or **Kenny**. Variants include the Welsh **Cenydd**.

**Kenny** *See* KENNETH.

**Kent** English name that may have its origins in the name of the English county of Kent, itself meaning 'border'.

**Kenton** English name possibly inspired by that of the river Kenn or else from an Old English place name derived from *cena* ('keen') or *cyne* ('royal') and the Old English *tun* ('settlement'). Sometimes shortened to **Ken**.

**Kenward** *See* KENNARD.

**Kenyon** English name based on a place name in Lancashire, itself from the Old English for 'Ennion's mound'. Sometimes shortened to **Ken**.

**Kermit** English version of the Gaelic surname Mac Dhiarmaid (also the source of DERMOT) meaning 'son of Diarmad'. It was taken up by English speakers in the USA in the nineteenth century.

**Kerr** English name taken from a place name based on the Old Norse *kjarr* ('rough ground with brushwood'). Variants include **Karr**.

**Kerry** English and Irish name probably modelled on that of the Irish county of Kerry (meaning 'descendants of Ciar'). In modern times it has been used chiefly as a name for girls.

**Kester** Scottish version of CHRISTOPHER. Fairly common in medieval times, it enjoyed a substantial revival in the twentieth century.

**Kev/Kevan** *See* KEVIN.

**Kevin** Irish name that developed out of the Gaelic Caoimhin (or Caoimhinn), itself meaning 'comely' or 'fair'. Also found as **Kevan**. Commonly shortened to **Kev**.

**Khalid** Arabic name meaning 'eternal'. The name was borne in the seventh century by Khalid ibn al-Walid, who won the praise of Muhammad for his conquests on behalf of Islam.

**Kian** *See* CIAN.

**Kiaran** *See* KIERAN.

**Kid** English nickname that has gradually won acceptance as a legitimate first name, especially in the USA. It began originally as a nickname for any man notable for his youthful good looks.

**Kiefer** German name meaning 'cooper' or 'barrel-maker'. It has become widely familiar through US film actor Kiefer Sutherland (b. 1966). Variants include **Keefer** and **Kieffer**.

**Kieffer** *See* KIEFER.

**Kieran** English version of the Gaelic **Ciaran**, itself based on the Irish *ciar* ('black') and usually interpreted to mean 'little dark-haired one'. The name was largely confined to Ireland until the middle of the twentieth century. Also found as **Cieran, Keiran, Kiaran, Kieron** or **Kyran**.

**Kieron** *See* KIERAN.

**Kilian** *See* KILLIAN.

**Killian** Irish name that represents an anglicization of the Irish Gaelic **Cillian**, meaning 'church'. Also encountered as **Kilian**.

**Kim** English name that

evolved as a shortened form of KIMBERLEY. In Rudyard Kipling's novel *Kim* (1901), however, it is explained that the full version of the central character's name is **Kimball** – probably from the Old English *cynebeald* ('kin bold').

**Kimball** *See* KIM.

**Kimberleigh** *See* KIMBERLEY.

**Kimberley** English name based on that of the South African town of Kimberley. The town was itself named after British statesman John Wodehouse, 1st Earl of Kimberley, whose family came from a place in England called Kimberley (meaning 'Cyneburga's wood'). Also found as **Kimberleigh** or **Kimberly**, it may be shortened to KIM.

**Kimberly** *See* KIMBERLEY.

**King** English name based on the royal title. It evolved in parallel with such equivalent names as DUKE and EARL, presumably in the belief that the bearer would thereby be distinguished by aristocratic qualities.

**Kingsley** English name that originated as a place name in Cheshire, Hampshire and Staffordshire. The original place name meant 'king's wood' in Old English. Notable bearers of the name have included British novelist Kingsley Amis (1922–95).

**Kirby** English name that originated as a place name based on the Old Norse *kirkja* ('church'). Its history as a first name dates from the nineteenth century.

**Kirk** Scottish and English name based on the Old Norse *kirkja* ('church') and formerly usually reserved for people living near a church. Well-known bearers of the name have included US film actor Kirk Douglas (Issur Danielovitch Demsky; b. 1916).

**Kishen/Kistna** *See* KRISHNA.

**Kit** *See* CHRISTOPHER.

**Korey/Korrie/Kory** *See* COREY.

**Kris** *See* CHRISTOPHER.

**Krishna** Indian name based on the Sanskrit for 'black' or 'dark'. As the name of the most widely venerated of Hindu gods, it has unique religious significance for Indians. **Kistna** and **Kishen** are variant forms.

**Kurt** German name that evolved as a diminutive of Konrad (*see* CONRAD). It was taken up on a limited scale among English speakers in the 1950s. Famous bearers of the name have included US rock singer Kurt Cobain (1967–94). Also encountered as **Curt**.

**Kyle** English name that originated as a Scottish surname, itself modelled on a place name from Ayrshire based on the Gaelic *caol* ('narrow'), as applied to narrow straits or channels.

**Kyran** *See* KIERAN.

# BOYS' NAMES

**Laban** Hebrew name meaning 'white'. It appears in the Bible and much later as the name of a character in Thomas Hardy's novel *Far From the Madding Crowd* (1874).

**Labhrainn/Labhras** *See* LAURENCE.

**Lacey** English name that originated in a surname based on a Norman place name, Lassy in Calvados. Also found as **Lacy**.

**Lachie** *See* LACHLAN.

**Lachlan** English version of the Scottish **Lachlann** or **Lochlann**, which means 'land of lochs' or 'land of fjords' and was originally reserved for

settlers from Norway. Another derivation suggests the name came from the Gaelic *laochail* ('warlike'). Shortened to **Lachie** or, in Canada, to **Lockie**.

**Lachlann** *See* LACHLAN.

**Lachtna** Irish name based on the Gaelic for 'milk-coloured'. It features in Irish legend as the name of an ancestor of King Brian Boru. *See also* LUCIUS.

**Lacy** *See* LACEY.

**Ladd** English name meaning 'manservant' or 'page'. Also found as **Laddie**.

**Laddie** *See* LADD.

**Ladislas** Polish name meaning 'rule of glory'.

**Laine** *See* LANE.

**Laing** *See* LANG.

**Laird** Scottish name meaning 'landowner'. It has made rare appearances as a first name, mostly in the USA.

**Lamar** French and German name variously meaning 'the

water' or 'land famous'.
Variants include **Lamarr** and
**Lemarr**.

**Lamarr** *See* LAMAR.

**Lambard** *See* LAMBERT.

**Lambert** English, French,
German and Dutch name based
on the Old German *lant*
('land') and *beraht* ('famous' or
'bright') and thus meaning
'famous landowner'. Also
found as **Lambard**, the name
came to England with the
Normans. Shortened to BERT.

**Lance** English name that
exists either as a shortened
form of LANCELOT or as a
name in its own right, based on
the Old German *lant* ('land') or
possibly on the French *lance*
('lance'). It was recorded in use
in England by the thirteenth
century, when it also appeared
as **Launce**.

**Lancelot** English name
possibly based on the Old
French *l'ancelle* ('servant') or
else on an unknown Celtic
name. Also found as
**Launcelot**, it became famous as
the name of one of King

Arthur's knights of the Round
Table. Shortened to LANCE.

**Landen** *See* LANDON.

**Landon** English name
meaning 'long hill'. Variant
forms include **Landen**.

**Lane** English name that
originated as a surname based
on the ordinary vocabulary
word. Variants include **Laine**,
**Laney** and **Layne**.

**Laney** *See* LANE.

**Lang** Scottish name that
originated as a surname
meaning 'tall' or 'long'. Also
found as **Laing**.

**Langford** English name that
originated in a surname
meaning 'long ford'.

**Langley** English name that
originated in a surname
meaning 'long meadow'.

**Langsden/Langsdon** *See*
LANGSTON.

**Langston** English name
meaning 'long stone' or 'long
town'. Variants include

**Langsden, Langsdon** and **Langton.**

**Langton** *See* LANGSTON.

**Lanty/Larrie/Larry** *See* LAURENCE.

**Lars** Scandinavian variant of LAURENCE. It emerged as one of the most popular of all masculine names in Scandinavia in the 1960s.

**Larsen** Scandinavian name meaning 'son of Lars'. Also found as **Larson.**

**Larson** *See* LARSEN.

**Lascelles** ('lasells') French name that originated as a surname meaning 'hermitage' or 'cell'.

**Laszlo** Hungarian name representing an equivalent of LADISLAS.

**Latham** English name that originated in a surname based on the Old Norse for 'barns'. Also found as **Lathom.**

**Lathom** *See* LATHAM.

**Latimer** English name that was based on the Old French for 'interpreter'.

**Launce** *See* LANCE.

**Launcelot** *See* LANCELOT.

**Laurence** English name based on the Roman Laurentius, which means 'man from Laurentum' (Laurentum being a town in Latium). The name also appears as **Lawrence,** the usual spelling in the USA and Canada. Shortened to **Larry** (or **Larrie**) or **Laurie** (or **Lawrie**). Other variants include **Lol, Laz** and the Irish **Lanty.** Variants in other languages include the Irish Gaelic **Labhras,** the Scottish Gaelic **Labhrainn,** the Dutch **Laurens,** the French **Laurent** and the German **Lorenz.** *See also* LARS.

**Laurens/Laurent/Laurie** *See* LAURENCE.

**Lawford** English name that originated as a surname meaning 'one who lives at the ford by the hill'.

**Lawrence/Lawrie** *See* LAURENCE.

**Lawson** English name that originated as a surname that was itself an elaboration of Law, a nickname inspired by **Lawrence**.

**Lawton** English name that originated as a surname meaning 'from the place on the hill'.

**Layne** *See* LANE.

**Layton** *See* LEIGHTON.

**Laz** *See* LAURENCE.

**Lazarus** Biblical name based ultimately on the Hebrew Eleazar (meaning 'God has helped' or 'God is my help'). It appears in the Bible but is rare today outside the Jewish community.

**Leal** English name based on the Old French for 'loyal'. Also found as **Leale**.

**Leale** *See* LEAL.

**Leander** Roman version of the Greek Leandros, based on *leon* ('lion') and *andros* ('man') and thus meaning 'lion man'. The name is famous from the Greek myth of Hero and Leander, in which the youthful Leander drowns while swimming the Hellespont to visit his lover Hero.

**Lee** English name based on the Old English *leah* ('wood', 'meadow' or 'clearing'). It has been employed as a first name for boys since the nineteenth century and for girls since the early twentieth century. Also found as **Leigh**.

**Leif** ('leef') Scandinavian name based on the Old Norse Leifr, meaning 'descendant' or 'heir'.

**Leigh** *See* LEE.

**Leighton** ('layton') English name that originated as a place name meaning 'herb garden'. Also found as **Layton** or **Leyton**.

**Leith** Scottish name that originated as a place name meaning based either on the Celtic for 'moist place' or on the Scots Gaelic for 'grey'.

**Leland** ('leeland') English name that originated as a surname based on the Old English *laege* ('fallow') and *land*

('land'). It has been in use as a first name, particularly in the USA, since the nineteenth century. Also found as **Leyland**.

**Lem** *See* LEMUEL.

**Lemarr** *See* LAMAR.

**Lemmy** *See* LEMUEL.

**Lemuel** Hebrew name meaning 'devoted to God'. A biblical name, it was later made famous by the character Lemuel Gulliver in Jonathan Swift's *Gulliver's Travels* (1725). Shortened to **Lem** or **Lemmy**.

**Len** *See* LENNOX; LEONARD; LIONEL.

**Lennard/Lennie** *See* LEONARD.

**Lennox** Scottish and English name that originated as a surname. Also found as **Lenox**, it is particularly associated with Scotland, where there is an earldom of the same name, referring to a district near Loch Lomond. Shortened to **Len** or **Lenny**.

**Lenny** *See* LENNOX; LEONARD; LIONEL.

**Lenox** *See* LENNOX.

**Leo** English name based on the Latin *leo* ('lion'). It made its first appearances among English speakers in the medieval period and enjoyed a peak in popularity in the late nineteenth and early twentieth centuries. *See also* LEON; LEOPOLD.

**Leolin/Leoline** *See* LLEWELYN.

**Leon** English, German and Irish Gaelic name that evolved out of LEO and thus means 'lion'. It is rare today outside the Jewish community, where it is used in remembrance of the dying words of Jacob, in which he likened the kingdom of Judah to a lion. *See also* LIONEL.

**Leonard** English name based via Old French on the Old German *leon* ('lion') and *hard* ('strong' or 'brave') and thus meaning 'brave as a lion'. It came to England with the Normans. Also found as **Lennard** and occasionally in

the Italian form **Leonardo**.
Shortened to **Len**, **Lennie** or
**Lenny**.

**Leonardo** *See* LEONARD.

**Leopold** German and
English name based on the Old
German Liutpold, meaning 'of
a bold people'. Popular among
European royal families, it was
taken up by English speakers
around the middle of the
nineteenth century.
Commonly shortened to LEO
or, more rarely, **Poldie**.

**LeRoi** *See* LEROY.

**Leroy** English name based on
the Old French *le roy* ('the
king'). Used initially as a
nickname, it is thought to have
been given initially to royal
servants. Variant forms include
**LeRoy** and **LeRoi**. *See also*
DELROY; ELROY.

**Les** *See* LESLIE; LESTER.

**Lesley** *See* LESLIE.

**Leslie** Scottish name that
originated in a place name
(Lesslyn in Aberdeenshire)
possibly based on the Gaelic
*leas cuilinn* ('garden of hollies').

It was first recorded as a first
name in the eighteenth
century, promoted by the
Robert Burns poem 'Bonnie
Lesley'. The alternate spelling
**Lesley** is now reserved chiefly
for girls. Shortened to **Les**.

**Lester** English name based on
a place name (now Leicester),
itself a combination of a tribal
name of unknown meaning
and *caester* ('Roman fort'). It
appears to have made its debut
as a first name around the
middle of the nineteenth
century.

**Levi** Jewish name based on
the Hebrew *lewi* ('associated',
'attached' or 'pledged'). It
features in the Bible and was in
use among English Jews as
early as the seventeenth
century. Also found as **Levy**.

**Levy** *See* LEVI.

**Lew** *See* LEWIS; LLEWELLYN.

**Lewie** *See* LEWIS.

**Lewin** English name based
on the Old English for
'beloved friend'.

**Lewis** English version of the

French LOUIS, also used in Wales as an anglicization of LLEWELLYN. First recorded among English speakers during the medieval period, it enjoyed a peak in popularity in the 1990s. Shortened to **Lew**. **Lewie** is a familiar form of the name.

**Lex** English name that is thought to have evolved as a shortened form of ALEXANDER, influenced perhaps by REX. **Lexie** and **Lexy** are familiar versions of the name.

**Lexie/Lexy** *See* LEX.

**Leyland** *See* LELAND.

**Leyton** *See* LEIGHTON.

**Liam** Irish variant of WILLIAM, via the Gaelic Uilliam. Notable bearers of the name have included Northern Irish actor Liam Neeson (b. 1952) and British rock musician Liam Gallagher (b. 1972).

**Lincoln** English name based on that of the city of Lincoln (meaning 'lake settlement'). It is more common in the USA than elsewhere, often bestowed in honour of President Abraham Lincoln (1809–65).

**Lindley** English name that originated in a place name meaning 'lime-tree meadow' or 'flax field'. Also found as Linley.

**Lindon** *See* LYNDON.

**Lindsay** English name inspired by Lindsey in Lincolnshire, meaning 'island of Lincoln' or 'wetland belonging to Lincoln'. Also found as **Lindsey**, it was taken up as a first name in the nineteenth century, reserved initially for males. Since the 1930s it has been used more often as a girls' name. *See also* LYNN.

**Lindsey** *See* LINDSAY.

**Linford** English name that originated in a place name in Berkshire, itself from the Old English *lin* ('flax') or *lind* ('lime tree') and *ford* ('ford'). Well-known bearers of the name have included British athlete Linford Christie (b. 1960).

**Linley** *See* LINDLEY.

**Linton** English name that originated in a place name based on the Old English *lin* ('flax' or 'cotton') or *lind* ('lime tree') and *tun* ('enclosure'). *See also* LYNTON.

**Linus** English name based on the Greek Linos, itself possibly from *lineos* ('blond' or 'flaxen-haired'). The name features in the Bible and today is more familiar in the USA than elsewhere. Notable bearers of the name have included US chemist Linus Pauling (1901–94).

**Lionel** English name that evolved from LEON, with the meaning 'little lion'. It was first recorded in use among English speakers in the medieval period but remained rare until the early twentieth century. Shortened to **Len** or **Lenny**.

**Lister** English name that originated as a surname meaning 'dyer'.

**Litton** *See* LYTTON.

**Lleu** Welsh name meaning 'bright' or 'shining'. It was borne by a Celtic Irish god and appears in the *Mabinogion*. Also found as **Llew**.

**Llew** *See* LLEU; LLEWELLYN.

**Llewellyn** Welsh name often thought to mean 'leader' or else to be linked to the Welsh *llyw* ('lion') and *eilun* ('likeness') but probably, in fact, descended from the older Celtic name Lugobelinos (of uncertain meaning). Also found as **Llywelyn** or **Fluellen**. Other variants include **Leolin** and **Leoline**. Shortened to **Lew**, **Lyn**, LYNN or **Llew**.

**Lloyd** English name based on a Welsh surname that in turn evolved as a nickname meaning 'grey' or 'grey-haired'. It was taken up by English speakers in the early twentieth century, when it became widely known through Prime Minister David Lloyd George (1863–1945). Occasionally found as **Loyd** or, in Wales, as **Llwyd**. *See also* FLOYD.

**Llwyd** *See* LLOYD.

**Llywelyn** *See* LLEWELLYN.

**Lochlann** *See* LACHLAN.

**Locke** English name that originated in a surname meaning 'enclosure' or 'stronghold'.

**Lockie** *See* LACHLAN.

**Logan** Scottish name based on a place name (from Ayrshire), possibly from the Gaelic for 'hollow'. It remains confined largely to Scotland.

**Lol** *See* LAURENCE.

**Loman** Irish name based on *lomm* ('bare'). It was borne by several early Irish saints.

**Lon** *See* LONNIE.

**Lonán** Irish name based on *lon* ('blackbird'). It was borne by a number of little-known Irish saints.

**Lonnie** English name that variously developed as an anglicized shortening of **Alonzo** or as a variant of **Lennie** (*see* LEONARD). Also found as **Lonny**, it appears to have been a twentieth-century invention. Famous bearers of the name have included Scottish pop musician Lonnie

Donegan (1931–2002). Shortened to **Lon**.

**Lonny** *See* LONNIE.

**Lorcan** Irish Gaelic name meaning 'fierce in battle'.

**Lorenz** *See* LAURENCE.

**Lorimer** English name that originated in a surname meaning 'harness maker'.

**Lorn** *See* LORNE.

**Lorne** English name that may have developed out of LORNA or may simply share the same origin in the Scottish place name Lorn (in Argyll). It is particularly popular in Canada and other countries with strong Scottish connections. Also found as **Lorn**.

**Lothario** *See* LUTHER.

**Lou/Louie** *See* LOUIS.

**Louis** ('looee') French name based on the German Ludwig, itself from the Old German *hlut* ('famous') and *wig* ('warrior'). The name was anglicized as LEWIS after it came to England in the medieval period but the

French form made a comeback from the eighteenth century. Shortened to **Lou** or **Louie**. *See also* ALOYSIUS.

**Love/Lovel** *See* LOVELL.

**Lovell** English name based on the Old French nickname Louvel ('wolf-cub' or 'little wolf'). Its use among English speakers dates back to at least the eleventh century. It also has strong Scottish connections. Sometimes found as **Lowell**, **Lovel** or **Lovet**. Shortened to **Love**.

**Lovet/Lowell** *See* LOVELL.

**Loyd** *See* LLOYD.

**Luc/Luca** *See* LUKE.

**Lucan** Irish name based on a place name meaning 'place of elms'.

**Lucas** Roman name meaning 'man from Lucania' (a region of southern Italy). Also the source of LUKE.

**Lucian** English version of the French Lucien and the Italian Luciano, both descendants of the Roman LUCIUS. As Lucianus, the name appeared among English speakers as early as the twelfth century. Occasionally found in the French form **Lucien**.

**Lucien** *See* LUCIAN.

**Lucius** Roman name derived from the Latin *lux* ('light'). It appears in the Bible and made its first appearances in English in the sixteenth century. In Ireland the name is sometimes used as an anglicized form of the Irish LACHTNA. *See also* LUCKY.

**Lucky** English name that developed either as a nickname or else as a familiar variant of such names as LUCIUS or LUKE. It has made irregular appearances as a first name since the early twentieth century, chiefly in the USA. One well-known bearer of the name was the notorious US gangster Charles 'Lucky' Luciano (1897–1962).

**Ludo** *See* LUDOVIC.

**Ludovic** English version of the Roman Ludovicus, also found in Scotland as an anglicization of the Gaelic

Maol Domhnaich, meaning 'devotee of the Lord'. It was taken up by English speakers in the nineteenth century. Commonly shortened to **Ludo**.

**Ludwig** German name based on the Old German Hlutwig, itself from *hlut* ('fame') and *wig* ('warrior'). Notable bearers of the name have included German composer Ludwig van Beethoven (1770–1827).

**Luke** English name based ultimately on the Greek for 'man from Lucania' (Lucania being an area in southern Italy). It features in the Bible as the name of the author of the third gospel. The name came to England with the Normans. Variants include the French **Luc** and the Italian **Luca**. *See also* LUCKY.

**Luther** German name based on the Old German *liut* ('people') and *heri* ('warrior') and thus meaning 'people's warrior' that was adopted among English speakers from the nineteenth century. As the surname of the German religious reformer Martin Luther (1483–1546) it has always had a special

significance for Protestants. Variants include the Italian **Lothario**.

**Lyall** Scottish name based on the Old Norse name Liulfr (possibly meaning 'wolf'). *See also* LYLE.

**Lyle** English name based on the French *de l'isle* ('of the island'). As a surname it originally referred to someone who came from any raised area of land, not just islands. Its popularity in Scotland may have been influenced by confusion with the otherwise unconnected Scottish name LYALL.

**Lyn** *See* LLEWELLYN.

**Lyndon** English name that originated as a place name (from Rutland) based on the Old English *lind* ('linden' or 'lime tree') and *dun* ('hill'). Awareness of the name in modern times is due in part to US president Lyndon Baines Johnson (1908–73). Also found as **Lindon**.

**Lynn** English name that developed as a shortened form of LLEWELYN or LINDSAY. As a masculine name it is rarely used outside Wales, where it seems to have made early appearances in the nineteenth century.

**Lynton** English name that originated as a place name meaning 'place on the torrent'. Also found as LINTON.

**Lytton** English name meaning 'loud torrent'. Also found as **Litton**, it is best known through English biographer Lytton Strachey (1880–1932).

# BOYS' NAMES

**Mabon** Welsh name based on the Old Celtic *mab* ('son'). It probably began as the name of a Celtic god. Like other ancient Celtic names it was revived in the twentieth century.

**Mackenzie** Scottish name meaning 'son of Kenneth'. It is particularly associated with Canada, where it is understood to be a reference to the Mackenzie River.

**Macsen** *See* MAXIM.

**Macy** English name based ultimately on French and roughly meaning 'from Matthew's estate'.

**Maddison** *See* MADISON.

**Maddock** Welsh name meaning 'beneficent'. Also found as **Maddox**.

**Maddox** *See* MADDOCK.

**Madison** English name derived either from Magdalen or meaning 'son of Maud'. Also encountered as **Maddison**, it is largely confined to the USA, where it was promoted through James Madison (1751–1836), the country's fourth president.

**Madoc** Welsh name meaning 'fortunate', or else based on the Celtic *aodh* ('fire'). Recorded as early as the eleventh century, it remains rare outside Wales. Also found as **Madog**.

**Madog** *See* MADOC.

**Mael** ('mile') Welsh name based on the Gaelic for 'prince'.

**Maelgwyn** Welsh name meaning 'fair prince'. Maelgwyn Gwynedd was a Welsh king of the sixth century.

**Maelmore** *See* MILES.

**Magnus** Roman name meaning 'great'. The name is usually traced back to the ninth-century Holy Roman Emperor Charlemagne, who was also known as *Carolus Magnus* ('Charles the Great'). It became more widespread among English speakers from the 1960s. Variants include the Irish **Manus**.

**Mahmood** *See* MAHMUD.

**Mahmud** Arabic name based on *hamida* ('to praise') and thus meaning 'praiseworthy'. Also found as **Mahmood, Mehmud** or **Mehmood**. *See also* MUHAMMAD.

**Mahomet** *See* MUHAMMAD.

**Mahon** English version of the Irish **Mathuin**, itself descended from Mathghambain, meaning 'bear'. In its earliest form it was borne by a brother of Brian Boru, a king of Ireland in the eleventh century.

**Maitland** English name of uncertain meaning. The original surname from which the first name came is of Norman French origin.

**Major** English name based on the Latin for 'greater'.

**Makepeace** English name that originated in a surname meaning 'peacemaker'. It became well known through British novelist William Makepeace Thackeray (1811–63).

**Mal** *See* MALCOLM; MALDWYN.

**Malachi** ('malakigh') Hebrew name meaning 'my messenger'. It features in the Bible as the name of the last of the twelve minor Old Testament prophets and was taken up by Puritans in the seventeenth century. Also found as **Malachy**, although this can also be interpreted to mean 'devotee of St Seachnall'.

**Malachy** *See* MALACHI.

**Malcolm** English version of the Gaelic Mael Colum ('disciple of St Columba'). It is also found in Scotland as an anglicized version of COLUM. The name Columba itself means 'dove' in Latin. St Columba's conversion of the Scots to Christianity in the sixth century ensured the name's popularity in Scotland. Shortened to **Mal** or **Malc**.

**Maldwyn** Welsh variant of the English BALDWIN. The name is relatively unknown outside Wales, where it is also a county name. **Mal** is a diminutive form of the name.

**Mallory** English name that originated as a surname that evolved from a Norman French nickname meaning 'unfortunate', from the French *malheure* ('unhappy' or 'unlucky').

**Malone** Irish name meaning 'follower of St John'.

**Malvin** *See* MELVIN.

**Man** *See* EMANUEL.

**Manasseh** Hebrew name meaning 'causing to forget'. It appears in the Bible and was recorded in use in England in the eleventh and twelfth centuries. It appears as the name of a character in William Makepeace Thackeray's *Vanity Fair* (1847–8). Also found as **Manasses**.

**Manasses** *See* MANASSEH.

**Manfred** English, German and Dutch name based on the Old German *mana* ('man') or *magin* ('strength') and *fridu* ('peace') and usually taken to mean 'man of peace'. The name was brought to Britain by the Normans but later became more common among German speakers than in Britain.

**Manley** English name possibly based on 'manly' or else on a place name combining the Old English *maene* ('common') and *leah* ('wood' or 'clearing'). Well-known bearers of the name have included British poet Gerard Manley Hopkins (1844–89).

**Manny** *See* EMANUEL.

**Mansel** English name that may have come originally from the French place name Le Mans. Also found as **Mansell**.

**Mansell** *See* MANSEL.

**Manuel** Spanish equivalent of EMANUEL.

**Manus** *See* MAGNUS.

**Maoileas/Maolmuire** *See* MILES.

**Marc** *See* MARCUS; MARK.

**Marcel** French name based on the Roman Marcellus, itself a variant of MARCUS. It was popularized in France through a third-century martyr of the name and was adopted on an occasional basis by English speakers in the late nineteenth century.

**Marco** *See* MARK.

**Marcus** Roman name possibly (though probably incorrectly) linked, like MARIUS, with Mars, the Roman god of war. Common in ancient Rome, it was taken up by English speakers around the middle of the nineteenth century. Sometimes shortened to **Marc**. *See also* MARK.

**Maredudd** *See* MEREDITH.

**Mario** Italian, Spanish and Portuguese name descended from the Roman MARIUS. Well-known bearers of the name have included the US singer Mario Lanza (Alfredo Cocozza; 1921–59).

**Marion** English name based, via Marianus, on the Roman MARIUS. The most famous bearer of the name to date has been US film actor John Wayne (Marion Michael Morrison; 1907–79).

**Marius** Roman name that may have come from that of Mars, the Roman god of war, or else possibly from the Latin *maris* ('male' or 'manly'). A suggestion that it comes from the Latin *mare* ('sea') is usually discounted. It has made occasional appearances among English speakers since the nineteenth century. *See also* MARCUS.

**Mark** English version of the Roman MARCUS, possibly linked to the Roman god of war Mars and thus meaning 'warlike'. The name appears in the Bible but it was not until the 1960s that it emerged as a popular boys' name among English speakers. Variants include the French **Marc** and the Italian and Spanish **Marco**. **Markie** and **Marky** are among familiar versions.

**Markie/Marky** *See* MARK.

**Marley** English name that originated as a place name meaning 'pleasant wood'. It has appeared more frequently in recent decades in tribute to Jamaican reggae musician Bob Marley (1945–81).

**Marlin** *See* MARLON; MERLIN.

**Marlo** *See* MARLON.

**Marlon** English name of uncertain origin, possibly a variant of **Marc** (*see* MARK) or else of MARION or MERLIN. It received a huge boost through US film actor Marlon Brando (1924–2004), who inherited the name from his father. Also found as **Marlo** or **Marlin**.

**Marlow** English name that originated in a place name meaning 'land of the former pool'. Also found as **Marlowe**.

**Marlowe** *See* MARLOW.

**Marmaduke** English and Irish name of uncertain origin. Attempts have been made to trace the name back to the Celtic name Mael Maedoc, meaning 'disciple of Maedoc' (Maedoc, or Madoc, being the name of several early Irish saints). Sometimes shortened to DUKE.

**Marsden** English name based on the Old English for 'boundary valley'.

**Marsh** English name based on the ordinary vocabulary word.

**Marshal** *See* MARSHALL.

**Marshall** English name that is ultimately German in origin, coming from *marah* ('horse') and *scalc* ('servant'), and was originally reserved for people connected with looking after horses. Also found as **Marshal**, it is more common in Canada and the USA than in the UK.

**Marston** English name that originated in a place name based on the Old English for 'place by a marsh'.

**Martin** English, French and German name based on the Roman Martinus, itself probably from the name of the Roman god of war Mars and meaning 'warlike'. Variant spellings include **Martyn**, originally a Welsh version of the name. Sometimes shortened to **Marty**.

**Marty/Martyn** *See* MARTIN.

**Marv** *See* MARVIN.

**Marvin** English name of uncertain origin that has been in use as a first name since the nineteenth century. It may have emerged as a variant of MERVYN, although another theory traces it back to the Old English name Maerwine, which meant 'famous friend'. Also found as **Marvyn**. Shortened to **Marv**.

**Marvyn** *See* MARVIN.

**Mason** English name that began as an occupational name for anyone working with stone. It is more common in the USA than elsewhere.

**Masterman** Scottish and English name meaning 'master's man' or 'servant' that has made occasional appearances as a first name. Traditionally considered an aristocratic name sometimes

given by barons to their first sons, it has never been very common.

**Mat/Mathew** *See* MATTHEW.

**Mathias** *See* MATTHIAS.

**Mathuin** *See* MAHON.

**Matt** *See* MATTHEW.

**Matthew** English name based on the Hebrew Mattathiah, meaning 'gift of God'. The name features in the Bible as the author of the first Gospel. It came to England with the Normans and reached a peak in popularity in the 1960s. Also found as **Mathew**. Shortened to **Mat** or **Matt**. *See also* MATTHIAS.

**Matthias** Greek version of the Hebrew Mattathiah (also the source of MATTHEW). It appears in the Bible as the name of the apostle who took the place of Judas Iscariot and was among the biblical names taken up by Puritans in the seventeenth century. Also found as **Mathias**.

**Maurice** ('morris') English

and French version of the Roman Mauricius, itself from the Latin *maurus* ('moor', 'dark-skinned' or 'swarthy'). Sometimes found as **Morris** and shortened to **Mo**, **Moss**, **Maurie** or **Morrie**. Variants include the Welsh **Meuric** or **Meurig** and the Irish **Muiris**.

**Maurie** *See* MAURICE.

**Max/Maxie** *See* MAXIMILIAN; MAXWELL.

**Maxim** Russian name based on the Latin *maximus* ('greatest'). Its modern adoption was promoted by its appearance in Daphne du Maurier's novel *Rebecca* (1938). Variants include the Welsh **Macsen**.

**Maximilian** English and German version of the Roman Maximilianus, based on the Latin *maximus* ('greatest'). The name became a favourite choice of the Habsburgs and also, from the sixteenth century, of the royal house of Bavaria. Shortened to **Max** or **Maxie**.

**Maxwell** Scottish name that originated as a place name

either meaning 'Magnus' well' or 'large spring'. Its history as a first name dates from the nineteenth century. Often shortened to **Max** or **Maxie**.

**Maynard** English name based via Norman French on the Old German *magin* ('strength') and *hard* ('brave' or 'hardy'). Notable bearers of the name have included British economist John Maynard Keynes (1883–1946).

**Medwyn** Welsh name based on that of a Welsh saint. It is often bestowed upon boys born on New Year's Day, the saint's festival.

**Mehmood/Mehmud** *See* MAHMUD.

**Meical** *See* MICHAEL.

**Meir** Jewish name based on the Hebrew for 'giving light'. Variants include **Meyer**.

**Meirion** Welsh name that may have its roots ultimately in the Roman Marianus, itself a variant of MARIUS. Also found as **Merrion**.

**Mel** *See* MELVILLE; MELVIN.

**Melville** English and Scottish name that originated in the Norman French place name Malville, meaning 'bad settlement'. It appeared as a surname in Scotland as early as the twelfth century and was taken up as a first name in the nineteenth century. Shortened to **Mel**.

**Melvin** Scottish name that was taken up among English speakers towards the end of the nineteenth century. Its roots are obscure, but it may be descended in part from the Old English *wine* ('friend') or linked to the Gaelic **Malvin** ('smooth brow'). Also found as **Melvyn**. Shortened to **Mel**.

**Melvyn** *See* MELVIN.

**Mercer** English name that originated as a surname meaning 'trader'.

**Meredith** English version of the Welsh **Maredudd** or **Meredydd**, meaning 'great chief'. The Welsh form of the name is little known outside Wales itself. Today the name is perhaps commoner among females than it is among men.

Sometimes shortened to MERRY.

**Meredydd** *See* MEREDITH.

**Merfyn** *See* MERVYN.

**Merle** English name that may be related to the French *merle* ('blackbird'). It made its first appearances as a boys' name early in the twentieth century, largely confined to the USA.

**Merlin** English version of the Welsh **Myrddin**, meaning 'sea-hill fort'. It is most famous as the name of the magician of Arthurian legend. Also found as **Marlin** or **Merlyn**.

**Merlyn** *See* MERLIN.

**Merrion** *See* MEIRION.

**Merry** English name that exists as a familiar form of MEREDITH and other names. It first won acceptance among English speakers in the nineteenth century.

**Merton** English name based on a place name meaning 'settlement by a lake'.

**Merv/Mervin** *See*
MERVYN.

**Mervyn** English version of
the Welsh **Merfyn**, probably
from the Old Celtic for 'sea
ruler'. It was largely confined
to Wales until the 1930s. Also
found as **Mervin**. Shortened to
**Merv**. *See also* MARVIN.

**Meuric/Meurig** *See*
MAURICE.

**Meyer** *See* MEIR.

**Micah** Hebrew equivalent of
MICHAEL, meaning 'who is like
Yah?' (Yah being an alternative
name for Jehovah or God.) It
appears in the Bible as the
name of one of the prophets
and was adopted by English
Puritans in the seventeenth
century.

**Michael** English and German
name based on the Hebrew for
'who is like God?'. St Michael
was the archangel who led the
angels against Satan. The name
was taken up by English
speakers in the twelfth century.
Shortened to **Mick**, **Mickey**
(or **Micky**), **Mike**, **Mikey** or
**Midge**. Variants include the
English **Mitchell** (or **Mitch**),

the Welsh **Meical**, the Spanish
**Miguel** and the Russian
**Mikhail**. *See also* MICAH;
MISHA.

**Mick/Mickey/Micky/
Midge/Miguel/Mike/
Mikey/Mikhail** *See*
MICHAEL.

**Milburn** English name that
originated as a place name
meaning 'mill stream'.

**Miles** English name of
uncertain origin. It may be
descended from the Roman
**Milo**, itself possibly from the
Latin *miles* ('soldier'), although
a link has also been suggested
with the Slavonic *mil* ('dear' or
'beloved') or with the Old
German for 'merciful' or
'generous'. In Ireland, it may
be linked to **Maoileas** ('servant
of Jesus'), **Maolmuire** ('servant
of Mary') or **Maelmore**
('majestic chief'). Also found as
**Myles**.

**Milford** English name that
originated as a place name
meaning 'mill ford'.

**Miller** English name based on
the ordinary vocabulary word,

originally a surname. Variants include **Milner**.

**Milner** *See* MILLER.

**Milo** *See* MILES.

**Milt** *See* MILTON.

**Milton** English name that originated as a place name meaning 'settlement with a mill'. The name's popularity was promoted through English poet John Milton (1608–74). Shortened to **Milt**.

**Mischa** *See* MISHA.

**Misha** Russian name that developed as a variant of MICHAEL. Also found as **Mischa**.

**Mitch/Mitchell** *See* MICHAEL.

**Mitya** *See* DMITRI.

**Mo** *See* MAURICE; MOSES.

**Moby** English name inspired by the name given to the monstrous white whale in Herman Melville's novel *Moby-Dick* (1851).

**Mohammad/ Mohammed** *See* MUHAMMAD.

**Moishe** *See* MOSES.

**Monro** *See* MONROE.

**Monroe** English and Scottish name that is thought to have had its roots in a Scottish place name meaning 'mouth of the Roe' (a reference to the River Roe in Ireland's County Londonderry, from which the Scottish Munro clan are supposed to have come). The name is especially popular in the USA. Also found as **Monro**, **Munroe** or **Munro**.

**Montagu** *See* MONTAGUE.

**Montague** English name that originated as a surname based on a Norman place name, Mont Aigu near Caen, itself from the Old French *mont* ('hill') and *aigu* ('pointed'). The name has strong aristocratic associations. Also found as **Montagu**. Shortened to **Monty**.

**Montana** English name based on the Latin for 'mountain'. It is largely confined to the USA, where it is also the name of a state.

**Montgomery** English name that began life as a Norman place name, Mont Goumeril, meaning something like 'mountain of the powerful one'. Postwar appearances of the name owed much to the popularity of Field Marshal Bernard Montgomery (1887–1976), otherwise known by the usual shortened form of the name, **Monty**.

**Montmorency** English name that originated as a Norman place name based on the Old French *mont* ('hill') and the Gallo-Roman name Maurentius. Sometimes shortened to **Monty**.

**Monty** *See* MONTAGUE; MONTGOMERY; MONTMORENCY.

**Moray** *See* MURRAY.

**Morcant** *See* MORGAN.

**Mordecai** Hebrew name probably borrowed from Persian and meaning 'devotee of Marduk' (Marduk being the most important of the gods of ancient Babylon). It features in the Bible and was taken up by English Puritans in the seventeenth century. Shortened to **Mordy** or **Morty** or, among Jews, to **Motke** or **Motl**.

**Mordy** *See* MORDECAI.

**Morgan** English name based on the Welsh **Morcant**, which may have come from the words *mor* ('sea') and *cant* ('circle' or 'edge') but is otherwise of unknown origin. It is sometimes suggested that the name means 'sea-bright'.

**Moriarty** English name that originated as a surname based on the Irish Muirchertach, meaning 'seafarer'. It is usually associated with Professor Moriarty, the arch-enemy of Sir Arthur Conan Doyle's fictional detective Sherlock Holmes.

**Morley** English name that originated as a place name based on the Old English *mor* ('moor' or 'marsh') and *leah* ('wood' or 'clearing').

**Morrie/Morris** *See* MAURICE.

**Mort** *See* MORTIMER;
MORTON.

**Mortimer** English name that
originated in a Norman place
name based on the Old French
for 'dead sea' (referring to a
stagnant lake or marsh).
Another suggestion is that it is
of Celtic origin, meaning 'sea
warrior'. Sometimes shortened
to **Mort**.

**Morton** English name that
originated as a place name
based on the Old English
*mortun* ('settlement on a
moor'). Having made its debut
as a first name in the mid-
nineteenth century, it is most
frequently found today within
the Jewish community as an
anglicized version of MOSES.
**Mort** and **Morty** are familiar
forms of the name.

**Morty** *See* MORDECAI;
MORTON.

**Mose** *See* MOSES.

**Moses** Hebrew name of
uncertain origin. It may have
evolved, via the Hebrew
Moshel, from the Egyptian *mes*
('child' or 'born of'). The story
of the biblical Moses

established the name as a
favourite among Jews. Early
records of the name in English,
dating from the eleventh
century, give it as **Moyses**.
Also found as **Moyse** or **Moss**.
Shortened to **Mo**, **Mose** or
**Moy**. **Moshe** (or **Moishe**) is a
Yiddish variant.

**Moshe** *See* MOSES.

**Moss** *See* MAURICE; MOSES;
MOSTYN.

**Mostafa** *See* MUSTAFA.

**Mostyn** Welsh name taken
from a place name in Clwyd,
itself based on the Old English
*mos* ('moss') and *tun*
('settlement'). Sometimes
shortened to **Moss**.

**Motke/Motl** *See*
MORDECAI.

**Moy/Moyse/Moyses** *See*
MOSES.

**Muhammad** Arabic name
based on *hamida* ('to praise')
and thus meaning
'praiseworthy'. As the name of
the founder of Islam, it has
long been one of the most
popular masculine names

among Muslims. Also found as **Mahomet**, **Mohammad** or **Mohammed**.

**Muir** Scottish name that originated in a place name meaning 'moor'. Notable bearers of the name have included the Scottish film music director Muir Mathieson (1911–72).

**Muireach** *See* MURRAY.

**Muireadhach** *See* MURDOCH.

**Muiris** *See* MAURICE.

**Mungo** Scottish name possibly based on the Welsh *mwyn* ('dear', 'gentle' or 'kind'). It was borne as a nickname meaning 'most dear' by a sixth-century Scottish saint, otherwise known as St Kentigern, and to this day is rare outside Scotland itself.

**Munro/Munroe** *See* MONROE.

**Murdie/Murdo** *See* MURDOCH.

**Murdoch** English name based on the Scottish Gaelic **Murdo** or **Muireadhach**, themselves from the Gaelic *muir* ('sea') and usually interpreted to mean 'seaman' or 'mariner'. Sometimes shortened to **Murdy** or **Murdie**. **Murtagh** is an Irish equivalent.

**Murdy** *See* MURDOCH.

**Murgatroyd** English name based on a place name (in Yorkshire). The original place name – unlocated – resulted from the combination of MARGARET and the Yorkshire dialect *royd* ('clearing') and thus means 'Margaret's clearing'.

**Murphy** Irish name based on the Irish Gaelic for 'sea hound'.

**Murray** Scottish name that originated in the Scottish place name Moray, itself from *mor* ('sea'). As a first name Murray may also be found as an anglicized version of the Gaelic **Muireach**. Also found as **Moray** or **Murry**.

**Murry** *See* MURRAY.

**Murtagh** *See* MURDOCH.

**Mustafa** Arabic name

meaning 'chosen'. As a title of MUHAMMAD, it has long been one of the most popular names among Muslims. Notable bearers of the name have included Mustafa Kemal (1881–1938), founder of the modern Turkish state. Also found as **Mostafa** or **Mustapha**.

**Mustapha** *See* MUSTAFA.

**Myles** *See* MILES.

**Myrddin** *See* MERLIN.

**Myron** Greek name meaning 'myrrh' that was taken up as a first name by English speakers in the twentieth century. Sometimes today interpreted to mean 'fragrant'. It was popular among early Christians because of its link with myrrh, one of the gifts presented to the baby Jesus.

# BOYS' NAMES

**Nadim** Arab name meaning 'drinking companion' or 'confidant'. The name has its origins in the verb *nadama* ('to drink') and is also commonly used in Indian communities.

**Nahum** ('naium') Hebrew name meaning 'comforter'. The name of an Old Testament prophet, it was among the biblical names taken up by Puritans in the seventeenth century. Nahum Tate (1652–1715) was a notable English playwright.

**Nairn** Celtic name meaning 'dweller by the alder tree'.

**Nandy** *See* FERDINAND.

**Naoise** ('naysee') Irish Gaelic name of uncertain meaning. It is best known as the name of the lover of Deirdre in ancient Irish legend: on Naoise's death at the hands of Conchobar, king of Ulster, Deirdre died of grief.

**Napier** English and French name based on the Greek for 'of the new city'.

**Napoleon** French name based on the Italian Napoleone, which was probably a reference to the city of Naples, combined with the Italian *leone* ('lion'). Through the Corsican-born French emperor Napoleon Bonaparte (1769–1821) it became one of the most feared names in Europe.

**Narcissus** English version of the Greek Narkissos, which may have been based on the Greek word *narkē* ('numbness'). The name is associated with the Greek legend of Narcissus, a beautiful youth who fell in love with his own reflection.

**Nash** English name that originated as a surname based

on the Old English for 'ash tree'.

**Nat/Nate** *See* NATHAN; NATHANIEL.

**Nathan** Hebrew name meaning 'gift' or 'he has given'. Borne by an Old Testament prophet, it was among the biblical names adopted by Puritans in the seventeenth century. It may also appear as a shortened form of NATHANIEL or JONATHAN. Commonly shortened to **Nat** or **Nate**.

**Nathanael** *See* NATHANIEL.

**Nathaniel** Hebrew name meaning 'gift of God' or 'God has given'. In the New Testament it is the personal name of the apostle Bartholomew. Famous bearers of the name have included American writer Nathaniel Hawthorne (1804–64). Also found as **Nathanael** and shortened to **Nat**, **Nate** or **Natty**. *See also* NATHAN.

**Natty** *See* NATHANIEL.

**Neal/Neale** *See* NEIL.

**Ned** *See* EDMUND; EDWARD.

**Neil** English name based on the Irish Gaelic *niadh* (variously thought to mean 'champion', 'cloud' or 'passionate'). Also found as **Neill**, **Neal**, **Neale**, **Niall** (the Irish Gaelic version of the name) and the Scottish **Neilie** or **Neillie**. *See also* NIGEL; NILS.

**Neilie/Neill/Neillie** *See* NEIL.

**Neirin** *See* ANEURIN.

**Nelson** English name meaning 'son of Neil' or 'son of Nell'. It was widely adopted as a first name in tribute to Admiral Horatio Nelson (1758–1805). Notable bearers of the name since then have included South African President Nelson Mandela (b. 1918).

**Nemo** Greek name meaning 'grove'.

**Nero** Roman name based on the Latin for 'black' or 'dark-haired'. It became notorious as the name of the Roman emperor Nero (AD 37–68).

**Nev** *See* NEVILLE.

**Neven** *See* NEVIN.

**Neville** English name taken from the French place name Neuville, meaning 'new town'. It was adopted as a first name in English-speaking countries after the Norman Conquest. Commonly shortened to **Nev**.

**Nevin** Irish Gaelic name that was originally a surname meaning 'little saint'. Also found as **Neven** or **Niven**.

**Newman** English name that began as a surname meaning 'newcomer'.

**Newt** *See* NEWTON.

**Newton** English name that originated as a place name meaning 'new town'. It remains rare outside the USA. The usual shortened form is **Newt**.

**Niall** *See* NEIL; NILES.

**Nichol** *See* NICHOLAS.

**Nicholas** First name based on the Greek Nikolaos, meaning 'victory of the people'. The fourth-century St Nicholas is widely familiar as

'Father Christmas' or 'Santa Claus'. Variants include **Nicolas**, **Nichol** and **Nicol** (popular in Scotland). Commonly shortened to **Nick**, **Nicky**, **Nico** or **Nik**. *See also* COLIN.

**Nick** *See* NICHOLAS.

**Nickson** *See* NIXON.

**Nicky/Nico/Nicol/ Nicolas** *See* NICHOLAS.

**Nige** *See* NIGEL.

**Nigel** English name that is thought to have been adopted as the Latin version of NEIL after the Norman Conquest. Sometimes shortened to **Nige**.

**Nik** *See* NICHOLAS.

**Niles** Variant of the Gaelic name **Niall** (*see* NEIL), thus meaning 'champion'.

**Nils** Scandinavian version of NEIL, similarly meaning 'champion'.

**Ninian** Scottish and Irish name of uncertain origin. It may possibly be related to VIVIAN, itself based on the

Latin *vivus* ('alive'). It was borne by a fifth-century saint who was responsible for bringing Christianity to the Picts of southern Scotland.

**Niven** *See* NEVIN.

**Nixon** English name that originated as a surname meaning 'son of Nicholas'. Also found as **Nickson**.

**Noah** Hebrew name meaning 'peaceful' or else 'long-lived', 'comforter' or 'wanderer'. It is commonly associated with the biblical Noah, builder of the Ark at the time of the Great Flood.

**Noam** ('nohm') Hebrew name meaning 'pleasantness', 'delight' or 'joy'. The name is popular chiefly among American Jewish families. Famous bearers have included the US linguist Noam Chomsky (b. 1928).

**Nobby** *See* NORBERT.

**Noble** English name of medieval origin inspired by the ordinary vocabulary word. Like DUKE and EARL, it was probably meant to convey a notion of social status and nobility of character.

**Noel** French and English name based on the French *Noël* ('Christmas'). Variously given with or without the diaeresis, the name has been reserved traditionally for children born on Christmas Day or during the Christmas period. **Nowell** is a variant form.

**Nolan** Irish name meaning 'descendant of a noble' or simply 'famous'.

**Noll/Nollie** *See* OLIVER.

**Norbert** English name based on the Old German for 'famous northman' (from words meaning 'north' and 'bright'). The name came to Britain with the Normans and was revived in the Victorian era. Informal versions of the name include BERT, BERTIE, **Norrie** and **Nobby**.

**Norm** *See* NORMAN.

**Norman** English name based on the Old English for 'Northman' (first applied to the Vikings). It also exists as an anglicization of the Norse name Tormod (from the name of the god Thor and the Norse for 'wrath'). **Norm** and **Norrie** are informal versions.

**Norrie** *See* NORBERT; NORMAN.

**Norris** English name that developed as a variant of NORMAN. It was fairly popular during the nineteenth century but has since become rare.

**Norton** English name that originated as a place name combining the Old English words for 'north' and 'settlement'. Its history as a first name dates from the nineteenth century.

**Nowell** *See* NOEL.

**Nye** *See* ANEURIN.

# BOYS' NAMES

**Oak** English name, based on that of the tree. **Oakie** and **Oaky** are informal versions of the name.

**Oakie** *See* OAK.

**Oakley** English name based on the Old English for 'from the oak tree meadow'.

**Oaky** *See* OAK.

**Obadiah** English name based on the Hebrew for 'servant of the Lord'. The name was among those adopted by the Puritans in the seventeenth century and became a slang term for anyone with Puritan leanings.

**Oberon** *See* AUBERON.

**Ocean** English name based on the ordinary vocabulary word 'ocean'. Oceanus was the name of a Greek sea-god.

**Ocky** *See* OSCAR.

**Octavian** Roman name based on the Latin *octavus* ('eighth'). Originally reserved for eighth-born children, it was adopted in the English-speaking world from the nineteenth century. **Octavius** is an equally rare variant form.

**Octavius** *See* OCTAVIAN.

**Odell** English name based on the Old English for 'hill of woad'.

**Odhran** *See* ORAN.

**Ogden** English name based on the Old English for 'valley of oak'. It has been in occasional use as a first name since the nineteenth century. Notable bearers of the name have included US humorous poet Ogden Nash (1902–71).

**Ogilvie** Celtic name meaning 'high peak'. Also encountered as **Ogilvy**.

**Ogilvy** *See* OGILVIE.

**Ol** *See* OLIVER.

**Olaf** Scandinavian name based on the Old Norse *anleifr* ('family descendant'). Borne by several Scandinavian kings, it came to Britain with the Vikings. Variants include **Olav** and the Scottish **Aulay**.

**Olav** *See* OLAF.

**Oleg** Russian variant of the Scandinavian Helge (*see* HELGA).

**Oliver** English name that may have developed either from the Scandinavian OLAF or from the Old German *alfihar* ('elf host'). Notable bearers of the name have included Oliver Cromwell (1599–1658). Variants include the French **Olivier** and the Welsh HAVELOCK. **Ol**, **Ollie**, **Nol** and **Nollie** are shortened forms.

**Olivier/Ollie** *See* OLIVER.

**Omar** *See* UMAR.

**Ombra** Italian name based on the Italian word for 'shadow'.

**Onda** Italian name based on the Italian word for 'wave'.

**Onslow** English name based on the Old English meaning 'hill of the zealous one'.

**Oran** Irish name, originally **Odhran**, based on the Gaelic *odhra* ('dark-haired'). Notable bearers of the name included one of St Columba's most loyal followers. Sometimes anglicized as **Orrin**.

**Oren** Hebrew name meaning 'laurel'.

**Orlando** Italian version of ROLAND, meaning 'famous land'. It has been in occasional use among English speakers since medieval times. It appears in Shakespeare and as the title of Virginia Woolf's novel *Orlando* (1928).

**Orli** *See* ORLY.

**Orly** Hebrew name meaning 'light is mine'. Also found as **Orli**.

**Ormond** Irish name,

originally a surname meaning 'from east Munster'. Also found as **Ormonde**.

**Ormonde** *See* ORMOND.

**Orrin** *See* ORAN.

**Orson** English and French name that developed, through Old French *ourson* ('bearcub'), from the Latin *ursus* ('bear'). In medieval legend, Orson was a child carried off and raised by a family of bears.

**Ortho** Cornish name based ultimately on the Greek *orthos* ('straight').

**Orval** *See* ORVILLE.

**Orville** English name invented by Fanny Burney for a central character in her book *Evelina* (1778), but possibly inspired by a French place name. It is famous as the name of US flight pioneer Orville Wright (1871–1948). **Orval** is a variant form.

**Os** *See* OSCAR.

**Osbert** English name based on the Old English *os* ('god') and *beorht* ('famous') and thus

meaning 'famous as a god'. It was in use in Northumberland prior to the Norman Conquest. Diminutive forms include **Oz** and **Ozzie**.

**Osborn** *See* OSBORNE.

**Osborne** English name based on the Old English *os* ('god') and *beorn* ('bear' or 'warrior') and thus meaning 'god-like warrior'. Occasionally found as **Osborn** or **Osbourne** and shortened to **Oz** or **Ozzie**.

**Osbourne** *See* OSBORNE.

**Oscar** English and Irish name based either on the Gaelic *os* ('deer') and *cara* ('friend'), and thus meaning 'gentle friend', or on the Old English *ansfar* ('god-spear'). It is strongly associated with the Irish playwright and wit Oscar Wilde (1854–1900). Occasionally shortened to **Ocky**, **Os** or **Ossie**.

**Osmond** English name based on the Old English *os* ('god') and *mund* ('protection'). Occasionally found as **Osmund**, it was in use prior to the Norman Conquest. Sometimes shortened to **Ossie**.

**Osmund** *See* OSMOND.

**Ossie** *See* OSCAR; OSMOND.

**Oswald** English name based on the Old English *os* ('god') and *weald* ('rule') and thus meaning 'rule of god' or 'divine power'. It was common in Anglo-Saxon England but was later linked to British fascist leader Oswald Mosley (1896–1980). **Oz** and **Ozzie** are shortened forms.

**Otis** English name based, via the German OTTO, on the Old German *ot* ('riches'). It is rare outside the USA, where notable bearers of the name have included soul singer Otis Redding (1941–67).

**Otto** German name based on the Old German *ot* ('riches'). It was brought to Britain by the Normans in the eleventh century. Like other German names it became virtually extinct among English speakers after the outbreak of the First World War.

**Owain** *See* OWEN.

**Owen** Welsh name that may have developed from EUGENE, meaning 'well-born', or else from the Welsh *oen* ('lamb'). Occasionally found in its original form **Owain**, it was borne by the Welsh rebel leader Owen Glendower (1359–1416).

**Oz/Ozzie** *See* OSBERT; OSBORNE; OSWALD.

# BOYS' NAMES

**Pablo** Spanish version of
PAUL, famous as the first name
of Spanish artist Pablo Picasso
(1881–1973).

**Paco** Spanish name that
developed as a variant of
FRANCIS. **Pancho** is a variant
form.

## Paddy/Padraic/Padraig
*See* PATRICK.

**Palmer** ('parma') English
name meaning 'pilgrim'. It is
thought that the name began as
'palm-bearer' and thus referred
to palm-bearing pilgrims to the
Holy Land.

**Pancho** *See* PACO.

**Paolo** Italian version of
PAUL.

**Paris** Greek name borne by
the son of King Priam of Troy,
a central character in the story
of the Trojan War. Also found
as **Parris**, the name is
traditionally a boys' name,
although in recent years it has
also been employed for girls.

**Parker** English name
meaning 'park keeper' that has
been in occasional use (chiefly
in the USA) as a first name
since the nineteenth century.
There is a Dr Parker Peps in
the novel *Dombey and Son*
(1848) by Charles Dickens.

**Parris** *See* PARIS.

**Parry** Welsh name from the
phrase *ap Harry* (meaning 'son
of Harry'). It is rarely
encountered outside Wales
itself.

**Pascal** French name based on
the Latin *Paschalis* ('of Easter').
It was taken up as a first name
by the early Christians, usually
reserved for boys born in the
Easter season. Occasionally
found as **Paschal** or **Pascoe**.

**Paschal/Pascoe** *See* PASCAL.

**Pat/Patraic/Patric** *See* PATRICK.

**Patrick** English and Irish name based on the Latin *patricius* ('nobleman'). The name is particularly popular in Ireland in tribute to St Patrick (c. 385–461), the patron saint of Ireland. Variants include the Irish **Padraic**, **Padraig**, **Patric** and **Patraic**. Often shortened to **Pat** or **Paddy**.

**Paul** Roman name based on the Latin *paulus* ('little' or 'small'). The name was borne by several saints and by the apostle St Paul (who changed his name from Saul on his conversion to Christianity). Variants include the Welsh **Pawl**.

**Pawl** *See* PAUL.

**Payn** *See* PAYNE.

**Payne** English name based ultimately on an Old French surname meaning 'countryman'. Also found as **Payn**.

**Payton** *See* PEYTON.

**Peadar** *See* PETER.

**Pearce** *See* PIERS.

**Pedr/Pedro** *See* PETER.

**Peers** *See* PIERS.

**Pelham** English name that originated as a place name meaning 'Peola's place'. Notable bearers of the name have included British novelist P. G. Wodehouse (Pelham George Wodehouse; 1881–1975), nicknamed 'Plum'.

**Pepe** ('pepay') Informal Spanish variant of JOSÉ that is also encountered among English speakers, chiefly in the USA.

**Perce** *See* PERCIVAL; PERCY.

**Percival** English and French name, apparently invented by the French poet Chrétien de Troyes for the hero of his poem *Percevale, a knight of King Arthur* (c. 1175). Chrétien himself indicated that the name came from the Old French *perce-val* ('one who pierces the valley'). Often shortened to PERCY, **Perce** or **Val**.

**Percy** English name that originated as a French place name. It also exists as a shortened form of PERCIVAL. The source place name, Perci in Normandy, appears to have had its roots in the Roman personal name Persius. Like Percival, the name is sometimes shortened to **Perce**.

**Peregrine** English name ultimately based (via Italian) on the Latin *peregrinus* ('stranger' or 'foreigner'). Notable bearers of the name include the central character in Tobias Smollett's *Peregrine Pickle* (1751). Sometimes shortened to PERRY.

**Perran** *See* PIRAN.

**Perry** English name based on the Old English *pirige* ('man who lives by a pear tree'). It is also encountered as a shortened form of PEREGRINE or PETER. The name is popular in Canada and the USA, partly in tribute to two nineteenth-century American admirals of the name.

**Pete** *See* PETER.

**Peter** English, German and Scandinavian name based ultimately on the Greek *petros* ('rock' or 'stone'). Its lasting popularity owes much to the apostle St Peter. The name was common during medieval times, often rendered as PIERS or in other variant forms. Variants in other languages include **Pedro**, the Welsh **Pedr** and the Scottish and Irish Gaelic **Peadar**. Commonly shortened to **Pete**. *See also* PETERKIN.

**Peterkin** English name that evolved as a variant of PETER. Of chiefly historical interest today, it was borne by a character in R. M. Ballantyne's adventure novel *The Coral Island* (1857).

**Peyton** English name based on a place name meaning 'farm of Paega'. The name, used for boys and girls, is more frequent in the USA than elsewhere, promoted perhaps by the US television drama series *Peyton Place* in the 1960s. Also found as **Payton**.

**Phelan** Irish name based on the Irish Gaelic for 'wolf'.

**Phelim** Irish name based on the Irish Gaelic for 'always good'. *See also* FELIX.

**Phil** *See* PHILIP.

**Philip** English name that developed from the Greek Philippos, itself based on the Greek words *philein* ('to love') and *hippos* ('horse'), and thus meaning 'lover of horses'. In medieval times the name was shared by both sexes. Variants include **Phillip**. Commonly shortened to **Phil**, **Pip** or **Flip**.

**Phillip** *See* PHILIP.

**Philo** ('fighlo') English and German version of the ancient Greek name Philon, meaning 'loved'. The name was adopted by English speakers in the eighteenth century. Well-known bearers of the name have included US typewriter and sewing-machine manufacturer Philo Remington (1816–89).

**Phineas** Biblical name possibly modelled on the Hebrew Phinehas ('serpent's mouth' or 'oracle'), but more likely descended from the Egyptian Panhsj ('the black'), a name used for Nubians. Notable bearers of the name have included US showman Phineas T. Barnum (1810–91).

**Piaras/Pierce** *See* PIERS.

**Piers** French equivalent of PETER that became familiar in England after the Norman Conquest, as evidenced by William Langland's poem *Piers Plowman* (c. 1362). Variant forms include **Pearce**, **Peers** and **Pierce**. The Irish also have the less common Gaelic variant **Piaras**.

**Pip** *See* PHILIP.

**Piran** Cornish name based on a place name of unknown meaning. It is suggested that the original place name was itself linked to the name PETER. Also found as **Perran**, the name was borne by the Celtic abbot St Piran, the patron saint of Cornish miners.

**Plaxy** Cornish name supposedly descended from the Greek name Praxedes, which was itself based on the Greek *praxis* ('action' or 'doing') and is usually taken to mean 'active'. Its use is confined mainly to Cornwall.

**Poldie** *See* LEOPOLD.

**Porter** English name based on the French for 'gatekeeper'.

**Powel** Welsh name meaning 'son of Hywel'.

**Presley** English name meaning 'priest's meadow'.

**Preston** English name taken from a place name based on the Old English *preost* ('priest') and *tun* ('enclosure'), thus meaning 'priest's farm' or 'priest's place'. Notable bearers of the name have included US film director and screenwriter Preston Sturges (Edmund Preston Biden; 1898–1959).

**Price** Welsh name meaning 'son of Rhys'. Also found as **Pryce**.

**Primo** Italian name based on the Latin *primus* ('first') and thus meaning 'first-born'.

**Prince** English name based on the royal title (itself from the Latin *princeps*, 'one who takes first place'). It was used originally as a surname by families with royal connections and by those who were in the service of a prince. Notable bearers of the name have included US pop star Prince (Prince Rogers Nelson; b. 1958).

**Prosper** French and English name based on the Latin *prosper* ('fortunate' or 'prosperous'). It was commonly found among the saints of the early Christian church and was later adopted by Puritans.

**Pryce** *See* PRICE.

**Pryderi** Welsh name meaning 'caring for' or 'anxiety'. There is a character of the name in the *Mabinogion*.

**Pugh** Welsh name meaning 'son of Hugh'.

**Pwll** *See* PWYLL.

**Pwyll** ('pull') Welsh name based on *pwll* ('wisdom' or 'prudence'). It is the name of a heroic prince in the *Mabinogion*. Also found as **Pwll**.

# BOYS' NAMES

**Quentin** English name of French origin, ultimately from the Latin *quintus* ('fifth') and formerly reserved for fifth sons. Also found as **Quintin** or **Quinton**. *See also* QUINN.

**Quincey** *See* QUINCY.

**Quincy** English name of French origin, ultimately (like QUENTIN) from the Roman *quintus* ('fifth') and often given to fifth sons. Also found as **Quincey**.

**Quinlan** Irish name meaning 'well-formed one'.

**Quinn** Irish name based on the Gaelic surname Ó Cuinn, meaning 'descendant of Conn' but generally taken to mean 'wise'. It may also be found as a shortened form of QUENTIN.

**Quintin/Quinton** *See* QUENTIN.

## BOYS' NAMES

**Rab/Rabbie** *See* ROBERT.

**Radcliff** English name based on an Old English place name meaning 'red cliff'.

**Radley** English name based on an Old English surname meaning 'red meadow'.

**Rafael** *See* RAPHAEL.

**Rafe** *See* RALPH.

**Raghnall** *See* RONALD.

**Rainer/Rainier** *See* RAYNER.

**Raleigh** English name taken from an Old English place name meaning 'clearing with roe deer'. The name evokes the memory of the celebrated English seafarer, writer and explorer Sir Walter Raleigh (c. 1552–1618).

**Ralf** *See* RALPH.

**Ralph** English name based via Norman French on the Old Norse Rathulfr, from *raed* ('counsel') and *wulf* ('wolf') and thus meaning 'wise and strong'. As **Ralf** or **Rauf** it was popular in medieval times. **Rafe** was the usual form in the seventeenth century, reflecting its contemporary pronunciation. A familiar version of the name is **Ralphie**.

**Ralphie** *See* RALPH.

**Ralston** English name based on an identical English place name. Its history as a first name goes back to the nineteenth century.

**Ramón** *See* RAYMOND.

**Ramsay** English and Scottish name taken from a place name based on the Old English *hramsa* ('wild garlic' or 'ram') and *eg* ('island'). The name's Scottish connections date back to the twelfth century. Notable bearers of the name include British prime minister James Ramsay MacDonald (1866–1937). Also found as **Ramsey**.

**Ramsden** English name meaning 'ram's valley'.

**Ramsey** *See* RAMSAY.

**Ran** *See* RANDOLPH; RANULF.

**Ranald** *See* RONALD.

**Randal/Randalf/ Randall/Randel** *See* RANDOLPH.

**Randi** *See* ANDREW; RANDOLPH.

**Randle** *See* RANDOLPH.

**Randolph** English name based on the Old English *rand* ('shield edge') and *wulf* ('wolf') and thus meaning, roughly, 'strong defender'. Historical versions included **Randal**, **Randall**, **Randel**, **Randle** and **Randalf**, though the -f ending had largely given way to -ph by the nineteenth century. Shortened to **Ran** or **Randy** (or **Randi**).

**Randy** *See* ANDREW; RANDOLPH.

**Ranulf** *See* RANULPH.

**Ranulph** English version of the Old Norse Reginulfr, which itself came from *regin* ('advice' or 'decision') and *ulfr* ('wolf'), thus meaning 'well-counselled and strong'. The original English form of the name was **Ranulf**. Shortened to **Ran**.

**Raphael** Hebrew name meaning 'God has healed'. As the name of a biblical archangel it was taken up by English speakers in the sixteenth and seventeenth centuries. Also found as **Rafael**. Notable bearers of the name have included the Italian Renaissance painter Raphael (Raffaello Santi; 1483–1520).

**Rastus** *See* ERASTUS.

**Rauf** *See* RALPH.

**Ray** *See* RAYMOND.

**Raymond** English name linked via the French Raimont to an Old German name combining *ragin* ('advice' or 'decision') and *mund* ('protection') and thus meaning 'well-advised protector'. Also found as **Raymund**. **Redmond** and **Redmund** are Irish versions of the name. **Ramón** is a Spanish variant. Often shortened to **Ray**.

**Raymund** *See* RAYMOND.

**Rayner** English name based on the Old German *ragin* ('advice' or 'protection') and *hari* ('army' or 'warrior'). The name was introduced to England by the Normans. Also found as **Raynor**, **Rainer** and **Rainier** (a French version).

**Raynor** *See* RAYNER.

**Read** *See* REID.

**Rearden** *See* RIORDAN.

**Red** English name that began life as a nickname for any person with red hair, or alternatively as a shortened form of EDWARD or RICHARD. Also found as **Redd**, it is more common in the USA than elsewhere.

**Redd** *See* RED.

**Redmond/Redmund**
*See* RAYMOND.

**Redvers** English name with strong aristocratic associations. It appears to have made its debut as a first name in the nineteenth century, when notable bearers included the British general Sir Redvers Buller (1839–1908).

**Reece** *See* RHYS.

**Reed** *See* REID.

**Rees** *See* RHYS.

**Reg/Reggie** *See* REGINALD.

**Reginald** English name based on the Old English *regen* ('counsel') and *weald* ('power') and thus meaning 'well-counselled ruler'. The anglicized form REYNOLD was more popular for many centuries, but Reginald revived after appearing in Sir Walter Scott's *Ivanhoe* (1820). Commonly shortened to **Reg**, **Reggie** or REX.

**Reid** English name based on the Old English *read* ('red') and usually reserved for children with red hair or a ruddy complexion. Occasionally found as **Reed** or **Read**.

**Remus** English name possibly based on the Latin *remus* ('oar') or else a reference to Remus, brother of Romulus, the legendary founder of Rome. The most famous bearer of the name is the fictional former slave Remus in Joel Chandler Harris' 'Uncle Remus' tales (1880–1910).

**Renatus** *See* RENÉ.

**René** French name based on the Latin *renatus* ('reborn'). As **Renatus** it was popular among early Christians and later taken up by Puritans in the seventeenth century. Its frequency in Canada and the USA reflects the influence of the French missionary St René Goupil (d. 1642).

**Reuben** Hebrew name meaning 'behold, a son'. The name appears in the Bible as that of Jacob's eldest son. Also found as **Ruben**, it was among the many biblical names adopted by Puritans in the seventeenth century. **Rube** and

**Ruby** are common abbreviations of the name.

**Rex** English name based on the Latin *rex* ('king'). It is sometimes considered to be a shortened form of REGINALD. Famous bearers of the name have included British actor Rex Harrison (Reginald Carey Harrison; 1908–90).

**Reynold** English name based via Norman French on the Old German *ragin* ('advice' or 'decision') and *wald* ('ruler') and thus meaning 'well-counselled ruler'. Also found as a variant of REGINALD, it has been in irregular use among English speakers since the nineteenth century. Other versions of the name include the Welsh **Rheinallt**.

**Rheinallt** *See* REYNOLD.

**Rhett** English name of uncertain origin, possibly based on the older BRETT or else on the Dutch surname de Raedt, itself from the Middle Dutch *raet* ('advice'). Another suggestion traces the name to the Greek *rhetor* ('speaker' or 'orator'). It became popular through Rhett Butler in

Margaret Mitchell's *Gone with the Wind* (1936).

**Rhodri** Welsh name based on the Old Welsh *rhod* ('wheel') and *rhi* ('ruler'), or alternatively treated as a Welsh variant of RODERICK.

**Rhys** Welsh name meaning 'ardour' or 'rashness'. Also found as **Reece** and in the anglicized form **Rees**, the name was borne by an eleventh-century king of Wales, Rhys ap Tewdwr (d. 1093), and by his grandson Rhys ap Gruffud (1132–97).

**Rian** *See* RYAN.

**Rich** *See* RICHARD; RICHMOND.

**Richard** English name based on the Old German Ricohard, itself from the German *ric* ('power') and *hard* ('strong') and thus meaning 'powerful ruler'. It appears in the 'Tom, Dick and Harry' list of common English names, DICK (or **Dickie**) being an informal version. Other informal versions include **Rich**, **Richie** (or **Ritchie**), **Rick** (or **Rik**) and **Ricky** (or **Rikki**).

**Richey** *See* RICHMOND.

**Richie** *See* RICHARD; RICHMOND.

**Richmond** English name that originated as a surname based on the Old French for 'strong hill'. Informal versions include **Rich**, **Richey** and **Richie**.

**Rick/Ricky** *See* ERIC; RICHARD.

**Rider** English name based on the ordinary vocabulary word. Its most famous bearer to date has been English novelist Sir Henry Rider Haggard (1856–1925). Also found as **Ryder**.

**Ridley** English name taken from a place name based on the Old English *hreod* ('reeds') and *leah* ('wood' or 'clearing'). The name became popular in tribute to the Protestant Bishop Nicholas Ridley (c. 1500–55), martyred during the reign of Mary Tudor.

**Rigby** English name that originated as an Old English surname meaning 'farm on a ridge'.

**Rik/Rikki** *See* RICHARD.

**Riley** English name taken from a place name based on the Old English *ryge* ('rye') and *leah* ('clearing' or 'meadow'). In Ireland it may also represent a development of the surname Reilly or be descended from the Irish first name Raghallach (of obscure meaning).

**Rio** Spanish name meaning 'river'. Well-known bearers of the name have included English footballer Rio Ferdinand (b. 1978).

**Riordan** English version of the Irish Gaelic name **Rordan**, derived from *riogh* ('king') and *bard* ('poet'). Also found as **Rearden**.

**Ritchie** *See* RICHARD.

**River** English name based on the ordinary vocabulary word. Famous bearers of the name have included US film actor River Phoenix (1970–93).

**Roald** Norwegian name based on the Old German *hrod* ('fame') and *valdr* ('ruler') and thus meaning 'famous ruler'. Famous bearers of the name

have included the Norwegian explorer Roald Amundsen (1872–1928) and the Norwegian-born British author Roald Dahl (1916–90).

**Roarke** Irish name based on the Gaelic meaning 'famous ruler'.

**Rob/Robb/Robbie/ Robby** *See* ROBERT.

**Robert** English, Scottish and French name derived via Norman French from the Old German Hrodebert, from *hrod* ('fame') and *berht* ('bright' or 'famous') and thus meaning 'bright famous one' or 'famously famous'. Informal versions include **Rob** (or **Robb**), **Robbie** (or **Robby**), BOB (or BOBBY) and BERT (or BERTIE). **Rab** and **Rabbie** are Scottish variants. *See also* ROBIN; RUPERT.

**Robin** English name that developed out of ROBERT but has long had its own independent existence. The name came to England from France in medieval times and subsequently emerged as a separate boys' name in its own right. It has been bestowed upon both sexes since the 1950s.

**Robinson** English name that originated as an Old English surname meaning 'son of Robert'.

**Rocco** Italian name based on the Old German *hrok* ('repose'). Variant forms of the name include **Rocky**. It is particularly associated with boxers, notably US boxer Rocky Marciano (Rocco Marciano; 1923–69).

**Rochester** English name that originated as a place name meaning 'Roman fort at the bridges'.

**Rocky** *See* ROCCO.

**Rod/Roddie/Roddy** *See* RODERICK; RODNEY.

**Roderic** *See* RODERICK.

**Roderick** English name based on the Old German Hrodic, from the words *hrod* ('fame') and *ric* ('power') and thus meaning 'famously powerful'. It was brought to England by the Normans. Also found as **Rodrick** and **Roderic**

and commonly shortened to **Rod**, **Roddie** or **Roddy**. **Rodrigo** is a Spanish version. *See also* RHODRI; RORY.

**Rodge/Rodger** *See* ROGER.

**Rodney** English name taken from a place name (from Somerset) meaning 'reed island'. Its popularity in England dates from the nineteenth century when it was associated with the naval exploits of Admiral Lord (George) Rodney (1719–92). Commonly shortened to **Rod**, **Roddie** or **Roddy**.

**Rodrick** *See* RODERICK.

**Rodrigo** *See* RODERICK.

**Roger** English and French name derived via Norman French from the Old German *hrod* ('fame') and *gar* ('spear') and thus meaning 'famous warrior'. The modern form of the name was introduced to England by the Normans. It is occasionally found as **Rodger**, which may be shortened to **Rodge**.

**Rohan** French or Irish name

alternately linked with a French place name or else with the Irish Gaelic for 'red'. Also found as ROWAN.

**Roland** English name based via Norman French on the Old German *hrod* ('fame') and *land* ('land' or 'territory') and thus meaning 'famous landowner'. In medieval legend, Roland was the most gallant of Emperor Charlemagne's knights. Also found as **Rowland**. Informal versions include **Roly**, **Rowley** and **Rollo**.

**Rolf** English, German and Scandinavian variant of RUDOLPH, derived from *hrod* ('fame') and *wulf* ('wolf'). In the Latinized form **Rollo** the name dates at least as far back as the Vikings. Rarely found in the variant form **Rolph**.

**Rollo** *See* ROLAND; ROLF.

**Rolph** *See* ROLF.

**Roly** *See* ROLAND.

**Roman** Russian, Polish and Czech first name based on the Latin Romanus ('man from Rome'). Notable bearers of the name have included Polish-born US film director Roman Polanski (b. 1933).

**Romeo** Italian name meaning 'pilgrim to Rome'. It became widely known through William Shakespeare's tragedy *Romeo and Juliet* (1595). It enjoyed new prominence in 2002 when English footballer David Beckham and his pop-star wife Victoria Beckham chose it for their second son.

**Romney** English name that originated as a place name meaning 'at the broad river'.

**Ron** *See* RONALD.

**Ronald** English and Scottish equivalent of REGINALD that developed from the Old Norse Rognvaldr. Also found in Scotland as **Ranald** or **Raghnall**, the name is no longer thought of as uniquely Scottish. Often shortened to **Ron** or **Ronnie** (or **Ronni**).

**Ronan** Irish name based on the Irish Gaelic *ron* ('little seal'). The most famous of several Irish saints to bear the name was a fifth-century Irish missionary working in

Cornwall and Brittany. Notable bearers of the name have included Irish pop singer Ronan Keating (b. 1977).

**Ronni/Ronnie** *See* RONALD.

**Rordan** *See* RIORDAN.

**Rorie** *See* RORY.

**Rory** Irish and Scottish name based on the Gaelic name Ruairi (or Ruaidhri), itself from *ruadh* ('red' or 'red-haired') and *ri* ('king') and thus meaning 'great king'. It may also be employed as an equivalent of ROGER or as a shortened form of RODERICK. Also found as **Rorie** or in the Gaelic forms **Ruari** or **Ruaridh**.

**Roscoe** English name that originated as a place name based on the Old Norse *ra* ('roe deer') and *skogr* ('wood' or 'copse').

**Ross** English and Scottish name taken from a Scottish place name, itself from the Gaelic *ros* ('peninsula' or 'promontory'). Other derivations suggest that it came

from the Old German *hrod* ('fame'), the French *roux* ('red') or the Anglo-Saxon *hros* ('horse').

**Rowan** English version of the Irish Gaelic **Ruadhan**, meaning 'little red-haired one'. It is also sometimes linked to the alternate name of the mountain ash, which bears red berries. It used to be an exclusively boys' name but is now used for both sexes. *See also* ROHAN.

**Rowland/Rowley** *See* ROLAND.

**Roy** English name that may have come from the French *roi* ('king') or else developed out of the Gaelic RORY, coming ultimately from the Gaelic *ruadh* ('red') and thus being reserved primarily for children with red hair or a ruddy complexion. Sir Walter Scott's novel *Rob Roy* (1817) promoted the name in the nineteenth century. *See also* LEROY.

**Royal** English name based either on the adjective 'royal' or on a surname meaning 'rye hill'. Its use as a first name is largely restricted to the USA.

**Royce** English name that has been in occasional use since the late nineteenth century.

**Royle** English name taken from a place name (from Lancashire), itself based on the Old English *ryge* ('rye') and *hyll* ('hill'). It probably developed under the influence of such similar-sounding names as **Doyle**.

**Royston** English name taken from a place name (from Hertfordshire) meaning 'settlement of Royce'. It appears to have made its debut as a first name in the eighteenth century and today is popular chiefly in England and Australia.

**Ruadhan** *See* ROWAN.

**Ruari/Ruaridh** *See* RORY.

**Rube/Ruben/Ruby** *See* REUBEN.

**Rudi/Rudolf** *See* RUDOLPH.

**Rudolph** English name

based on the Old German Hrodulf, from *hrod* ('fame') and *wulf* ('wolf') and thus meaning 'famous warrior'. The name has been in use among English speakers since the nineteenth century, occasionally in the modern Germanic form **Rudolf**. Commonly shortened to **Rudi** or **Rudy**.

**Rudy** *See* RUDOLPH.

**Rudyard** English name inspired by Rudyard Lake in Staffordshire. It was made lastingly famous through the British writer Rudyard Kipling (1865–1936).

**Rufus** English name based on the Latin for 'red-haired'. A biblical name, it was later borne by William Rufus (1056–1100), who ruled England as William II. It is unclear whether William acquired the name through the colour of his hair or through the colour of his complexion.

**Rupert** English version of the Dutch Rupprecht, which like ROBERT comes ultimately from the Old German for 'bright fame'. The name came to England with Prince Rupert of the Rhine (1619–92), the soldier–nephew of Charles I.

**Russ/Russel** *See* RUSSELL.

**Russell** English name based on the French nickname *rousel* ('little red one'). It was originally reserved for children with red hair or a ruddy complexion. Also found as **Russel**, it has strong aristocratic connections and is the family name of the dukes of Bedford. Sometimes shortened to **Russ** or **Rusty**.

**Rusty** *See* RUSSELL.

**Rutland** English name taken from the name of the English county. It has been in occasional use as a first name since the nineteenth century.

**Ryan** Irish name of uncertain origin. The original Gaelic surname meant 'descendant of Rian', Rian probably coming from *ri*, meaning 'king'. An alternative derivation links the name with that of an ancient sea or river god (also the inspiration behind the name of the River Rhine). Occasionally found as **Rian**.

**Ryder** *See* RIDER.

# BOYS' NAMES

**Sacha** *See* SASHA.

**Sacheverell** English name that is thought to have been taken from a place name in Normandy, Saute-Chevreuil (meaning 'roebuck leap'). Famous bearers of the name have included the British writer Sacheverell Sitwell (1897–1985). Sometimes shortened to **Sachie**.

**Sachie** *See* SACHEVERELL.

**Said** ('sigheed') Arabic name meaning 'happy' or 'lucky'.

**Sal** *See* SALVADOR.

**Salah** Arabic name meaning 'goodness' or 'righteousness'. Also found as **Saleh**, it is one of the most popular of all Arab names.

**Salamon** *See* SOLOMON.

**Saleem** *See* SALIM.

**Saleh** *See* SALAH.

**Salim** ('saleem') Arabic name meaning 'safe' or 'secure'. Also found as **Saleem** or **Selim**.

**Salman** *See* SOLOMON.

**Salvador** Spanish name meaning 'saviour'. Its use is largely confined to Roman Catholic countries. Shortened to **Sal**.

**Sam/Sammy** *See* SAMSON; SAMUEL.

**Sampson** *See* SAMSON.

**Samson** English version of the Hebrew Shimshon, itself based on *shemesh* ('sun'), thus meaning 'sun child'. It features in the Bible as the name of the immensely powerful leader of the Israelites who was deceived by Delilah. Sometimes found as **Sampson**. **Sam** and **Sammy** are familiar forms of the name.

**Samuel** English version of
the Hebrew Shemuel or
Shmuel, meaning 'name of
God' or 'He has hearkened'.
Another derivation links it to
the Hebrew *shaul meel* ('asked
of God'). It is also sometimes
considered to be an anglicized
version of the Gaelic
Somhairle, from the Old Norse
for 'summer wanderer' or
'Viking'. Shortened to **Sam** or
**Sammy**.

**Sancho** Spanish name of
uncertain meaning, possibly
linked to the Latin *sanctus*
('holy').

**Sandford** *See* SANFORD.

**Sandor** *See* ALEXANDER.

**Sandy** *See* ALEXANDER;
SAWNEY.

**Sanford** English name that
originated as a place name,
originally **Sandford**, from Old
English *sand* ('sand') and *ford*
('ford'). It is more common in
the USA than elsewhere,
sometimes appearing in tribute
to an early governor of Rhode
Island called Peleg Sanford.

**Sanjay** Indian name based on

the Sanskrit *samjaya*
('triumphant'). It is borne by
several characters in Indian
mythology and figures in the
*Mahabharata*. Bearers of the
name in more recent times
have included Indira Gandhi's
son Sanjay Gandhi (1948–80).

**Santiago** Spanish name
based on the Spanish rendering
of 'Saint James' (the patron
saint of Spain). *See also* DIEGO.

**Sasha** Informal version of
ALEXANDER. Originally a
Russian variant, it was
introduced to the English-
speaking world in the early
twentieth century. **Sacha** – as
borne by the French singer
Sacha Distel (1933–2004) – is a
common French version.

**Saul** Hebrew name meaning
'asked for' or 'desired'. It
features in the Bible as the
name of one of the first kings
of Israel and as the Jewish name
of St Paul. It is rare outside the
Jewish community.

**Sawney** Scottish variant of
Sandy (*see* ALEXANDER). The
name has lost ground since the
nineteenth century, perhaps
because it acquired a new

vocabulary sense meaning 'fool'.

**Saxon** English name taken from the name of the fifth-century Germanic invaders of Britain, the Saxons. The Old German *sachs* originally meant 'dagger' or 'short sword'. It was taken up as a first name during the nineteenth century.

**Scot** *See* SCOTT.

**Scott** Scottish and English name meaning 'Scotsman' or 'Scottish'. Also found as **Scot**, the name increased in popularity around the middle of the twentieth century, perhaps in tribute to US novelist F. Scott Fitzgerald (1896–1940). Familiar variants include **Scottie** and **Scotty**.

**Scottie/Scotty** *See* SCOTT.

**Seaghdh** ('shor') Scottish name based on the Gaelic for 'fine' or 'hawk-like'. **Seaghdha** is an Irish Gaelic variant. Anglicized versions of the name include SETH and SHAW.

**Seaghdha** *See* SEAGHDH.

**Seamas** *See* SEAMUS.

**Seamor/Seamore/ Seamour** *See* SEYMOUR.

**Seamus** ('shaymus') English version of the Irish **Seamas**, itself an equivalent of the English JAMES. Commonly encountered in Ireland, it remains rare elsewhere. Also found as **Seumas** or **Shamus** and shortened to **Shay**. Famous bearers of the name include Irish poet Seamus Heaney (b. 1939). *See also* HAMISH.

**Sean** ('shorn') Irish name that is an equivalent of the English JOHN. Also encountered as **Shane** (from the Northern Irish pronunciation of the name), **Shaun** and **Shawn**.

**Seanan** *See* SENAN.

**Seaton** English name that originated as a place name meaning 'farmstead at the sea'. Also found as **Seton**.

**Seb** *See* SEBASTIAN.

**Sebastian** English form of the Roman Sebastianus, meaning 'of Sebasta' (a town in Asia Minor). Another derivation links it to the Greek *sebastos* ('respected' or 'august').

It was borne by the third-century martyr St Sebastian, who was shot with arrows and then beaten to death. Shortened to **Seb**, **Sebbie**, **Bastian**, **Baz** or **Bazza**.

**Sebbie** *See* SEBASTIAN.

**Sefton** English name that originated as a place name meaning 'settlement in the rushes'. Its history as a first name began in the nineteenth century.

**Seiriol** ('sighreeol') Welsh name based on the Welsh *serennu* ('sparkle') and thus meaning 'bright one'.

**Selby** English name that originated as a place name meaning 'willow farm'. It was taken up as a first name in the nineteenth century.

**Selden** English name that originated as a surname meaning 'place by the willow trees'.

**Selim** *See* SALIM.

**Selwin** *See* SELWYN.

**Selwyn** English name that

may have evolved out of the Old English *sele* ('prosperity') or *sele* ('hall') and *wine* ('friend') or else, via Old French, from the Roman Silvanus, from *silva* ('wood'). A third derivation links the name to Welsh words meaning 'ardour' and 'fair'. Also found as **Selwin**.

**Senan** English version of the Irish **Seanan**, from the Gaelic *sean* ('old' or 'wise'). The name was borne by several early Irish saints.

**Sencha** ('senha') Irish name based on the Gaelic for 'historian'.

**Septimus** Roman name meaning 'seventh'. It was taken up by English speakers in the nineteenth century, usually reserved for seventh-born male children.

**Serge** *See* SERGEI.

**Sergei** ('sairgay') Russian name based on the Roman Sergius, itself of uncertain origin. Variants include the Italian **Sergio** and the French **Serge**.

**Sergio** *See* SERGEI.

**Seth** English name based on
the Hebrew *sheth* ('appointed'
or 'set'). It appears in the Bible
as the name of the third son of
Adam and Eve. It is also used
by Indian peoples, who trace it
back to the Sanskrit *setu*
('bridge') or *sveta* ('white').

**Seton** *See* SEATON.

**Seumas** *See* SEAMUS.

**Seward** English name based
on the Old English for 'sea' or
'victory' and 'guard'. It was
first used as a first name in the
nineteenth century.

**Sexton** English name based
on the Old French for
'sacristan'. It is most familiar
from Harry Blyth's fictional
radio detective Sexton Blake.

**Seymour** English name that
originated as a Norman French
place name, Saint-Maur in
Normandy, which itself took
its name from the little-known
sixth-century North African St
Maurus (Maurus meaning
'Moor'). Occasionally found as
**Seamor**, **Seamore** or
**Seamour**.

**Shamus** *See* SEAMUS.

**Shane** *See* SEAN.

**Shanley** Irish name meaning
'son of the hero' in Irish
Gaelic.

**Shaun** *See* SEAN.

**Shaw** English name based on
the Old English *sceaga* ('wood'
or 'copse') and used as a first
name since the nineteenth
century. It can also be found in
Scotland as an anglicized
equivalent of SEAGHDH.

**Shawn** *See* SEAN.

**Shay** *See* SEAMUS; SHEA.

**Shea** Irish name based on a
surname meaning 'stately' or
'courageous'. Also found as
Shay.

**Sheldon** English name that
originated in a place name
(from Derbyshire, Devon and
the West Midlands) meaning
'steep-sided valley' or 'flat-
topped hill'. It appears to have
made its debut as a first name
in the early twentieth century,
initially in the USA.

**Shem** Hebrew name
meaning 'renown'. It appears

in the Bible as the name of one of Noah's sons. Rare outside Jewish communities.

**Sherborne** English name that originated in a place name meaning 'clear stream'. Also encountered as **Sherbourne**.

**Sherbourne** *See* SHERBORNE.

**Sheridan** Irish name of uncertain meaning, possibly from the Gaelic *sirim* ('to seek'). It made its debut as a first name in the middle of the nineteenth century, boosted by the popularity of Irish playwright Richard Brinsley Sheridan (1751–1816). Sometimes shortened to **Sherry**.

**Sherlock** English name based on the Middle English for 'shear lock' (possibly reserved for people with closely cropped hair). The name is strongly associated with Sherlock Holmes, the fictional detective created by Sir Arthur Conan Doyle in the late nineteenth century.

**Sherman** English name based on the Old English *sceara* ('shears') and *mann* ('man'). It began as a medieval trade name reserved for those whose job it was to trim the nap of woollen cloth after weaving. Its popularity in the USA was boosted by US general William Tecumseh Sherman (1820–91).

**Sherry** *See* SHERIDAN.

**Sherwin** English name meaning 'loyal friend' or 'fast-footed'.

**Sherwood** English name that originated in a surname meaning 'shore wood'.

**Shilo** *See* SHILOH.

**Shiloh** Hebrew name meaning 'His gift'. Also found as **Shilo**, **Shylo** or **Shyloh**.

**Sholto** English version of the Scottish Gaelic Sioltach (meaning 'sower' or 'fruitful'). It is largely confined to Scotland, where it first emerged in the nineteenth century.

**Shug/Shuggie** *See* HUGH.

**Shylo/Shyloh** *See* SHILOH.

**Si** *See* SIMON.

**Sid** *See* SIDNEY.

**Sidney** English name that may have originated as a Norman French place name, Saint-Denis, or, more likely, came from the Old English *sidan* ('wide') and *eg* ('river island' or 'wide island'). Also found from the nineteenth century as **Sydney**, a form of the name that is now usually reserved for females. Shortened to **Syd** or **Sid**.

**Siegfried** German name based on the Old Germanic *sige* ('victory') and *frid* ('peace'). It has made rare appearances among English speakers, being borne by, among others, the British war poet Siegfried Sassoon (1886–1967). Sometimes shortened to **Sigi**.

**Sigi** *See* SIEGFRIED; SIGMUND.

**Sigmund** German and English name based on the Old German *sige* ('victory') and *mund* ('defender') and thus meaning 'victorious defender'. Notable bearers of the name have included a legendary German hero and the Austrian

psychiatrist Sigmund Freud (1856–1939). Sometimes shortened to **Sigi**.

**Silas** English name based via Hebrew on the Latin Silvanus, from *silva* ('wood'). Silvanus was the Roman god of trees. The name was originally applied to people who lived in wooded areas or who worked with wood in some way.

**Silvain** French name based on the Roman Silvanus, itself based on the Latin for 'of a wood'.

**Silver** English name based on the Old English *siolfor* ('silver'). It was reserved originally for children with silvery hair.

**Silvester** *See* SYLVESTER.

**Sim/Simeon/Simmy** *See* SIMON.

**Simon** English version of the Hebrew **Simeon** or **Shimon**, meaning 'hearkening' or 'he who hears' (although another derivation traces it back to the Greek *simos*, meaning 'snub-nosed'). The name is borne by several biblical figures.

Shortened to **Si** or **Sim** (or **Simmy**).

**Sinclair** Scottish name that originated as a Norman French place name, Saint-Clair, which in turn may have been named after the French St Clair. It appears to have made its debut as a first name towards the end of the nineteenth century.

**Sion** Welsh equivalent of JOHN. **Sionyn** is a familiar form.

**Sionyn** See SION.

**Skeeter** English name that began as a nickname for any small or energetic person. It may have come from 'mosquito' or else from 'skeets' or 'scoots'. It is a twentieth-century introduction of US origin.

**Skelton** English name that originated as a surname based on the Old English for 'farmstead on a hill'.

**Skerry** Scandinavian name based on the Old Norse meaning 'sea rock'.

**Skip** English name adopted as a shortened form of **Skipper**. It may have come ultimately from a Dutch word meaning 'ship's captain'.

**Skipper** See SKIP.

**Sky** See SKYE.

**Skye** English name based either upon the ordinary vocabulary word or else intended as a reference to the Scottish island of Skye. Also found as **Sky**.

**Slade** English name that originated as a surname meaning 'valley'.

**Sly** See SYLVESTER.

**Smith** English name that originated as a surname meaning 'blacksmith'.

**Snowden** See SNOWDON.

**Snowdon** English name that originated in a surname meaning 'snowy hill'. Also found as **Snowden**.

**Sol/Solly** See SOLOMON.

**Solomon** Hebrew name based on the word *shalom*

('peace') and meaning 'man of peace'. It appears in the Bible as the name of the son of David and Beersheba, whose wise rule over Israel brought about a lengthy peace. Rare outside the Jewish community. Variants include **Salamon** and **Salman**. Shortened to **Sol** or **Solly**.

**Somerset** English name based on the name of the county, meaning 'summer farmstead'. The most notable bearer of the name to date has been English novelist William Somerset Maugham (1874–1965).

**Sonnie** *See* SONNY.

**Sonny** English variant of SAUL, SOLOMON and other names. Notable bearers of the name have included US boxer Sonny Liston (Charles Liston; 1932–70). Also found as **Sonnie**.

**Spencer** English name meaning 'dispenser' that was originally reserved for the stewards who dispensed supplies in English manor houses. As a surname, it is identified with the Churchill family and also with Diana, Princess of Wales, whose maiden name was Spencer.

**Spike** English name that began life as a nickname for anyone with tufty or spiky hair. Famous bearers of the name have included British comedian Spike Milligan (Terence Alan Milligan; 1918–2002) and US film director Spike Lee (Shelton Jackson; b. 1956).

**Squire** English name based on the Old French for 'shield-bearer'.

**Stacey** *See* STACY.

**Stacy** English name that evolved out of EUSTACE. Well-known bearers of the name have included US actor Stacy Keach (Walter Stacy Keach; b. 1941). Also found as **Stacey**.

**Stafford** English name that originated as a place name based on the Old English *staeth* ('landing place') and *ford* ('ford'). Notable bearers of the name have included British politician Sir Stafford Cripps (Richard Stafford Cripps; 1889–1952).

**Stamford** *See* STANFORD.

**Stan** *See* STANLEY.

**Standish** English name that originated in a surname meaning 'stony pasture'.

**Stanford** English name that originated as an Old English place name meaning 'stony ford'. Occasionally found as Stamford.

**Stanhope** English name that originated as a surname meaning 'stony hollow'.

**Stanley** English name based on the Old English *stan* ('stone') and *leah* ('wood' or 'clearing') and thus meaning 'stony field'. As a surname it was strongly associated with the earls of Derby. Commonly shortened to Stan.

**Steafan/Steenie/ Steffan/Stephan** *See* STEPHEN.

**Stephen** English version of the Greek name Stephanos, meaning 'garland', 'wreath' or 'crown'. The name features in the Bible as that of the first Christian martyr, who was stoned to death on false charges. Shortened to **Steve** or **Stevie**. Variants include Steven, Stephan, the Welsh Steffan, the Irish Steafan and the Scottish Steenie.

**Sterling** *See* STIRLING.

**Steve/Steven/Stevie** *See* STEPHEN.

**Stew** *See* STEWART; STUART.

**Stewart** English name that developed either from a Scottish surname, based on the Old English *stigweard* ('steward'), or as a variant of STUART. Well-known bearers of the name have included British film actor Stewart Granger (James Lablanche Stewart; 1913–93). **Stew, Stu** and **Stewie** are common diminutive forms.

**Stewie** *See* STEWART; STUART.

**Stig** Scandinavian name based on the Old Norse Stigr, itself meaning 'wanderer'. The name became familiar to English speakers through Clive King's children's novel *Stig of the Dump* (1963).

**Stirling** English and Scottish name variously linked to the place name Stirling (of uncertain meaning) or to the ordinary vocabulary word 'sterling', itself from the Middle English *sterrling* ('little star'). As a first name Stirling (or **Sterling**) is a relatively recent introduction.

**St John** ('sinjun') English name that developed out of the French place name Saint-Jean, itself a reference to John the Baptist. Mostly confined to the Roman Catholic community.

**Stoddard** English name that originated as a surname meaning 'horse keeper'.

**Storm** English name based on the ordinary vocabulary word, suggesting a passionate, lively nature. The name does not seem to have been used before the late nineteenth century.

**Strachan** ('strakan') Scottish name that originated in a place name meaning 'little valley'. Also found as **Strahan**.

**Strahan** *See* STRACHAN.

**Stratford** English name that originated in a place name meaning 'ford on a Roman road'.

**Struan** Scottish name based on the Scottish Gaelic *sruthan*, meaning 'streams'.

**Stu** *See* STEWART; STUART.

**Stuart** Scottish name that developed as a French version of STEWART. It came to Scotland in the sixteenth century with Mary Stuart, Queen of Scots, who had spent her childhood in France. **Stew**, **Stu** and **Stewie** are familiar forms of the name.

**Sullivan** Irish name that originated as a surname with the Irish Gaelic meaning 'black-eyed'.

**Sven** Swedish name based on the Old Norse *sveinn* ('boy' or 'lad'). Well-known bearers of the name have included Swedish-born England football manager Sven-Göran Eriksson (b. 1948).

**Swithin** English name based on the Old English *swith* ('strong' or 'mighty'). The most famous bearer of the name was St Swithin (or Swithun), the ninth-century bishop of Winchester whose feast day falls on 15 July: according to tradition, if it rains on St Swithin's Day then it will continue to rain for another forty days.

**Sy** *See* CYRUS.

**Syd/Sydney** *See* SIDNEY.

**Syl** *See* SYLVESTER.

**Sylvester** English and German name based on the Latin for 'wood-dweller' or 'of the woods'. Notable bearers of the name have included US film actor Sylvester Stallone (b. 1946). Also found as **Silvester**. Shortened to **Syl** or **Sly**.

# BOYS' NAMES

**Tad** *See* THADDEUS.

**Tadhg** ('teeg') Irish name meaning 'poet' or 'philosopher'. A traditional nickname for a Roman Catholic, it is also found as **Taig**, **Teague** or **Teige**.

**Taff** *See* TAFFY.

**Taffy** Welsh version of DAVID that has made occasional appearances as a name in its own right. Widely known as a nickname for anyone with Welsh ancestry, the name evolved from the Welsh **Dafydd** in the nineteenth century. Also found as **Taff**.

**Taig** *See* TADHG.

**Tait** *See* TATE.

**Talbot** English name possibly based on the Old French *taillebotte* ('cleave faggot' or 'cut bundle') or else from obscure Germanic roots. It has strong aristocratic connections, being the family name of the earls of Shrewsbury.

**Talfryn** Welsh name that was originally a place name meaning 'high hill'. Its use as a first name is a relatively recent phenomenon.

**Tam/Tammy** *See* THOMAS.

**Tanner** English name that originated as a surname meaning 'leather worker'.

**Tari** *See* TARIQ.

**Tariq** Arabic name meaning 'night star' or 'one who knocks at the door at night'. The name is borne by the morning star and also by a celebrated eighth-century Berber leader, Tariq ibn Ziyad (d. c. 720). Sometimes found as **Tari**.

**Tarquin** Roman family name of obscure Etruscan

origin. Two early Roman kings bore the name. It also appears as the name of a knight in Arthurian legend.

**Tasgall** Scottish Gaelic name derived from Old Norse words meaning 'god' and 'sacrificial cauldron'. The name is sometimes rendered as **Taskill** by English speakers.

**Taskill** *See* TASGALL.

**Tate** English name based ultimately on the Old Norse for 'cheerful'. Also found as **Tait** or **Teyte**.

**Tayler** *See* TAYLOR.

**Taylor** English name based on a surname originally reserved for those engaged in the business of tailoring. Notable bearers of the name have included British poet Samuel Taylor Coleridge (1772–1834). Also found as **Tayler**.

**Teague** *See* TADHG.

**Tebald** *See* THEOBALD.

**Ted/Teddy** *See* EDMUND; EDWARD; THEODORE.

**Teige** *See* TADHG.

**Teive** *See* TEYVE.

**Tel** *See* TERENCE; TERRY.

**Tennyson** *See* DENNISON.

**Terance** *See* TERENCE.

**Terence** English name based on the Roman Terentius, itself of obscure origin. It is also used as an anglicization of the Irish **Turlough** (meaning 'instigator' or 'one who initiates an idea'). Also found as **Terance**, **Terrance**, **Terrence** or **Terrell**. Commonly shortened to **Tel** or TERRY.

**Terrance/Terrell/ Terrence** *See* TERENCE.

**Terry** English name of Germanic origin, from words meaning 'tribe' and 'power'. It is also a shortened form of several other names, including TERENCE and THEODORE. Sometimes itself shortened to **Tel**.

**Tertius** ('tershus') Roman name based on the Latin for 'three' and thus reserved for third-born sons.

**Tex** American name inspired by the state name Texas and originally reserved for inhabitants of that state. It remains confined largely to the USA.

**Teyte** *See* TATE.

**Teyve** ('toyvay') Jewish name representing a Yiddish version of the Hebrew Tuvia, which is itself a version of **Tobias** (*see* TOBY). The most famous bearer of the name is the central character in the musical *Fiddler on the Roof* (1967). Also found as **Teive**.

**Thad** *See* THADDEUS.

**Thaddeus** Hebrew first name possibly meaning 'valiant' or 'wise' or else based on THEODORE. It appears in the New Testament as the name of one of the apostles. **Tad** and **Thad** are shortened forms.

**Thelonious** *See* THELONIUS.

**Thelonius** English name of Roman origins. It is also found as **Thelonious**, in which form it was borne by the celebrated US jazz musician Thelonious Monk (1920–82).

**Theo** *See* THEOBALD; THEODORE.

**Theobald** German name descended from the Old German Theudobald, which was based on words meaning 'people' or 'race' and 'bold' or 'brave'. Ancient variants of the name included **Tebald** and **Tybalt**. Sometimes shortened to **Theo**, **Tibby** or **Tibs**.

**Theodore** English name based on the Greek for 'God's gift'. The name was popular with early Christians and was borne by no fewer than twenty-eight saints. Variants include the Russian **Fyodor**. Commonly shortened to **Theo** or, in the USA, to **Ted** or **Teddy**. *See also* TUDOR.

**Theophilus** Greek name based on the Greek words *theos* ('god') and *philos* ('loving') and meaning 'loved by God' or 'one who loves God'. It appears in the New Testament and was adopted by the Puritans in the sixteenth century. Often shortened to **Theo**.

**Thom** *See* THOMAS.

**Thomas** English name based on the Aramaic for 'twin'. The name appears in the Bible, notably as the name of one of the apostles. Commonly shortened to **Tom** (occasionally **Thom**) or **Tommy**, it appears in the proverbial 'Tom, Dick and Harry' list of common boys' names. **Tam**, **Tammy** and **Tomas** are Scottish variants.

**Thorley** English name that was originally a place name meaning 'thorn wood'. It has been in occasional use as a first name since the Victorian era.

**Thornton** English name derived from a place name meaning 'settlement among the thorns'. A notable bearer of the name was US writer Thornton Wilder (1897–1975).

**Thurstan** English name that was originally an Old Norse place name meaning 'Thor's stone'. Also found as **Thurston**, the name came to England with the Vikings. *See also* DUSTIN.

**Thurston** *See* THURSTAN.

**Tiarnan** Irish name based on the Gaelic for 'lord'. Also found as **Tiernan** or **Tierney**.

**Tibby** *See* THEOBALD.

**Tibor** Slavonic name that originated as a place name meaning 'holy place'.

**Tibs** *See* THEOBALD.

**Tiernan/Tierney** *See* TIARNAN.

**Till** *See* DIETRICH.

**Tim/Timmy** *See* TIMOTHY.

**Timothy** Hebrew name based on the Greek Timotheos (meaning 'honouring God' or 'honoured by God'). The name was apparently unknown in England prior to the Reformation. Commonly shortened to **Tim** or **Timmy**.

**Tirell** *See* TYRELL.

**Titus** Roman name of uncertain origin (possibly meaning 'honoured', from Latin *titulus*, 'title of honour'). The name was adopted by English speakers after the

Reformation and was borne by the English conspirator Titus Oates (1649–1705).

**Tobias/Tobin** *See* TOBY.

**Toby** English version of the Hebrew **Tobias** (meaning 'the Lord is good'). The name features in William Langland's poem *Piers Plowman* (late fourteenth century). Variants include **Tobin**.

**Tod** *See* TODD.

**Todd** English name meaning 'fox'. The name enjoyed a considerable vogue during the 1970s, especially in Canada and the USA where it ranked among the fifty most popular boys' names. Also found as **Tod**.

**Tolly** *See* BARTHOLOMEW.

**Tom/Tomas/Tommy** *See* THOMAS.

**Tony** *See* ANTHONY.

**Torcail/Torcall/ Torcul/Torkel** *See* TORQUIL.

**Torquil** Scottish version of the Old Norse name Thorketill (meaning 'Thor's cauldron'). The name came to Britain with the Danes and entered Gaelic culture as **Torcall**, **Torcul** or **Torcail**. **Torkel** is another variant.

**Torr** English name based on the Old English for 'from the tower'.

**Trae** *See* TREY.

**Trafford** English name of Germanic origin meaning 'dweller beyond the ford'.

**Trahearn** Welsh first name meaning 'iron'. Also found as **Traherne**.

**Traherne** *See* TRAHEARN.

**Travers** *See* TRAVIS.

**Travis** English name meaning 'toll-keeper' or 'crossing', originally from the French *traverser* ('to cross'). Also found as **Travers**, the name figured among lists of the fifty most popular boys' names in the 1970s.

**Trefor** *See* TREVOR.

**Trelawney** *See* TRELAWNY.

**Trelawny** Cornish name that was originally a place name meaning 'from the church town'. Also found as Trelawney.

**Tremaine** Cornish name meaning 'homestead on the rock'. Also found as Tremayne.

**Tremayne** *See* TREMAINE.

**Trent** English name based on that of the River Trent in the Midlands of England. It is more commonly encountered in the USA than it is on the British side of the Atlantic.

**Trev** *See* TREVOR.

**Trevelyan** ('treveleean') Cornish name that was originally a place name meaning 'place of Elian'.

**Trevor** English and Welsh name that was originally a place name meaning 'great homestead'. Rendered in Welsh as Trefor, it has been in use as a first name since the 1860s. Commonly shortened to Trev.

**Trey** ('tray') English name that is thought to have been based on the word 'three' and is thus often reserved for third-born children. Also found as Trae.

**Tris** *See* TRISTAN.

**Tristan** English version of the Celtic Drystan, which may have been based on the Celtic *drest* or *drust* ('din' or 'tumult') or on the Latin *tristis* ('sad'). As Tristram, it made its first appearance in England in the twelfth century. Also found as Trystan. Commonly shortened to Tris.

**Tristram** *See* TRISTAN.

**Troy** English and Irish name taken from that of the French city of Troyes or else from the Irish for 'foot soldier' or a phrase meaning 'from the place of the people with curly hair'.

**Trueman** *See* TRUMAN.

**Truman** English name based on the Old English for 'trusty man'. It is uncommon outside the USA, where notable bearers of the name have included the writer Truman

Capote (1924–84). Also found as **Trueman**.

**Trystan** *See* TRISTAN.

**Tudor** Welsh first name that evolved from the Celtic Teutorix (meaning 'people's ruler'). Also found in Wales as **Tudur**, the name has strong royal connections, being borne by the royal house of Tudor.

**Tudur** *See* TUDOR.

**Turlough** *See* TERENCE.

**Turner** English name that originated as a surname meaning 'lathe worker'.

**Ty** *See* TYLER; TYRONE; TYSON.

**Tybalt** *See* THEOBALD.

**Tye** *See* TYRONE.

**Tylar** *See* TYLER.

**Tyler** English name that was originally an occupational surname given to workers employed to tile roofs. Also found as **Tylar**. Commonly shortened to **Ty**.

**Tyrel** *See* TYRELL.

**Tyrell** English name that may have begun as a reference to the Scandinavian god of war, Tyr, or else has French origins, meaning 'stubborn'. Variants include **Tirell**, **Tyrel** and **Tyrrell**.

**Tyrrell** *See* TYRELL.

**Tyrone** Irish name based on the county name, meaning 'Eoghan's (or Owen's) land'. Celebrated bearers of the name have included US film star Tyrone Power (1913–58). Sometimes shortened to **Ty** or **Tye**.

**Tyson** English name that originated as a surname meaning 'son of the German'. Shortened to **Ty**.

# BOYS' NAMES

**Udo** ('oodoh') German name meaning 'prosperous'.

**Ughes** *See* UISDEAN.

**Ugo** ('oogoh') Italian equivalent of HUGH.

**Uilleam** *See* WILLIAM.

**Uisdean** ('ooshtyeean') Scottish Gaelic name meaning 'always stone' in Old Norse, otherwise an equivalent of HUGH. Another Gaelic version is **Ughes**.

**Ulick** *See* ULYSSES; WILLIAM.

**Ulric** *See* ULRICH.

**Ulrich** ('ulrik') German name meaning 'powerful'. Also found as **Ulric** or **Ulrik**. A shortened form of the name is **Utz**.

**Ulrik** *See* ULRICH.

**Ulysses** Roman equivalent of the Greek Odysseus, famous as the hero of Homer's *Odyssey*. It may have meant 'hater' in the original Greek. **Ulick** is a shortened form.

**Umar** ('oomah') Arabic name meaning 'populous' or 'flourishing'. Also found as **Omar**, it was the name of one of Muhammad's most loyal followers.

**Unique** ('yooneek') English name meaning 'one and only'. A relatively recent introduction, confined chiefly to the US.

**Unwin** English name derived from Old English, meaning 'not a friend'. More commonly encountered as a surname.

**Upton** English name meaning 'upper settlement' or 'town on the heights' in Old English. Its history as a first name dates from the nineteenth century.

**Urban** Roman name meaning 'from the city' or 'citizen'. It has been borne by several saints and eight popes. *See also* URIEN.

**Uri** ('yooree') Hebrew name meaning 'light'. Well known as the name of Israeli illusionist Uri Geller (b. 1943).

**Uriah** ('yooriah') Hebrew name meaning 'God is light'. Famous from Uriah Heep, an unlikeable character in the Charles Dickens novel *David Copperfield* (1850).

**Urien** ('yoorien') Welsh equivalent of the Roman URBAN, meaning 'citizen'. It appears in the *Mabinogion*.

**Utah** ('yootah') US name derived from that of the US state.

**Utz** *See* ULRICH.

# BOYS' NAMES

**Vadim** Russian name of uncertain origin, though possibly a variant of VLADIMIR.

**Vail** English name, originally a surname, from the Old English for 'valley'.

**Val** *See* PERCIVAL; VALENTINE.

**Valentine** English and French name based on the Latin *valens* ('strong' or 'healthy'). The link with St Valentine's Day (14 February) has long given the name romantic associations. Sometimes shortened to **Val**.

**Van** *See* IVAN; VANCE.

**Vance** English name,

originally a surname, from the Old English for 'fen-dweller'. It is sometimes shortened to **Van**.

**Vanya** Russian name meaning 'right'.

**Varden** English name meaning 'from a green hill'. Variants include **Vardon** and **Verdon**.

**Vardon** *See* VARDEN.

**Vaughan** ('vorn') English and Welsh name, from the Welsh *fychan* ('little one'). Also found as **Vaughn**. Famous bearers of the name have included the British composer Ralph Vaughan Williams (1872–1958).

**Vaughn** *See* VAUGHAN.

**Veejay** *See* VIJAY.

**Venn** English name, from the Old English meaning 'handsome'.

**Verdon** *See* VARDEN.

**Vere** ('veer') French name derived from the Old French *ver* ('alder'). It was introduced to Britain from France at the time of the Norman Conquest.

**Vergil** *See* VIRGIL.

**Vern/Verne** *See* VERNON.

**Vernon** English name derived from a French place name meaning 'place of alders' or 'alder grove'. It has strong aristocratic associations. **Vern** and **Verne** are shortened forms.

**Vic** *See* VICTOR.

**Victor** English version of the Roman Victorius, itself from the Latin for 'conqueror'. Commemorating Christ's victory over sin and death, the name was fairly common among early Christians. Commonly shortened to **Vic**.

**Vidal** Spanish name based ultimately on the Hebrew *hayyim* ('life').

**Viggo** Scandinavian name meaning 'exuberant'. It became well known among English speakers through film actor Viggo Mortensen (b. 1958).

**Vijay** ('veejay') Indian name, from the Sanskrit *vijaya* ('victory' or 'booty'). The name of one of Krishna's grandchildren, it has been popular as a first name for many centuries. Variants include **Veejay** and the Bengali **Bijay**.

**Vikram** Indian name, from the Sanskrit *vikrama* ('stride' or 'pace', but later interpreted as meaning 'heroism' or 'strength'). It was borne by Vishnu in the *Mahabharata*.

**Vin/Vince** *See* VINCENT.

**Vincent** English, French, Dutch and Scandinavian name, from the Latin *vincens* ('conquering'). Notable bearers of the name have included the Dutch painter Vincent van Gogh (1853–90). **Vin**, **Vince**, **Vinnie** and **Vinny** are shortened forms.

**Vinnie/Vinny** *See* VINCENT.

**Vinson** English name, originally a surname, that probably shares the same root as VINCENT and thus means 'conquering'.

**Virgil** Roman name of obscure meaning originally adopted by English speakers in tribute to a revered French bishop or Irish monk so-called. Also found as **Vergil**, it is associated today with the first-century Roman poet Publius Vergilius Maro (or Virgil).

**Vito** *See* VITUS.

**Vitus** Roman name meaning 'life'. Variants include the Italian **Vito**.

**Viv** *See* VIVIAN.

**Vivian** English name based on the Latin *vivus* ('alive' or 'lively'). Borne by a fifth-century martyr called St Vivianus, it was originally reserved for males but came to be used for both sexes. Also spelled **Vivien**, **Vivyan** or **Vyvyan** and commonly shortened to **Viv**.

**Vivien/Vivyan** *See* VIVIAN.

**Vladimir** Russian name based on the Slavonic *volod* ('rule') and *meri* ('great'). St Vladimir (956–1015) was largely responsible for the Christianization of Russia. *See also* VADIM.

**Vyvyan** *See* VIVIAN.

# BOYS' NAMES

**Wade** English name meaning 'ford' or 'dweller by the ford'. Long-established as a surname, its popularity as a first name increased after it appeared as the name of a character in Margaret Mitchell's novel *Gone with the Wind* (1936).

**Wadsworth** English name based on an Old English place name meaning 'Wade's homestead'. **Wordsworth** is a variant form.

**Wainwright** English name taken from an Old English surname meaning 'cart-maker'.

**Wake** English name taken from an Old English surname meaning 'alert'.

**Wal** *See* WALLACE; WALTER.

**Waldemar** *See* WALDO.

**Waldo** English name that developed as a shortened form of the German **Waldemar**, meaning 'rule' or 'power'. Borne by the celebrated US writer and philosopher Ralph Waldo Emerson (1803–82), it remains rare outside the USA.

**Walid** ('waleed') Arabic name meaning 'newborn baby'. Its use was much promoted by the military successes of Arab armies during the reign of Walid I (d. 715).

**Walker** English name, originally a surname, meaning 'fuller'.

**Wallace** English name that began life as a Scottish surname meaning 'Welsh' or 'Welshman' or (from Old French *waleis*) simply 'foreign' or 'stranger'. Also found as **Wallas**, it became popular among Scots in tribute to Sir William Wallace (1274–1305). Shortened forms include **Wal** and **Wally**.

**Wallas** *See* WALLACE.

**Wally** *See* WALLACE; WALTER.

**Walsh** English name based on the Irish term for the Welsh, or foreigners in general. Variants include **Welsh**.

**Walt** *See* WALTER; WALTON.

**Walter** English, German and Scandinavian name based on the Old German *waldhar* ('army ruler' or 'folk ruler'). It was originally pronounced with a silent 'l' (as 'water'), giving rise to such variants as **Wat**, **Watkin** and the Scottish **Wattie** or **Watty**. Shortened forms include **Wal**, **Wally** and **Walt**.

**Walton** English name based on an Old English surname meaning 'farmstead of the Britons'. Sometimes shortened to **Walt**.

**Ward** English name based on the Old English *weard* ('guard' or 'watchman'). Originally a surname, it was taken up as a first name around the middle of the nineteenth century.

**Warne** English name taken from the Cornish for 'alder wood'.

**Warner** English name equivalent to the German **Werner**, itself from the German tribal name Warin (meaning 'guard') and the German *heri* (meaning 'army'). Warner has been used as a first name among English speakers since the nineteenth century.

**Warren** English name that may have been introduced originally as a Norman surname meaning 'game park' or else came from the Old German tribal name Warin (meaning 'to guard'). It was adopted as a first name in the nineteenth century.

**Warrie** *See* WARWICK.

**Warwick** ('worrik') English name based on that of the county town of Warwickshire, which itself means 'farm by the weir'. It was adopted as a first name in the nineteenth century. **Warrie** is an informal version.

**Waseem** *See* WASIM.

**Wash** *See* WASHINGTON.

**Washington** English name based on an Old English place name meaning 'settlement of Wassa's people'. It is particularly popular in the USA, where it evokes memories of the first president, George Washington (1732–99). Sometimes shortened to **Wash**.

**Wasim** Arabic and Indian name meaning 'handsome' or 'good-looking'. An Indian variant is **Waseem**.

**Wat/Watkin/Wattie/ Watty** *See* WALTER.

**Waverley** English name taken from a place name meaning 'meadow by a swamp'.

**Wayland** *See* WAYLON.

**Waylon** English name based on the Old English **Wayland**, meaning 'land by the road'. Famous bearers of the name have included US country musician Waylon Jennings (1937–2002).

**Wayne** English name based on a surname meaning 'cart-maker'. It became popular in tribute to US film actor John Wayne (Marion Michael Morrison; 1907–79), whose stage name was inspired by the fame of Anthony Wayne (1745–96), a general in the War of Independence.

**Webb** English name taken from an Old English surname meaning 'weaver'.

**Webster** English name taken from an Old English surname meaning 'weaver'. It is more common in the USA than elsewhere in the English-speaking world.

**Wellington** English name taken from an Old English place name meaning 'Weola's farmstead'. It is strongly associated with the British soldier and statesman Arthur Wellesley, Duke of Wellington (1769–1852).

**Welsh** *See* WALSH.

**Wendel** *See* WENDELL.

**Wendell** English name based on a Germanic surname usually interpreted as meaning 'wanderer'. Also found as **Wendel**, it has been in occasional use as a first name since the nineteenth century.

**Wentworth** English name taken from an Old English place name meaning 'winter enclosure'. It is more common in Australia than elsewhere in the English-speaking world in tribute to Australian political leader William Wentworth (1790–1872).

**Werner** *See* WARNER.

**Wes** *See* WESLEY.

**Wesley** English name based on an Old English place name meaning 'west meadow'. It was taken up as an occasional first name in tribute to John Wesley (1703–91), founder of the Methodist movement. **Wes** is a shortened form.

**West/Westie** *See* WESTON.

**Weston** English name taken from a place name meaning 'west settlement'. Also found in the shortened forms **West** or **Westie**, it is popular chiefly in the USA.

**Whitaker** English name based on the Old English

meaning 'white acre'. Also found as **Whitakker**.

**Whitakker** *See* WHITAKER.

**Whitman** English name based on the Old English surname meaning 'fair-haired'.

**Whitney** English name derived from a place name meaning 'at the white island'. Originally a surname, it has been used as a first name for both sexes since the early twentieth century.

**Wilberforce** English name derived from a place name in North Yorkshire, meaning 'Wilbur's ditch'. It became popular in tribute to English politician William Wilberforce (1759–1833), who led the campaign to end the slave trade.

**Wilbert** English name derived from the Old English *will* ('will') and *beorht* ('bright'). Its use is largely confined to the USA.

**Wilbur** English name of obscure origins, possibly from the Old English *will* ('will') and *burh* ('defence'). It is more common in the USA than elsewhere in the English-speaking world, having been taken there (probably) by Dutch settlers.

**Wiley** *See* WYLIE.

**Wilf/Wilfie** *See* WILFRED.

**Wilfred** English name derived from the Old German *wil* ('will' or 'desire') and *frid* ('peace') and thus meaning 'desiring peace'. Also found as **Wilfrid**. Shortened forms include **Wilf** and **Wilfie**. *See also* WILKIE.

**Wilfrid** *See* WILFRED.

**Wilhelm** *See* WILLIAM.

**Wilkie** English name that developed out of WILFRED or WILLIAM. It has been in occasional use as a first name since the nineteenth century. Notable bearers of the name have included British novelist Wilkie Collins (1824–89).

**Will** *See* WILLIAM.

**Willard** English name based on the Old German *wil* ('will') and *heard* ('hardy'). Notable

bearers of the name have included Jamaican-born opera singer Willard White (b. 1946).

**Willem** *See* WILLIAM.

**William** English name based on the Old German *wil* ('will') and *helm* ('helmet' or 'protection'). It came to Britain with the Normans under William the Conqueror. Variants include the Germanic **Wilhelm** and **Willem**, Scottish Gaelic **Uilleam**, the Irish Gaelic **Ulick** and the Welsh **Gwilym**. Commonly shortened to **Bill**, **Billy**, **Will** and **Willy** (or **Willie**). *See also* LIAM.

**Willie** *See* WILLIAM.

**Willis** English name meaning 'son of Will'. It has been in occasional use as a first name since the nineteenth century.

**Willoughby** English name taken from a place name meaning 'farm among the willows'. It was taken up as a first name in the nineteenth century.

**Willson** *See* WILSON.

**Willy** *See* WILLIAM.

**Wilmer** English name that evolved either as a masculine version of Wilma (*see* WILHELMINA) or from the Old German *wil* ('will' or 'desire') and *meri* ('famous') and thus meaning 'resolute'.

**Wilmot** English name that developed from WILLIAM or else from the Old German *wil* ('will' or 'desire') and *muot* ('mind' or 'courage'). Its use as a first name dates from the nineteenth century.

**Wilson** English name meaning 'son of Will'. Also found as **Willson**.

**Wilt** *See* WILTON.

**Wilton** English name taken from a place name meaning 'floodable place'. Sometimes shortened to **Wilt**.

**Win** *See* WINSTON; WINTHROP.

**Windham** *See* WYNDHAM.

**Windsor** English name taken from an Old English place name meaning 'river bank with a windlass (for hauling boats)'. Famous for its royal connections, it has been employed as an occasional first name since the nineteenth century.

**Winnie** *See* WINSTON.

**Winston** English name taken from that of the village of Winston in Gloucestershire, itself meaning either 'boundary stone of a man called Wynna' or 'friend's settlement'. It is indelibly associated with British wartime leader Sir Winston Churchill (1874–1965). **Win** and **Winnie** are shortened forms.

**Winthrop** English name taken from an Old English place name meaning 'village of Wynna'. More familiar as a surname, it has been employed occasionally as a first name, chiefly in the USA. Sometimes shortened to **Win**.

**Winton** English name taken from a place name found in both Cumbria and North Yorkshire, meaning 'pasture enclosure' or 'willow enclosure'.

**Wolf** German and Jewish name that probably evolved as a shortened form of WOLFGANG. Variant forms include **Wolfe**, as borne by Irish nationalist Wolfe Tone (1763–98).

**Wolfe** *See* WOLF.

**Wolfgang** German name based on the Old German *wolf* ('wolf') and *gang* ('going'). Its occasional use as a first name in the English-speaking world owes much to Austrian composer Wolfgang Amadeus Mozart (1756–91).

**Woodrow** English name taken from an Old English place name meaning 'row of houses by a wood'. Its popularity in the USA was boosted through US President Thomas Woodrow Wilson (1856–1924). *See also* WOODY.

**Woodward** English name based on an Old English surname meaning 'forest guardian'.

**Woody** English name that developed as a shortened form of WOODROW. Notable bearers of the name have included US comedian and film director Woody Allen (Allen Stewart Konigsberg; b. 1935).

**Wordsworth** *See* WADSWORTH.

**Wyatt** English name ultimately based on the Old German *wido* ('wood' or 'wide'). It has been used as an occasional first name since the nineteenth century. Notable bearers of the name have included US lawman Wyatt Earp (1848–1929).

**Wye** *See* WYLIE.

**Wylie** English name meaning 'clever' or 'crafty'. Variant forms are **Wiley** and **Wye**.

**Wyn** *See* WYNN.

**Wyndham** English name taken from a place name from Norfolk meaning 'Wyman's homestead'. Famous bearers of the name have included British novelist Percy Wyndham Lewis (1882–1957). Also found as **Windham**.

**Wynfor** *See* GWYNFOR.

**Wynford** Welsh name taken

from a place name meaning 'white stream' or 'holy stream'. Its use as a first name dates from the early twentieth century.

**Wynn** English name variously derived from the Welsh *wyn* ('white' or 'blessed') or else from an Old English surname meaning 'friend'. Also found as **Wyn** or in use as a variant of GWYN.

**Wystan** English name based on the Old English *wig* ('battle') and *stan* ('stone'). It became widely familiar in the mid-twentieth century through British poet Wystan Hugh Auden (1907–73).

# BOYS' NAMES

**Xan/Xander** *See*
ALEXANDER.

**Xavier** ('zayvya' or 'zavvya')
Spanish name derived from the
Arabic word for 'bright', or
else from the Basque for 'new
house'. Also found as **Javier** or
**Zavier**.

## BOYS' NAMES

**Yael** *See* JAEL.

**Yale** English name from the Welsh for 'fertile upland'.

**Yance** *See* YANCEY.

**Yancey** US name possibly from a native American term for an Englishman. Also found as **Yance**, **Yancie** or **Yancy**.

**Yancie/Yancy** *See* YANCEY.

**Yardley** English name from the Old English meaning 'from the enclosed meadow'.

**Yehudi** *See* JUDAH.

**Yestin** Welsh name meaning 'just'.

**Yoel** Hebrew variant of JOEL.

**Yorath** *See* IORWERTH.

**Yorick** Danish equivalent of the English GEORGE. It is best known as the name of the deceased court jester in William Shakespeare's *Hamlet* (1599).

**York** English name meaning 'yew tree'. Also encountered as **Yorke**.

**Yorke** *See* YORK.

**Yul** Mongolian name meaning 'beyond the horizon'. Best known as the name of Russian-born film actor Yul Brynner (1920–85).

**Yuri** Russian equivalent of the English GEORGE. Also found as **Yury**.

**Yury** *See* YURI.

**Yves** (eevs) French name meaning 'yew tree'. *See also* IVES.

# BOYS' NAMES

**Zac** *See* ZACHARY.

**Zachary** English name based on the Hebrew Zachariah, Zacharias or Zechariah, meaning 'Jehovah has remembered'. The name of John the Baptist's father, it is commonly shortened to **Zac**, **Zack**, **Zak** or **Zakki**.

**Zack/Zak/Zakki** *See* ISAAC; ZACHARY.

**Zane** English name either from JOHN or possibly of Danish origin or otherwise inspired by an unidentified surname or place name.

**Zavier** *See* XAVIER.

**Zeb** Shortened form of the Hebrew name Zebulun (meaning 'exaltation') or otherwise of the biblical Zebedee or Zebediah (meaning 'my gift').

**Zed** Shortened form of the Hebrew name Zedekiah (meaning 'the Lord is just'). The full form of the name appears in the Old Testament as the name of a king of Judea.

**Zeke** *See* EZEKIEL.

**Zeph** *See* ZEPHANIAH.

**Zephaniah** ('zefaniah') Hebrew name meaning 'hidden from God'. It was the name of an Old Testament prophet. Often shortened to Zeph.

**Zero** Arabic name meaning 'nothing'. Also found as Zeroh.

**Zeroh** *See* ZERO.

**Zoltan** Hungarian name that may have developed from the Turkish *sultan*.

# APPENDICES

## Saints' Days

### January

1   Basil, Fulgentius, Justin, Telemachus
2   Abel, Basil, Caspar, Gregory, Macarius, Seraphim
3   Daniel, Frances, Genevieve
4   Angela, Benedicta, Roger
5   Paula, Simeon
6   Balthasar, Gaspar, Raphaela
7   Cedda, Crispin, Lucian, Raymond, Reynold, Valentine
8   Atticus, Gudule, Lucian, Severinus
9   Adrian, Alix, Hadrian, Peter
10  Agatho, Marcian, William
11  Brandan
12  Ailred, Benedict, Tatiana
13  Godfrey, Hilary
14  Felix, Hilary, Kentigern, Malachi
15  Isidore, Ita, Macarius, Maurus, Micah, Paul
16  Henry, Honoratus, Marcellus, Otto, Priscilla
17  Antony, Rosclinc
18  Dermot, Faustina, Priscilla, Susanna
19  Gerontius, Henry, Marius, Martha, Pia, Wulfstan
20  Euthymius, Fabian, Sebastian
21  Agnes, Fructuosus, Josepha, Maximus, Meinrad
22  Dominic, Timothy, Vincent
23  Aquila, Bernard, Ildefonsus, Raymond
24  Babylas, Francis, Timothy
25  Artemas, Gregory, Joel
26  Aubrey, Conan, Paula, Timothy, Titus, Xenophon
27  Angela, Candida, John, Julian, Marius, Theodoric
28  Ephraem, Paulinus, Peter, Thomas
29  Francis, Gildas
30  Hyacintha, Martina, Matthias

31  Adamnan, Aidan, Cyrus, John, Julius, Marcella, Tryphena

## February

1  Bridget, Ignatius, Pionius
2  Joan, Theodoric
3  Anskar, Blaise, Ives, Laurence, Margaret, Oliver, Simeon, Werburga
4  Andrew, Gilbert, Isidore, Joan, Joseph, Nicholas, Phileas, Theophilus
5  Adelaide, Agatha, Avitus, Caius, Joachim, Matthias
6  Dorothy, Gerald, Luke, Mel, Paul, Silvanus, Titus, Vedast
7  Juliana, Luke, Moses, Richard, Theodore
8  Isaiah, Jerome, Sebastian, Stephen, Theodore
9  Apollonia, Cyril, Teilo
10  Hyacinth, Scholastica, Silvanus
11  Benedict, Blaise, Caedmon, Gregory, Jonas, Lazarus, Lucius, Theodore, Victoria
12  Alexis, Eulalia, Julian, Marina, Meletius
13  Agabus, Beatrice, Catherine, Priscilla
14  Abraham, Adolf, Cyril, Methodius, Valentine
15  Claud, Georgia, Jordan, Sigfrid
16  Elias, Flavian, Gilbert, Jeremy, Juliana, Pamphilus, Philippa, Samuel, Valentine
17  Reginald
18  Bernadette, Colman, Flavian, Leo, Simeon
19  Boniface, Conrad
20  Amata, Wulfric
21  George, Peter
22  Margaret
23  Lazarus, Martha, Mildburga, Milo, Polycarp
24  Adela, Lucius, Matthias
25  Ethelbert, Tarasius, Walburga
26  Alexander, Isabel, Porphyrius, Victor
27  Gabriel, Leander
28  Antonia, Hedwig, Hilary, Louisa, Oswald

*March*

1  Albinus, David, Felix, Roger
2  Agnes, Chad, Simplicius
3  Ailred, Anselm, Camilla, Marcia, Owen
4  Adrian, Casimir, Humbert, Lucius, Peter
5  Kieran, Piran, Virgil
6  Chrodegang, Colette, Cyril, Felicity, Jordan, Perpetua
7  Felicity, Paul, Perpetua, Thomas
8  Beata, Felix, Humphrey, John, Julian, Philemon, Pontius, Stephen
9  Catherine, Dominic, Frances, Gregory, Pacian
10 Anastasia, Caius, John, Macarius, Simplicius
11 Alberta, Aurea, Constantine, Oengus, Sophronius, Teresa
12 Bernard, Gregory, Maximilian, Paul, Seraphim
13 Gerald, Nicephorus, Patricia, Roderick, Solomon
14 Benedict, Eustace, Matilda
15 Clement, Louise, Lucretia, Zachary
16 Abraham, Julian, René
17 Gertrude, Joseph, Patrick, Paul
18 Alexander, Anselm, Christian, Cyril, Edward, Egbert, Narcissus, Salvator
19 Joseph
20 Alexandra, Claudia, Cuthbert, Euphemia, Herbert, Hippolytus, John, Martin, Sebastian, Theodosia
21 Benedict, Clementia, Serapion
22 Basil, Catherine, Nicholas, Octavian
23 Aquila, Theodosia, Turibius
24 Catherine, Gabriel, Simon
25 Harold, Humbert, Lucy, Richard
26 Basil, Emmanuel
27 Augusta, John, Lydia, Matthew
28 Gwendoline, John
29 Berthold, Gladys, Jonas, Mark, Rupert
30 John
31 Aldo, Amos, Benjamin, Cornelia, Guy

## April

1 Gilbert, Hugh, Ludovic, Mary, Melito
2 Constantine, Drogo, Francis, Leopold, Mary, Theodosia, Urban
3 Alexandrina, Irene, Richard
4 Benedict, Isidore
5 Gerald, Juliana, Vincent
6 Celestine, William
7 George, Hegesippus, Herman, John, Llewellyn
8 Agabus, Dionysius, Walter
9 Hugh, Mary, Reginald
10 Ezekiel, Fulbert, Hedda, Michael, Terence
11 Gemma, Guthlac, Hildebrand, Isaac, Leo, Stanislaus
12 Damian, Julius, Zeno
13 Ida, Martin
14 Bernard, Caradoc, Eustace, Justin, Lambert
15 Anastasia, Aristarchus, Pudus, Silvester, Trophimus
16 Benedict, Bernadette, Drogo, Hervé, Lambert, Magnus
17 Agapetus, Elias, Robert, Stephen
18 Andrew, James
19 Alphege, Leo
20 Agnes
21 Anastasius, Anselm, Beuno, Conrad, Januarius, Simeon
22 Alexander, Caius, Theodore
23 Fortunatus, George, Gerard, Giles, Helen
24 Egbert, Fidelis, Ives, Mellitus
25 Mark, Phaebadius
26 Alda, Franca, Stephen
27 Zita
28 Louis, Patrick, Paul, Peter, Theodora, Valeria, Vitalis
29 Antonia, Ava, Catherine, Hugh, Peter, Robert, Wilfrid
30 Catherine, Hildegard, James, Miles, Pius, Sophia

## May

1 Asaph, Bertha, Isidora, Joseph, Peregrine, Sigismund, Walburga
2 Athanasius, Zoë
3 Antonina, James, Maura, Philip, Timothy

4 Ethelrad, Florian, Gotthard, Monica, Silvanus
5 Angelo, Hilary
6 Benedicta, Prudence
7 Augustus, Flavia, Gisela, John, Stanislas
8 Benedict, Boniface, John, Michael, Peter, Victor
9 Gerontius
10 Antoninus, Aurelian, Beatrice, Comgall, Job, John, Simon
11 Aloysius, Cyril, Ignatius, James, Mamertus, Methodius, Philip, Walter
12 Achilleus, Dominic, Epiphanius, Gemma, Nereus, Pancras
13 Robert
14 Carthage, Giles, Mary, Matthias, Michael, Petronilla
15 Bertha, Dionysia, Dympna, Hilary, Isidore, Magdalen, Rupert, Silvanus
16 Brendan, John, Peregrine, Simon
17 Basilla, Paschal, Robert
18 Alexandra, Camilla, Claudia, Eric, John, Julitta
19 Celestine, Dunstan, Pudens, Pudentia, Yves
20 Aquila, Basilissa, Bernardino, Ethelbert, Orlando
21 Helena, Theobald, Theophilus
22 Julia, Rita
23 Ivo, William
24 David, Joanna, Patrick, Susanna, Vincent
25 Aldhelm, Bede, Dionysius, Gregory, Madeleine, Urban
26 Augustine, Lambert, Philip, Quadratus, Zachary
27 Augustine, Frederick, John, Julius
28 Augustine, Bernard
29 Theodosia, William
30 Felix, Ferdinand, Hubert, Isaac, Joan
31 Camilla, Petronilla

## June

1 Angela, Justin, Pamphilus, Simeon, Theobald
2 Erasmus, Eugene, Marcellinus, Nicephorus, Nicholas, Peter, Pothinus
3 Charles, Clotilda, Isaac, Kevin, Matthias, Paula
4 Cornelius, Francis, Optatus, Petrock, Vincentia, Walter

5  Boniface, Ferdinand, Franco, Marcia, Valeria
6  Claud, Felicia, Martha, Norbert, Philip
7  Paul, Robert, Willibald
8  Melania, William
9  Amata, Cecilia, Columba, Cyril, Diana, Ephraem, Richard
10 Margaret, Olive, Zachary
11 Barnabas, Bartholomew, Fortunatus
12 Antonia, Christian, Humphrey, Leo
13 Anthony, Lucian
14 Basil
15 Alice, Germaine, Guy, Orsisius, Vitus, Yolanda
16 Aurelian, Julitta
17 Alban, Botolph, Emily, Harvey, Manuel, Sanchia, Teresa
18 Elizabeth, Fortunatus, Guy, Marina, Mark
19 Bruno, Gervase, Jude, Juliana, Odo, Protasius, Romuald
20 Alban, John
21 Alban, Aloysius, Lazarus, Ralph, Terence
22 Alban, Ederhard, John, Niceta, Pantaenus, Paulinus, Thomas
23 Audrey
24 Bartholomew, Ivan, John
25 Prosper, Solomon, William
26 John
27 Cyril, Ferdinand, Ladislaus, Madeleine, Samson
28 Irenaeus, Marcella, Paul
29 Emma, Judith, Paul, Peter, Salome
30 Bertrand, Lucina, Theobald

## July

1  Aaron, Cosmas, Damian, Oliver, Simeon, Theodoric
2  Marcia, Otto, Reginald
3  Aaron, Anatolius, Julius, Leo, Thomas
4  Andrew, Aurelian, Bertha, Elizabeth, Odo, Ulrich
5  Anthony, Blanche, Grace, Gwen, Philomena, Zoë
6  Isaiah, Mary
7  Cyril, Hedda, Palladius, Pantaenus
8  Adrian, Aquila, Arnold, Edgar, Elizabeth, Kilian, Morwenna, Priscilla, Raymund

9 Alberic, Barnabas, Cornelius, Everild, Godfrey, Jerome, Nicholas, Thomas, Veronica
10 Amelia, Emmanuel, Maurice
11 Benedict, Olga, Oliver, Pius
12 Fortunatus, Jason, John, Monica, Veronica
13 Eugene, Henry, Joel, Mildred, Silas
14 Camillus, Deusdedit, Humbert, Nicholas, Ulric
15 Baldwin, Bonaventure, David, Donald, Edith, Henry, Jacob, Swithin, Vladimir
16 Eustace, Milo, Valentine
17 Alexis, Antoinette, Ennodius, Kenelm, Leo, Marcellina, Margaret, Nahum
18 Arnulf, Bruno, Camillus, Edith, Frederick, Marina, Philastrius
19 Ambrose, Aurea, Jerome, Symmachus, Vincent
20 Aurelius, Elias, Elijah, Jerome, Margaret, Marina
21 Angelina, Constantine, Daniel, Julia, Laurence, Praxedes, Victor
22 Joseph, Mary, Theophilus
23 Anne, Apollinaris, Balthasar, Bridget, Gaspar, Susanna
24 Boris, Christiana, Christina, Declan, Felicia
25 Anne, Christopher, James, Joachim, Thea, Valentina
26 Anne, Joachim
27 Berthold, Celestine, Natalia, Pantaleon, Rudolph, Theobald
28 Innocent, Samson, Victor
29 Beatrice, Felix, Flora, Lucilla, Lupus, Martha, Olaf, Urban
30 Everard, Julitta, Peter, Silas
31 Giovanni, Helen, Ignatius, Joseph

## *August*

1 Alphonsus, Charity, Eiluned, Ethelwold, Faith, Hope, Justin, Kenneth
2 Alphonsus, Eusebius, Stephen
3 Gamaliel, Lydia, Nicodemus
4 Dominic, Jean-Baptiste, Perpetua
5 Afra, Oswald
6 Hormisdas, Octavian
7 Albert, Cajetan, Claudia, Sixtus
8 Dominic, Myron

9 Matthias, Oswald, Samuel
10 Geraint, Laurence, Oswald, Philomena
11 Alexander, Blane, Clare, Lelia, Susanna
12 Clare, Murtagh
13 Hippolytus, Maximus, Pontian, Radegunde
14 Marcellus, Maximilian
15 Arnulf, Mary, Napoleon, Stanislaus, Tarsicius
16 Joachim, Roch, Serena, Simplicianus, Stephen, Titus
17 Benedicta, Cecilia, Clare, Hyacinth, Myron, Septimus
18 Evan, Helena, Milo
19 John, Louis, Magnus, Sebaldus, Thecla, Timothy
20 Bernard, Herbert, Oswin, Philibert, Ronald, Samuel
21 Abraham, Jane, Pius
22 Andrew, Hippolytus, Sigfrid, Timothy
23 Claudius, Eleazar, Eugene, Philip, Rose, Sidonius, Zacchaeus
24 Alice, Bartholomew, Emily, Jane, Joan, Nathanael, Ouen
25 Joseph, Louis, Lucilla, Menas, Patricia
26 Dominic, Elias, Elizabeth, Zephyrinus
27 Caesarius, Gabriel, Hugh, Margaret, Monica, Rufus
28 Adelina, Alexander, Augustine, Julian, Moses, Vivian
29 Basilla, John, Merry, Sabina
30 Felix, Pammachius, Rose
31 Aidan, Paulinus, Raymund

### September

1 Anna, Augustus, Gideon, Giles, Joshua, Simeon, Verena
2 John, René, Stephen, William
3 Dorothy, Euphemia, Gabriel, Gregory, Phoebe, Simeon
4 Babylas, Boniface, Candida, Hermione, Ida, Marcellus, Moses, Rosalia, Rose
5 Laurence, Urban, Vitus, Zacharias
6 Beata, Magnus, Zechariah
7 Eustace, Regina
8 Adrian, Natalia, Sergius
9 Isaac, Kieran, Louise, Peter, Seraphina, Sergius, Wilfrida
10 Aubert, Candida, Finnian, Isabel, Nicholas, Pulcheria
11 Daniel, Ethelburga, Hyacinth, Paphnutius, Theodora

12 Guy
13 Amatus, John
14 Cormac
15 Albinus, Catherine, Roland
16 Cornelius, Cyprian, Edith, Eugenia, Euphemia, Lucy, Ninian, Victor
17 Ariadne, Columba, Hildegard, Justin, Lambert, Narcissus, Robert, Satyrus, Theodora
18 Irene, Sophia
19 Constantia, Emily, Januarius, Susanna, Theodore
20 Candida, Eustace, Philippa, Vincent
21 Jonah, Matthew, Maura
22 Felix, Jonas, Maurice, Thomas
23 Adamnan, Helen, Linus, Thecla
24 Gerard
25 Albert, Aurelia, Herman, Sergius
26 Cosmas, Cyprian, John, Justina, René
27 Adolphus, Caius, Cosmas, Damian, Frumentius, Terence, Vincent
28 Exuperius, Solomon, Wenceslas
29 Gabriel, Michael, Raphael
30 Jerome, Otto, Simon, Sophia

## *October*

1 Francis, Nicholas, Remigius, Romanos, Teresa
2 Leodegar, Theophilus
3 Gerard, Thérèse, Thomas
4 Ammon, Aurea, Berenice, Francis, Petronius
5 Flavia, Flora
6 Aurea, Bruno, Faith, Magnus, Mary, Thomas
7 Augustus, Julia, Justina, Mark
8 Bridget, Laurentia, Sergius, Simeon
9 Abraham, Demetrius, Denis, Dionysius, Gunther, James, John, Louis
10 Daniel, Francis, Paulinus, Samuel
11 Atticus, Bruno, Juliana, Kenneth, Nectarius
12 Cyprian, Edwin, Maximilian, Wilfrid

13 Edward, Gerald, Magdalen, Maurice, Theophilus
14 Callistus, Cosmas, Dominic
15 Aurelia, Leonard, Lucian, Teresa, Thecla, Willa
16 Baldwin, Bertrand, Gall, Gerard, Hedwig, Lullus, Margaret
17 Ignatius, Margaret, Rudolph, Victor
18 Blanche, Candida, Gwen, Gwendoline, Luke
19 Cleopatra, Isaac, John, Laura, Lucius, Paul, Peter
20 Adelina, Andrew, Irene, Martha
21 Hilarion, Ursula
22 Abercius, Philip
23 Bartholomew, Ignatius, James, John, Josephine
24 Anthony, Martin, Raphael, Septimus
25 Balthasar, Crispin, Crispinian, Dorcas, Gaudentius, George, Tabitha, Thaddeus, Theodoric
26 Albinus, Cuthbert, Damian, Demetrius, Lucian
27 Antonia, Sabina
28 Anastasias, Firmilian, Godwin, Jude, Simon, Thaddaeus
29 Narcissus, Terence
30 Alphonsus, Artemas, Dorothy, Marcellus, Serapion, Zenobia
31 Quentin, Wolfgang

## November

1 Cledwyn, Cosmas, Damian, Mary
2 Eustace, Maura, Tobias, Victorinus
3 Hubert, Malachy, Martin, Pirminius, Sylvia, Valentine, Winifred
4 Agricola, Charles, Frances, Vitalis
5 Cosmo, Elizabeth, Martin, Zacharias
6 Illtyd, Leonard, Paul
7 Carina, Florentius, Gertrude, Rufus, Willibrord
8 Elizabeth, Godfrey, Willehad
9 Simeon, Theodore
10 Florence, Justus, Leo, Tryphena
11 Bartholomew, Martin, Menas, Theodore
12 Josaphat, Martin, Matthew, Nilus, René
13 Abbo, Brice, Eugene, John, Nicholas, Stanislaus
14 Dubricius, Gregory, Laurence
15 Albert, Leopold, Machutus

16 Agnes, Edmund, Eucherius, Gertrude, Margaret, Matthew
17 Dionysius, Elizabeth, Gregory, Hilda, Hugh, Victoria, Zacchaeus
18 Constant, Odo, Romanus
19 Crispin, Elizabeth, Mechtild, Nerses
20 Edmund, Octavius, Silvester
21 Albert, Gelasius, Rufus
22 Cecilia, Philemon
23 Amphilochius, Clement, Columban, Felicity, Gregory, Lucretia
24 Flora, John, Thaddeus
25 Catherine, Clement, Mercurius, Mesrob, Moses
26 Conrad, Leonard, Peter, Silvester, Siricius
27 Barlam, Fergus, James, Josaphat, Virgil
28 James, Simeon, Stephen
29 Blaise, Brendan, Cuthbert, Frederick
30 Andrew, Frumentius, Maura

## December

1 Eligius, Nahum, Natalia, Ralph
2 Aurelia, Chromatius, Viviana
3 Claudius, Francis Xavier, Jason, Lucius
4 Ada, Barbara, Bernard, John, Osmond
5 Bartholomew, Clement, Sabas
6 Abraham, Dionysia, Gertrude, Nicholas, Tertius
7 Ambrose, Josepha
8 Mary
9 Peter
10 Brian, Eulalia, Gregory, Julia, Miltiades, Sidney
11 Damasus, Daniel, Franco
12 Agatha, Cormac, Dionysia, Jane Frances, Spyridon, Vicelin
13 Aubert, Judoc, Lucy, Ottilia
14 Conrad, John, Spyridon
15 Christiana, Mary
16 Adelaide, Albina, Azariah, Eusebius
17 Florian, Lazarus, Olympias
18 Frumentius, Rufus
19 Thea, Urban
20 Dominic, Ignatius

21 Peter, Thomas
22 Adam, Anastasia, Chrysogonus
23 John, Victoria
24 Adam, Adela, Eve
25 Anastasia, Eugenia
26 Christina, Dionysius, Stephen, Vincentia
27 Fabiola, John, Stephen, Theodore
28 Theophila
29 David, Marcellus, Thomas, Trophimus
30 Sabinus
31 Columba, Cornelius, Fabian, Melania, Sextus, Silvester

# Popular Names *(based on latest available official records)*

## *Girls*

| | England and Wales | Scotland | USA | Australia |
|---|---|---|---|---|
| 1 | Grace | Sophie | Emily | Ella |
| 2 | Ruby | Emma | Isabella | Emily |
| 3 | Olivia | Lucy | Emma | Mia |
| 4 | Emily | Katie | Ava | Chloe |
| 5 | Jessica | Erin | Madison | Charlotte |
| 6 | Sophie | Ellie | Sophia | Isabella |
| 7 | Chloe | Amy | Olivia | Olivia |
| 8 | Lily | Emily | Abigail | Sophie |
| 9 | Ella | Chloe | Hannah | Sienna |
| 10 | Amelia | Olivia | Elizabeth | Lily |
| 11 | Lucy | Hannah | Addison | Ava |
| 12 | Charlotte | Jessica | Samantha | Jessica |
| 13 | Ellie | Grace | Ashley | Hannah |
| 14 | Mia | Ava | Alyssa | Arace |
| 15 | Evie | Rebecca | Mia | Amelia |
| 16 | Hannah | Isla | Chloe | Ruby |
| 17 | Megan | Brooke | Natalie | Georgia |
| 18 | Katie | Megan | Sarah | Emma |
| 19 | Isabella | Niamh | Alexis | Lucy |
| 20 | Isabelle | Eilidh | Grace | Madison |
| 21 | Millie | Eva | Ella | Jasmine |
| 22 | Abigail | Abbie | Brianna | Sarah |
| 23 | Amy | Skye | Hailey | Zoe |
| 24 | Daisy | Aimee | Taylor | Hayley |
| 25 | Freya | Mia | Anna | Chelsea |
| 26 | Emma | Ruby | Kayla | Matilda |
| 27 | Erin | Anna | Lily | Holly |
| 28 | Poppy | Sarah | Lauren | Imogen |
| 29 | Molly | Rachel | Victoria | Jade |
| 30 | Holly | Caitlin | Savannah | Sophia |
| 31 | Phoebe | Lauden | Nevaeh | Isabelle |
| 32 | Jasmine | Freya | Jasmine | Caitlin |

| | England and Wales | Scotland | USA | Australia |
|---|---|---|---|---|
| 33 | Caitlin | Keira | Lillian | Lara |
| 34 | Imogen | Lily | Julia | Maddison |
| 35 | Madison | Leah | Sofia | Scarlett |
| 36 | Elizabeth | Holly | Kaylee | Alyssa |
| 37 | Sophia | Millie | Sydney | Zara |
| 38 | Keira | Charlotte | Gabriella | Lilly |
| 39 | Scarlett | Abigail | Katherine | Tahlia |
| 40 | Leah | Molly | Alexa | Eva |
| 41 | Ava | Kayla | Destiny | Amy |
| 42 | Georgia | Zoe | Jessica | Summer |
| 43 | Alice | Eve | Morgan | Samantha |
| 44 | Summer | Iona | Kaitlyn | Paige |
| 45 | Isabel | Cara | Brooke | Kayla |
| 46 | Rebecca | Ella | Allison | Molly |
| 47 | Lauren | Evie | Makayla | Abigail |
| 48 | Amber | Nicole | Avery | Dakota |
| 49 | Eleanor | Morgan | Alexandra | Tayla |
| 50 | Bethany | Jenna | Jocelyn | Jorja |

## Boys

| | England and Wales | Scotland | USA | Australia |
|---|---|---|---|---|
| 1 | Jack | Lewis | Jacob | Jack |
| 2 | Thomas | Jack | Michael | Joshua |
| 3 | Oliver | Ryan | Ethan | Lachlan |
| 4 | Joshua | James | Joshua | Riley |
| 5 | Harry | Callum | Daniel | Thomas |
| 6 | Charlie | Cameron | Christopher | William |
| 7 | Daniel | Daniel | Anthony | James |
| 8 | William | Liam | William | Ethan |
| 9 | James | Jamie | Matthew | Cooper |
| 10 | Alfie | Kyle | Andrew | Daniel |
| 11 | Samuel | Matthew | Alexander | Noah |
| 12 | George | Logan | David | Samuel |
| 13 | Joseph | Finlay | Joseph | Lucas |
| 14 | Benjamin | Adam | Noah | Oliver |
| 15 | Ethan | Alexander | James | Liam |

| | | | |
|---|---|---|---|
| 16 Lewis | Dylan | Ryan | Ryan |
| 17 Mohammed | Aiden | Logan | Jacob |
| 18 Jake | Andrew | Jayden | Matthew |
| 19 Dylan | Ben | John | Benjamin |
| 20 Jacob | Aaron | Nicholas | Luke |
| 21 Luke | Connor | Tyler | Alexander |
| 22 Callum | Thomas | Christian | Jayden |
| 23 Alexander | Joshua | Jonathan | Tyler |
| 24 Matthew | David | Nathan | Charlie |
| 25 Ryan | Ross | Samuel | Jake |
| 26 Adam | Luke | Benjamin | Dylan |
| 27 Tyler | Nathan | Aiden | Nicholas |
| 28 Liam | Charlie | Gabriel | Max |
| 29 Harvey | Ethan | Dylan | Harrison |
| 30 Max | Aidan | Elijah | Blake |
| 31 Harrison | Michael | Brandon | Isaac |
| 32 Jayden | John | Gavin | Bailey |
| 33 Cameron | Calum | Jackson | Mitchell |
| 34 Henry | Scott | Angel | Cameron |
| 35 Archie | Josh | José | Jackson |
| 36 Connor | Samuel | Caleb | Oscar |
| 37 Jamie | Kieran | Mason | Michael |
| 38 Muhammad | Fraser | Jack | Angus |
| 39 Oscar | William | Kevin | Jordan |
| 40 Edward | Oliver | Evan | Hayden |
| 41 Lucas | Rhys | Isaac | Harry |
| 42 Isaac | Sean | Zachary | Nathan |
| 43 Leo | Harry | Isaiah | Alex |
| 44 Owen | Owen | Justin | Seth |
| 45 Nathan | Sam | Jordan | Tyson |
| 46 Michael | Christopher | Luke | Taj |
| 47 Finley | Euan | Robert | Zachary |
| 48 Ben | Robert | Austin | Henry |
| 49 Aaron | Kai | Landon | Adam |
| 50 Noah | Jay | Cameron | Connor |

# Celebrity Names *(Parents' names in brackets)*

## *Girls*

Aanisah (Macy Gray)
Anaïs (Noel Gallagher)
Apple (Gwyneth Paltrow and Chris Martin)
Assisi (Jade Jagger)
Ava (Myleene Klaas)
Betty Kitten (Jonathan Ross)
Bluebell Madonna (Geri Halliwell)
Bria (Eddie and Nicole Murphy)
Carys Zeta (Catherine Zeta Jones and Michael Douglas)
Coco Reilly (Courteney Cox and David Arquette)
Cosima (Nigella Lawson)
Daisy Boo (Jamie Oliver)
Dandelion (Keith Richard)
Fifi Trixibelle (Bob Geldof and Paula Yates)
Gaia (Emma Thompson)
Greta (Phoebe Cates and Kevin Kline)
Heavenly Hiraani Tiger Lily (Michael Hutchence and Paula Yates)
Ireland (Alec Baldwin and Kim Basinger)
Iris (Jude Law and Sadie Frost)
Isadora (Björk)
Jaz Elle (Steffi Graf and André Agassi)
Kenya (Natassja Kinski and Quincy Jones)
Lark Song (Mia Farrow and André Previn)
Little Pixie (Bob Geldof and Paula Yates)
Nell Marmalade (Helen Baxendale)
Peaches Honeyblossom (Bob Geldof and Paula Yates)
Phoenix Chi (Mel B)
Poppy Honey (Jamie Oliver)
Princess Tiaamii (Jordan and Peter Andre)
Rumer Glenn (Bruce Willis and Demi Moore)
Scout LaRue (Bruce Willis and Demi Moore)
Shiloh Nouvel (Brad Pitt and Angelina Jolie)
Sonnet (Forest Whitaker)

Suri (Tom Cruise and Katie Holmes)
Tallulah Belle (Bruce Willis and Demi Moore)
Willow Camille Reign (Will Smith)
Zola (Eddie and Nicole Murphy)

## Boys

Aurelius Cy (Elle Macpherson)
Billy Ray (Tim Burton and Helena Bonham-Carter)
Brandon Thomas (Pamela Anderson and Tommy Lee)
Brooklyn (David and Victoria Beckham)
Caspar (Claudia Schiffer)
Cruz (David and Victoria Beckham)
Deacon (Reese Witherspoon)
Dylan Jagger (Pamela Anderson and Tommy Lee)
Eja (Shania Twain)
Elijah Blue (Cher and Gregg Allman)
Elijah Bob Patricius Guggi Q (Bono)
Ellery (Laura Dern)
Giacomo (Sting and Trudie Styler)
Gulliver (Gary Oldman)
Jayden (Will Smith)
Jett (John Travolta and Kelly Preston)
Kal-El (Nicholas Cage)
Lennon (Liam Gallagher and Patsy Kensit)
Maddox (Angelina Jolie)
Moon Unit (Frank Zappa)
Moses (Gwyneth Paltrow and Chris Martin)
Pedro (Frances McDormand and Joel Coen)
Prince Michael (Michael Jackson)
Prince Michael II (Michael Jackson)
Rafferty (Jude Law and Sadie Frost)
River Jude (Bruce Willis and Demi Moore)
Rocco (Madonna)
Rolan (Marc Bolan)
Romeo (David and Victoria Beckham)
Sage Moon Blood (Sylvester Stallone)

Satchel (Woody Allen and Mia Farrow)
Zowie (David Bowie)

# PENGUIN REFERENCE LIBRARY

**THE PENGUIN DICTIONARY OF FIRST NAMES**

EDITED BY DAVID PICKERING

What's in a name? Rather more than you might at first suspect, for names are steeped in history and myth and have much to tell us about our past, our beliefs – even our personality traits. Now fully updated for its second edition, with 150 new entries, *The Penguin Dictionary of First Names* is much more than just an inspiration for expectant parents. Each entry is a carefully researched mini-masterpiece in cultural and linguistic history, as David Pickering offers a wealth of information fitted for the twenty-first century reader. He takes a close look at over 5000 examples – ranging from the familiar to the comparatively obscure – drawn from all parts of the English-speaking world. No other book provides the same authoritative detail and quality of definition.

- Gives the meaning or origin of each name, its variants and diminutives
- Highlights names that have become popular from literature, films, culture and celebrities
- Shows how names have changed in use and popularity over time
- Lists the most popular girls' and boys' names from 1700 to the present, from *Siobhan* and *Iolanthe* to *Hayden* and *Sherlock*
- Examines trends and changing tastes in the twenty-first century

**ONLY PENGUIN GIVES YOU MORE**

# PENGUIN POCKET REFERENCE

## THE PENGUIN POCKET DICTIONARY OF QUOTATIONS
### EDITED BY DAVID CRYSTAL

*The Penguin Pocket Dictionary of Quotations* is essential reading for anyone searching for the perfect quotation – whether you need a snappy one-liner for a speech or a remark of brilliant insight for your written work. With this pithy and provocative selection of wit and wisdom, you will never be lost for words again.

- Includes quotations from a vast range of people, from film stars to politicians

- Arranged alphabetically by name of person quoted, with the original source for each quotation given

- Provides a full index of key words to help you find each quotation quickly and easily

www.penguin.com

# PENGUIN REFERENCE LIBRARY

**THE PENGUIN BOOK OF FACTS**

EDITED BY DAVID CRYSTAL

'One of the greatest reference books ever published' *Independent on Sunday*

Funafuti is the capital of which south Pacific island? Which dog-toting film star's real name is Frances Gumm? How far is Brussels from Paris? *The Penguin Book of Facts* is the most comprehensive and authoritative general factbook available. Calling upon his famously encyclopaedic knowledge, David Crystal has compiled this international information bible with meticulous precision, layering fact upon fact in a logical order, from the beginnings of the universe to the World Water Skiing Union. It is not only the authoritative and infinite breadth of knowledge that sets this dictionary apart; Crystal has added an invaluable and comprehensive index that makes finding that elusive fact all the easier.

- Contains more facts than any other book of its kind and is illustrated throughout

- Includes contributions from over 250 experts

- This is the updated edition of *The New Penguin Factfinder*

**ONLY PENGUIN GIVES YOU MORE**

# PENGUIN REFERENCE LIBRARY

**THE PENGUIN HANDBOOK OF LIVING RELIGIONS**

EDITED BY JOHN R HINNELLS

'Excellent ... This whole book is a joy to read'
*The Times Higher Education Supplement*

Religion is more relevant than ever. From Islam to fundamentalism to the Kabbalah, faith is never far from the headlines, making our understanding of it utterly crucial. *The Penguin Handbook of Living Religions* is designed with this in mind. Crammed with charts, maps and diagrams, it comprises lengthy enlightening chapters on all of today's major religions, from Hinduism to Christianity to Baha'ism, as well as additional essays on cross-cultural areas, such as gender and spirituality. Each chapter represents a book's worth of information on all twenty-first century religions, featuring detailed discussion of the history, culture and practices of each. Comprehensive, informative and compiled by a team of leading international scholars, it includes discussion of modern developments and recent scholarship.

- Explains the sources and history of the world's religions, from Buddhism, Christianity, Hinduism, Islam, Sikhism and Zoroastrianism to regional groups in Africa, China and Japan

- Describes different doctrines, practices and teachings, including rites of passage and specific rituals

- Explores the role of gender and diaspora in modern religion

**ONLY PENGUIN GIVES YOU MORE**

# PENGUIN REFERENCE LIBRARY

**THE PENGUIN DICTIONARY OF BIOLOGY**
EDITED BY M. THAIN & M. HICKMAN

'A marvellous compendium: accurate, clear and complete'
Matt Ridley, author of *Genome*

Worried about your *maternal effect* or *biological clock*? Need to know a *rhizoid* from a *rhizome*? Think you're going to fail your *zoology* or *botany* exam? *The Penguin Dictionary of Biology* is your saviour, defining some 6000 terms relating to this rich, complex and constantly expanding subject – from *amino acids*, *bacteria* and the *cell cycle* to *X-ray diffraction*, *Y chromosome* and *zygotes*. Long established as the definitive single-volume source, this dictionary has sold over 200,000 copies and is extensively updated for its eleventh edition.

- Contains over 400 new entries to take account of the latest thinking on *genetics*, *human physiology*, *disease* and *cell biology*
- Superbly complemented by *The Penguin Dictionary of Human Biology*, due in Autumn 2007
- Ideal for students, teachers, professionals and amateur biologists
- Extensively illustrated throughout, with charts demonstrating *vertebrate spermatogenesis*, *primate evolution* and much more

**ONLY PENGUIN GIVES YOU MORE**

# PENGUIN REFERENCE LIBRARY

**THE PENGUIN DICTIONARY OF CLASSICAL MYTHOLOGY**

EDITED BY PIERRE GRIMAL

'An essential source' *Library Journal*

Who bore children by a bear and was transformed into a bird as punishment? Why exactly did Zeus turn his lover into a cow? Classical myth is a vibrant and entertaining world, and Pierre Grimal's seminal text *The Penguin Dictionary of Classical Mythology* is indisputably the finest guide available. Meticulously researched and thoroughly cross-referenced, the text is accessible and informative, sweeping in its breadth and comprehensive in its detail. You will find the no less than *four* versions of the beautiful *Helen*'s birth, as well as lengthy explanations of all the major figures and events – from *Odysseus* to *Heracles* to *Troy* to the *Jason* and the *Argonauts*.

- Discusses all the heroes and heroines of Homer, Sophocles, Aeschylus and Euripides (amongst many others), from *Venus* to *Pandora* via *Apollo* and *Aphrodite*

- Demonstrates how and where classical mythology has resurfaced and influenced the works of later painters and writers, from Freud to James Joyce

- Includes comprehensive cross-referencing and genealogical tables to show the complex links between different characters and myths

**ONLY PENGUIN GIVES YOU MORE**

# PENGUIN REFERENCE LIBRARY

**THE PENGUIN DICTIONARY OF GEOGRAPHY**

EDITED BY AUDREY N. CLARKE

*Winner of the Association of College and Research Libraries Choice Award*

*Global warming, ethnic cleansing, plate tectonics*: our world is changing fast, and geography is at the core of it all. *The Penguin Dictionary of Geography* is the leading guide to the subject, giving clear, concise definitions of key concepts in physical and human geography, from the *shadow effect* to *eluviation* to *cladistics*. This award-winning text is targeted at students and teachers from GCSE upwards, and also takes account of new developments in this fast-changing subject.

- Ideal for any student from GCSE to undergraduate

- Includes clear, easy-to-read diagrams and illustrations for entries such as *cliff formation*, *plate tectonics* and *population pyramids*

- Explains terms used in human geography, from *sociology* to *psychology*, *population studies* to *economics*

- Covers terms connected with all aspects of the natural environment, from *geology* to *economy*, *climatology* to *soil science*

- Discusses recent developments in such areas as *feminist geography*, *sustainability* and *globalization*

- Ranges from core vocabulary to specialist terms and concepts

**ONLY PENGUIN GIVES YOU MORE**

# PENGUIN REFERENCE LIBRARY

**THE PENGUIN DICTIONARY OF LITERARY TERMS
& LITERARY THEORY**

EDITED BY J. A. CUDDON

'Scholarly, succinct, comprehensive and entertaining ... an indispensable work of reference' *The Times Literary Supplement*

Now over thirty years old, J. A. Cuddon's *The Penguin Dictionary of Literary Terms and Literary Theory* is a reference classic, a stunning survey of literature and theory that stands as the first port of call for any reader or student of literature. Consistently updated since, Cuddon's work illuminates the history and complexity of literature's movements, terms and major figures in relaxed, accessible prose. From *existentialism* to *caesura* to *doggerel*, the text ranges authoritatively over both high and low literary culture and theory, and is the primary reference source for anyone interested in writing or reading.

- Gives definitions of technical terms (*hamartia, iamb, zeugma*) and critical jargon (*aporia, binary opposition, intertextuality*)

- Explores literary movements (*neoclassicism, romanticism, vorticism*) and schools of literary theory (*feminist criticism, new historicism, structuralism*)

- Covers genres (*elegy, fabliau, pastoral*) and literary forms (*haiku, ottava rima, sonnet*)

**ONLY PENGUIN GIVES YOU MORE**

# PENGUIN SUBJECT DICTIONARIES

Penguin's Subject Dictionaries aim to provide two things: authoritative complimentary reference texts for the academic market (primarily A level and undergraduate studies) *and* clear, exciting and approachable reference books for general readers on subjects outside the core curriculum.

**Academic & Professional**

ACCOUNTING
ARCHEOLOGY
ARCHITECTURE
BUILDING
BUSINESS
CLASSICAL MYTHOLOGY
CRITICAL THEORY
ECONOMICS
INTERNATIONAL RELATIONS
LATIN
LITERARY TERMS & THEORY
MARKETING (forthcoming)
MEDIA STUDIES
MODERN HISTORY
PENGUIN HUMAN BIOLOGY (forthcoming)
PHILOSOPHY
PSYCHOLOGY
SOCIOLOGY

**Scientific, Technical and Medical**

BIOLOGY
CHEMISTRY
CIVIL ENGINEERING
COMPUTING
ELECTRONICS
GEOGRAPHY
GEOLOGY
MATHEMATICS
PHYSICAL GEOGRAPHY
PHYSICS
PSYCHOANALYSIS
SCIENCE
STATISTICS

**English Words & Language**

CLICHÉS
ENGLISH IDIOMS
PENGUIN ENGLISH GRAMMAR
PENGUIN RHYMING DICTIONARY
PROVERBS
SYNONYMS & ANTONYMS
SYNONYMS & RELATED WORDS
ROGET'S THESAURUS
THE COMPLETE PLAIN WORDS
THE PENGUIN A–Z THESAURUS
THE PENGUIN GUIDE TO PLAIN ENGLISH
THE PENGUIN GUIDE TO PUNCTUATION
THE PENGUIN WRITER'S MANUAL
USAGE AND ABUSAGE

**Religion**

BIBLE
ISLAM (forthcoming)
JUDAISM (forthcoming)
LIVING RELIGIONS
RELIGIONS
SAINTS
WHO'S WHO IN THE AGE OF JESUS

**General Interest**

BOOK OF FACTS
FIRST NAMES
MUSIC
OPERA
SURNAMES (forthcoming)
SYMBOLS
THEATRE

**Penguin Reference – making knowledge everybody's property**